QUIXOTIC FRESCOES: CERVANTES AND ITALIAN RENAISSANCE ART

As a young man, Miguel de Cervantes left his home in Spain and travelled extensively through Italy, experiencing all that the Italian Renaissance had to offer. In his later writings, Cervantes sought to recapture his experience through literature, and literary critics have often pointed to Italian texts as models for Cervantes' writing. The art of the period, however, has seldom been examined in this context.

Focusing on *Don Quixote,* Frederick A. de Armas unearths links between Cervantes' text and frescoes, paintings, and sculptures by Italian artists such as Cambiaso, Michelangelo, Raphael, and Titian. His study seeks to re-engage the critics of today by formulating the link between Cervantes and the Renaissance through an interdisciplinary dialogue that establishes a new set of models and predecessors. This dialogue is used to explore a variety of issues in Cervantes including the absence of a single guiding pictorial program, the doubling of archaeological reconstruction, and the use of ekphrasis as allusion, interpolation, and an integral component of the action. *Quixotic Frescoes* delves into the politics of imitation, self-censorship, religious ideology expressed through the pictorial, as well as the gendering of art as reflected in Cervantes' work. This detailed and exhaustive study is an invaluable contribution to both Hispanic and Renaissance studies

FREDERICK A. DE ARMAS is the Andrew W. Mellon Professor in Humanities and chair of the Department of Romance Languages and Literature at the University of Chicago.

FREDERICK A. DE ARMAS

Quixotic Frescoes:

Cervantes and Italian Renaissance Art

UNIVERSITY OF TORONTO PRESS
Toronto Buffalo London

Toronto Buffalo London

Reprinted in paperback 2009

ISBN 978-0-8020-9074-4 (cloth)
ISBN 978-1-4426-1031-6 (paper)

Library and Archives Canada Cataloguing in Publication

De Armas, Frederick A.
Quixotic frescoes : Cervantes and Italian Renaissance art / Frederick A. de Armas.

Includes bibliographical references and index.
ISBN 978-0-8020-9074-4 (bound) – ISBN 978-1-4426-1031-6 (pbk.)

1. Cervantes Saavedra, Miguel de, 1547–1616. Don Quixote. 2. Ekphrasis. 3. Cervantes Saavedra, Miguel de, 1547–1616 – Knowledge – Art. 4. Cervantes Saavedra, Miguel de, 1547–1616 – Knowledge – Italy. 5. Art in literature. 6. Cervantes Saavedra, Miguel de, 1547–1616 – Technique. I. Title.

PQ6353.D38 2006 863′.3 C2006-900893-0

Cover illustration: *St George and the Dragon* by Raphael. Louvre, Paris, France. Scala / Art Resource, NY

University of Toronto Press acknowledges the financial assistance to its publishing program of the Canada Council for the Arts and the Ontario Arts Council.

University of Toronto Press acknowledges the financial support for its publishing activities of the Government of Canada through the Book Publishing Industry Development Program (BPIDP).

Contents

List of Illustrations vii

Preface xi

1 The Exhilaration of Italy 3

2 A Museum of Memories: From *Numancia* to *La Galatea* 14

3 At School with the Ancients: Raphael 29

4 The Fourfold Way: Raphael 52

5 Textual Terribilitá: Michelangelo 71

6 The Merchants of Trebizond: Luca Cambiaso 93

7 Drawing Decorum: Titian 113

8 Dancing with Giants: Philostratus 134

9 A Mannerist Theophany / A Cruel *Teichoskopia*: Pontormo and Parmigianino 153

10 Dulcinea and the Five Maidens: Zeuxis 170

11 Love's Architecture: Giulio Romano 189

12 The Last Enchantment: Epilogue 205

Notes 213

Works Cited 253

Index 227

Illustrations follow p. 126

Illustrations

1.1 *Apollo Belvedere*. Roman marble copy of a Greek original, 4th BCE. Palazzo Farnese, Rome, Italy.

2.1 Raphael/Giulio Romano. *The Cross Appearing to Constantine the Great, flanked by portraits of two popes*. Stanze de Raffaello, Vatican Palace, Vatican State.

2.2 Raphael. *The Triumph of Galatea*. Palazzo Farnese, Rome, Italy.

2.3 Sebastiano del Piombo. *Polyphemus*. Palazzo della Farnesina, Rome, Italy.

2.4 Botticelli, Sandro. *Primavera*. Uffizi, Florence, Italy.

2.5 Raphael. *The Three Graces*. Musée Condé, Chantilly, France.

3.1 Raphael. *Parnassus*. Stanza della Segnatura, Vatican Palace, Vatican State.

3.2 Raphael. *Poetry*. Detail from the ceiling of the Stanza della Segnatura. Stanza della Segnatura, Vatican Palace, Vatican State.

3.3 Raphael. *The School of Athens*. Stanza della Segnatura, Vatican Palace, Vatican State.

3.4 Raphael. *Disputa* (Disputation over the Blessed Sacrament). Stanza della Segnatura, Vatican Palace, Vatican State.

3.5 Raphael. *The Virtues, Fortitude, Prudence (with Janus head) and Temperance*. Stanza della Segnatura, Vatican Palace, Vatican State.

4.1 Raphael. *The School of Athens,* detail of Pythagoras with a boy. Stanza della Segnatura, Vatican Palace, Vatican State.

4.2 Raphael. *Ceiling of the Stanza della Segnatura.* Stanza della Segnatura, Vatican Palace, Vatican State.

4.3 Ripa, Cesare (edited by J. Georg Hertel). *Castitas.* 1760.

5.1 Raphael. *The School of Athens,* detail of left half. Stanza della Segnatura, Vatican Palace, Vatican State.

5.2 Michelangelo. *David* (frontal view). Accademia, Florence, Italy. Ufizzi, Florence.

5.3 Bandinelli, Baccio. *Hercules and Cacus.* Piazza della Signoria, Florence, Italy.

5.4 Michelangelo. *St. Matthew.* Accademia, Florence, Italy.

5.5 Michelangelo. *Last Judgment.* Sistine Chapel, Vatican Palace, Vatican State.

5.6 Michelangelo. *Saint Bartholomew,* detail of *Last Judgment.* Sistine Chapel, Vatican Palace, Vatican State.

6.1 Romano, Giulio. *The Stoning of Saint Stephen.* S. Stefano, Genoa, Italy.

6.2 Cambiaso, Luca. *La Gloria.* Real Monasterio de San Lorenzo de El Escorial, Madrid.

7.1 Titian. *Charles V at Mühlberg.* Museo del Prado, Madrid, Spain.

7.2 Raphael. *Saint George fighting the dragon.* Louvre, Paris, France.

7.3 Dürer, Albrecht. *The Knight, Death, and the Devil.* Musée du Petit Palais, Paris, France.

7.4 Titian. *Portrait of Charles V, Holy Roman Emperor.* Museo Nazionale di Capodimonte, Naples, Italy.

8.1 Doré, Gustave. *Miséricorde! S'Écria Sancho.* 1863.

8.2 Doré, Gustave. *L'aile emporte après elle le cheval et le chevalier.*

8.3 Titian. *David and Goliath.* S. Maria della Salute, Venice, Italy.

8.4 Romano, Giulio. *Room of the Giants.* Palazzo del Té, Mantua, Italy.

9.1 Pontormo, Jacopo. *Vertumnus and Pomona*. Villa Medici, Poggio a Caiano, Italy.

9.2 Pontormo, Jacopo. *The Entombment*. S. Felicita, Florence, Italy.

9.3 Parmigianino. *Altarpiece: The Madonna and Child with Saints John the Baptist and Jerome*. 1527.

10.1 Cromberger, Iacobo, and Iuan Cromberger, eds, *Amadís de Gaula. Oriana*.

10.2 Juan de la Corte. *El rapto de Helena*. 1631.

10.3 Titian. *Tarquin and Lucrecia*. 1571.

10.4 Raimondi, Marcantonio. *The Death of Lucretia*.

11.1 Romano, Giulio. *The Wedding Banquet of Psyche and Cupid*. Palazzo del Té, Mantua, Italy.

11.2 Raphael. *The Banquet of the Gods*. Palazzo della Farnesina, Rome, Italy.

11.3 Romano, Giulio. *Wedding Banquet of Amor and Psyche*. Palazzo del Té, Mantua, Italy.

Preface

Throughout his literary works, Cervantes repeatedly textualizes his desire for Italy. This desire often takes the form of evocations and descriptions of the art and architecture of the Italian peninsula. In many cases, these moments carry a second, deeper, and more concealed aspiration, that of recapturing the ancient world. These two yearnings coexist within many of the textual images since a number of the Italian frescoes and edifices described in Cervantes' prose fiction evoke antiquity. Although some theorists such as Michel Foucault view *Don Quixote* as 'the negative of the Renaissance world' (1970, 47) a whole school of criticism, starting with Américo Castro and culminating with Alban Forcione, has discussed how Cervantes' *Don Quixote* owes much to the Northern and the Italian Renaissance. However, most if not all critics have ignored Italian art while discussing Cervantes' models. This book seeks to reengage the critics of today on this topic by formulating the link between Cervantes and the Renaissance through an interdisciplinary dialogue that establishes a new set of models and predecessors. This study also continues a journey started some years ago in my *Cervantes, Raphael and the Classics*. In the previous volume, I focused on Cervantes' voyage to Italy, showing how his keen interest in the frescoes of Raphael and Giulio Romano at the Vatican led him not only to incorporate images and structures from these paintings in his tragedy *La Numancia*, but also to become interested in the archaeology of the ancients as exhibited in these frescoes. When writing of Numancia, then, Cervantes would not only be picturing images from Raphael, but he would be attempting to reconstruct the ruins of the Celtiberian city from those of ancient Rome and Troy. Although often giving examples from other texts by Cervantes, I felt that a focus on one play would yield very specific and tangible results. It was my intention to point to a way of dealing with the artistic and classical models of Cervantes' major prose works. But as I lectured on the subject, the persistent question, 'Can we discover a similar imitation of Italian Renaissance art in Cervantes' prose works?' led me reluctantly to face these texts and seek to establish how Cervantes dealt with his Italian sojourn after he wrote his early tragedy, *La Numancia*.

My first impulse was to turn to *La Galatea* (1585) and *Los trabajos de Persiles y Sigismunda* (1617) in order to begin to assess the impact of Italian Renaissance art and architecture in Cervantes' prose. It would be easier to deal with the first and last of his prose works since Edward Dudley has already pointed to the presence of Raphael's *The Triumph of Galatea* in Cervantes' pastoral romance, while the *Persiles* contains a detailed description of Rome and its works of art, including allusions to Raphael and Michelangelo. And yet, what puzzled me most was what could be found in between these two books. How could the adventures of a melancholy knight who does battle with peasants and windmills as he travels down the dusty roads of La Mancha have anything to do with Italian Renaissance art? Had Cervantes turned away from his almost continuous desire to exhibit Italian art, architecture, and culture? I was unable to set aside this problem. Thus, I was led, reluctantly, to search for Quixotic frescoes, for traces of Italian art within Cervantes' canonical text. In order to show the shift in the uses of art, ekphrasis, and imitation in the 1605 *Don Quixote*, I have decided to begin this book with a discussion of earlier Cervantine texts. After an introductory section on Cervantes' desire for Italy (and for the Renaissance) and his use of ekphrasis, to textualize this desire, this volume briefly discusses the importance of mnemonics and visual representation in *La Numancia* and *La Galatea*. The other eight chapters are devoted to *Don Quixote*, Part I. In the previous book, I moved from imitation of art to imitation of the classics. In this volume the impact of classical literature will be folded into discussions of Italian art. Indeed, Cervantes' use of the ancients will be foregrounded in discussions of artificial memory, ekphrasis, *invention*, *imitatio*, and *techné*. The use of *techné*, for example, ranges from classical figures such as Daedalus and Archimedes to Charles V's favourite inventor Juanelo Turriano. Cervantes' use of mnemonics, on the other hand, reflects elements from Cicero's *De Oratore* as well as the *Ad Herennium* attributed to this Roman writer. Of the many Renaissance texts on mnemonics, the author of *Don Quixote* seems to prefer Giambattista della Porta's *L'Arte del ricordare*. In his conception of ekphrasis, Cervantes reflects a knowledge of Philostratus, Homer, and Virgil – but he also refers to Garcilaso's imitation of ancient ekphrasis. Although Cervantes points to Greek literature, he does not read it in the original language, but constructs his perceptions of its meanings through translations, summaries, and adaptations. Even when dealing with some of the Latin writers, mediation is utilized. Perhaps Cervantes did read Cicero, Lucan, and Virgil in the original, but he also read translations (into Spanish and Italian) and commentaries that impinged upon his models. This book will not embark upon a search for the specific mediators (although some will be pointed out). Rather, it will point to imitation of the ancients as part of a desire for Italy, a desire to refashion a Renaissance through art and its antique models.

There are at least three levels of memory in Cervantes' *Don Quixote*. First, there is the memory of the knight himself who is constantly recalling his readings. Second, there is the memory the knight creates for others as he paints over the landscape, people, and architecture of La Mancha with images taken from his books. These 'paintings' are particularly appealing to the memory since they combine two key elements recommended by Giambattista Della Porta's art of memory: the idealized valour of heroes and the ridiculous and risible way in which these are reconfigured in Cervantes' text. Although there will be some discussion of this second level, this book concentrates on a third mnemonic level, searching for hidden images from Italian art, placed as memory markers by the narrators or imagined by the mad knight. While some paintings emerge only through allusive and fragmented ekphrasis, others are more fully represented through a number of more traditional modes of ekphrasis, a pause in the narrative that allows for the description of an art object or painting. The notion of ekphrasis and the many forms it takes in the novel will of necessity lead us to touch upon imitation of the classics since some of the objects described or evoked bring forth a memory of the ancients.

Ekphrasis and pictorial allusion in *Don Quixote* is a topic much more difficult to approach than in Cervantes' other works since we have a constant erasure of artistic models. It is as if we have to look beneath writings and rewritings to discover the remnants of an Italian fresco, oil painting, or sculpture. The text is thus exhibited as a site for archaeological reconstruction where remnants from the past (scattered objects and figures from early modern art and its antique models) can be discovered beneath a sixteenth-century Spanish ideological and physical landscape. The knight's dusty tomes also cover up Italian and classical elements in spite of their chivalric medievalizing. In these textual excavations the reader can unearth partially preserved shapes from antiquity or objects from pictures of the Renaissance which lend the surface texture of the narrative both new patterns and images. This rediscovery foregrounds the revival of the ancients during the Renaissance. And indeed, Cervantes was clearly aware that, by utilizing High Renaissance art, he was turning to a style that emulated the ancients and attempted to bring art to a new pinnacle. In this vision he was aided by Giorgio Vasari's *Lives of the Artists*, which describes the continuous rise, flowering, and decline of art, focusing on the high point of art in the Renaissance as exemplified in the works of Leonardo da Vinci, Raphael, and Michelangelo.

Once this rediscovery takes place, however, the reader is faced with a number of other problems including the absence of one pictorial program to serve as a guide, except for the consequent presence of a pictorial impetus – the desire for Italy; the doubling of archaeological reconstruction by using Italian art as a doorway for the ancient world; and the use of ekphrasis not so much as a momentary pause in the action, but as allusion, interpolation, and even as an integral part of the action – what has been called dramatic ekphrasis – thus breaking with the very descriptive basis of this rhetorical technique. The reader is also faced with the politics of imitation in a text that deals with the imperial epic and paintings of conquest and empire; with the religious ideology expressed through the pictorial – the counterreligion of paganism in Counter-Reformation Spain; and the gendering of art within the text. Discussion of these topics is further problematized by the parodic nature of the novel and by the grotesque uses of classical topics. Many of these issues will be broached as different images are taken up for perusal. But one motif that continues to reappear is the link between Don Quixote and Charles V. Perhaps the novel represents a desire to recapture a Renaissance ruled by Charles, an emperor who was twice crowned in Italy, who was partially responsible for the sack of Rome in 1527, and who much later entered the same city in triumph, in the guise of a Roman emperor.

It would be impossible to exhaust in a single book the topic of *Don Quixote*, Italian art, the art of memory, and classical ekphrasis, with all of its concomitant problems. This volume, then, is but a beginning, a first look at hidden works that serve to enrich even further one of the most studied texts in the Western literary tradition. It focuses on the first part of the novel published in 1605, leaving the 1615 volume for another time. This study will highlight only some of the more powerful examples of the many frescoes, paintings, buildings, and ancient objects that are contained within the novel. After an introductory section the book will follow *Don Quixote*, starting with the Prologue to Part I and ending with Don Quixote's defeat through an enchantment. The classical painter (Zeuxis) as well as seven Italian artists are discussed (Cambiaso, Giulio Romano, Michelangelo, Parmigianino, Pontormo, Raphael, and Titian), in addition to ekphrastic descriptions from Dante, Garcilaso, the Homeric poems, Philostratus, Virgil, and other classical and Renaissance writers. The importance of libraries is also foregrounded, from Julius II's Vatican Library to Philip II's library at the Escorial. The latter grounds some of the Italian influences within Spanish soil. After all, the pictorial program for the library at the Escorial is based, in part, on works by Michelangelo and Raphael. Many of the paintings inscribed in the text are frescoes – thus the title for the book. But the technique of fresco will also be used as metaphor for the knight's (and the 'author's') production of images. The ability to preserve a fresco is based on the drying of the plaster, much like the ability to fix images in the mind was said to entail first a moist brain to capture the image and then a dryness of the humours to hold it in place. It is no coincidence that both Don Quixote and the novel are depicted as dry in nature.

As with *La Numancia* and *La Galatea*, Cervantes includes in *Don Quixote* many of Raphael's frescoes – although there is an attempt to distance the text from an artist best known for his grace, harmony, and balance. In addition, I believe that the artistic battle between Raphael and Michelangelo also participates in the oppositions found in the narrative. Raphael's disciple, Giulio Romano, may have provided Cervantes with a vision of valued caskets, beautiful ladies, love's architecture, and epic shields, images that appear in *Don Quixote*. Luca Cambiaso's view of an ancient empire may be part of the quixotic dream. As the artist whom Cervantes may have first confronted when arriving in Italy, he serves as prelude to many of the topics and techniques that the Spanish writer would later view in paintings and frescoes by other artists. Titian is not used at first for his mythological or antique subjects. Rather, it is his vision of empire, the portrayal of Charles V as a Christian knight who commands attention. When picturing Dulcinea and Maritornes, however, a vision of violent desire from Titian disrupts Platonic contemplations. The mannerist art of Pontormo and Parmigianino serves to problematize the question of pastoral in the novel, showing Marcela as a sublime but also perverse dream which serves to fulfil Grisóstomo's aspirations as a writer. The prevalence of the pictorial representation of Cupid and Psyche in Italian art serves as background for the architecture of love in Cervantes' interpolated tale, *El curioso impertinente* (*Tale of Foolish Curiosity*) – and interpolation is in itself a type of ekphrasis. The aesthetics of Part I as evinced by these painters is very different from that of Part II, where a new set of artists will lead to a different vision. The artist of the 1605 novel will be quirky, grotesque, and exotic: Botticelli, Arcimboldo, Pinturicchio.

Portions of this book are derived from previously published material, but all have been revised, rethought, and expanded. Chapter 10 derives from 'Painting Dulcinea: Italian Art and the Art of Memory in *Cervantes' Don Quixote*,' *Yearbook of Comparative and General Literature*. References to Della Porta and his art of memory derive from 'Cervantes and Della Porta: The Art of Memory in *La Numancia, El retablo de las maravillas, El Licenciado Vidriera,* and *Don Quijote*,' *Bulletin of Hispanic Studies*. Since the introductory section of this book owes much to my previous *Cervantes, Raphael and the Classics*, it has been impossible to avoid some repetition. I have tried to keep it to a minimum. All citations in Spanish have been left in the original. However, all other references are given in English translation. When citing *Don Quixote*, I use the Murillo edition and the Rutherford translation and I always give the part and chapter in addition to the page. All other Spanish translations are my own. References to authors from ancient Greece and Rome include the page number of the actual edition used (most often from the Loeb Classical Library), followed after a semicolon by the standard book and line numbers. With Philostratus I include the chapter number only after the book page number.

I would like to thank *The Yearbook of Comparative and General Literature* and the *Bulletin of Hispanic Studies* for permission to include material from these essays. Many Golden Age scholars have helped me to focus and rethink my arguments through discussions and letters. I would like to thank in particular Emilie Bergmann, Jean Canavaggio, Anne J. Cruz, Edward Dudley, Edward H. Friedman, Eric Graf, James Parr, and Christopher Weimer. Many of my present and past colleagues at the University of Chicago have graciously listened to my readings of parts of this book and made valuable suggestions. I would like to thank in particular Elizabeth Amman (now at Columbia), Armando Maggi, Patrick O'Connor (now at Oberlin), Thomas Pavel, Mario Santana, Lisa Voigt, and Elissa Weaver. During the summer of 2003, I presented many of the ideas found in this book at an NEH Summer Seminar for College and University Faculty which I directed at the University of Chicago. I would like to express my deep appreciation to the members of the seminar for their interest, patience, and valuable suggestions. The dynamics of the seminar, where art historians and literature specialists dialogued with each other, impelled me to look at many of the questions they raised as I attempted to complete the book. The participants included Kathleen Bollard, Deborah Cibelli, Pamela Decoteau, Eric Graf, Polly Hoover, Ignacio López, Ana Laguna, Alvaro Molina, Cristina Muller, Rosina Neginsky, Jaime Pérez, John Slater, Steven Wagschal, William Worden, and Barbara Watts. I would also like to thank my former students Ronald Friis, Rogelio Miñana, Antonio Sanchez Jimenéz, Peter Thompson, Julio Vélez, and Kerry Wilks for all their valuable help in researching and assembling this volume. I could not have completed this book in a timely fashion without the constant, conscientious, and inestimable editorial work of my research assistant, Benjamin J. Nelson. And, I would like to thank Carmela Mattza for her work assembling and locating many of the illustrations. Research for this book has been made possible by a research leave from the University of Chicago, and by a Fellowship from the National Endowment for the Humanities. Any views, findings, conclusions, or recommendations expressed in this publication do not necessarily reflect those of the National Endowment for the Humanities.

QUIXOTIC FRESCOES

1 The Exhilaration of Italy

The exhilaration, then, derives from the dream – and the pursuit – of a language that can, in spite of its limits, recover the immediacy of a sightless vision built into our habit of perceptual desire since Plato. It is the romantic quest to realize the nostalgic dream of the original, pre-fallen language of corporeal presence ...

Murray Krieger, *Ekphrasis: The Illusion of the Natural Sign*

Italian sojourns were almost de rigueur for Spanish poets and other thinkers during the Golden Age. Learning Italian metres and perusing the canonical texts of the Renaissance were thought to be almost indispensable in the making of a poet's career. Cervantes' voyage, then, resembled the ones of Acuña, Aldana, the brothers Argensola, Cetina, Figueroa, Garcilaso, Hurtado de Mendoza, Medrano, Santillana, and Villamediana. The Italian Renaissance also beckoned writers of prose fiction such as Francisco Delicado, who left Spain for Venice in 1492 never to return; Agustín de Rojas Villandrado, who travelled to Italy around 1596–7;[1] and Francisco de Quevedo, who spent many years in Naples. And humanists were, of course, most interested in the cultural riches of the Italian states. Juan de Valdés settled in Naples in 1534, but Ambrosio de Morales almost drowned attempting to climb from a small boat aboard a ship bound to Italy. He immediately abandoned his cherished desire to travel to Rome, interpreting the incident as an evil omen (1791, 3.17). Being awarded the *cátedra* of rhetoric at the University of Alcalá, he wrote a history which became Cervantes' main source for the historical elements in his tragedy *La Numancia*. It should not come as a surprise, then, that Cervantes spent part of his youth in the

Italian peninsula, spending more than five years there (from 1569 to 1575). Of course, it was during this period that he also joined the Holy League and fought in the battle of Lepanto.

Italy was for Cervantes and others both a familiar and a foreign land. In parts of Italy, Spaniards would find institutions and a language of their own. After all, the island of Sicily had been part of the kingdom of Aragon since 1282, while the kingdom of Naples enjoyed a major revival of culture during the reign of Alfonso V of Aragon, who conquered it in 1443. Although separated from Spanish rule for more than fifty years, Naples was again to be part of Aragon and later Castile with the intervention of Ferdinand the Catholic (1503–4). Indeed, this largest of Italian kingdoms remained in Spanish control until the eighteenth century. Spanish soldiers were not an uncommon sight in the Italian peninsula. Whether fighting against French intervention, threatening the pope and even sacking Rome, or aiding the Vatican and Venice to conquer the Turks in the Mediterranean, these soldiers and their commanders were well acquainted with Italian soil and its spoils. As for poets, nobles, clerics, expelled Jews, and even *pícaros*, they filled the streets of Rome and roamed the countryside and the many city-states in search of fame and favour. Those who did not go to the Italian peninsula knew of its cities from the oral accounts by the travellers and by the numerous commonplaces published in the literature of Spain.

I would argue that Cervantes spent his life 'desiring Italy' – and that this desire is often represented in his literary texts through allusions to the art, architecture, and culture of the Italian peninsula.[2] We can document Cervantes' attempts to return to the Italian peninsula on at least two occasions. The first when he tries to follow Ascanio Colonna to Italy in 1585 – the year in which Cervantes publishes his pastoral romance *La Galatea* and only five years after his return to Spain. This desire for Italy can be gleaned from his dedicatory to Colonna at the beginning of *La Galatea* (151). But Cervantes was not granted his wish. Colonna took with him instead a friend of Cervantes, Luis Gálvez de Montalvo. Gálvez and Cervantes were almost of the same age, the former having been born in 1549. Their close literary friendship can be documented by a sonnet written by Gálvez proclaiming that with Cervantes' return from captivity in Algier in 1580, 'cobra España las perdidas Musas' (Spain recovers the lost Muses) (*La Galatea* 1995, 160). Gálvez had published his own pastoral romance *El pastor de Fílida* three years before Cervantes' own pastoral and Cervantes praises him in the *Canción de Calíope* included in his *La Galatea* (1995, 550, stanza 28) – and Cervantes lauds him again in *Don Quixote*. Once in Italy Gálvez turns to translations from the Italian. He dies suddenly in 1591 without having completed his version of Tasso's epic poem.

The second time when we can document Cervantes' desire for Italy is in itself a series of moments.[3] The many dedicatory prefaces to Lemos hint at Cervantes' continuing desire for Italy. Wanting to be at the Neapolitan court of his patron, Cervantes dedicates to him many of his most important works: the *Novelas ejemplares, Ocho comedias y ocho entremeses*, the second part of *Don Quixote*, and the posthumously published *Trabajos de Persiles y Sigismunda*. He was never invited. But, the memory of a youth spent in Italy would be preserved in many of his works. The tale of Timbrio and Silerio in *La Galatea* includes 'una descripción típicamente cervantina de Génova' (a typically Cervantine description of Genoa) (Stamm 1981, 341). Bologna is the setting for *La señora Cornelia,* while Florence is the background for *El curioso impertinente.* Italian art works may also have impinged on the depiction of a murder in *La Galatea*.[4] Naples has a prominent role in *La fuerza de la sangre* and in *El viaje del Parnaso,* while Rome is a constant presence in Cervantes' texts, from *La española inglesa* and *El licenciado Vidriera* to *Don Quixote II* and *Persiles y Sigismunda.*

Cervantes' voyage to Italy, as mirrored in many of his literary texts, is more than an eclectic enjoyment of Renaissance art, architecture, and poetry. His learning experience took on a distinctive aspect. At the service of the future Cardinal Acquaviva in Rome around 1569–71, he came in contact with a papal court saturated with political subtexts whose laudatory thrust often stemmed from the authority of classical cultures. But the ancients represented for Cervantes much more than a source for poetic praise. The constant reminder of classical civilizations through both visual (art and architecture) and verbal means aroused in the Spanish author a yearning to visualize the brilliant past of Greece and Rome. While in the service of Acquaviva at the Vatican, the young poet must have been anxious to view works by the Italian masters whose 'pagan' subjects differed so much from Spanish paintings of the Golden Age. Jonathan Brown reminds us: 'It has often been observed that Spanish painting of the Golden Age is largely restricted to religious subjects (mostly from the New Testament), portraiture, and still life, in that order. Absent, or nearly absent, are mythological and allegorical subjects ...' (1991, 4). What David Darst has called the 'actitud anti-mitológica y anti-clásica' (antimythological and anticlassical attitude) (1985, 23–4) is found in a number of Spanish treatises which complain of the indecencies and immorality of mythological paintings: 'pinturas desnudas de hombres y mujeres profanas, llenas de tantas indecencias contra la pureza christiana, que no hay ojos castos que aun a larga distancia se atrevan a mirarlas' (nude paintings of profane men and women, full of so many indecencies against Christian purity, that no chaste eyes even at a far distance shall dare to gaze upon them) (Darst 1985, 23). While at the Vatican, Cervantes would have been able to view these works and understand their precarious position during the Counter-Reformation. Indeed, many were being dispersed by the papacy. The Spanish poet, taught in his youth by a humanist, must have wanted to comprehend how Renaissance Italian artists were able to foreground the pagan while embracing the Christian at the very centre of Catholic power, the Vatican – an ability that was suspect by the time he came to Rome.

Walking through the Vatican, Cervantes would have been aware of the contrast between a Counter-Reformation ideology that labelled the Sistine Chapel 'a bathroom full of nudes,' as it wished to flush away all traces of paganism, and the remnants of a brilliant Renaissance whose syncretism made it impossible to exorcize the ancient while retaining the Christian message. Surrounded by the ruins of the Roman Empire and decorated with frescoes and sculptures which sought to revive the ancient past, the prelates at the Vatican could only banish the past by destroying the edifice of thought and art that had been built over the past century. Renaissance popes had wished to be praised with words and images of the ancients. And now these canonical words and drawings could not be wiped away without impoverishing the might and culture of the Roman church. Many of Cervantes' conceptual and imagistic elements could derive from this frisson between ancient, Renaissance, and Counter-Reformation cultures. By obscuring a past that had so recently been rediscovered, the papacy may not have achieved its aim to make Cervantes and other visitors/pilgrims more religiously minded. Instead, these pilgrims may have sought to discover what the church was hiding – the alluring forms of an ancient culture.

During the second half of the sixteenth century, the famous statue of *Apollo Belvedere* 'was hidden behind a wooden partition placed over its niche in the Cortile' (*Vatican Collections* 1982, 63; fig. 1.1). While this ancient image was enclosed in a coffinlike structure that sought to convey the death of pagan deities, Cervantes could witness other images of this antique god. Raphael, for example, had thrice designed this deity in the Stanza della Segnatura at the Vatican. The frescoes for this hall, which was to serve as Pope Julius II's library, were executed between 1508 and 1510. Here, Cervantes would have seen a statue of Apollo within one of Raphael's most famous frescoes, *The School of Athens*, and it was Apollo who presided over the poets in Raphael's *Parnassus*. The vault exhibited a disturbing yet brilliant *Apollo and Marsyas* over the *Parnassus*. Thus, the 'pagan idol' of Apollo, god of poetry, would beckon the writer though interred in a coffinlike enclosure in the old pleasure garden of the Belvedere. Raphael's archaeological interest had resurrected the ancient statue, replicating it at least three times in the papal apartments. Some art critics even claim that the *Apollo Belvedere* was transmuted by Michelangelo into the central figure of the *Last Judgment*. Loren Partridge asserts: 'Christ – modeled on the famous *Apollo Belvedere* in the sculpture court ... is a new Apollo, the eternal radiance of truth ...' (1996, 136). But it is not just Christ that challenges the viewer to rethink the break between Christianity and the classical past. Pierluigi de Vecchi explains: 'In the figures of Christ, Sebastian and numerous others, Michelangelo seems to want to rival the classical models of the heroic nude. Here, in this portrait of the resurrection, the beauty of the unclothed human body has become a symbol for the glory of the chosen ones' (1996, 226). In Michelangelo the resurrection is also a revivifying of the ancient world.

Michelangelo's powers of resuscitation were well known, as in the famous story of an ancient statue which was unearthed but lacked a foot. Michelangelo provided the missing extremity, explaining that he had actually sculpted the work and buried it so that it would appear to be an archaeological find.[5] Surrounded by works of art with a keen interest in the disinterment of the ancient past, Cervantes would undoubtedly come to mirror their feats through his own textual necromancies.[6] But Cervantes would attempt an even more troubling resuscitation. His would entail a second awakening, one that would attempt the feats of the Renaissance at a time when the recovered ancient past was once again being buried through the weight of the Counter-Reformation. In this voyage to recover the Renaissance, he would be guided by Giorgio Vasari's *Lives of the Artists*, a text that not only canonizes certain artists of the period, but also labels the period as a Renaissance. Vasari, who establishes an analogy between the development of art and the ages of a human being, studies painting and sculpture through the four stages of childhood, adolescence, maturity, and decrepitude (Haskell 1993, 120; Rubin 1995, 164–5). He thus sees three causes for the decline of Roman art starting with Constantine:

'Christian iconoclasm, the displacement of the capital of the Empire to Constantinople and the barbarian invasions' (Haskell 1993, 121). But this excursus into the ancients has a major purpose. It allows him to invent Renaissance art (Rubin 1995, 1). At the end of the *Preface* to the *Lives*, Vasari comes up with the notion of 'rinascita' or rebirth of the arts. Having declined in late Roman times, the arts are now born again. His book, divided into three parts, deals with three centuries, the fourteenth to the sixteenth. Vasari shows 'the progress of her second birth and of that very perfection whereto she has risen again in our times' (1996, 1.46). It is this moment of perfection as canonized by Vasari that Cervantes seeks to picture in his mind during his Italian sojourn.

As Cervantes walked through the Vatican, he would view many of the masterpieces of the Renaissance as recorded by Vasari. They would become part of the images and structures of his plays, stories, and novels. In the fourth and final book of the *Persiles y Sigismunda*, for example, the pilgrims arrive in Rome and witness great art works from classical times and from the Italian Renaissance: 'Parrasio, Polignoto, Apeles, Ceuxis y Timantes tenían allí lo perfecto de sus pinceles ... acompañados de los del devoto Rafael de Urbino y de los del divino Micael Angelo' (Parrhasius, Polygnotus, Apelles, Zeuxis, and Thimantes had there the perfection of their brushes ... accompanied by those of the pious Raphael of Urbino and those of the divine Michelangelo) (1969, 445).[7] This passage testifies not only to Cervantes' archaeological interest,[8] but also to his fascination with Michelangelo and Raphael, artists who contributed extensively to the decoration of the Vatican.[9] The pairing of these two Renaissance artists in the *Persiles* is significant since Raphael was commissioned to decorate the Stanza della Segnatura in the Vatican at the same time as Michelangelo began to work on the ceiling of the Sistine chapel. Cervantes' *Numancia*, his pastoral novel *La Galatea*, and the chivalric tale of *Don Quixote* will utilize key images and structures from Raphael's famous hall. But these images would bear the weight and danger of necromancies[10] performed at a time when pagan idols (and artists who sought to revivify the power of these images) were again being demonized. Even Michelangelo's *Last Judgment*, a work that strove through contortion and ascension to incorporate the new thought, was deemed lewd and even heretical (Vecchi 1996, 216). Indeed, in 1564 the Council of Trent 'decreed the "correction" of the parts of the fresco deemed indecent' (Vecchi 1996, 216). Cervantes would thus view a censored original. This fresco, like those of Raphael who revealed the hidden *Apollo Belvedere*, would be like palimpsests where the Spanish author could rediscover the hidden beauties of the past. But they would also teach how to conceal so as not to be censored by others. It is this double movement of revelation of the ancients and Counter-Reformation concealment that will flow back and forth in Cervantes' *Don Quixote*.

The Vatican as a school for Cervantes' future fiction would teach him effectively concerning images and structure, laudatory politics and artistic integrity, origins and originality, imitation and concealment. But the Spanish author would have to learn how to clearly visualize the frescoes, statues, chapels, and palaces. Visualization thus became a key to Cervantes' art. While looking at Italian art, the Spanish poet must have been guided by Giorgio Vasari, who in his *Lives of the Artists* stresses visualization on the part of the reader. Patricia Rubin explains: 'Vasari's address to the judicious eye of his reader depended in part on a definition of imagination as the inner sense (the *imaginativa*) that formed mental images of sense experience and impressed them upon memory. The assumed link between perception and cognition made it possible for Vasari confidently to produce a book about images without illustration' (1995, 133). Cervantes' *Galatea*, *Persiles*, and *Don Quixote* are also works laden with images – but without illustrations. This should come as no surprise since, as Javier Portús Pérez reminds us, in the days of Lope de Vega, painting had become an important motif for writers (1999, 12). Subsequent urges to create engravings from the major events in these novels exemplify the narrative's pictorial thrust. Some of the pictorial elements in the text, I would argue, are partially derived from Italian art and its descriptions in Giorgio Vasari.

All three works of fiction, then, make extensive use of ekphrasis. This term from classical rhetoric meant at first the description of any object. But as time went on, it was refined to mean the description in words of a work of art. It appears as such in Philostratus the Younger's *Imagines*. Ekphrasis is thus often defined as 'a pause in the narrative when art looks at and continues art' (Putnam 1998, ix). This rhetorical technique was repeatedly used in the Renaissance where it was expanded and metamorphosed – with the help of modern literary theory that seeks to reenvision ekphrasis.[11] Perhaps the least important type and the most difficult to classify is ekphrasis according to subject. As such, it can be hagiographic, mythological, grotesque, historical, or based on a landscape, to name but a few. In terms of form and function, ekphrasis can be allegorical, emblematic, decorative, or veiled;[12] and it can serve as a rhetorical or mnemonic device (or both) – the latter leading to the proliferation of occult or magical theatres of memory. In terms of pictorial models and how these are used, ekphrasis can be notional (based on an imagined work of art),[13] or actual or true (based on a real work of art).[14] It can also be combinatory (combining two or more works of art), transformative (changing some elements in the art work into others that can be connected to the original ones), metadescriptive (based on a textual description of a work of art which may or may not exist), or fragmented (using parts of a work). Ekphrasis can conform to the traditional pause in a narrative to describe an object (descriptive ekphrasis),[15] or it can tell the story depicted in the art work – and even expand on the incidents (narrative ekphrasis). There is also the ekphrasis of an object that is being created, such as Vulcan's forging of Achilles' shield – a shaping ekphrasis. Finally, an ekphrasis can be contained within another ekphrasis, creating a metaekphrasis such as the drawing of the battle with the Basque within the description of the discovered manuscript of Don Quixote in chapter nine of the novel.[16]

There are other types of ekphrasis that do violence to the term. For example, some have pointed to allusive ekphrasis.[17] Here, the work of art is not described, nor is a narrative created from its images. Instead, the poet, playwright, or novelist simply refers to a painter, a work of art, or even to a feature that may apply to a work of art. This becomes an ekphrasis only in the mind of the reader/spectator who can view the work in his memory and imagination. This mnemonic and visual effect has the ability to make words capacious. Even more transgressive (albeit returning to its meaning in Hellenistic rhetoric) is the ekphrasis that takes into account the pause in a narrative, but does not use it to describe an art object.[18] This pause can allow for the insertion of an interpolated tale (as in the case of Cervantes' *Curioso impertinente*). This could be called an interpolated ekphrasis which is framed by the novel itself, much as the shield of Achilles is framed by the Ocean.[19] Paradoxically, ekphrasis can also be dramatic, using the art object to construct a developing action – thus taking to an extreme the narrative ekphrasis. And, beyond this, the device can become an ur-ekphrasis, existing as a concept of ekphrasis in a character's mind (as seen when Don Quixote imagines giants out of the stones from which windmills are built), thus foregrounding the process of artistic creation.

Even the reading of Vasari's *Lives* can be considered an ekphrastic exercise, for here, Cervantes would read countless descriptions of paintings. Although for Patricia Rubin, Vasari reverses the process of what constitutes an ekphrasis for Philostratus, her definition of what he did is very close to what we consider to be ekphrasis: 'Starting from extant works, he placed them in the mind's eye, seizing and expounding upon details and episodes that made them compelling and lifelike' (1995, 275). Vasari's work is the first art history every written. Its lack of illustrations of the works described calls for visualization. Subsequent works of art history are often filled with illustrations, but even here, descriptions can be seen as ekphrasis. Indeed W.J.T. Mitchell asserts: 'Insofar as art history is a verbal representation of visual representation, it is an elevation of ekphrasis to a disciplinary principle' (1994, 157).

Art historical books are but one type of collection of ekphrases. There are also sets of ekphrases of paintings and/or sculptures that can be grouped together as collectionist ekphrases, constituting a gallery or museum within a literary text. In Cervantes, they often reflect existing collections of art such as those at the Vatican, the Villa Farnesina, the Palazzo del Té in Italy, or even the Escorial in Spain. But, these collectionist ekphrases can also be notional as in Ariosto's *Orlando furioso* in which a room of supernatural or prophetic art conceived by Merlin is described in detail. This way the characters and readers may 'view' the textual artistic objects and ponder on their placement and significance. The purpose of such groupings may be to reflect (and reflect upon) the aristocratic impetus for artistic collections which gained impetus during the seventeenth-century.[20] These collections can also be mnemonic in nature, recalling the architectural art of memory which places images in a series of rooms within the mind so as to later use them as a tool for recalling a speech.

In addition to his collectionist mode, Cervantes uses many of the types of ekphrasis categorized above. Often works of art are presented through allusive ekphrasis rather than description. When a description does emerge, it seldom serves as a pause and much less as an interruption (except in interpolated ekphrasis). In some cases, they are narrative or shaping in nature, thus closer to the locus classicus of this rhetorical device, the shield of Achilles in the *Illiad*. Some are also dramatic. Discussing twentieth-century Spanish theatre, Phyllis Zatlin has defined ekphrasitic theatre as 'A play in which actual or imaginary visual art works by historical or fictional artists are described, interpreted or made to come to life as an integral part of the play's dramatic action' (1990, 203).[21] It may be that in adapting ekphrasis to theatre as in *La Numancia* (De Armas 1998, 22–39), Cervantes learned to make it into a dynamic and dramatic device.

In *Don Quixote*, the art object is seldom contemplated. If it is derived from an Italian painting, it is inserted in the narrative already fragmented and ready to comply to the purposes of the action. At times, a pictorial program rather than its images serves to structure portions of the work. Thus, ekphrasis in the novel is a dynamic principle, one that must be caught as we move along the text. And, even dramatic ekphrasis is often kept to a minimum in contradistinction to what happens in *La Numancia* and *La Galatea*. More often, as noted above, Italian art is represented through allusive ekphrases, which run against the very nature of pause and description, basic elements of this rhetorical term.

The pictorial impetus, the ekphrastic thrust in Cervantes, may well derive from the exhilaration of Italy, the exhilaration felt by the poet when viewing masterpieces of art and architecture that he felt could somehow be transposed into a verbal medium. Murray Krieger states: 'The exhilaration, then, derives from the dream – and the pursuit – of a language that can, in spite of its limits, recover the immediacy of a sightless vision built into our habit of perceptual desire since Plato. It is the romantic quest to realize the nostalgic dream of an original, prefallen language of corporeal presence' (1992, 10). The Cervantes of *La Numancia* is the poet of exhilaration, the one who seeks this magical transformation of language into the visual. Much of this impetus is still present in *La Galatea* and reappears in the *Novelas ejemplares* and in the *Persiles*. *Don Quixote*, on the other hand, although preserving this quest for enchantment through the mad visions of its hero, the constant flickering of hidden art, and the dim perception of a faraway yet unfathomable luminescence of origins, confronts the opposite movement – the exasperation encountered in the inability to achieve this purpose. As Krieger explains, it is 'the incapacity of words to come together at an instant (*tout à coup*), at a single stroke of sensuous immediacy, as if in an unmediated impact ... words cannot have capacity, cannot be capacious, because they have, literally, no space' (1992, 10). The failures of Don Quixote, then, may parallel the apparent failures of ekphrasis. And yet, Don Quixote strives over and over again to impose the images from his memory and imagination upon the reality of La Mancha. This double vision, although representing a failure, paradoxically provides the reader with pictorial amplitude. It is within this double vision that exphrasis and pictorial allusions are folded within the text. Exasperation seeks new spaces.

Instead of an extended ekphrasis, *Don Quixote* experiments with flickers of pictorial images, with allusions that give the illusion that in these sudden bursts – so quick and vague that they are almost invisible – there can be space within language. More often, a brief allusion (allusive ekphrasis) to a feature in a painting (fragmented ekphrasis) or a programmatic structure is all that is presented. This is very different from the *Galatea* where Raphael's frescoes clearly frame the pastoral. *Don Quixote*, on the other hand, combines quick bursts of imitative textual material with pictorial flickers, detached objects and lengthy but diffuse luminosity so as to problematize the authority of the textual word and of the pictorial image while at the same time attempting to revive the impossible exhilaration of a pre-fallen language. Don Quixote's quest for a new Golden Age is a quest for a return to the Renaissance;[22] but it is also a metaphor for the novel's quest for the impossible in the minimal and the diffuse.

2 A Museum of Memories: From *Numancia* to *La Galatea*

A network of museums ... grew up across Europe in the later sixteenth and seventeenth centuries. From Oxford to Vienna, from Naples to Nuremberg, kings and merchants, doctors and professors set spaces aside for collections of the wonderful works of nature and art.

Anthony Grafton, 'The Rest vs. the West'

Cervantes, as we have seen in the first chapter, inscribes his desire for Italy into his texts through allusions, quick pictorial bursts, dramatic ekphrasis, and pictorial programs from the Renaissance. But how can the verbal and the visual coexist? And how can Cervantes recollect the many images seen long ago so as to include them in his works? Frances Yates reminds us of the antiquity of the relationship between poetry and painting. Simonedes of Ceos, she tells us, believed that 'the poet and the painter both think in visual images which the one expresses in poetry and the other in pictures' (1966, 28).[1] The transposition of the visual and the verbal, then, was based on the supremacy of sight. Furthermore, transposition and visualization are related to memory. In his *Memory and Reminiscence*, Aristotle states: 'There is in us something like an impression or picture ... For when one actually remembers, this impression is what he contemplates and this is what he perceives.' It is 'a picture painted on a panel' which in turn is a 'likeness' of the original memory (1941, 610).

This mnemonic faculty for the ancients and up to the Renaissance had a much greater value than the imagination. Indeed, it held many of the functions of what would later be thought as imagination. For Aristotle, what sets humans apart from animals was the rational soul, composed of reason, memory, and will. Memory was the highest creative power since it combined what the twenty-first century considers as memory with learning. Indeed, as Mary Carruthers explains, 'Whereas now geniuses are said to have creative imagination which they express in intricate reasoning and original discovery, in early times they were said to have richly retentive memories which they expressed in intricate reasoning and original discovery' (1990, 4). She shows how: 'It was memory that made knowledge into useful experience, and memory that combined these pieces of information-become-experience into what we call "ideas," what they were more likely to call "judgment."' (1). The imagination, on the other hand, was more often considered of lesser ranking since it was part of the sensitive soul. It received sensory images from the outside world. These phantasms produced by the imagination through its image-making power, 'are recorded in memory like a seal in wax' (Carruthers 1990, 55). Although the *imaginativa* can only retain phantasms briefly, these can be aroused through humoral imbalance or in sleep as residual elements (Carruthers 1990, 58). With the Renaissance, the imagination acquired a more prominent role. Marcilio Ficino, for example, exalts the imagination in its role in producing and retaining healing images and in eliciting magical results.[2] And indeed, Juan Huarte de San Juan, one of the authors used by Cervantes in his development of Don Quixote's psychology, assigns a high value to the imagination.[3] The importance of memory and imagination in Don Quixote will be discussed in chapter 4. At this time, what is important is the construction of mental images in Cervantes' texts.

Cervantes, then, would have been most concerned with the retentive memory as a storehouse or inventory of images and ideas that would enable him to produce his own textual constructions through *ingenio* or wit. Not only did Cervantes have to remember the multiple patterns and images of the architects and painters of the Italian Renaissance, works that Giorgio Vasari considered as the high point in development, but he had to recall these many years later. While *La Galatea* was written only a decade after his Italian sojourn, *Don Quixote*, Part I, was written some thirty years after his visit to the Vatican and other Italian churches and palaces. Finally, Cervantes' detailed evocation of Rome in the *Persiles y Sigismunda* was penned forty years after his Italian visit. To accomplish these feats of memory Cervantes had to do what most of the mnemonic treatises counselled: 'One must be careful to form one's *imagines* securely and distinctly in the first place, and by repetition and practice ensure that they are in 'long-term' memory' (Carruthers 1990,

61). Memory, as the *Ad Herennium* explains, is of two kinds: natural and artificial. 'The natural memory is that memory which is imbedded in our minds, born simultaneously with thought. The artificial memory is that memory which is strengthened by a kind of training and system of discipline' (1954, 207; 3.16.28). Simonides of Ceos, who was so preoccupied with visual images as the source for both poetry and painting, was said to be the inventor of this art of (artificial) memory.[4] He conceived of 'poetry, painting and mnemonics in terms of intense visualization' (Yates 1966, 28).

According to ancient and Renaissance thinkers, even a person with a good memory would benefit from the artificial art. The *Ad Herennium*, once attributed to Cicero, declares: 'Thus the natural memory must be strengthened by discipline so as to become exceptional' (1954, 207; 3.16.29). Among the many artificial systems, perhaps the best known is the 'Architectural Mnemonic' found in the *Ad Herennium*, in Cicero's *De Oratore*, and in Quintilian's *Institutio* (Carruthers 1990, 72; Yates 1966, 115). The orator, or in this case, the writer, would use two elements to develop the art of memory: 'The artificial memory includes backgrounds and images' (Cicero 1954, 209; 3.16.29). The images are placed in the backgrounds or loci to remind the practitioner of specific arguments, words, or notions. The backgrounds could be 'a house, an intercolumnar space, a recess, and arch' (209; 3.16.30). But they should be chosen with care 'so that they may cling lastingly in our memory' (211; 3.17.31). As for the images, they need to be 'strong and sharp and suitable for awakening recollection' (219; 3.21.35). During the Renaissance, these images were often associated with paintings, a notion authorized by Cicero who in *De Oratore* compares 'the forming of images and painting' (Carruthers 1990, 72).

Cervantes must have been acquainted with the *Ad Herennium* and other ancient arts of memory. There is little evidence that Cervantes turned to the sixteenth-century Spanish Arts of Memory, carefully catalogued by Fernando R. de la Flor. These were based either on Lullian principles or in Augustinian and Thomistic didacticism which saw this art as a way to develop the virtues, particularly prudence (De la Flor 1996, 29–30); they tended towards religious oratory and Christian practices. Cervantes probably turned to practical guides, and revivals of the ancient texts. Pedro Mexía, whose *Silva de varia lección* was repeatedly used by Cervantes in his works, includes two chapters on memory and gives a summary of 'Architectural Mnemonics.' Citing Quintilian and the *Ad Herennium*, he describes the loci as 'lugares señalados y muy conoscidos, como si en una casa muy grande o camino o calle señalásemos con la ymaginación y tuviéssemos en la memoria muchos lugares y puertas' (marked and well known places, as if in a very large house or path or street we would mark with our imagination and we would have in our memory many places and doors) (1991, 2.58). He goes on to describe how one must 'pintar con la ymaginación' (paint with the imagination) (1991, 2.58) the necessary mnemonic images that are to be places in these loci.

Cervantes, I would argue, also used at least one Italian Renaissance text, Giovan Battista (Giambattista) della Porta's *L'Arte del ricordare* (De Armas 2005b). Della Porta, a Neopolitan, travelled to Spain in the early 1560s where he presented to Philip II his book on ciphers, *De furtivus literarum* (1563). The third edition of his *Magiae* (1561) also contains a brief dedication to the Spanish Philip. As his biographer, Louise George Clubb asserts that Della Porta 'was well received by the Spanish king, a fact which added to his prestige at home in Spanish-ruled Naples' (1965, 13). Cervantes may have heard of Della Porta at this time since his trip to Spain put him in contact with learned men as the Italian savant searched for new secrets to include in later editions of his *Magiae*. But Cervantes could certainly have met Della Porta during his travels in Italy from 1569 to 1575. Although he does not name him, he was well aware of the humanistic milieu of Naples, referring to Telesio, another famous humanist and poet from Naples, in his *Galatea*. During the period Cervantes spent in Naples, Della Porta was composing plays – his *Turca* seems to be of 1572 (Clubb 1965, 14). His dramatic work could have impacted Cervantes and led him to try his hand at drama during the following decade. Della Porta's *Turca*, like several of Cervantes' plays, focuses on the Islamic corsairs of the Mediterranean and their abduction of Europeans to Algiers. But more importantly, *L'Arte del Ricordare* was published only four years before Cervantes' 1570 arrival in Naples, a city that viewed Della Porta as one of its greatest writers. While Della Porta's book is of 1566, the second edition of Vasari's *Lives of the Artists* came out in 1568. These two texts may well have provided Cervantes with the necessary theoretical background for his utilization of Italian Renaissance art.

Della Porta alludes both to Simonides of Ceos and to Cicero in his treatise, and there are sections in *L'Arte del Ricordare* that seem to derive directly from the *Ad Herennium*. The treatise begins with an antique fable: the muses are daughters of Jupiter/Jove and Mnemosine. Thus, the knowledge of Jove and the memory of Mnemosine are essential to the poet (who is inspired by the muses). A writer like Cervantes should then take heed of this manner of approaching the muses. In *Don Quixote,* Cervantes will evoke the muses[5] as he fashions a character who exhibits deep flaws in memory and a paradoxical ability to develop strongly mnemonic images. Don Quixote as a 'machine of figuration' will transform the outer landscape by imposing upon it one derived from his memories of the romances of chivalry. Since Don Quixote is described as having a predominance of dryness in his physiology, he would have had a rather poor memory. This faculty thrives in humidity. So, how then, can Don Quixote remember so many characters and events from the chivalric romances?[6] One possible explanation would be that he, like his creator, practised the artificial art of mnemonics. This art, as noted, allows the subject to paint images in his mind and place them in appropriate places so as to remember them. The humidity the knight once possessed in his brain (before too much reading and vigils dried up this organ) recalls the wet plaster that is spread over the wall surface to create a fresco. Once it dries, the image is retained. The knight's dryness makes retention of his former readings even more enduring.

The association between mnemonics and frescoes (and other types of painting) is clearly seen in Don Quixote's recollections. In many ways, we can say that the knight 'paints' upon reality the images his memory retained from the romances of chivalry. These images are often particularly easy to remember; they are strong mnemonic devices since they follow some of the precepts outlined by Della Porta. But it is not so much the chivalric memories painted on the canvas of reality that will be of concern in this book. Some of these have been brilliantly discussed by Aurora Egido.[7] Rather, the more hidden images taken from Italian art and classical ekphrasis will be singled out for discussion.[8]

Della Porta makes several other points that would have a major impact on Cervantes' writings. As already noted, he stresses the importance of places or loci for memory images. Second, he includes a number of comparisons between the art of memory and theatre. Third, he emphasizes how artificial mnemonics is related to painting, how pictoric images are to be inserted in the appropriate places created by the student of this art. He actually states that strong images are ideal for memorizing and that these often derive from Italian Renaissance art. And fourth, he argues that images that produce laughter or are particularly ugly or lewd, can also be easily impressed on the memory. It is precisely the fusion between the ideal images of chivalric valour from the romances and their ludicrous application to a quotidian reality that make of Don Quixote's vision of the world a gallery of excellent mnemonic images (1996, 79).[9]

The first problem encountered by a practitioner of 'Architectural Mnemonics' would be where to place the images. Johannes Romberch, in his *Congestorium artificiose memorie* (1520), points to three place systems: the cosmos, the zodiac, and real buildings (Yates 1966, 115–17). Cosmas Rossellius, in his *Thesaurus artificiosae memoriae* (1579), uses hell and paradise as memory places, but also points to the zodiac and to churches and abbeys (Yates 1966, 122). Della Porta, although noting Cicero's choice of a city and of Metrodorus of Scepsis's zodiacal system (1996, 66-7), firmly directs the reader to the construction in the mind of a real building, having different parts such as entrances, balconies, halls, loggias, gardens, etc. All these rooms must have sufficient light for the images to be seen clearly.[10] In his search for an appropriate building with many different types of rooms, Cervantes could well have conceived of the Vatican, as well as other palaces, villas, and churches he visited. After all, churches, palaces, and monasteries were often recommended for such loci or backgrounds during the Renaissance. And, what greater hall for the mind than the centre of Catholic power? Vatican halls, together with Florentine and Mantuan palaces, with their many frescoes, paintings, and other decorations could well have become the loci containing those striking images recommended by Della Porta. In other words, the buildings would become the background and the paintings and art objects within would become appropriate images to be used in the future. Della Porta adds that places we know well (having lived there)[11] or places that give us a 'sweet satisfaction' (1966, 63) should be chosen. And Cervantes certainly experienced a sweet satisfaction in viewing Renaissance Italian art, something that can be concluded from his many recollections of it in his writings.

Even if Cervantes had no desire to create loci of memory from these great edifices, we have Della Porta's assurance that paintings can be powerful images for the memory: 'It is useful to take pictures by good artists as memory images for these are more striking and move more than pictures by ordinary painters. For example, pictures by Michelangelo, Raphael, Titian, stay in the memory' (Yates 1966, 206; Della Porta 1996, 79).[12] And visualization was key to both painting and poetry. The young writer would have treasured these images as mimetic keys for his own poetry. These images from Renaissance Italian art would then be used to create texts that would have unforgettable images. This type of training is not so different from the one used by apprentices in the art of painting. In his *Arte de la pintura*, Francisco Pacheco states: 'Enriquecida la memoria y llena la imaginación de las buenas formas que de la imitación ha criado, camina adelante el ingenio del pintor' (The memory enriched and the imagination full of the good forms that have been bred by imitation, the genius of the painter advances) (1982, 42). Having established his own mnemonic museum or Vatican of the mind, the writer can then easily view these images and choose what he needs in order to create memorable scenes in his works. Again, this recalls Pacheco's notion of how the more mature painter operates: 'Donde quiere que se hallare el tal artífice, sin particulares cosas, ni originales ajenos, con sólo su ingenio y mano, tiene la sabiduría y riqueza competente para obrar libremente y lleva sus bienes consigo, sin aparato de cosas exteriores' (Wherever such an artist may find himself, without his own items, nor anybody else's originals, with only his genius and hand, he has the wisdom and competent richness to work freely since he carries his goods within him, without the apparatus of exterior items) (1982, 42).

Of course, memory alone cannot lead to excellent composition. After all, the images must be placed correctly and harmoniously within a work. Referring to exactly the same painters evoked by Della Porta, Lodovico Dolce makes a striking remark: 'Consider, that is, the case of a painter who has culled some worthwhile element from antiquity or from some capable modern artist (whether it be Michelangelo, Raphael, Titian or someone else again), but does not know how to place it where it belongs ... for putting things in place or out of place is emphatically that important' (Roskill 1968, 145). While Cervantes at this time learns to place images in the Vatican of his mind, he would later have to learn how to place them appropriately in a text of his own. His first attempts to place images from Italian art in his works are to be found in the theatre, particularly in his early tragedy, *La Numancia*. Cervantes, as noted above, could well have been acquainted with Della Porta's dramatic works such as *La Turca*, and could have related the mnemonics of this writer to his theatre. The romance plot and the events of captivity could well have been an inspiration for Cervantes' *El trato de Argel*.

It should not come as a surprise that Cervantes first turned to theatre for the placement of images from Italian art. Both the *Ad Herennium* and *L'Arte del ricordare* repeatedly relate memory to theatre. Other arts of memory also show this link. As noted previously, the *Thesaurus artificiosae memoriae* of Cosmas Rossellius uses as places the different rooms in heaven and hell. Such locations recall the *Divina commedia* and the whole notion of theatre (Yates, 1966, 122). The very beginnings of *La Numancia* foregrounds the importance of memory by showing how the Roman general Scipio can deliver a powerful harangue to his soldiers from memory. As a skilled orator he must organize in his mind and remember all the topics and images he wishes to raise. His grandfather was considered one of the great orators of Rome,[13] while his grandfather's brother was known for his memory. According to Pliny he, 'knew the names of the whole Roman people (1952, 7.88). Della Porta knows this anecdote well, claiming in his *Arte* that both Cyrus and Scipio are great generals because they can recollect the names of their soldiers (1996, 2.59). The Scipio of Cervantes' play, on the other hand, was reputed to have a poor memory.[14] Thus he has a heavy burden and a challenging task. He must compose like his grandfather and remember like his granduncle. The only way to improve memory is to rely on artificial mnemonics. Only thus can he successfully organize and remember his harangue.

The images from Scipio's speech are derived from Raphael/Giulio Romano's *The Cross Appearing to Constantine the Great, flanked by portraits of two popes* (De Armas 1998, 62–76 fig. 2.1), a fresco that itself deals with the art of artificial memory as made explicit by the presence of the dwarf in the lower right-hand corner. In *De memoria et reminiscentia,* Aristotle asserts: 'Those whose upper parts are abnormally large, as in the case of dwarfs, have abnormally weak memory, as compared to their opposites, because of the great weight which they have resting upon the organ of perception' (1941, 617). Dwarves thus find it difficult to relay such images or impressions to the mind where they are collected and sorted out by the imagination and stored by the memory. In Giulio Romano's fresco, we are alerted to the dwarf's importance by the fact that he does not belong in the battlefield. Furthermore, he stands at the very foreground of the painting, stealing the viewer's gaze away from the centre, from the *allocutio.* This enigmatic dwarf holds a helmet but does not seem to be able to put it on. He cannot protect the head, one of two seats of memory (the other being the heart). His presence serves to point to Constantine's dilemma. How can he store and protect the images needed for his speech? In an imitation that reverses time, the Roman general in Cervantes' tragedy is following the objects of memory used by Constantine. Thus, *La Numancia* in this initial scene uses images from a Renaissance painting as mnemonic keys for Scipio's speech so as to demonstrate the importance of Italian art in the representation and development of artificial mnemonics. But the scene is also a dramatic ekphrasis that both enriches the visual texture of the play and shows its author as a worthy rival to a famed Renaissance artist. The play, then, is related to the mnemonic dramatic scenes proposed by treatises on the art of memory.

Perhaps the most famous theatre of memory was the one actually built by Giulio Camillo. Apparently it existed as a wooden model of a theatre, but big enough for a couple of people to enter. In it, Camillo sought to place 'certain corporeal signs in such a way that the beholder may at once perceive with his eyes everything that is otherwise hidden in the depths of the human mind' (Yates 1966, 131–2). This hermetic, occult theatre where all human memory can be found is not that far removed from Cervantes' conception, as depicted in *La Numancia,* where each of the four acts represents one of the four elements that constitute the cosmos (De Armas, 1998, 12–13). Furthermore, the text draws from all sixteen frescoes found in Raphael's Vatican Stanze. The replication of these images in Cervantes' text, together with its constant allusions to the ruined remains of the ancients, would transform *La Numancia* into a museum where a reader could view the art and architecture of the classical world and the Renaissance. Anthony Grafton reminds us that 'a network of museums ... grew up across Europe in the later sixteenth and seventeenth centuries. From Oxford to Vienna, from Naples to Nuremberg, kings and merchants, doctors and professors set spaces aside for collections of the wonderful works of nature and art' (1998, 14). For those readers or audiences who had seen some of these Italian works, Cervantes' hidden museum would be a clever and enjoyable reminder. Others would remember many of these works from the myriad prints that circulated throughout Europe, while others would have merely read about them in Vasari, Dolce, or Pacheco. For those who had not travelled to Italy, these flickers of classical and Renaissance art and architecture would provide a tantalizing glimpse of realms yet to be discovered.

Soon after his epic play, *La Numancia,* Cervantes pens *La Galatea.* He dedicates the work to Ascanio Colonna (1559–1608) in the hopes that he can go with him to Italy. After all, Cervantes' friend and fellow writer, Gálvez de Montalvo, author of the pastoral romance *El pastor de Fílida,* had been invited to accompany Colonna in Rome. Cervantes' dedicatory further emphasizes his desire to visit Italy by recalling his earlier stay in Rome when he worked as chamberlain for the future Cardinal Giulio Acquaviva around 1570. But the desire for Rome finds full fruition in the depiction of Italian Renaissance art within the novel. *La*

Galatea is a work framed by frescoes, as Books I and VI introduce works by Raphael. Other Italian artists also appear: Sebastiano del Piombo and Botticelli. In addition, there are numerous other ekphrases of famous fountains, gardens, and villas. Finally, the work also includes references to at least one other ekphrastic text, Garcilaso's *Third Eclogue*.

In this chapter, I want to briefly discuss the most important scene in the pastoral that utilizes this technique, so that the reader may see how notions of ekphrasis continue to evolve here, leading to the very complex representations in *Don Quixote*. The first appearance of the eponymous heroine of the romance signals the introduction of Italian art in the text. Edward Dudley has argued that Cervantes could have viewed Raphael's *The Triumph of Galatea* while in Rome (fig. 2.2). After all, this fresco was at a loggia in the Villa Farnesina, which was open to the public (1995, 33). However, city maps from the period seem to show that the villa was walled in on three sides while the fourth was framed by the Tiber River. If such was the case, then Cervantes would have had to rely on accounts by other visitors, printed descriptions of the villa or prints of the painting, which we know existed.[15] Cervantes' knowledge of this and other paintings at the Farnesina are so detailed that I believe with Dudley that he somehow had access to the loggia. According to Dudley, both the painting and the pastoral partake of a Neoplatonic aesthetics which discards Venus's lascivious voluptuousness in favour of Galatea's chastity. In both works, he argues, the nymph, although surrounded by eroticism, is able to stand apart from it. In Raphael's painting, 'she cuts diagonally through the scenario, avoiding all attempts to involve her in the goings on. She is herself sexually exciting but not ... sexually excited' (Dudley 1995, 36). Pointing to Cervantes' passage, 'encaminóla a otra parte diferente de la que los pastores llevan' (she turned to another path different from the one the shepherds are following) (Cervantes 1995, 205), this critic claims that in Cervantes's novel, 'this effect is even more pronounced ... because he has the shepherds call out to her as she changed direction within the movement of the scene. Cervantes also reminds us of the contrast between her erotically stimulating appearance and the untouchable and inaccessible demeanor of her movements' (Dudley 1995, 38). Galatea's 'triumph' in Raphael's painting thus parallels her triumph in Cervantes' novel where Erastro accuses her of leaving, 'triunfando sobre nuestras voluntades' (triumphing over our will) (Cervantes 1995, 206).

But we must remember that the painting of Galatea is not merely inserted in Cervantes' work as a true or actual ekphrasis. There is no stop of the narrative. Instead, Cervantes places his figures in motion, creating what is in a way a contradiction in terms, a dramatic ekphrasis. He is beginning to create a museum or a collectionist ekphrasis in which his paintings are in motion. By turning ocean waves into pastoral hills and dolphins into sheep, Cervantes may be playfully recalling a text which urges the mixture of painting and poetry ('ut pictura poesis'). Horace's *Ars Poetica* had warned against the poet who takes his leave of all restraints and paints dolphins in forests. This citation was well known in the Renaissance. Lodovico Dolce, for example, quotes Horace and stresses that 'since the painter's business is the imitation of nature, there is no call for variety to appear artificially elaborated' (Roskill 1968, 147). Both Horace and Dolce revel in the sisterhood of the arts, in the (con)fusion of art and painting. Cervantes may be taking up their lead as he playfully inserts a painting located at sea into an earthly pastoral. The result is not artificial, as Dolce warns, since the painting is only recalled, the sheep only remind the reader of Raphael's dolphins. While the playful use of Horace recalls the sisterhood of the arts, the use of rustic musical instruments introduces yet a third manner into the text: painting, text, and music come together to create a certain Neoplatonic concordance that underlines Ficino's notions of harmony. But yet again, Cervantes plays with the concept. The 'chaste' Galatea of Cervantes' novel is playing a *zampoña,* while the male shepherds are associated with the *rabel*: 'al subir de una ladera oyeron el sonido de una suave zampoña que luego por Elicio y Erastro fue conocido que era Galatea quien la sonaba' (upon climbing up the hillside they heard the sound of a sweet *zampoña* and it was later known by Elicio and Erastro that it was Galatea who was sounding it) (1995, 204). The *zampoña* is a wind instrument like a flute[16] while the *rabel* is a string instrument akin to the lyre. In this way, the contrast between Galatea and the male shepherds who wish for her attention is foregrounded by the musical instrument each of them uses. While the wind instrument is 'traditionally seen as appealing to the baser parts of the soul' (Damiani 1983, 89), the string instruments, like the lyre and the harp, were thought to be nobler, and were related to ancient embodiments of poetry, such as Orpheus and Apollo. Galatea plays baser and more bodily sounds, thus bringing into question notions of chastity.

It is surprising that the embodiment of the new Raphaelesque chastity would be playing a wind instrument, representative of the more corporeal instincts of the soul. In fact, Raphael's 'chaste' Galatea is often contrasted with the figure that appears next to her in the loggia of the

Farnesina, Sebastiano del Piombo's *Polyphemus* (fig. 2.3). This gigantic figure, representing eroticism and sexual violence, looks at Galatea with desire but is outside of Raphael's frame. Critics have often compared Piombo's 'robusta maniera' (robust manner) with Raphael's 'gentile o bella maniera' (gentle or lovely manner). Let us recall that for Giorgio Vasari, Raphael was the representative of grace (1996, 1.710). And he mentions that the *Triumph of Galatea* was painted 'in his softest manner' (1996, 1.710).

This disparity of styles on one wall of the loggia has often been viewed with disapproval by art critics. Recently, Rona Goffen has stressed the notion of confrontation and competition. She quotes Vasari (1996, 2.141), who thought there was competition here between Baldassare Peruzzi, Sebastiano, and Raphael. But, Goffen argues that Peruzzi and Sebastiano, were friends. She shows instead that 'the stylistic disparity ... may have been intended as a purposeful confrontation of their two styles – or rather, the art of Raphael in confrontation with that of Michelangelo as interpreted by Sebastiano ... Sebastino combined several *Ignudi*, evoking all of them though not replicating any one of them exactly in the *Polyphemus*' (2002, 230–1).[17] Indeed, Vasari himself explains that Sebastiano del Piombo became one of Michelangelo's pupils, turning away from Raphael's style (1996, 2.142). So, Cervantes is representing a clash of styles between Michelangelo's *terribilitá* and Raphael's grace, a clash that exists between a story of violent murder and the adjacent appearance of Galatea 'cuya hermosura era tanta' (whose beauty was so great) (1995, 204). What we have is a collectionist set of ekphrasis that exhibits contrasting styles.

In addition, the text uses combinatory ekphrasis (combining two works of art) as well as fragmented ekphrasis (using just a fragment of the *Polyphemus*, the musical instrument). The clash between the two styles in painting (Raphael vs. Michelangelo) is problematized by Cervantes' playful combinatory (con)fusion between the two canvases. We may ask: why then is Galatea contaminated with the *zampoña*, an instrument of carnal love that is held by Polyphemus in the painting' It is not my purpose here to discuss in detail my theories of Galatea's turning away from heterosexual love for the male shepherds while preferring the company of her female friend Florisa. This relationship acts as a countermirror to the perfect Platonic male friendship so much praised in the Renaissance. Galatea and Florisa share a true friendship and their deepest thoughts – they also share an erotic attraction expressed in the music of the *zampoña* and their blush (as they wash themselves alone in the river).[18] What is important here is Cervantes' use of painting and music to both veil and reveal the major topics of his narrative (veiled ekphrasis). At the same time, Cervantes covertly unveils the love between the two women so that the reader as voyeur can enjoy their seductive pleasures. Without knowledge of the placement of frescoes in the Villa Farnesina, some of this material would remain hidden. Thus, in a Counter-Reformation move, Cervantes censors his own novel by veiling erotic female friendship in the same manner as detractors of Michelangelo painted over his offending nudes. But the irony is that Cervantes turns to offending Renaissance art to both veil and display what was forbidden.

But there is yet one final twist that must be pointed out in the artistic collection that Cervantes is showing his public through words. In the scene at the river, Galatea and Florisa are compared to the Three Graces as they gather flowers. For George Camamis, we see here fragments of Botticelli's painting of the *Primavera* (fig. 2.4). In Cervantes' museum of words, the reader must suddenly move from two frescoes at the Farnesina in Rome to a painting in Florence. The reason for the sudden shift is unclear. Whatever the answer may be, I would turn away from Camamis's reading where Galatea/Venus is 'the spirit of Renaissance arts and letters and a truly worthy object of the love of shepherd-poets inspired by the humanistic spirit of those times' (1988, 186). Rather, the meeting between Galatea and Florisa (who certainly stands for Botticelli's Flora) recalls both the love of Corydon for Alexis in Virgil's *Second Eclogue* and the imagery of Poliziano's *Orpheus*. In Virgil, Corydon sings of his unrequited love using floral images. If Alexis comes to him, he would have the nymphs gather flowers such as lilies, violets, and the narcissus (1978, 1.13; Eclogue 2.45ff). While Galatea and Florisa can gather flowers together, Corydon can only imagine doing so since his homoerotic desire is unfulfilled. Poliziano's text sings of same-sex relations through floral imagery: 'Henceforth I prefer to gather different flowers ... / This is a love more sweet, more soft, more deep' (Saslow 1986, 122). While Orpheus turns away from women, Galatea turns away from men to gather Florisa herself into her arms.

Although their meeting takes place at the fountain of the Pizarras, the text later reveals that these two women also know of 'un lugar secreto y apartado' (a secret and secluded place) (1995, 214), which is shaded by myrtles and thus hidden from view ('sin ser vistas de ninguno' [without being seen by anyone]) (214). Even though at this time Galatea and Florisa go there to listen to the story of a foreign shepherdess, it is made clear that they know this hidden place and have been there before. The shade of myrtles recalls Botticelli's *Primavera* and the fact that this tree was sacred to Venus. As a symbol of marriage and sexual union, the myrtle thus represents the union between Galatea and Florisa.

Finally, it might be argued that Cervantes turns away from Botticelli's painting since in the *Primavera* the Graces are clothed, while Cervantes pictures them nude. But their thin, translucent gossamer veil in Botticelli reveals more than it conceals. In like manner, the ekphrastic passages in Cervantes' pastoral, while attempting to hide the erotic feelings between women through a thin veil of pastoral pleasures, actually reveal more than they conceal. However, the representation of the naked Graces has an ancient tradition, and Cervantes does note that the ancient Greeks painted them in this manner (1995, 209). Thus, Cervantes is relating classical antiquity to Renaissance art, which sought to recover the ancients. Among the many Renaissance images of the Graces, Cervantes' citation may also bring to mind a painting by Raphael, which is now at the Musée Condé in Cantilly (fig. 5). Here, the three are represented naked except for wearing strings of red coral. In addition, one wears a transparent loin-cloth. In their hands they have either golden apples or golden orbs/balls. While the orbs or balls may be linked to the theme of friendship,[19] the nudity is linked to *voluptas*. The three nude Graces, for example, were held as a sign for a brothel in Pompeii (Van Lohouizen-Mulder 1977, 89). Cervantes makes it clear that this nakedness serves to demonstrate 'que eran señoras de la belleza' (that they were mistresses of beauty) (1995, 209). The fact that Raphael's Graces have corals clearly relates them to Venus/*voluptas* (Ficino 1989, 201). But Cervantes admits 'otros efectos' (other effects) (1995, 209). From antiquity to the Renaissance, the Graces were held as symbols for giving and receiving and thus for *amicitia* or friendship. The Graces stand for friendship in Aristotle, Seneca's *De Beneficiis*, Boccaccio's *Genealogia deorum*, and even in Leon Battista Albert's *De Pictura* where they are related to *liberalitas*, a key condition for friendship. Thus, we can read Cervantes' Graces as representing both friendship and *voluptas*. What Cervantes does is to combine these attributes establishing an erotic friendship between Galatea and Florisa.

Earlier in the pastoral romance, the entrance of Galatea enacted the contest between Sebastiano del Piombo and Raphael, one robust and the other one graceful. Now, if we follow Vasari, we have a contest between the whimsical and the graceful. Vasari thought of Botticelli as 'restless,' with a father 'weary of the vagaries of his son's brain' (1996, 1.535). Raphael, as noted, was depicted by Vasari as pure grace.[20] By pointing to the naked Graces, Cervantes could be underlining the sincerity and grace of Raphael's art, and thus to the very qualities that flourish in the erotic friendship between the two loving shepherdesses in Cervantes' pastoral.

Galatea's is a friendship that reverses male-centred Platonic dialogues, thus empowering the love of women. Through the lustful and homoerotic *zampoña*, the mutual blush, the shaded myrtle, and the reference to the nude Graces, this love is unveiled as an erotic passion. Galatea, who is indeed the chaste Galatea when confronted by men, turns into a beautiful loving Venus who shares the pleasures of spring with her companion, the goddess Flora/Florisa. Together they gather flowers and emerge from their erotic encounter with loose and attractively dishevelled hair (1995, 209), the final sign of their erotic encounter.

In the textual museum of his works, *La Numancia* and *La Galatea*, Cervantes places images of strong mnemonic power. Be they canvases of war and exhortation to battle as in his epic tragedy or images of erotic play in his pastoral, Cervantes always places them in strategic locations as required in the treatises on artificial memory. Scipio's allocution is the ideal place for Giulio Romano's fresco, while the first entrance of Galatea into the pastoral romance becomes unforgettable through the utilization of Raphael's *Triumph of Galatea*. As she moves through the open canvas of the text, she seems to be a chaste nymph who knows how to avoid men's desire. The male gaze is upon her, but she deflects their desire through a diagonal movement. Her thoughts are elsewhere. When alone or with Florisa, she becomes a new Venus, playing the sounds of passionate desire for the goddess of Flowers, thus reenacting in erotic fashion a glorious moment captured by Botticelli's *Primavera*. Carefully transmuting the male-love of the Platonists into a scene of woman's desire for her like, Cervantes gives us a glimpse of Galatea bathing (if only her face) with her true friend. In one stroke of the pen, Cervantes subverts not only the platonic male-love tradition and the consequent superiority of men but also the allegorically charged images of Botticelli's *Primavera*. In this textual museum of antique and Renaissance art, Raphael's glorious painting of *The Triumph of Galatea* is left as a mere foil for the love between two women, a sincere friendship ruled by Venus and expressed in ancient statues and in Raphael's painting of *The Three Graces*. Italian art and the classics furnish a museum and library that seek to recapture a Renaissance where beauty, antique myths, harmony, and erotic friendships can flourish. Carefully concealed, these verbal pictures and antique tales are at play in a text that veils through combinatory ekphrasis what the Counter-Reformation would censure.

3 At School with the Ancients: Raphael

Early Europeans ... must have resembled not the robed sages of Raphael's *School of Athens* but the naked inhabitants of pre-Conquest Virginia and Mexico: they had been not the masters of a universally valid Great Tradition but the prisoners of a little one ... Europeans, not Indians, were the real barbarians. Antiquity lost authority.

Anthony Grafton, 'The Rest vs. the West'

La Numancia and *La Galatea* are works that revel in the art of imitation. Using the structures and images from Raphael' frescoes and following many of the classical and Renaissance writers represented in them, these two texts find a way to approach the ancients. While these early texts revel in *imitatio* and *auctoritas, Don Quixote* presents itself as a celebration of the artist's freedom. Instead of following ancient authorities, it foregrounds Leonardo's heresy (Greene 1982, 44); that is, it resists and even mocks the urge to imitate other texts or even visual representations. There are thus curious similarities between the Prologue to Part I of *Don Quixote* and Leonardo's views. Very much like the Cervantes of the Prologue, Leonardo asserts: 'They will say that since I do not have literary learning I cannot possibly express the things I wish to treat ... I may not know, like them, how to cite from the authors' (1989, 9). While Leonardo turns away from *auctoritas* emphasizing that nature and experience are the true teachers, Cervantes uses parody to show the apparent pitfalls found in reliance on textual authority. Don Quixote surely acts according to what Michel Foucault has called the prose of the world: 'There is no difference between the visible marks that God has stamped upon the surface of the earth, so that we may know its inner secrets, and the legible words that the Scriptures, or the sages of Antiquity, have set down in the books preserved for us by tradition' (1970, 33). But these 'Scriptures' and 'sages' are mocked in the prologue. The text also questions Don Quixote's quest after authority. After all, the knight goes mad because he not only reads too much but he lends full authority to what he reads – and the world and its authorities as texts no longer provide proof of their truth. Foucault argues that '*Don Quixote* is a negative of the Renaissance world; writing has ceased to be the prose of the world' (1970, 47). Not only is chivalric 'authority' at fault; in his madness, Don Quixote also envisions epic models (seeming a mad Ajax in the battle of the sheep) only to be humiliated. This failure emerges from the fact that 'it is his task to recreate the epic, though by a reverse process: the epic recounted (or claimed to recount) real exploits, offering them to our memory; Don Quixote, on the other hand, must endow with reality the signs-without-content of the narrative. His adventures will be ... a diligent search over the entire surface of the earth for the forms that will prove that what the books say is true' (Foucault 1970, 47). But Foucault is only partially correct. The very instability of the novel also allows for a counterreading, one that supports notions of classical authority: the Homeric epics, Virgil, Apuleius, Plutarch, Pythagoras, etc. In the end, the text and its multiple narrators may be mocking its hero simply because he is unable to follow authorities that are appropriate for his status, situation in life, and concerns. In breaking with decorum and the order of the cosmos, the hero fails to emulate the 'order of the world.'

Cervantes' novel both questions and reaffirms the prose of the world, showing how this writing manifests itself in amazing varieties of literature and art, including the epic and the chivalric, Italian frescoes and manuscript drawings. Numerous other forms are upheld while also being represented as noxious. Pastoral literature, for example, leads to Grisóstomo's suicide, while Italian *novelle* may be the cause of the tragic mistakes in the interpolated tale of *El curioso impertinente*. Too much reliance on authority, then, leads to loss or failure. What the characters show within the text is what the text itself does with its models. Although the *Quixote* incorporates scores of genres and points to a dizzying abundance of models, it conjures them up in an attempt to transform or escape them. As opposed to the classical *Numancia* and *Galatea* with their precise and elaborate program based on imitation of art and literature, *Don Quixote* revels in the freedom to repeatedly evoke and veer away from an artistic or poetic authority. While *La Numancia* and

La Galatea had rejected the extremes of *contaminatio*, that is, the anachronistic mixture of a number of models, *Don Quixote* takes this type of imitation to an extreme. Juxtaposing the epic and the chivalric, Aristotelian concepts and Neoplatonic images, the work creates a chain of motifs that flicker and disappear only to be rekindled in later pages and once again fade.

Very much like the burning of Don Quixote's library in the sixth chapter, the novel itself is formed from the dying embers of previous texts, pictures, and authorities. From the textual ashes of a myriad of forms rises something new. Although accepting the notion of origin, it strives for originality. According to David Quint, the Renaissance debate between origin and originality, that is, between locating 'the text's value in a source of truth and authority that lies outside the text itself – normally in an earlier text or series of texts that have been granted authoritative or sacred status' and the 'historicist reading' that focuses on 'the craftsmanship of the human author' finally shifted to the second mode with *Don Quixote*. 'This shift is felt when Cervantes asks that *Don Quixote* be judged on the basis of its intrinsic qualities as a literary work of art, perhaps ultimately for its inimitable originality' (1983, 22).

Don Quixote does not seem to follow through with a particular program of literary imitation, much less of Italian art. Whenever imitation seems to appear, an extreme *clinamen* invalidates the predecessor.[1] It would thus seem almost futile to search for the graphic representations that underlie some of these literary flickers within the text. Such a search may seem as disjointed and episodic as some of the narratives. And yet, the novel itself invites such an analysis. Helena Percas de Ponsetti has repeatedly pointed to the pictorial nature of the narrative, demonstrating that any reader must understand this distinctive characteristic of Cervantes' art. His pictorial narrative points to the very ancient competition between poetry and painting encapsulated in Horace's famous dictum 'ut pictura poesis.' But it is not just that Cervantes wants to join this ancient competition between the sister arts. What Percas de Ponseti leaves unsaid in her erudite and important book *Cervantes y su concepto del arte* is the fact that the epic relies heavily upon ekphrasis, the depiction of an object or work of art with such detail that it seems to be visible. From Achilles' shield in the *Iliad* to the paintings of the Trojan War found in Juno's temple in the *Aeneid*, the epic thrives on the pictorial. And yet, the matter is not so simple. Cervantes' novel repeatedly undoes attempts at rapprochement with the epic through fragmentation. It often turns away from traditional ekphrasis and chooses allusive ekphrasis instead. At times, the text even turns away from famous images, using only the program or structure on which they were drawn. *Don Quixote* also mocks a number of genres starting with the chivalric romances through overstatement, minimization, humorous characterization, etc.

Margaret Anne Doody (among others) has recently argued that Cervantes was not the creator of the novel. Rather than being heir to the epic, the novel derives from the ancient Greek romances, which she views as early novels. Curiously, she demonstrates that ekphrasis is one of its main elements (1996, 136–42). And Cervantes clearly includes this type of fiction within his novel. Indeed, the novel may even have religious origins, unfolding from the stories of Isis and Osiris (Doody 1996, 19). If we look beyond the ubiquitous novels of chivalry, it may be possible to find in *Don Quixote* a constant wavering between two ancient forms, the epic and the classical/Egyptian novel.

It is thus very difficult to search for the origins of Cervantes' images since the stress on minimalism and variety stem from the myths of a madman, from the narrative of a 'lying' Arab, rather than from a single pictorial program. Thus these chapters on *Don Quixote* will move among the flickering images and the tenuous lights of origins showing a series of possible models both from Italian art and from notional ekphrasis. It may well be that the knight's memory is intent in recollecting a chivalric past, imposing upon reality images from his mind that can surely please those who prefer the risible and the ridiculous in artificial memory. But beyond (and sometimes within) these amazing images of a modern landscape made over into a chivalric site the reader can detect more ancient echoes. It is these that interest us in this book, since they are often connected with Renaissance art. Is this museum so personal that it cannot be arranged without the presence of its owner? Susan A. Crane explains: 'The collector was able to maintain whatever sense of order he desired as long as the collection remained in his cabinet ... What for him was representative of plenitude became to observers a sign of disorder' (2000, 76). Is this a text where the order of the collection is now lost? And whose collection is it? Don Quixote's, Cide Hamete Benengeli's? Or should it be ascribed to a virtual Cervantes who brings these images from Italian soil? And can we see these collections amidst the dusty and rustic landscape of La Mancha and amidst the accumulation of chivalric texts? And if we can see them, how do they appear to us – as ekphrases, as dramatic ekphrases, as allusive ekphrases and citations, or as remnants from artistic programs? The books of chivalry will not help us in most instances to review a museum of Italian Renaissance art and architecture. Instead, we must turn to the classics, to the ancients, and see if they point to some sort of order.

While the epic with its imperial connotations seems to dominate the beginnings of Part 1 of the novel, as the knight's adventures lead to increasing failures, the search for love, be it the search for Dulcinea or the interpolation of amorous digressions, becomes more important. These are often modelled on classical and Renaissance texts such as Ariosto's *Orlando furioso*, Heliodorus' *Aethiopica*, and Apuleius's *Golden Ass*. In the 1615 *Quixote* (which is beyond the scope of this book), the search for a Renaissance and classical Dulcinea gives way to images of the grotesque; and this search, in turn, leads once again to Apuleius and to the Egyptian mysteries. In terms of images, there are also major shifts. The novel begins with evocations of Raphael and turns to Michelangelo's *terribilitá*; it draws Titian's imperial portraits while later turning to Titian's, Giulio Romano's, and Raphael's portraits of desire in a combinatory ekphrasis. And while Part I has a strong heroic and parodic quality, Part II turns to defeat, deformity, and the grotesque through Arcimboldo. Furthermore, the 1605 novel shows itself to be circular; it begins with the wisdom of Pythagoras and ends with the astral magic of Ficino, who made use of Pythagoras in his Platonic commentaries. By evoking ancient wars and antique wisdoms through Renaissance art and ekphrasis, the following chapters strive to celebrate the exhilaration of Italy, the desire to recapture the Renaissance, as found in the novel, an impetus which is accompanied by a movement for exasperation within the knight, when the dusty roads of La Mancha fail to provide with ease and abundance not only his cherished chivalric adventures, but the images found in the classical and oriental worlds.

The prologue to *Don Quixote* I may serve as vestibule, as an entrance to the Quixotic worlds, one that not only beckons the visitor but also warns the reader that this abode is very different from previous Cervantine creations. While Cervantes' *La Numancia* exhibits all sixteen frescoes from Raphael's Stanze at the Vatican and *La Galatea* is framed by two frescoes by Raphael, the prologue to *Don Quixote* carefully conceals an extended commentary on the earliest of the Stanze decorated by Raphael, the Stanza della Segnatura. While the prologue evokes Raphael's images through fragmented ekphrases, it also replicates the structure or program utilized by Raphael. This program is far from unique, and thus it may be possible to argue that Cervantes could have found such a program elsewhere. Thus, the program would not be a model, but simply a way to clarify the structure of the prologue. In my view, there can be little question that Cervantes turns specifically to Raphael's Stanza della Segnatura in order to structure his prologue. Indeed, he develops it by repeatedly alluding to Raphael's vivid images, thus making his vision conjoin that of Raphael. We know from mnemonic treatises that paintings that represent vivid images are unforgettable, but Cervantes takes both the program and its images and mocks them through comic repetition, inversion, and trivialization. Although the pictorial and classical imitative models from *La Numancia* and *La Galatea* have not been abandoned, the tone and manner of imitation have changed from monumental or elegiac to parodic, and from necromantic and sacramental to eclectic. The grace, balance, and majesty of Raphael's frescoes seem to have no place in Cervantes' text.

The prefatory pages begin with a portrayal of a poet. It should be noted from the start that presenting similarities between this fictional 'author' and Cervantes is one of the many methods used in the novel to weave a myth of the author. Mary Gaylord reminds us: 'The personified author is not interchangeable with the historical Cervantes, but rather another character within the author's fiction, one who serves as another reminder of the distance between the real author and his subject' (1983, 84). But it is this fictional Cervantes which interests us here, since he will mythologize his role through constant references to the great artists of the Italian Renaissance. We have seen already how the prologue echoes Leonardo's 'heresy.' It also serves to distance the new book from the works of Raphael. The poet/author begins by pointing to the place where the novel was conceived, one from which the muses were absent. These nine goddesses immediately remind the reader of their presence in *La Galatea*. But here, images of pastoral are immediately dashed. This new book, the author-narrator claims, was born in a prison, a place whose melancholy sounds and harsh ambience deprived him of appropriate inspiration: 'El sosiego, el lugar apacible, la amenidad de los campos, la serenidad de los cielos, el murmurar de las fuentes, la quietud del espíritu son grande parte para que las musas más estériles se muestren fecundas ...' (Tranquility, peaceful surroundings, the pleasures of the countryside, the serenity of the skies, the murmuring of the springs, and the quietude of the spirit – these are the things that encourage even the most barren muses to become fertile) (1978, 1.50; 11) (fig. 3.1). *Parnassus*, Raphael's depiction of the haven for poets, is just such a *locus amoenus* with a terrain moulded for human contemplation. Laurel trees provide shade and the promise of poetic fulfilment; a Castalian spring murmurs of nature's secrets, its sounds blending with the harmonies of the gods. In the quiet and pleasant place imagined by Cervantes and depicted by Raphael, the muses provide inspiration even to the most prosaic of poets. The 'serenidad de los cielos' is further replicated in the allegorical figure of *Poetry* (fig. 3.2) which stands above *Parnassus*: 'Her blue gown, with a girdle strewn with stars and wings, symbolizes the flight of the imagination' (Hersey 1993, 142). While the author of *La Numancia* and *La Galatea* revelled in such ekphrasis, the fictional Cervantes,[2] portrayed in the prologue of *Don Quixote*, has a difficult time evoking Raphael's *Parnassus*. The 'author' is concerned that his tale of Don Quixote, not having been watered by the Castalian spring, is as dry as a rush. He also has writer's block and cannot compose the prologue.

But a friend appears and offers his help. 'Cervantes' wishes to learn not just how to write the prologue but also how to adorn it as well as his novel with learned allusions. One need only look at *The School of Athens* to be overwhelmed by the wisdom of antiquity (fig. 3.3). The friend's advice alludes not only to this fresco but to all four compositions in the Stanza della Segnatura. These four frescoes painted by Raphael served to decorate Pope Julius II's private library. They may be mnemonic devices to recall what books are included.[3] For example, the right foreground of *The School of Athens* depicts Pythagoras, Empedocles, and Averroes, 'authors of books originally shelved in the room' (Hersey 1993, 133). Noting that the prominent figure in white right behind these three authors has been identified as Francesco Maria della Rovere, Pope Julius's nephew, George Hersey explains that the young man is portrayed as a student of these philosophers 'in the sense that he would, or could, read their books' (133). More important, as the pope's heir Francesco 'would inherit the library housed here. He will thus eventually receive these philosophers in the sense that he becomes the owner of their works' (133). The description of Don Quixote's library in chapter 6 can be seen as a reflection of Julius's collection. While the knight's books, according to his critics, should be burnt as heretics ('y quemaran todos estos descomulgados libros, que tiene muchos, que bien merecen ser abrasados como si fueren herejes' (and burned those unchristian books of his ...; he's got lots and lots of them, and they do deserve to be put to the flames, like heretics) [1978; 1.5.108; 50]), Julius's library, if it had remained at the Vatican at the time of Cervantes' visit, may have been judged too 'pagan' for the ideology of the Counter-Reformation.

Before continuing with the prologue, a brief discussion of Don Quixote's library in terms of the Stanza della Segnatura may be in order. As the priest and the barber peruse the knight's shelves so as to discover and destroy the most heretical books, they encounter three basic clusters or types of works: romances of chivalry, pastoral romances together with lyric poetry, and epics. This tripartite division could well be a reflection of the three main frescoes of the Stanza della Segnatura, paintings that could well reflect the division of Julius's library according to three main topics. For Don Quixote, the romances of chivalry form the foundation of his belief. Since the knight strays from accepted behaviour and the books are his models, they are associated with heretics who stray from approved dogma. *Amadís de Gaula*, Don Quixote's chief chivalric model, is called 'dogmatizador de una secta tan mala' (the prophet of such a pernicious sect) (1978, 1.6.110; 52). It becomes, in a sense, Don Quixote's Gospel or Bible. Since chivalric books are the source of dogma, they can be linked to Raphael's *Disputa*, in which the four Gospel writers and numerous fathers of the church are depicted. Thus, the theological section of Julius's library corresponds to the chivalric cluster in Don Quixote's study.

The pastoral romances are replete with doctrines of love taken from the Neoplatonic philosophers of the Renaissance. *La Diana*, for example, the first of the pastorals discovered by the priest and the barber (1978, 1.6.118), contains lengthy discussions on love taken directly from Leo Hebreus's *Diálogos de amor*. It is no coincidence that Cervantes mentions Leo Hebreus in the prologue as a source for amorous doctrines. These romances, as Pero Pérez, the priest, states are 'libros de entendimiento' (books for the intellect) (1.6.118; 56), which, as Mary Cozad explains, means that they are books of 'intellect' and 'meaning,' 'a sort of Neo-Platonic higher knowledge' (1988, 172). And citing other critics she shows how they ought to have 'a philosophical content' (161). As exponents of Neoplatonic philosophies, these romances can be linked to *The School of Athens* in which Plato is one of two main figures. Let us recall that in *La Galatea* (one of the works found in Don Quixote's library) Cervantes proclaims in the preface that his work includes 'razones de filosofía' (concepts of philosophy) (1985, 158). Thus, the cluster on ancient philosophy in Julius's library corresponds to the pastoral romances in the Spanish knight's study. Finally, the epic cluster in Don Quixote's library, is represented in Raphael's *Parnassus* where the great epic poets stand next to Apollo and his muses. Next to blind Homer stands Virgil, dressed in green, and next to him the author of the great Christian epic, Dante. Thus, the literary cluster in Julius's library, a grouping that foregrounds the epic, appears as the poetry section in Don Quixote's study where epic is again the chief genre. Indeed, the prominence of epic may serve to alert the reader to the link between Cervantes' novel and this ancient genre.

In order to confirm these relationships, the text includes a clear reminiscence of Raphael's Stanza in the chapter dealing with Don Quixote's library. The priest praises the *Palmerín de Inglaterra* by comparing it to Homer's epics. He argues for its preservation, evoking Alexander: 'y se haga para ello otra caja como la que halló Alejandro en los despojos de Darío, que la diputó para guardar en ella las obras del poeta Homero' (and a casket be made for it like the one Alexander the Great found among the spoils of Darius and designated as a case for the works of the poet Homer) (1978, 1.6.115; 55). This tale is the subject of 'a grisaille painting' in the Stanza della Segnatura. It is entitled *Alexander the Great Places Homer's 'Iliad' in Safe Keeping* (Jones and Penny 1983, 74). Although this painting may appear to be a minor addition to Raphael's Stanza and perhaps not worth this detailed attention, it was engraved by Marcantonio Raimondi, the famous popularizer of Raphael during the Renaissance. Thus, the allusion would not have been at all an obscure one during the period (Shoemaker and Brown 1981, 10). The grisaille painting next to this one, *Augustus Prevents the Burning of Virgil's 'Aeneid,'* will be evoked by Vivaldo when he wants to save Grisostomo's poems in chapter 13 (1978, 1.179).[4]

But let us return to Cervantes' prologue. Here, the friend is showing the fictional Cervantes how to pretend to 'own' a series of authorities. Although the friend's advice serves to call attention to Lope de Vega's exhibitionist erudition, it also leads back to Raphael's intense interest in the archaeology of knowledge. The friend, then, is teaching the author how to become a counterfeit Raphael. In contrast to the Renaissance painter, the friend of the prologue counsels 'Cervantes' to engage in a show of erudition rather than in an intensive investigation of the past. This is not to say that there is not a kind of exhibitionism in *The School of Athens*, which may have led Cervantes to choose Raphael as model. After all, this virtuoso representation of past authorities exhibits not only them but also the painter's own knowledge. Furthermore, the Italian artist includes himself in this vast fresco of antique learning. Draped in white and wearing a black beret, he peers at the viewer from the right foreground – but not as 'shyly' as Hersey would have us believe (1993, 135).[5] The presence of Raphael in his own fresco recalls the portrayal of the author in Cervantes' prologue to his novel. While *La Numancia* had seriously entered into competition with Raphael's authorities, *Don Quixote*, as a debunking of useless references to authority, of necessity takes aim, although indirectly, at Raphael's fresco through the figure of the friend. Of course, we will eventually discover that this debunking is mere play; that the text is truly engaged in the representation of the ancients through Italian Renaissance art.

Each of the figures included in *The School of Athens* is a famous thinker from the remote past.[6] In a glaring anachronism, Raphael unites learned men from diverse times and places, bringing them together in what the viewer might think to be fifth-century Athens since Plato and Aristotle preside over the crowd and stand in a building that includes statues of the pagan gods. The supposed absence of such learning from Cervantes' novel propels the fictional author to contrast his 'leyenda seca como un esparto' (a book as dry as esparto grass) (1978, 1.52; 12) with books 'tan llenos de sentencias ... de toda la caterva de filosófos' (so crammed with maxims from ... the whole herd of philosophers) (1.52; 12). Pointing to this statement, Robert B. Alter asserts that 'the novel begins out of an erosion of belief in the authority of the written word' (1975, 3). More specifically, the sentence seems to question the authority of the ancients.[7] Such an entourage of philosophers is precisely one of the elements provided to Cervantes by his friend. Just as *The School of Athens* foregrounds the figures of Plato and Aristotle by placing them at the centre of the gathering, Cervantes' prologue also singles them out in this mock-school by alluding to books 'tan llenos de sentencias de Aristóteles, de Platón' (so cramned with maxims from Aristotle, Pato) (1.52; 12). This again constitutes a humorous allusion to Raphael's *School of Athens*, in which Plato and Aristotle do indeed stand at the centre of a 'herd of philosophers.' Lope de Vega, who must have felt ridiculed in this prologue for his showy erudition, takes up Cervantes' mocking allusion and repackages it with dignity and authority. He begins his *Arte nuevo de hacer comedias* (*New Art of Writing Comedias*) (1609/1613) by pointing to the lyceums and academies of Greece and Rome. The modern Spanish Academy that asked him to write a treatise on theatre will soon excel the ancient ones, he claims. In praising the new Academy, he also praises himself, becoming one of Raphael's great sages, and thus seeking to overturn Cervantes' mocking remarks in *Don Quixote*.

The fictional Cervantes continues his humorous lament, bemoaning the fact that his book is also lacking quotes from holy scripture, while other texts insert whole sermons next to pictures of a distracted lover. Mockingly, he claims that these writers will claim that they are 'unos santos Tomases y otros doctores de la Iglesia' (so many St Thomases and other doctors of the Church) (1978, 1.52; 12). Continuing Cervantes' move through the Stanza della Segnatura, this is an allusion to Raphael's *Disputa* (fig. 3.4), which stands opposite the *School of Athens*, and where, among the doctors of the church, we find St Thomas on the lower right hand of the fresco. He is easily recognizable 'by the inscription on his halo' (Cornini 1993, 256).[8] According to Hersey, this fresco 'represents Christianity's triumph over, and transformation of, the sources of thought portrayed in the *School [of Athens]*' (1993, 135). However, Raphael presents both traditions independently. There is nothing to show that the wisdom of the pagans is inferior to that of the Christians. Indeed, by placing St Thomas in a different fresco from the one that includes Plato, Aristotle, and Averroes, Raphael may be breaking with the pictorial tradition of the 'Triumph of St Thomas,' in which this doctor of the church is depicted as standing above Plato and Aristotle (representatives of reason) on the altar at Santa Caterina in Pisa. In addition, Filippino Lippi's *St Thomas in Triumph over the Heretics* at the Carafa Chapel in Santa Maria Sopra Minerva in Rome depicts Thomas defeating a number of heresies. The Arabic philosopher Averroes lies at his feet. Steffi Roettgen explains: 'The scene is based on Thomas's major writings. In his *Summa theologica* he engages in an imaginary debate with various third-to fifth-century thinkers who opposed Church doctrine ... This debate is combined with Thomas' demonstration in his *Summa contra gentiles* of the triumph of faith over reason' (1996, 209).[9] Cervantes, like Raphael, fails to authorize Christians over pagans.[10] His portrayal of the doctors of the church is presented as mockingly as that of the philosophers. We thus see a series of playful swerves that characterizes Cervantes' treatment of authorities, be they Renaissance artists, classical writers, church fathers, or even chivalric fictions.

Although the prologue presents the three frescoes in a parodic manner, seemingly rejecting biblical, philosophical, and literary authorities, the novel will actually include a sustained imitation of some of the authorities in all three frescoes. For example, Plato's *Timeus* will buttress the numerological architecture of the text, while Aristotle's *Ethics* will provide material for the characterization of Don Quixote. The central figures of *Parnassus*, Virgil, Homer, and Dante will add an epic dimension to the knight's quest. And the image St Thomas whose *Summa contra gentiles* demonstrates the triumph of faith over reason echoes the challenge of Don Quixote who orders the merchants to believe in Dulcinea's beauty without proof: 'Lo importante es que sin verla lo habéis de creer, confesar, afirmar, jurar y defender' (The whole point is that, without seeing her, you must believe, confess, affirm, swear and uphold it) (1978, 1.4.100; 46). The prologue, then, is not mocking all authority, but the unimaginative and servile use of ancient and biblical texts. While humbly proposing that his text lacks erudition, Cervantes, in contradistinction to Lope de Vega, makes use of imitation in subtle and suggestive ways.

Having finished his lament, the 'author' informs his friend that he has decided to bury his *Don Quixote* 'hasta que el cielo depare quien le adorne de tantas cosas como le faltan' (until heaven provides someone to adorn him with all these attributes that he lacks) (1978, 1.53; 13). But the friend replies that this lack is easily remedied. He offers two major pieces of advice: the addition of Latin maxims so as to include references in the margins (*acotaciones*) and the inclusion of names that can be easily footnoted (*anotaciones*). The *acotaciones*, like the fictional author's initial lament, include allusions to the three main frescoes of the Stanza della Segnatura. The *anotaciones* are divided into three clusters, the first and third also including the three frescoes. Let us look first of all at the *acotaciones*. Here, the friend singles out a series of maxims in Latin in a show of erudition. The first two appear to derive from Horace.[11] Many art critics believe that this Roman poet plays a key role in Raphael's *Parnassus*.[12] Some locate Horace at the extreme right front of the fresco, drawing the viewer into the painting with his gesture. According to Matthias Winner, the gesture is a eulogy to the pope who would enter the room by the door under the fresco: 'Horace's Odes provide the best examples of eulogies (*laudes*) that might legitimately be related to the entrance of the Pope through the door at the poet's feet' (1993, 288). Given the neo-Pythagorean program of the Stanza,[13] it is possible that this figure stands for Pindar, in which case, Horace is the standing figure to the right of the seated Pindar who not only listens to him but also 'expresses his rapture with his outstretched arms' (Joost-Gaugier 1996, 65). The 'rapture' derives from the fact that Horace imitated Pindar, acknowledging the Greek poet's superiority. While Raphael's portrayal of Horace serves to praise either the viewer or the seated figure, the two Horatian *sententiae* found in Cervantes' text have a more critical content. These two maxims are linked thematically in that both show the powerlessness of gold to bring about liberty and to avert death. The first one evokes Cervantes' long captivity and questions the reasons for Spain's forgetfulness of its heroic soldiers. The second shows the equalizing power of death thus warning the wealthy and powerful that they too will be its victims. Popes and emperors, soldiers and commoners will all come to the same end.

The worldly disillusionment present in these two *sententiae* is carried over into the next two maxims which are religious in nature. They derive from the apostle Matthew, thus veering away from the *Parnassus* and returning to the *Disputa*, where the evangelist may well be the third figure from the right in the upper or celestial tier of the fresco, sitting between Abraham and Moses (Hersey 1993, 136).[14] Indeed, Matthew's Gospel is the first of four texts opened at the very centre of the painting, lying between the celestial and earthly realms. Not only is Cervantes foregrounding here the first of the Gospels, but one that, in contrast to Mark's, 'records many more sayings' (Kermode 1987, 377). This abundance of maxims may thus have led the friend to recommend this book to the fictional Cervantes.

It is very likely that Cervantes had read Giorgio Vasari's interpretation of the frescoes in the Stanza della Segnatura – after all, the revised and augmented second edition of the *Lives* was published in 1568, the year before Cervantes' arrival in Italy. In Vasari's well-known text, the Pythagoras of *The School of Athens* is confused with the Matthew of the *Disputa*. Vasari writes: 'Nor is one able to describe the beauty and goodness that are to be seen in the heads and figures of the Evangelists, to whose countenances he gave an air of attention and intentness very true to life, and particularly in those who are writing. Thus, behind St. Matthew, who is copying the characters from the tablet wherein are the figures ... he painted an old man' (1996, 1.718). As Patricia Rubin has shown, Vasari's mistake derives from the fact that 'he surely did not write the polished and intricate passages about the *Stanze* while standing in front of the paintings. He worked, probably in Florence, from his notes, his drawings, and his memory ...' (1995, 365). More important, he may have recalled the details of the left foreground of *The School of Athens* by looking at a print of the fresco by Agostino Veneziano, who substitutes an evangelist for Pythagoras, intending 'to facilitate the sale of the print as a sacred subject' (Rubin 1995, 365). Thus, Cervantes' inclusion of Matthew would underline Vasari's vision of the Stanza della Segnatura as a place depicting 'theologians reconciling Philosophy and Astrology with Theology: wherein are portraits of all the sages in the world, disputing in various ways' (1996, 1.717). It is this sense of a wholeness of knowledge, a 'universally valid Great Tradition' (Grafton 1997, 57), where the ancient Greeks and Romans prefigured the truths of Christianity, which is replicated in a parodic manner in Cervantes' prologue. This quaternity of maxims by Horace and Matthew establishes a dialogue between pagan verses and Christian sacred writings. The notion of quaternity points both to the Christian tradition in which the Gospels are four in number and to the pagan wisdom of Pythagoras, as depicted in *The School of Athens*, who foregrounds the number four as key to the cosmos.

A fifth *sentencia* dangles at the end of the passage dealing with *acotaciones*. It is wrongly attributed to Cato by Cervantes' friend, thus providing an added element of satire on those who revel in a show of erudition, while knowing little. In an age when classical learning was pervasive among the educated, it would be clear that this maxim came from Ovid. It is fitting that the Roman poet be included here since he is portrayed as one of the figures standing above Horace in the *Parnassus* (Hersey 1993, 140). The two verses derive from the *Tristia*, Ovid's meditations on exile, and tell how the poet was abandoned by his friends in times of need. Cervantes' friend is telling the writer that he is a true friend since he has not abandoned him in his suffering. He is instead providing him with a solution to his problems. This friend, as noted, is attempting to transform 'Cervantes' into a counterfeit or mock-Raphael. His solutions to Cervantes' problems, which emphasize the fake erudition of rival authors such as Lope de Vega, are not in themselves helping the fictional Cervantes, although he pretends they are. At a deeper level, however, both the pictorial and classical allusions will help to enrich any reading of *Don Quixote*. While surface erudition is satirized, the text will invite the reader to delve into the hidden flickers of *contaminatio*, a mode of imitation that reverberates beneath a seemingly seamless clarity of style.

Thus far, the fictional Cervantes has alluded to the three principal frescoes in the Stanza della Segnatura, while the friend, discussing maxims (*sentencias*) and annotations (*acotaciones*), has twice evoked the three frescoes.[15] The next element in the friend's advice has to do with *anotaciones* – how to include words that can be footnoted at the end. These can be divided into three clusters of three, six, and four figures each. The three names suggested by the friend in the first cluster of *anotaciones* are simple but effective. Instead of using the term 'giant,' the fictional Cervantes should use Goliath; instead of any body of water, the river Tagus should be mentioned; and in dealing with thieves, the author should refer to Cacus. Curiously, the first and third suggestions have to do with giants. The importance of these beings is further emphasized by the fact that they are actually alluded to within the novel.[16] An innkeeper is compared to Cacus in the second chapter of Part I,[17] while the size of Goliath is discussed in the first chapter of Part II using the Bible as authority.[18] Thus, the two giants of the prologue stand as great exponents of two opposing traditions, the biblical and the classical. But these are not the traditions that are supposed to help to shape them in Cervantes' novel. As Augustin Redondo has pointed out, the giant is a key figure in the chivalric romances, the genre that is most consistently imitated and parodied in *Don Quixote*: 'Es una manera para el novel caballero, que ha llegado al final de su recorrido iniciático y ha triunfado de múltiples dificultades, de ostentar su valor y su maestría al derrocar a un adversario superior a los anteriores, el cual es símbolo además de las fuerzas del Mal' (It is a way for the new knight, who has arrived at the end of his process of initiation and has triumphed over multiple difficulties, of displaying his valour and mastery upon knocking down an adversary superior to the preceding ones, who is also a symbol of the forces of Evil') (1998, 325). Given the confluence of three major traditions, it should come as no surprise that the figure of the giant is present in Don Quixote's mind from the very first chapter. Here, he imagines himself defeating one of these legendary figures (Cervantes 1978, 1.77; Redondo 1998, 326) and perhaps sending the defeated creature as a trophy to his lady.

Although both Eduardo Urbina (1987) and Augustin Redondo (1998) rightly search for models of Cervantine imitation in the chivalric romances, the prologue to *Don Quixote* makes it clear that there are other traditions of giants, the biblical and the classical. It is fitting that the friend would mention Goliath soon after citing Matthew's gospel. After all, the biblical text begins by claiming that Christ is the son of Abraham and of David. Christ/David came to be envisioned by writers such as Lope de Vega (whom Cervantes satirizes in this prologue) as the defeater of Goliath, 'es decir, de los enemigos de la fe' (meaning, of the enemies of the faith) (Vosters 1977, 1.101).[19] The dialogues between Don Quixote and Sancho contrasting the roles of the knight and the saint, which are scattered throughout the novel, can be viewed in terms of the symbolism of David and Goliath: 'El degollador de Goliat personificaba la heroica lucha de los justos para ganar el cielo a fuerzas' (The beheader of Goliath personified the heroic fight of the just to win heaven through by force) (Vosters 1977, 1.224). In this manner, the biblical figure of the giant with its symbolic meanings serves to construct the malefic statue of this creature and moulds it as a key foe. A knight who can battle and conquer giants is thus a figure akin to Christ.

The second giant mentioned by the friend in the prologue is Cacus, thus pairing biblical with classical authorities, since this figure plays a significant role in Virgil's *Aeneid*. In book 8, as King Evander performs rites in honour of Hercules, Aeneas sails up the Tiber to meet him. In the place where Rome would stand someday, Evander tells Aeneas the tale of Hercules and Cacus. This 'foul-featured, half-human monster' (1991, 195) who vomited fire from his mouth was a robber who had stolen some of Hercules' cattle and hidden them in his subterranean abode on Mount Aventine. But Hercules heard the sounds of one of his cows and was able to find the entrance and destroy Cacus. It is this triumph that Evander recounts, one that prefigures Aeneas's victories and the future founding of Rome.

And yet, the question of thieving is a complex one. Aeneas appears on the scene at a time when the myth of a thief is recounted. In many ways Aeneas himself is a thief. He will appropriate for himself the lands of others in order to establish a new Troy. And Rome, in both its republican and imperial incarnations, believed in wars of conquest where booty was seen as 'the outward sign of the inner glory which is the heart of *Romanitas* and its destiny' (W.R. Johnson 1984, 5). It can be argued then that Aeneas's vision is one based on thievery or booty, and that Cacus is a giant empire who robs others. While Rome stole treasures and lands while becoming the centre of 'culture,' the friend in the prologue suggests the stealing of authorities so that the fictional Cervantes may expand his literary empire. The allusion to Cacus, then, is a complex one, suggesting on the one hand Herculean triumph and on the other the failures of political and literary empires. The latter is further explicated by Cervantes when he discusses notions of imitation. In the *Adjunta al Parnaso*, he defines the limits of imitation. An artist who goes beyond these prescribed boundaries is nothing more than a thief. It is not a coincidence that Cervantes names this thief Cacus (Riley 1962, 110; Cervantes 1984b, 190). Thus, the friend's appropriation of Cacus in the prologue to the *Quixote* must be seen in terms of literary thievery. The text pokes fun at those who pretend erudition, at those who steal bits and pieces from others to appear authoritative. Lope de Vega, as noted, is Cervantes' model for literary pretensions.

Two myths, one biblical and one Virgilian, struggle for authority.

Between them is found the allusion to the river Tagus, perhaps signifying that a vast divide separates Christian and pagan visions of the giant – a figure of otherness. This separation may seem somewhat illusive. Pagan myths had survived in different guises during the Middle Ages and thrived in the Renaissance. The pagan myth of Cacus is related by Sebastián de Covarrubias to the biblical tale of David. In his *Tesoro de la lengua*, the Spanish writer describes 'Cacodaemon' as an evil spirit who tormented Saul, David's father (1987, 259). But the syncretism of the Renaissance had given way to a more critical view of the ancients. Written during the aftermath of the Counter-Reformation, Cervantes' prologue includes the river as a great divide between ancient and Christian conceptions.

As noted, the opposition between Christian and pagan visions is represented in the Stanza della Segnatura by the *Disputa* (which depicts religious texts) and the *Parnassus*. Here, the opposition is one of competition and syncretism rather than the more open hostility that will prevail during the aftermath of the Renaissance. In the *Parnassus*, Virgil stands in a prominent position, second only to the blind Homer. Both epic writers foreground the importance of rivers, whether to establish epic catalogues or to present them as prophesying entities. In Cervantes' prologue the friend calls for a reference to the Tagus so as to authorize Cervantes as both a connoisseur of the classics and a cosmographer ('para mostraros hombre erudito en letras humanas y cosmógrafo' [to show that you're erudite in the humanities and a cosmographer] [1978, 1.56; 15]). The passage then serves to interpose a third fresco between the Homeric and Virgilian *Parnassus*[20] and the biblical *Disputa*. In addition to philosophers of antiquity, *The School of Athens* portrays mathematicians and cosmographers. These figures are located in the right foreground and include Euclid (geometry) and Ptolemy (astronomy and geography). A third figure, once considered to be Zoroaster, is really the geographer Strabo.[21] In the fresco, Ptolemy holds a sphere of the world while Strabo carries a celestial sphere since he offers 'celestial "proofs" that the earth is a sphere. In several places Strabo urges the reader to observe a globe in order to understand the position of the earth surrounded by its celestial "universe"' (Joost-Gaugier 1998, 774). The friend in Cervantes' prologue may be alluding to the pair of Greek geographers and in particular to Ptolemy, the major authority on geography throughout the Middle Ages and into the Renaissance. His *Geography* lists the Tagus as one of the main rivers of Hispania. Some Renaissance editions have maps showing the course of this stream.[22]

Although the details of the friend's description are not in Ptolemy, his reputation as the foremost ancient geographer and his mention of the river serve to point to this figure in *The School of Athens*.[23] Thus, the authorities who speak of a classical robber, a biblical giant, and the qualities and location of a river are found in three of the four frescoes of the Stanza della Segnatura.

While the first cluster of *anotaciones* includes all three of Raphael's main frescoes from the Stanza della Segnatura, the second cluster is particularly intriguing since it breaks with the decorative program for the Stanza. This cluster is made up of allusions to six women of antiquity. Homer and Virgil, the key figures in Raphael's *Parnassus*, are singled out for their depiction of enchantresses rather than for their epic qualities. The evocation of these enchantresses point to a major absence in Raphael's Stanza della Segnatura. The 'robed sages' of the 'great tradition' (Grafton 1997, 57) pictured here are for the most part white European males. Women are conspicuously absent. Only one female is shown among the countless theologians, philosophers, and poets. Joost-Gaugier has noted: 'Only one figure carries a *titulus*, and that figure is the only female inhabitant not only (aside from the mythological Muses) of the *Parnassus*, but of the entire chamber' (Joost-Gautier 1993, 124). Sappho, the single exception, serves merely to reinforce the rule: only males possess wisdom. In order to camouflage woman's absence, Raphael includes a number of women as allegories within the Stanza. The ceiling, for example, depicts Philosophy, Theology, Poetry, and the virtues (Justice) in the guise of women. Although women can represent a discipline, they are never their practitioners. Their role is to reflect male learning. The vault's depiction of Adam and Eve may well serve to warn of woman's ill-fated curiosity.

While *The Virtues* includes three women, they are allegorical figures, each representing one of the virtues. The woman in *The School of Athens* is a goddess, Minerva. Indeed, this deity is not even present. Only her statue stands above the philosophers, opposite Apollo. Mirroring the one goddess of *The School of Athens* is the figure of Mary, mother of Christ, in the *Disputa*. Her contribution to the Western tradition, so richly represented through the fathers of the church, the apostles, and saints, is very different from that of the men. She is not portrayed because she has generated new texts, concepts, or ideas, but because she has given birth to Jesus, whose Gospels, written down by his apostles, will be one of the major influences on the West. Only in *Parnassus* is this absence of women mitigated. The fresco depicts nine muses at the service of Apollo. Again, their role is not to produce text. Rather, they serve to inspire the men-poets of the painting. Sappho, then, is the only woman who is part of the wisdom tradition. The well-known battle between philosophy and poetry is here resolved by showing how the 'higher' discipline does not allow women in its midst while poetry includes the nine muses and even one female practitioner.

In order to problematize Raphael's vision of male-dominated wisdom, Cervantes' prologue names two enchantresses (Circe and Calypso), one child murderer (Medea), and three courtesans. These women break with the ideals represented in Raphael's frescoes. Instead of exhibiting the virtues of temperance, prudence, and fortitude as depicted in Raphael's *The Virtues*, Medea breaks with these qualities. She is characterized as a woman whose excessive passion and cruelty leads her to kill her own children in a show of rage. Instead of personifying the highest knowledge achieved through a contemplation of the heavens and knowledge of reason and natural philosophy as portrayed in *The School of Athens*, Circe and Calypso utilize forbidden magic and the occult arts to control nature and ensnare men. And instead of inspiring men as the muses in the *Parnassus*, Laida, Lamia, and Flora, attract them with their voluptuous bodies.[24] Indeed, the figure of Sappho in the *Parnassus*, although representing Pythagorean wisdom, can also be associated with prostitution. In the encyclopedia of Raffaello Maffei, we read: 'But Aelian says that Sappho of Lesbos was not a poet, but a well known prostitute' (cited in Joost-Gaugier 1993, 128).[25]

While in *Don Quixote* Cervantes characterizes prostitutes such as Maritornes as 'ugly, poor, weak and from a low social standing' (Nadeau 1997, 12), the ones described by Guevara and alluded to in Cervantes' prologue come from the classical tradition of courtesans such as the hetairae and are 'intelligent, cultivated, and artistic; they were spiritually and politically powerful' (Nadeau 2002, 55). Like Circe and Calypso, these are women of power. But their power is suspect, being related to carnal delights or occult undertakings. Their presence in the prologue may have a double purpose: the representation of imperial enchantments and the critical textualization of artistic misogyny. As José Antonio Maravall has shown, Antonio de Guevara's works reflect the utopian vision of empire common to a number of Spanish thinkers writing under Charles V (1991, 17). By turning to Guevara as model in the representation of three courtesans, Cervantes' prologue may be hinting that the alluring textuality of Guevara hides a false or ineffective vision, one that is grounded on a past that cannot be resurrected.

Indeed, Maravall notes that Guevara's utopian slant would be taken up by Don Quixote, but he adds that the novel itself shows the defeat of such ideals. The play between the utopian imperial vision and the characterization of the knight will be taken up in a later chapter in relation to Titian's portraits of Charles V.

What is important here is to emphasize that the Cervantine allusion to six women of suspect power serves to take to an extreme the latent misogyny of Raphael's Stanza della Segnatura. These alluring but dangerous women show how the female sex should be cut off from the highest pursuits of wisdom. Indeed, they are often characterized as subverting and betraying the tradition. The question of a woman's role is reiterated in the text of *Don Quixote,* in which the absence of women is also a glaring element. Few women appear in the main narrative of Part I of the novel. Their presence is generally relegated to the seven interpolated stories. Even though here they play an important role, it is always a problematic one in a society that is suspicious of women who exercise wisdom or power. Although the portrayal of Marcela in the first interpolated tale is certainly an admirable example of female agency, it is tempered through the many male voices that attempt to condemn, marginalize, or restrict her words, actions, and will.[26] After contemplating the fate of Marcela's words, a reader is led to wonder if the women of the prologue have not been condemned by male writers for 'inappropriate' behaviour. Their portrayal may well reflect patriarchal suspicions in the face of female power and wisdom.

The women of the prologue can also be envisioned in a more positive light as representing two triads. Renaissance syncretism was always searching for ways to validate pagan images and structures through Christian ideals. For Edgar Wind, one of the most prevalent Neoplatonic doctrines was that of the 'vestiges of the Trinity' (1968, 41), pagan triads that reflect the Christian Trinity. Of the many triads, the three Graces were 'the archetype on which all other triads of Neoplatonism appeared to be modeled' (Wind 1968, 39). Even though the double triad in Cervantes' prologue serves to recall the elevated syncretism of Neoplatonic Renaissance philosophers, these two sets of three also problematize and even subvert this ideal. Calypso, Circe, and Medea form a pagan female trinity whose godlike powers are meant to enchant and seduce. The second trinity is one of the flesh, where enchantments lose their supernatural powers to become mere feminine wiles. Both of these unholy trinities will be recast by Cervantes in the 1615 *Quixote* through an imitation of the double trinity in Botticelli's *Primavera*

(De Armas 2001a). Furthermore, the second triad shows how a courtesan like Lamia in antiquity 'teaches simultaneously the receiving and giving of pleasure and the receiving and giving of knowledge' (Bell 1994, 19; Nadeau 2002, 60). This is precisely one of the main attributes of the three Graces, who form a circle related to giving and receiving in either love or friendship.

In addition, Carolyn Nadeau has shown how the six women of the prologue are metamorphosed into actual female characters in Part I of the novel. Indeed, a number of other suggestions by the 'author's' friend will be clearly included by Cervantes in his text. The fictionality of the prefatory Cervantes and the friend is upheld by including figures already found in the text. It thus seems as if the book was polished after the friend's advice. We may even come to believe that many of the characters come into being only after this conversation. This is, of course, one of the text's many illusions since the prologue was written after the book had been completed and is in many ways a supplement to the text. The author's friend has unwittingly demonstrated the misogyny of the Western tradition by subtly exposing how Raphael camouflaged the absence of women through allegorizing and deification. Although this absence is replicated in Cervantes' text, the women of the interpolations show both female agency and marginality and help to question the portrait of the classical women encountered in the prologue. After all, the six female characters were delineated by male writers who, unlike the perspectivist Cervantes, may have succeeded in transforming their intelligence and agency into a negative vision of female power.

The friend now turns to the third and final cluster of *anotaciones*, which is the most distant from Raphael's Stanza. It is as if the friend's witty evocations have got out of control and escaped Raphael's room, although vague reminiscences may be encountered.[27] After this very lengthy and careful mock-mirroring of the Stanza della Segnatura as a place where authorities vie with each other, the friend ends up claiming that *Don Quixote* has no need of embellishments because his whole work 'es una invectiva contra los libros de caballerías, de quien nunca se acordó Aristóteles, ni dijo nada San Basilio, ni alcanzó Cicerón' (is an invective against books of chivalry – which Aristotle never dreamed of, St Basil never mentioned and Cicero never came across) (1978, 1.57; 16). Just as all authorities are rejected, so are the three main frescoes by Raphael, Aristotle standing for *The School of Athens*, St Basil for the *Disputa*,[28] and Cicero for *Parnassus*. In their place, the prologue foregrounds the figure of Don Quixote. He becomes a hero who upholds in mock-heroic fashion two of the virtues that are reflected in the fourth fresco in the Stanza della Segnatura, *The Virtues* (fig. 3.5). As 'el más casto enamorado' (the chastest lover) (1978, 1.58; 16), he is the embodiment of temperance. Standing at the right-hand side of the fresco, the allegorical figure representing this virtue holds a bridle in her hand, an image of how the knightly spirit controls the equine passions. The novel will later mock Don Quixote's temperance, showing Rocinante as wilful and unchaste. The prologue further refers to Don Quixote as the 'más valiente caballero' (the bravest knight) (1978, 1.58; 16). He thus embodies *fortitudo* on the left-hand side of Raphael's fresco.[29] The allegory of this virtue has a 'pet lion and a leonine boot ornament' (Jones and Penny 1983, 80) and recalls Don Quixote's famous adventure with the lion (1978, 2.17). Once again the text belies the praises of the prologue.

The third virtue represented in the fresco, Prudence, is not mentioned in the prologue since it is clear that the knight's exploits deny her power. Her main attribute in the fresco is a mirror and it is thus not surprising that Don Quixote will be confronted by the Knight of the Mirrors (1978, 2.15) and later defeated by the same person, now under the guise of the Knight of the Moon – and the moon is a heavenly body that *mirrors* the rays of the sun. Absent from the fresco is the fourth cardinal virtue, Justice. She is represented in the vault above. It is to her restoration that Don Quixote directs all his misguided efforts. Indeed, the knight invokes her as a key figure in the Golden Age of humankind – an age he wishes to restore. His speech is prompted by some acorns given to him by goatherds since this was the staple of the inhabitants of the Golden Age (1978, 1.155–7). Curiously, the figure of *Fortitudo* in Raphael's fresco holds 'an oak branch with acorns (which was also the emblem of Julius II)' (Jones and Penny 1983, 80). If nothing else, Don Quixote wishes by mere force and valour to bring back this elusive first age of humankind.

The prologue, then, foregrounds a series of wars of authority, battles inscribed in the Stanza della Segnatura, where ancient philosophy, Christian theology, and Christian and pagan poetry vie with each other for prominence. But Raphael's battles are not Cervantes.' Through the friend, the prologue problematizes the authority of erudite citations from any of the three disciplines. What is left is a fresco dealing with the virtues. In other words, the prologue minimizes conceptual debates in order to foreground fashioning of a very human representation of a would-be knight. But his character is inseparable from his vision – a vision of a Golden Age restored and already present in Raphael's *Cardinal Virtues* through the presence of the acorn, symbol of that first mythical epoch. In order to re-establish this time of perfection, the knight, together with the author and the reader, have to rediscover the meaning of the cosmos. The text must then return to beginnings, return to the origins of Raphael's frescoes where Plato and Pythagoras hold out the written keys to the mysteries of the world and the world as text.

4 The Fourfold Way: Raphael

What is the oracle at Delphi?
The tetractys.

Iamblicus, *Life of Pythagoras*

Before turning from the work done at the Vatican by Raphael, let us return to the school where Cervantes learned how to structure texts so as to reflect the elemental forces of nature. Cervantes utilized this form to forge his *Numancia*. This chapter will argue that such a numerological structure is key to the first part of the 1605 *Quijote* and is foregrounded through constant recapitulation in the first two chapters of the novel. Although many patterns can emerge from a study of Raphael's Stanze, there is one structuring principle that is signalled from within one of the paintings. The Stanza della Segnatura was the first of the four halls decorated by Raphael. Its most famous fresco, *The School of Athens*, has at least one ordering element at work.[1] At the very centre of all the great thinkers of ancient Greece stands Plato, pointing to the heavens and holding in his hand the *Timaeus*. S.K. Heninger has shown that this Platonic dialogue was, for the Renaissance, 'the most important single vehicle of Pythagorean doctrine' (1974, 47). This text foregrounds numerology, studying the notion of harmony through mathematical ratios and structuring the four elements (earth, water, air, and fire) into a unified system called tetrad or quaternion.[2] In order to underline the importance of the Pythagorean connotations of the number four as found in Plato's dialogue, *The School of Athens* includes the figure of Pythagoras himself in the left foreground (fig. 4.1), viewing a tablet that shows his tetractys: I+II+III+IV=X. This arithmetical formula was the 'sacred symbol by which Pythagoreans sealed their oaths' (Heninger 1974, 152) since it was thought that all things were governed by the number four, and that their sum symbolizes perfection. That Empedocles is seen perched behind Pythagoras in Raphael's fresco should come as no surprise, since he was the one who codified the system of the four elements or roots that combine and separate through Love and Strife. His theories were associated with those of Pythagoras who used the number four as focus for his mathematical philosophy and cosmology.

A young man dressed in white stands in back of this group, looking out into space rather than at the writing of Pythagoras and his followers. Some have speculated that this is Hermes Trismegistus, the Egyptian priest who, according to Renaissance thinkers, had composed the *Corpus Hermeticum* and the *Asclepius*. His prominent position in the fresco and his outward gaze derives from his alleged antiquity and wisdom. He must have had an eminent place among the ancient philosophers of Raphael's work since he precedes them and surpasses them in wisdom. Although it was later proven that the Hermetic writers derive from the early Christian era, the Renaissance thinkers believed in his antiquity. Explaining Marsilio Ficino's translation priorities, Frances Yates asserts: 'Egypt was before Greece; Hermes was earlier than Plato. Renaissance respect for the old, the primary, the far-away, as nearest to divine truth, demanded that the *Corpus Hermeticum* should be translated before Plato's *Republic* or *Symposium*, and so this was in fact the first translation that Ficino made' (1964, 14). Thus, the *Corpus Hermeticum* became accessible and in it Renaissance writers found echoes of Pythagoreanism. The *Corpus Hermeticum* shows the importance of numbers in creation, foregrounding the seven governors (planets), the four elements, and the monad which 'contains every number' (*Hermetica* 1992, 17). Although in Hermes the number four is less important than the number seven, since it depicts materiality, its importance was passed on and transformed by later Platonists. The Renaissance was well aware of the Hermetic origin of numerology. It was from Pythagoras and the *Hermetica* that the Renaissance Platonist, Pico della Mirandolla took the idea that number was 'the root of all truth' (Yates 1964, 146). Even Johannes Kepler turns to these ancient texts when dealing with number, identifying 'the Hermetic teachings with those of Pythagoras' (Yates 1964, 441). Thus, the visionary figure in white who towers above the seated philosophers on the left-hand side of *The School of Athens* could well be identified with Hermes Trismegistus, the Egyptian sage revered by Renaissance thinkers. His ancient theories of number and cosmos which were utilized, transformed, and expanded by Plato, Empedocles, and Pythagoras, became a central ingredient in Renaissance Platonism and cosmology.

Although many structuring principles may be found in *The School of Athens*, the number four, as seen through the works of Hermes, Empedocles, Plato, and Pythagoras, is the most obvious. Indeed, the prominence of the quaternion is not restricted to this one fresco. The number four is highlighted in the Stanza della Segnatura not only by the presence of four large paintings but also by the representation of the four cardinal virtues. While three appear in one fresco, the fourth is found in the ceiling, forming a tetrad of allegorical figures: Poetry, Philosophy, Theology, and Justice. Although a number of art critics claim that the fourfold division of the ceiling was made before Raphael and has little to do with his program for the hall,[3] I would argue that Raphael preserved the structure so as to underline the importance of quaternity, which is further emphasized by four sets of paired scenes next to these larger figures in the ceiling (fig. 4.2).[4] The upper pictures deal with Roman history, while the lower ones have mythological subjects. As Edgar Wind has noted, each pair represents one of the four elements (1938, 75–9) and each is also linked to the four larger allegorical figures that refer to the pursuits of the mind. Although Wind does not mention them, there are also four rectangular scenes that are clearly linked to the allegories.

The four allegories, the four rectangular figures that comment on these representations, the four histories, and the four mythologies that foreground the elements create four sets of four pictures each. This double quaternity invites the spectator not only to view and interpret this particular hall in terms of the four elements, but also to consider each of the four rooms as representing a particular element, a guess that would seem to be supported by the fact that the third hall to be painted was later referred as the Stanza dell'Incendio (fire).[5] Observing this suite of rooms from the Cortile del Pappagallo, the Incendio would be at the extreme left, while the Stanza di Constantino would be at the far right. They represent the two extreme elements: fire as the highest for the Incendio and earth as the lowest, represented by Constantine's donation of land to the church. In between these two, stand the Stanza della Segnatura and the Stanza d'Eliodoro, with a reversed elemental order since the first foregrounds water (as seen in the fountain of Parnassus) while the latter indicates the prominence of air through the movement and flight of the figures in the frescoes.[6]

The tetractys held by Pythagoras in *The School of Athens* thus points to the importance of the number four for Pythagoras and his followers, and for Raphael and his disciples. It is representative of the physical emergence of cosmos from the mind of God. Thus, the world in which humanity abides is founded upon this number: 'In the world, all things are comprised in the quaternary, elements, numbers, seasons of the year and ages of life. Neither can you name any thing which does not depend upon the quaternary as its root or foundation' (Heninger 1974, 152).[7] *Don Quixote* follows this numerological structure indicative of cosmos found not only in Raphael's Stanze but also in Cervantes' own *La Numancia*. Rudolf Wittkower explains: 'Renaissance artists firmly adhered to the Pythagorean conception "All is Number" and, guided by Plato and the Neo-Platonists and supported by a long chain of theologians from Augustine onwards, they were convinced of the mathematical and harmonic structure of the universe and all creation' (1952, 24).[8] Discussing how Pythagoras 'invented' the word *cosmos* with the dominant motifs of beauty, perfection, reconciliation, of opposites (*discordia concors*), and 'unity arising of a multeity, *e pluribus unum*' (1974, 147), Heninger asserts: 'During the Renaissance, as at most times in our intellectual history, the longing for order was so strong that the belief in cosmos persisted despite all evidence to the contrary ... And with increasing insistence and ingenuity the dogma of cosmos was proclaimed' (1974, 147–8).[9]

The sixteenth and seventeenth centuries often viewed the poets as emulating God. Their art would attempt to 'rival' the divine creation. Raphael's frescoes imitate a *Deus pictor*[10] as he not only recreated, but even perfected through heroic magnification the kings, warriors, poets, prelates, and philosophers he portrayed. In *La Numancia*, Cervantes signals a new creation by dividing his play into four acts, each representing one of the four elements that constitute the world, and each imitating one classical author in order to authorize and perfect his text (De Armas 1998, 27). The 1605 *Quixote* is also divided into four parts. This quaternion seems to contrast with the recurring love triangles in the interpolated tales of the novel. Such a structure appears to be far removed from Pythagorean harmony since, as Ruth El Saffar has noted, 'the love triangle is an emblem of a misplaced desire for God. Lacking an Absolute Other on which to attach itself, the desire is displaced onto a secondary other who then acquires the attributes of God ... The third term ... emerges as a rival ... preventing discovery of the object's mundane reality' (1984, 5). But, the triangle can be Pythagorean in nature, as seen in Raphael's *Parnassus*. As Christiane L. Joost-Gaugier has explained, the three key Pythagorean figures (Apollo, Sappho, and Pindar) in this fresco create a triangle which 'dominates the design' (1996, 71).

And yet, Apollo, the apex of harmony in the fresco and in Pythagorean writings, is also the god of frustrated desire as in the Apollo/Daphne and Apollo/Hyacinth relations. It should come as no surprise, then, that the relation between Grisóstomo and Marcela in the first interpolated tale of the novel has been linked to Apollo's pursuit of Daphne (McGaha 1977). But Apollo is also present in this tale in his role as the deity who presides over poetry. While Grisóstomo fails at love, he triumphs in art. Even Marcela reflects divine inspiration when she delivers her speech. Viewing the first interpolated tale in Cervantes' novel through Raphael's fresco one may perceive Marcela as a new Sappho and Grisóstomo as a new Pindar. They express divine harmony through poetry, speech, and song. The death of Grisóstomo and the aloneness of Marcela, who in spite of her brilliant rhetoric cannot communicate with the male audience at the end of the story, is sung in a Pythagorean manner since the lyre served to detach 'mankind from material concerns' and provoke 'the desire for divine love' (Joost-Gaugier 1993, 130).

The divine Apollonian triangle in the Cervantine text represents both poetic inspiration and the frustrations of earthly love. The latter can be resolved by embracing the divine triangle and thus accepting separation from the material. This separation can also ensue without divine intervention, in which case death and solitude are the result. Both Grisóstomo and Marcela are at the tip of the triangle tottering between divinity and aloneness. Of course, the agony and ecstasy of the Pythagorean triangle can be avoided by embracing earthly quaternities. While some Cervantine triangles lead to divine loneliness, others are surmounted and turn into a 'love fulfilled in marriage,' which comes about 'through the introduction of a fourth figure who had formerly been neglected by the characters who saw themselves locked into the endless frustration of the triangle' (El Saffar 1984, 10).

Such harmony based on quaternity is found not only in certain love triangles in the novel. More important, it is one of the basic structuring principles in the making of the knight. His frame will reflect the novel's structure and vice versa. Consequently the first part of the 1605 novel strongly mirrors Raphael's frescoes and the author's own *Numancia* through the inclusion of microquaternities that reflect the overall fourfold division. According to Karl-Ludwig Selig, the device of *enumeratio* occurs with remarkable frequency in the first part of *Don Quixote*.[11] Although Cervantes makes use of the most common type, that is the *paragon* or epic catalogue of heroes, the text, according to Selig, also includes many other types. What this critic neglects to mention is that the first chapters of the novel take *enumeratio* to an extreme, constantly using it as quaternity. Let us first look at how a fourfold listing is foregrounded in the making of a knight in the first two chapters of the novel.

José Antonio Madrigal, one of the few critics who has noticed the importance of quaternity, points to the four days needed by Don Quixote to name his horse (1981, 571). For this critic, the number four appears at a point in the initiatory rites of the knight when he sees the horse as vehicle for his chivalric adventures. Although Madrigal does not search for the presence of these quaternities elsewhere in the novel, his observation should receive careful consideration since many of the tetrads he mentions are structuring principles in the first chapter of the novel. Indeed, Hermann Iventosch tells us that the first chapter of the novel is onomastic in nature, dealing with the Platonic vision of the creation of a new world through naming (1963–4, 60). This Platonic vision proposed by Iventosch is represented by Raphael in his depiction of Plato holding the *Timaeus* in *The School of Athens*. Let us recall that this dialogue has a strong Pythagorean flavour. Thus, in the first chapter of *Don Quixote*, the Platonic vision is conflated with the Pythagorean notion of cosmos so as to establish this initial sequence as the foundation of creation, be it the creation of a poetic world or the *hidalgo*'s re-creation of himself as a knight.

Explaining the originality of the opening of Cervantes' novel, Avalle-Arce contrasts it with the beginning of the *Amadís de Gaula*, its acknowledged predecessor, and with the first lines of the *Lazarillo de Tormes*, the first Spanish picaresque novel, written, according to some, as a reaction to the romances of chivalry. The *Amadís* begins with a detailed genealogy of the chivalric hero. This foregrounds 'la plentitud de *datos deterministas* que se acumulan sobre Amadís de Gaula, y que lo disponen, *a nativitate*, para su heroico sino' (the plentitude of *determining facts* which are gathered concerning Amadeus of Gaul, and which prepare him, at birth, for his heroic destiny) (1975, 229). A similar determinism can be found in the *Lazarillo*, but it is one that connotes the creation of an antihero (Avalle-Arce 1975, 229). What is different in Cervantes' novel is that all the genealogical data is absent, thus giving a new type of freedom to the protagonist. His past is not important since the novel deals with his desired freedom to create his own future.

Rather than discussing genealogy, the work begins by setting up a series of quaternities. It starts by listing the four major objects which serve as the emblem for the *hidalgo*: a lance, a leather shield, a horse, and a hound. The text then lists the four types of food eaten by this country gentleman: what he consumes during the week ('olla'/'salpicón' [stew/leftovers]); his Friday meal ('lentejas' [lentil broth]); Saturday's feast ('duelos y quebrantos' [lardy eggs]); and the best meal, Sunday's, with 'algún palomino de añadidura' (an occasional pigeon) (1978, 1.1.69; 25). And if the reader has not been attentive to these fourfold divisions, the narrative will now emphasize that this food takes up three-fourths of the knight's income. The last fourth is given over to clothing and again, four types are mentioned (1978, 1.1.70). The novel, then, begins by presenting four sets of four: possessions, food, income, and clothing.

Once the notion of quaternities is set, the text can become more playful and less restrictive in its utilization of this principle. The reader is then told of the members of the household: the housekeeper, the niece, and a *mozo* who works in the field. The fourth member is, of course, the gentleman-owner. Even the *mozo* is described through a set of four jobs that he performs. The text then tells of the different surnames authors have given the *hidalgo*. Three are mentioned here (Quijada, Quesada, Quejana), a tetrad to be completed later in the chapter by the gentleman's own creation of the name Don Quixote.[12] Discussion soon turns to his major preoccupation, the perusing of romances of chivalry. In order to be able to spend his time reading, he neglects the hunt as well as the administration of his household. Indeed, in order to purchase more books, he has to sell much of his land. Thus, the protagonist of the novel is seen practising two occupations while neglecting two others, to form a quaternity: hunting and administering (appropriate occupations) and excessive reading and selling (inappropriate). This second set of four, then, has to do with names and occupations: the members of Quixote's household, his own name, his occupations, and the occupations of the *mozo* who works in the household.

Although Alonso Quijano is unique in his compulsive and constant reading of romances of chivalry, the next tetrad shows that others are also interested in these texts. The *hidalgo*'s two friends, the priest and the barber, attempt to decide who is the best of all knights. Predictably, each mentions two possible contenders to create a quaternity of heroes (Amadís de Gaula, Palmerín de Inglaterra, Caballero del Febo, and don Galaor [1978, 1.173]). Alonso Quijano, however, is not thinking of these four chivalric heroes at this time, but is considering other texts instead.

He is said to enjoy the 'entricadas razones' (intricate language) of Feliciano de Silva, whose obscure and witty concepts he considered as pearls of wisdom (1978, 1.1.72; 26). He is also worried about the many wounds received by the protagonist of Jerónimo Fernández's *Don Belianís de Grecia* since they were so numerous that 'no dejaría de tener el rostro y todo el cuerpo lleno de cicatrices y señales' (his face and body must have been covered with gashes and scars) (1978, 1.1.72; 26). But this concern does not prevent him from thinking of writing a continuation to the romance. This sudden duality in the midst of quaternities is not gratuitous – It helps to explain Don Quixote's madness. The most important lines on the subject of his *locura* are well known: 'En resolución, él se enfrascó tanto en su letura, que se le pasaban las noches leyendo de claro en claro, y los días de turbio en turbio; y así, del poco dormir y del mucho leer se le secó el celebro, de manera que vino a perder el juicio' (In short, our hidalgo was soon so absorbed in these books that his nights were spent reading from dusk till dawn, and his days from dawn till dusk, until the lack of sleep and the excess of reading withered his brain, and he went mad) (1978, 1.1.73; 26–7). Day and night, wakefulness and sleep form a tetrad not heeded by the country gentleman whose constant reading leads him to madness.[13] Although the resulting dryness of the brain ('se le secó el celebro') may seem like a humorous expression to a modern reader, it in fact signals the utilization of several of the most important quaternities in the novel. This dryness found within Don Quixote's physiology had already been located as the central quality of Cervantes' novelistic world. In the prologue, the fictional author speaks of his creation, of his novel, as 'un hijo seco' (a dry ... child) (1978, 1.50; 11). Thus, the dryness of the text and the dryness of the protagonist are inextricably interrelated.

Heninger has quoted 'the plainest verbal statement of the tetrad' or quaternity during the Renaissance: 'All things are born from hot, cold, moist and dry' (1974, 160). These four qualities are basic to the composition of the four elements that form the material world (earth, water, air, and fire), since each of the elements shares two of the qualities. The elements, often pictured in a circle, act in ways contrary to each other and are thus at war, disrupting the system of cosmos they are meant to create. But an opposite movement holds them together without allowing them to fully merge into each other: 'By sharing qualities, however, the elements build up a force for stasis around the circumference of the figure – what Empedocles described as primordial love' (Heninger 1974, 163). The figure of Empedocles pictured in *The School of Athens* points to the Pythagorean tetractys and to this philosopher's musical ratios. The harmony of cosmos comes about when the four qualities and elements are able to lovingly join with each other without losing their identity. And yet, the son (or stepson as he is called in the prologue) engendered by Cervantes, his fictional creation, has an excess of dryness. This quality is shared by two of the elements, earth and fire. According to Plato's *Timaeus* (a book pictured in *The School of Athens*): 'God started to construct the body of the universe from fire and earth – from fire to give his creation visibility and from earth to give it solidity and consequent tangibleness' (Heninger 1974, 160). Earth and fire with their dryness form the conflictive and arid landscape of Cervantes' fiction, a novelistic cosmos that lacks equilibrium since it has a diminished portion of the other two elements and qualities.

This disruption in the macrocosm of the novel is replicated in the microcosm of Don Quixote's physiology – his madness is also related to dryness. As Heninger explains: 'Just as the four basic qualities interact to produce the four elements that comprise the world's body, they similarly produce the four humours that compose the body of man and make him a microcosm' (1974, 168). The four bodily humours (blood, choler, melancholy, and phlegm) not only led to the establishment of four body types, but also served to categorize the many forms of behaviour of an individual from classical times. The humours were also key to medical examination and practice from the antique world to the Spanish Golden Age. As Daniel L. Heiple states: 'The Western theory of medicine began, possibly in the sixth century B.C. with the Greek philosopher Alcmaeon of Crotona, and certainly with Hippocrates ... This medical theory was quite simple. It postulated that the body is healthy if its chemical composition is in balance and unhealthy if one of its humors ... predominates over the others. As a corollary, it ascribed humoral properties to those things that man must experience such as air, food, sleep, etc., and in this way all health and sickness could be attributed to the patient's personal habits or his environment' (1979, 65). Heiple goes on to explain how Don Quixote's habits, as described in chapter 1, lead him to madness through an excess of melancholy.

Like the four elements, the four humours are composed by the four qualities: dryness, humidity, coldness, and heat. And like the elements, each of the humours is said to partake of two of these qualities. Dryness, as we have seen, corresponds to the elements fire and earth. It is also associated with the choleric and melancholy humours. Since Cervantes' novel makes it explicit that Alonso Quijano suffers from dryness, this has served to fuel a critical debate as to whether the knight is choleric or melancholic.[14] These two humours take us back to Don Quixote's favourite reading. His first interest is Feliciano de Silva with his many obscure concepts. Intense study is both a cause and a result of the melancholy humour. The student who is engrossed in deciphering obscure concepts partakes of the maddening heaviness of this black bile. Not surprisingly, one of the passages from Feliciano de Silva most appreciated by the knight contrasts *razón* with *sinrazón*.[15] Don Quixote will eventually succumb to *sinrazón*, to a madness created by excessive conceptual imaginings and study. His second favourite reading is a book of chivalry by Jerónimo de Fernández. Reading it, Don Quixote does not worry about concepts, but about scars on the protagonist's body (1978, 1.1.72; 26). These signs point to an excess of violence, which can serve to exacerbate the choleric or warlike disposition. Don Quixote is thus adept at reading not only chivalric texts but also bodily texts. While the first inclines him to melancholy, the second stirs in him a choleric response. Thus, the two texts read by Don Quixote lead him towards two humoral excesses that share the quality of dryness.

Although beginning with a tetrad from Empedocles/Raphael, Cervantes' novel shows the analogical structure of cosmos through a series of tetrads that grow out of the initial elemental structure, the humoral structure being central to the development of the knight's character. This humoral supplement serves to reinforce the Pythagorean aspects of Raphael's *School of Athens*. As Teresa Soufas states: 'The roots of humoral theory itself can be traced to Pythagorean philosophy and is insistence on tetradic categories of time and natural elements, a system that eventually merged with other notions to accommodate the idea of four substances within the body, each with physical properties of heat, cold, dryness, and moisture that match it to one of the four elements, to a season, to a planetary or stellar body, and to one of the ages of man' (1990, 5). Indeed, a number of these and other Pythagorean tetrads will be developed in these early chapters and in the work as a whole.

Before turning to some of these, let us look briefly at the steps taken by the gentleman from La Mancha to become a knight. While the number four has been used as a foundational device in this chapter to create a fictional world in which characters and setting must arise from a Pythagorean quaternity, it is also used by the knight to create his fictive universe. Indeed, Don Quixote pinpoints four elements that he needs in order to ride out into the countryside in search of adventure: arms and armour, a horse, himself, and his lady. All foundations require naming. In fact, idealistic theories of language sought to link name and form. Thus, the future knight must be careful to choose the appropriate name for all, since the name provides the foundational frame for future action. In chapter 1 he names his horse, himself, and his lady, only neglecting to name his weapons.[16] The time he takes to ponder these names must also conform to the foundational frame. Thus, he takes four days to name his horse and twice four days to name himself. This doubling of four reflects the fact that his name is a compound one. Having called himself Don Quixote he needs to complete the name in the way Amadís had done by using place, 'de Gaula.' He decides on don Quijote de la Mancha because 'declaraba muy al vivo su linaje y patria, y la honraba con tomar el sobrenombre della' (he declared in a most vivid manner both his lineage and his homeland, and honoured the latter by taking it as his surname) (1978 1.1.77; 29). We are not told how long he takes in naming his lady. Very much like the absence of women in Raphael's Stanza della Segnatura, there is an absence of foundational time in the naming of Dulcinea del Toboso. In many ways, she is not part of the fourfold foundation of the novel – only in chapter 25 will the reader come to recognize her literary provenance.

Chapter 2 continues the concern with establishing foundations, whether the foundations of the fictive novelistic world or the knight's foundations for his future adventures. The beginnings of this chapter make it clear that the novel takes place in July, which is the high point of summer. According to the many Renaissance diagrams that juxtaposed seasons, elements, and humours, summer with its dry heat corresponds to the element of fire and to the choleric disposition. It is thus not surprising, as Otis Green has stated, that Don Quixote is 'quick to anger' and has a fiery temperament (1970, 174). A number of quaternities are at play here, as Don Quixote is related to the choleric humour, the summer season, and the element of fire. To complete a quaternity of tetrads, it should be added that a particular planet is associated with each humour, element, and season. Don Quixote is born under Mars, the celestial body that corresponds to choler, summer, and fire: 'Yo tengo más armas que letras, y nací, según me inclino a las armas, debajo de la influencia del planeta Marte' (I myself am more arms than letters, and, to judge from this inclination of mine, I must have been born under the influence of the planet Mars) (1978, 2.6.84; 524).

Although Don Quixote's ruling planet, according to his humoral and elemental constitution, seems to be Mars, there is a second Ptolemaic body which is key to his character. Sol is as fiery as Mars and certainly dominates the arid and hot landscape of La Mancha. It is under the hot summer sun that Don Quixote begins his chivalric career. The sun, however, does not exert a benefic influence upon don Quixote: 'el sol entraba tan apriesa y con tanto ardor que fuera bastante a derretirle los sesos, si algunos tuviera' (the sun was rising so fast and becoming so hot, that his brains would have melted, if he'd had any (1978, 1.2.81; 31). The humoral imbalances of the knight are exacerbated by the excessive heat and dryness of this Ptolemaic luminary. Thus, the solar planetary influences appear to have a negative impact upon Don Quixote – and Mars does not seem to help him to win battles. However, Don Quixote is labelled as *ingenioso*. And, as Huarte de San Juan states, mental ability or *ingenio*, when it is derived from heat 'would create a strong imagination capable of producing poets, artists, inventors, and such, depending on the degree of excess' (quoted in Heiple 1991, 123). Both the heat of the sun and the heat of choler (Mars) make Don Quixote into a person akin to the artist. It should come as no surprise that these two planets are singled out by Marsilio Ficino as the heavenly bodies that create a powerful imagination.[17] Even though Don Quixote will fail at both arms (Mars) and letters (Apollo), he will amaze those around him by his ability to recreate the environment. Through an active and overheated imagination, he can rearrange chivalric images retrieved from his dried-up memory and place or 'paint' them upon the landscape of La Mancha. Thus, both his excessive or deranged imagination and his dry memory lead him to become a mad artist, whose portraits are done upon nature itself.[18] The irony, of course, is that such art is commonplace in the postmodern world. Don Quixote's imaginative abilities lead us to recall that Della Porta clearly states that a strong imagination is key to the construction of an architectural structure for recollection through artificial mnemonics (1996, 57–8).

We have seen how the sun dries out the knight's brain. And yet, Don Quixote revels in the solar presence. He purposefully sallies forth at dawn, linking the dawning of a new day with the beginnings of his chivalric pursuits. In fact, he envisions the telling of his own tale as beginning with a reference to Apollo/Sol. This deity reflects the dawn of his career: 'Apenas había el rubicundo Apolo tendido por la faz de la ancha y espaciosa tierra las doradas hebras de sus hermosos cabellos ... cuando el famoso caballero don Quijote de la Mancha, dejando las ociosas plumas, subió sobre su famoso caballo Rocinante, y comenzó a caminar por el antiguo y conocido campo de Montiel' (Scarce had ruddy Apollo spread over the face of the wide and spacious earth the golden tresses of his beauteous hair ... when the famous knight Don Quixote de la Mancha, quitting the slothful feathers of his bed, mounted his famous steed Rocinante and began to ride over the ancient and far-famed Plain of Montiel) (1978, 1.2.80; 30–1).

Don Quixote thus envisions himself as a solar hero, as someone whose adventures will follow the brilliant course of the luminary. Furthermore, he also perceives the link between heroic and poetic pursuits. After all, the brilliant and heroic Sol is also Apollo, the god who presides over the poets in Parnassus. Let us recall that this deity stands at the pinnacle of the Pythagorean triangle in Raphael's *Parnassus*. Don Quixote claims that he has given up the pen ('plumas') in order to become a warrior – he has given up the pursuits of Apollo for the deeds of the solar hero. Through allusions to the Stanza della Segnatura and references to famous warriors and poets, the prologue had already established links between these two pursuits. As opposed to Julius Caesar, who writes of his own deeds, Don Quixote abandons the pen for the sword or lance in hopes that a wise one, a writer, will chronicle his tale and make him famous. Although in the *Parnassus*, Apollo is related to the triangle rather than to the tetrad, he is surrounded by a series of tretrads that emphasize his foundational purpose, his ability to inspire humans to become great poets. The triadic and celestial god has a quaternal influence on his subjects. Furthermore, Sol is always linked to the number four. In Ptolemaic astronomy, this celestial body is located in the fourth sphere, being the fourth of seven planets that revolve around the earth. Thus, Don Quixote perceives Apollo/Sol as the foundational fourth planet. It will help to establish his career as hero in texts to be written about the knight – texts under the influence of the poetic Apollo. He is unaware of the planet's malefic influence and of his own humoral imbalances. He is also mistaken as to the style and tone of the work that will be written concerning his adventures. Apollo will not choose an epic poet to accompany the knight. A lying Arab will become narrator and antagonist to the hero from La Mancha.[19]

The perfect analogies established by Platonists and Pythagoreans to demonstrate the harmony of the cosmos seem to break down in the Cervantine text through the knight's misreading of the book of the world. We have seen how the novel takes place in summer, a time of heat and choler when the knight can display his martial disposition and his solar heroic tendencies. In most of the tetradic diagrams prepared during the Renaissance, the seasons are related to the four ages of the human being. According to tradition, Pythagoras was the first to establish the correspondence between the two. Diogenes Laertius explains that Pythagoras divides man's life into four quarters thus: 'Twenty years a boy, twenty years a youth, twenty years a young man, twenty years an old man; and these four periods correspond to the four seasons, the boy to spring, the youth to summer, the young man to autumn, and the old man to winter' (Diogenes Laertius viii.10; quoted in Burrow 1986, 14). Don Quixote, then, is in the autumn of his life as he moves out into the world of chivalric adventures. Summer is not his season. As James Parr asks: 'What could be more topsy turvy than for a man of Alonso Quijano's age – relatively more advanced in his time that it might be in ours – to emulate a strapping, young knight errant?' (1988, 91). This break in the tetradic analogies does not represent a break in cosmic order but an infraction on the part of the gentleman from La Mancha. In the carefully planned structures of the period, he is too late to begin his quest. Chivalry is a profession for youth and for summer. This break between the microcosm (Don Quixote) and the macrocosm will lead to defeat and failure. Although Don Quixote has carefully prepared the foundational structure for his journey, he cannot fulfil this particular requirement. He can point to Mars and choler as his allies, but the summertime of chivalric adventures is not his to command.

Don Quixote of necessity overlooks this break with quaternity but he does attempt to remedy two other lapses. Interestingly, these two lapses are brought out in the second chapter. In terms of the numerology of the times, which owes so much to Pythagoras, the number two is inauspicious. Cornelius Agrippa reports: 'Pythagoras ... said, that Unity was God and a good intellect; and that Duality was a Divell, and an evill intellect, in which is a materill multitude' (1986, 178). In fact the number two is particularly inauspicious 'whence the Soothsaying is taken, be Saturnall, or Martiall' (Agrippa 1986, 178). We know that Don Quixote partakes of these two celestial influences since his dryness makes him both a melancholic, a humour ruled by Saturn, and a choleric, a temperament guided by Mars. Thus, although in the second chapter Don Quixote will try to remedy the foundational problems of becoming a knight, his actions will not be successful.

Don Quixote recognizes that he cannot name his arms/armour/shield since so far he has not triumphed over any foes. As a novice knight he should wear plain armour, 'armas blancas' (white arms) (1978, 1.2.79; 30) without device on the shield. Don Quixote's solution to this problem evinces his ability to manipulate language in order to construct his own reality. Since his shield is white or plain he thinks that he will clean it quite carefully so as to make it look as white as an ermine (1978, 1.2.80). Although he is not allowed to carry a marked shield, the very whiteness of it, he believes, will evoke the ermine which was a common heraldic device. Once again, Don Quixote is intent on naming and has chosen a very telling device. But this onomastic event is also tied to the tradition of ekphrasis. Let us recall that Homer, in the locus classicus of ekphrasis, describes how the shield of Achilles is forged. This shaping ekphrasis is parodied in Cervantes' text since the knight is also intent in having figures in his shield, and the only way he can think of doing this is to clean it so that it can appear as white as an ermine. As we will see, this nonexistent figure in the shield is also, according to its subject, a heraldic or emblematic ekphrasis. Again Cervantes takes this type of device to its limit by having the figure be invisible.

The story that the ermine, when encircled in mud, 'would prefer to be captured rather than to sully itself while trying to escape' (Beryl Rowland 1973, 74) was to be found in emblems and dictionaries of the Renaissance and Golden Age (Covarrubias 1987, 146). Indeed, it appears at a telling point in Cervantes' interpolated tale of the *Curioso impertinente* (1978, 1.33.408–9). This legendary behaviour made this small animal a symbol of chastity or 'of the wearer's personal integrity' (Rowland 1973, 74). From Ferdinand I of Naples to Elizabeth I of England,[20] the ermine became a prized symbol of royalty, decorating robes of princes and prelates and appearing in heraldic devices, emblems, and paintings. Indeed, the pictorial aura surrounding the ermine makes it a particularly apt choice for a narrative that revels in the competition between the visual and the verbal. Cesare Ripa's depiction of *Castitas* evinces the sisterhood of these two competing modes of expression (fig. 3). The illustration shows a woman dressed in white with an ermine at her feet. In the verbal component of his emblem, Ripa explains that 'the white ermine, which takes such great care that its coat remains immaculate, demonstrates the necessity to keep one's honor and reputation unsullied and as pure as the snow' (1971, 48). Don Quixote thus seeks to preserve and augment his honour and reputation through chivalric deeds. But there is an alternate interpretation given by Ripa in the 1603 edition of his work. The ermine 'also represents a man who seems pure, but is totally lascivious underneath, as is the beast' (1971, 48). Don Quixote's new weapon is thus a double-edged sword. It can fulfil his imaginings or it can show his lasciviousness, a quality that will later be foregrounded when the knight's open eyes are compared to those of the hare, an animal always associated with lust (1978, 1.16.202). Naming, then, is essential to creation – and Don Quixote has unwittingly chosen for his device a creature that may reveal a hidden side of his being.

Not only is Don Quixote without a device as he ventures out into the world of adventure. He also realizes that 'no era armado caballero, y que, conforme a la ley de caballería no podía ni debía tomar armas con ningún caballero' (he hadn't been knighted and by the laws of chivalry shouldn't and indeed couldn't take up arms against any knight) (1978, 1.2.79; 30). As with his lack of device, Don Quixote immediately thinks of a way to overcome this obstacle. Both decisions, taking place in a chapter representing duality will bring about both positive and negative results. He will ask the first person he encounters to knight him. The first place he comes to is an inn. It should come as no surprise that, in his desire to be knighted, Don Quixote transforms this humble abode into a castle and constructs it in his imagination with drawbridge and a moat. But there is one element lacking, one that casts doubt on his imagined painting. He stops his horse, Rocinante, waiting 'que algún enano se pusiese entre las almenas a dar señal con alguna trompeta de que llegaba caballero al castillo' (for some dwarf to appear upon the battlements and announce with a trumpet-blast the arrival of a knight) (1978, 1.2.78; 32). Then, he moves on to the castle after a short wait, meeting two ladies/prostitutes at the entrance. At this point, the full picture that arose in his mnemonic imagination is confirmed: 'En esto sucedió acaso que un porquero que andaba recogiendo de unos trastrajos una manada de puercos ... tocó un cuerno, a cuya señal se recogen, y al instante se le representó a don Quijote lo que deseaba, que era que algún enano hacía señal de su venida' (At this point a swineherd who was gathering together some pigs ... happened to sound his horn to round them up, and Don Quixote thought that his wish had been fulfilled and that a dwarf was announcing his arrival) (1978, 1.2.78; 32). The presence of the dwarf confirms for Don Quixote the reality of the painting he is creating upon the canvas of reality. Ironically, since the time of Aristotle, the dwarf came to represent difficulties in memorizing. Here, Don Quixote can no longer separate the images stored in his memory from the new images brought to the memory by the senses through the imagination. The dwarf, then, is both a symbol of his triumph and of his failure. He can memorize, but cannot use it to write or paint. Instead, his life, as critics have argued, becomes a work of art.

This is true in the sense that he paints uncontrollably upon reality. And his paintings validate the chivalric ideals he holds dear. The castle, which to him is like those that 'se pintan' (are painted) (1978, 1.2.82), has one more important feature.[21] It has four towers which, as a foundational number, confirm to Don Quixote that this place will grant him a knighthood and thus become the foundation for his future adventures.

Indeed, the novel itself replicates Don Quixote's foundational desires. The 1605 text is divided into four parts, recalling the four stanze decorated by Raphael. The first of four parts consists of eight chapters, a doubling of the tetrad and the Pythagorean number of justice.[22] Continuing the Cervantine structure of fours, we discover that in these eight chapters the knight participates in four adventures. Two of these occur in chapter 4 and the other two in chapter 8. The knight's failure in all four adventures can be related to his failure to construct a proper foundational structure for himself. His lapses in chapter 2 culminate in his request to have the castle-keeper or innkeeper arm him as a knight. Not only is the innkeeper not a gentleman, but instead of reflecting chivalric qualities, his adventures evince his picaresque leanings. Thus, he comes to represent the genre that is opposed to the chivalric. By arming Don Quixote as a knight he subverts the whole hierarchical conception of knighthood and imparts in Don Quixote the spirit of plebeian humour and picaresque carnival.[23]

The innkeeper is described as thievish as Cacus ('no menos ladrón que Caco' [no less a thief than Cacus]) (1978, 1.2.84; 33), thus returning us to the friend's advice to *Don Quixote* in the prologue. Cacus, it will be recalled, was a giant and a thief who stole Hercules' cattle. The ancient hero is able to recover his cows after he defeats the giant in battle. From the beginning of the novel, the knight sees himself as an exemplar of chivalric valour and virtue fighting evil foes. The latter are often related to giants. In chapter 1, for example, Don Quixote discusses a quaternity of heroes: the Cid, the Knight of the Burning Sword, Morgante,[24] and Reinaldos de Montalbán. But, for the knight, the greatest of all is Bernardo del Carpio, a Spanish hero who was able to defeat Roland/Orlando at Roncesvalles using the same stratagem that Hercules had utilized to defeat the giant Anteus (1978, 1.1.78). Thus, at the apex of heroic grandeur stands a Spanish hero who, like his classical ancestor, can defeat a great foe – one related to the evils of giants. When faced with a castle-keeper whose thieving deeds are akin to those of Cacus, one would expect that Don Quixote would be reminded of Hercules and immediately do battle with this foe. Don Quixote should have taken on the role of Hercules, a solar hero whose twelve labours were often related to the twelve signs of the zodiac through which the sun must journey. But the knight sinks to the ground instead, kneeling before this modern Cacus, and requests that the 'giant' innkeeper arm him as a *caballero* (1978, 1.3.87). This is one of Don Quixote's greatest transgressions in the novel. In his desire to be knighted he fails to perform his first Herculean task. The gentleman from La Mancha not only succumbs to the giant but becomes his vassal. In fact, he accepts the castle-keeper's advice, returning home to search for clothes, money, medicine, and a squire. These four items are again foundational, forming the nucleus of Don Quixote's needed possessions in his second sally.

The failures of Don Quixote, then, can be linked to the failures in establishing a proper tetradic foundation for the construction of his 'self' as knight. The Pythagorean harmony and balance depicted by Raphael in the Vatican Stanze are replicated in the quaternities used to begin the task of writing the novel. But the knight's own madness leads the text away from a Raphaelesque harmony. Cervantes had already provided a glimpse at Don Quixote's failures in the prologue through allusions to Raphael's *The Virtues*. Although the knight wishes to embody all four virtues, and justice in particular, he fails in all four, his lack of prudence leading to his final defeat. Raphaelesque harmonies, then, are replaced by an elemental, humoral, and seasonal imbalance in the characterization of the gentleman from La Mancha. Don Quixote also transgresses against the harmonious tetrad by embarking in chivalric adventures in the wrong 'season' of life. Although he calls upon Apollo, the fourth Ptolemaic planet, to be his guide, he is unaware that this deity can become a malefic influence by further disrupting the qualities and humours that serve as foundations for his character. In his role as god of poetry, Apollo also takes on a malefic role. Instead of appearing as the god of Raphael's *Parnassus* who keeps close to him the epic poets, he is shown in Cervantes' novel as a deity who refuses to honour the knight's plea to have his adventures narrated in an epic tone. But perhaps the greatest foundational transgression has to do with the knight's subservience to Cacus. Under the influence of this picaresque innkeeper/giant, Don Quixote will be unable to perform truly heroic, epic, and Herculean deeds. No matter how high his ambitions and how daring his imaginings, Don Quixote's actions will be imbued with the comic and the picaresque. As vassal to a thieving giant, his imaginings will never prove to be his own, but scenes stolen from other texts, from other images – as the very image of Cacus is itself 'stolen' from Virgil and even from Renaissance art. The thieving Cacus, then, leads the reader to ponder the role of imitation in the creation of a text. When is imitation a slavish repetition of ancient authorities, a thieving art that merely replicates the past, and when is it an emulation, a competition with authoritative models so as to rival and even surpass what was once considered as *auctoritas*? While Don Quixote merely attempts to replicate his readings, the novel establishes a space for emulation in the gap between the representation of the knight's environment and the imagined textual and visual spaces that Don Quijote wishes to impose upon his milieu.

5 Textual Terribilitá: Michelangelo

I do not see that, where narrative composition is concerned, Michelangelo yields place to Raphael. Indeed, I maintain the opposite: to wit, that Michelangelo comes out a good way ahead. I venture to say, that is, that his stupendous *Last Judgment* embodies in its arrangement certain allegorical meanings of great profundity which few people arrive at understanding.

Lodovico Dolce, *The Dialogue on Painting*, edited by Mark W. Roskill

The presence of Raphael in the 1605 *Don Quixote* does not mean an unquestioned incorporation of his art as a 'sacramental' imitation of the Stanza della Segnatura. Although the first part of the novel (chapters 1–8) follow the Pythagorean tetractys and the numerology of cosmos found in the Vatican frescoes of Raphael, other elements create a countermovement that strains the well-ordered creation of cosmos in the first eight chapters of the novel and eventually lead to a break with Raphael. The tone of the prologue clearly proclaims that the novel will come to reject the correct, measured, and 'divine' classicism of Raphael. In order to assume a more monstrous and modern form, Cervantes' text uses the figure of the friend to mock the aspirations of the artist. Rather than the monumental and epic quality of Raphael's frescoes, the prologue's 'friend' presents fragmented, minimized, and humorous replicas. The sacred geometry, the Pythagorean numerology of Raphael, will break down in Cervantes' text under the tremendous strain of tenuous links and textual *terribilitá*. The burlesque tone of the prologue points to the burlesque imitation of the 'epic' that will follow. Don Quixote may well be a new Aeneas, but his feats are failures and his bumbling attempts to reestablish a Golden Age are far from the Virgilian hero's high tone and civilizing influence as viewed by Renaissance readers and commentators. The audacious yet foolish knight from La Mancha may well be signalling that the new Spanish empire has failed to live up to the valour of ancient Troy, the cunning of the Greek alliance, and the majesty of Rome. In so doing, it may also be questioning the whole impulse for empire and the desire for territorial and ideological conquest.

Although this chapter belongs to Michelangelo, it is impossible to speak of him without mention of Raphael. The rivalry between these two painters is replicated in the prologue as the text subverts the imitative strategies of the former and points to Cervantes' new link to the latter. One way to come to an initial understanding of the admiration and rivalry that existed between these two painters is to return to Raphael's most famous fresco in the Stanza della Segnatura, a work that, as noted before, is central to the creation of Cervantes' prologue to the novel. At the beginning of the prologue, the fictionalized author is portrayed in a melancholy pose, as he attempts to write, he describes himself as being: 'en suspenso, con el papel delante, la pluma en la oreja, el codo en el bufete y la mano en la mejilla, pensando lo que diría' (in this quandary, with the paper in front of me, the pen behind my ear, my elbow on the desk and my cheek in my hand, wondering what I could write) (1978, 1.51–2; 12). Cervantes' self-depiction recalls a fascinating portrayal in the *School of Athens* (fig. 5.1).[1] In the fresco, there is a figure in the foreground who is also portrayed seated, with his elbow on a block, and hand on the cheek. Both Raphael's painting and Cervantes' text include the necessary materials for a writer – paper and pen. But, while the figure in Raphael's painting has written some lines and is again thinking, the Cervantes figure has been unable to write. It is his friend's advice that will provide him material for the prologue. Commenting on Raphael's portrayal, Jones and Penny assert: 'More than anyone else in the fresco he powerfully does what one expects philosophers to do – sit and think –' (1983, 77). And yet, they believe that this philosopher cannot be identified. Many art critics, on the other hand, believe he represents Heraclitus. Cervantes would hardly have missed the opportunity to include him in his prologue as Fernando de Rojas had done in *La Celestina*.

Rojas's prologue begins with a reference to this pre-Socratic philosopher: 'Todas las cosas ser criadas a manera de contienda o batalla, dice aquel gran sabio Heráclito' (All things are created through struggle or battle, says the great sage Heraclitus') (1974, 47). Rojas goes on to present numerous examples of this *sententiae*, as found in the cosmos, the beasts, the birds, and human beings. This universal conflict is specifically related to the art of writing and to the reception of the *Celestina*. Since the prologue to *Don Quixote* also deals with the art of writing and is also concerned with reception, it would seem appropriate that the figure of the author be presented in terms of Heraclitus. The pre-Socratic philosopher is reputed not to have wanted to publish his works. Instead, he offered his texts to the goddess Artemis, leaving them in her temple. The fictional Cervantes also evinces qualms as to publishing: 'ni menos sacar a luz las hazañas de tan noble caballero' (still less publish the exploits of this noble knight) (1978, 1.52; 12). And in the second volume of *Don Quixote*, the narrator will allude to the dubious fame acquired by writing in terms of the temple of Artemis/Diana (1978, 2.8.95). Although Heraclitus focused on the elemental conflict in the universe, he also believed in one unifying principle, fire. When Rojas claims that his examples are like tales told by the fire (1974, 48), he may also have had in mind the Heraclitan unifying fire. In this sense the fiery passions of his text lead to both conflict and a vision beyond conflict, the eternal fire of the cosmos. But those who cannot reach the philosopher's vision are caught in the opposition symbolized by the seasons: 'El verano vemos que nos aqueja con calor demasiado, el invierno con frío y aspereza' (In the summer we see that too much heat distresses us, the winter with cold and roughness) (1974, 48). In *Don Quixote*, the seasonal opposition is immediately felt by the protagonist who is subjected to the intense heat of summer ('el sol entraba tan apriesa y con tanto ardor que fuera bastante a derretirle los sesos, si alguno tuviera' [the sun was rising so fast and becoming so hot, that his brains would have melted, if he'd had any'] (978, 1.2.81; 31]).

From the start, Don Quixote is a symbol of conflict, unable to attain that Golden Age of peace for which he wishes to do battle. The fire he exudes is one of elemental conflict and not the transcendental fire of unity. This opposition is reflected in his humoral composition. As noted in chapter 4, many have argued as to whether he is ruled by choler (fire) or melancholy (dryness). As the heir to his Heraclitan father, he must evince both humours: the choleric since it denotes both the fire of conflict and the flames of transcendence; and the melancholic since the philosopher was repeatedly labelled as being ruled by this temper. While Heraclitus and Don Quixote are seen as melancholic, the fictional Cervantes is also depicted this way in the prologue ('tan imaginativo' [so imaginative]).[2] Since melancholy belongs to Saturn, a planet that is responsible for both creativity and incarceration, it should come as no surprise that *Don Quixote* is said to have been conceived by its author 'en una cárcel' (in prison) (1978, 1.50; 11). This offspring is as melancholic as his father: 'hijo seco, avellando' (a dry, shrivelled child) (1978, 1.50; 11). As noted, dryness is the chief quality of the melancholy humour. And yet, this dry and saturnine knight invites laughter.

This paradoxical creation symbolizes the oppositions which form the basis of Heraclitus's philosophy and which are described in the prologue to *Celestina* where, for example, the elephant, an animal so powerful and strong, becomes frightened and flees at the sight of a mouse (Rojas 1974, 48). Valour and fear, power and weakness can be found within the same animal. Thus, Rojas argues that it should not be unexpected that readers have battled over the type of work he has written: is it a comedy that provides pleasure or a tragedy that elicits sadness? This opposing vision of life and fiction recalls how the Renaissance viewed Heraclitus. As the 'weeping philosopher,' he was contrasted with Democritus, the 'laughing philosopher,' in a play of opposites typical of universal conflicts. While pleasure and sadness battle for supremacy in *Celestina*, laughter and melancholy are at odds in *Don Quixote*. Indeed, the battle over the meaning and tone of *Don Quixote* from those who see it as a funny book to those who view it in a heroic and 'romantic' fashion was prefigured by the hidden allusion to Raphael's Heraclitus, as conflated with Fernando de Rojas's prologue.[3]

Raphael's portrayal of Heraclitus was added late, once the cartoon of the fresco was already finished. Thus, it mirrors the prologue of Cervantes' novel, which was the last section written by the author. Asking himself why there was a need to add an additional philosopher to the painting, D. Redig de Campos has shown that the figure is not only a portrayal of Heraclitus but also one of Michelangelo (1946, 85). He goes on to explain the link between the ancient philosopher and Michelangelo through their melancholy character:[4] 'The love for reflection, the tendency towards solitude, and his melancholy were fundamental traits of his character ... he wanted to refigure his great rival in Heraclitus, the obscure and misunderstood philosopher' (1946, 96). Although Penny and Jones argue that 'his features have, implausibly, been seen as those of Michelangelo' (1983, 78), many agree with Redig de Campos. George L. Hersey, noting that in the fresco the figure is reclining on a block of marble in order to highlight Michelangelo's role as sculptor, explains: 'This is probably Michelangelo, who many years later was in fact to write a poem about a statue imprisoned in a marble block. Michelangelo even wore a famous pair of boots like those shown here. His sulky resentment of Bramante and Raphael is readable' (1993, 134).

We cannot be certain that Cervantes was aware of this identification, although many art historians assert that this link was well known during the Renaissance. Given Cervantes' knowledge of Renaissance art as shown in this volume, I think there can be little doubt that he would have known of this famous portrait of Michelangelo by Raphael. Indeed, Cervantes' prologue can be studied in terms of the artistic rivalry between Raphael and Michelangelo. In *La Numancia* and *La Galatea*, Cervantes had followed the classicizing bent of Raphael. The first part of *Don Quixote* serves to break with the model by mocking the careful archaeology, erudite allusiveness, and the majesty, harmony, and order of the frescoes. This break aids in the creation of something new, something more akin to Michelangelo's *terribilitá* than to the piety and grace of Raphael. Here, classical allusions are turned against themselves, questioning *auctoritas* and distorting the ancients so as to establish what on the surface appears to be an anti-classical stance. While the author's friend becomes a humorous, petty, and rather ignorant counsellor who wants to turn 'Cervantes' into a mock-Raphael, the author portrays himself in a somber, sulky, and melancholy manner, thus cloaking himself in Michelangelo's mannered pose. Thus, the portrayal of the author figure in the prologue to the 1605 *Don Quixote* is a fragmented ekphrasis, taking as its model a key figure from Raphael's *School of Athens*.

In the *The School of Athens*, Raphael both pays tribute to Michelangelo and portrays him as a figure rather alien to the classical harmony depicted in the fresco. His odd boots contrast with the bare-footed or sandalled philosophers. His musings seem to shelter him from the crowd of thinkers, isolating him from their classicizing influence. Indeed, he shares the centre of the painting with the other eccentric figure, Diogenes, 'who sounds the only other note of discord in the scene's harmony' (Hersey 1993, 134). At this early date, when he worked on the Stanza della Segnatura, Raphael was still in awe of Michelangelo, carefully measuring his own talents against those of his rival. As time goes on, the rivalry – but also the admiration of Raphael for Michelangelo – becomes more pronounced.

This is not the only placement of Michelangelo as rival to Raphael in the prologue to Cervantes' *Quixote*. When the friend recommends that the author include in his text allusions to Goliath and Cacus, he may not have been alluding only to Raphael's contest between the Christian (Matthew in the *Disputa*) and the pagan (Virgil in the *Parnassus*) in the Stanza della Segnatura; he may well have been pointing also to Michelangelo, whose 'curious preoccupation with giants' in both his sculptures and his poetry has been noted by many art historians (Clements 1966, 166). Indeed, Michelangelo's interest in David and Goliath was so keen 'that he executed young David three times' (Clements 1966, 167). There may be a series of artistic and textual rivalries hidden in the Goliath/Cacus allusion. In his attempt to understand Italian Renaissance art, Cervantes certainly consulted Vasari's *Lives* – its second and definitive edition was published in 1568, the year before his arrival in Italy. Although Vasari clearly preferred 'praise to blame' (Rubin 1995, 231), he at times did succumb to strong criticism. In reading Vasari, Cervantes may well have noted the rivalry between this biographer and Baccio Bandinelli. The latter labelled Vasari 'as a pretentious incompetent and sneak, not fit to lick Bandinelli's shoes or call himself Bandinelli's student' (Rubin 1995, 53). Vasari follows suit, telling all manner of negative anecdotes of Bandinelli in the *Lives*, including the story that in 1512, when the Medici were restored to power, Baccio entered the palace in secret and tore a cartoon by Michelangelo. This was caused, according to Vasari, by the 'hatred he felt against Michelangelo and afterwards demonstrated as long as he lived' (1996, 2.267). Vasari adds that in 1515 Bandinelli received a commission from Leo X for a colossal *Hercules* which Baccio claimed would surpass Michelangelo's *David*. Vasari asserts: 'But the act did not correspond to the word, nor the work to the boast, and it robbed Baccio of much of the estimation in which he had previously been held by the craftsmen and by the whole city' (Vasari 1996, 2.270). But it was his *Hercules and Cacus*, a commission he 'stole' from Michelangelo, which was the climactic moment of the rivalry between the two Florentine artists (Vasari 1996, 2.274–5). I believe that the mention of David/Goliath and Cacus in Cervantes refers to the battles between Bandinelli and Michelangelo over the fashioning of giants.

Michelangelo's *David* (fig. 5.2) was completed in 1504, its beauty and originality creating quite a stir in Florence. After all, the biblical boy hero was transformed into a gigantic nude figure, which borrowed much from the ancients. Indeed its torso 'represents Michelangelo's version of a Hellenistic athlete' (Hibbard 1974, 56). Rather than depicting the biblical figure in the midst of its struggle with Goliath (as in Michelangelo's fresco in the Sistine Chapel) or showing David immediately after his triumph (as in Donatello's statue at the Palazzo Vecchio or Raphael's fresco at the Vatican Loggia), Michelangelo chose to represent him before the battle. His pose is one 'hallowed by Greco-Roman statuary – neither walking nor still, it is a version of the *contrapposto* pose that had become the norm for standing male statues in the later 5th century B.C.' (Hibbard 1974, 56). Such a moment would be particularly significant for Cervantes when writing the prologue, since here the writer represents himself in the act of wanting to write. Like a new David, Cervantes portrays himself ready to do battle with the blank page. He must also do battle with his would-be friend, who would turn him into a mock-Raphael. He must stand up for himself. And this agonic self is akin to Heraclitus and Michelangelo.

Bandinelli's statue was not sculpted for another thirty years. His rivalry with Michelangelo, fueled by Pope Clement VII (Pope-Hennessy 1970, 71), led to the placement of his *Hercules and Cacus* at Florence's Piazza della Signoria, opposite Michelangelo's *David* (fig. 5.3). Such a placement worked to the detriment of Baccio's statue since it lacks the striking beauty and originality of Michelangelo's work. But the placement did speak of the rivalry between the two artists. The allusion to the giants Goliath and Cacus made by the author's friend in the prologue immediately evokes a series of artistic contests. It recalls the hatred between Vasari and Bandinelli and the contest between Michelangelo and Bandinelli, artists who loved to sculpt giants; it reminds the reader of the two gigantic figures in front of the Palazzo della Signoria, a *David* readying to kill Goliath and a *Hercules and Cacus*. If we accept that the friend in the prologue is trying to remake Cervantes into a mock-Raphael, we have yet a fourth contest, that between Raphael and Michelangelo. These contests as depicted in the prologue would later be replicated in the novel. Don Quixote, in his sleep, will slay the giant Pandafilando (actually, he will use his sword to battle with the innkeeper's wineskins). Thus, the main character becomes a new David, a new Hercules who, in mock-heroic fashion, destroys his gigantic opponent.

In addition to the fragmented ekphrasis of Raphael's Heraclitus/ Michelangelo as a figure that represents the fictionalized Cervantes, the prologue provides us with glimpses of other artistic rivalries through allusive ekphrases. An attentive reader who notes the veiled references in the prologue to the rivalries between Michelangelo, Raphael, Vasari, and Bandinelli may well ask: Why place an allusion to the Tagus River in between Goliath and Cacus? When Cervantes viewed these two figures in Florence, they were not separated by a river. It is true that there was a door in between, an entrance to the palace. But this does not suggest a watery realm. What Cervantes would have perceived on entering the Piazza della Signoria was the construction of a fountain which was to be topped by a gigantic sea god, Neptune. The watery realm, then, does exist in the sculpted world of the Piazza. It stands between two giants as if to separate rival artists (Michelangelo and Bandinelli) and rival legends, one representing biblical *auctoritas* and the other embodying the authority of the ancients. Indeed, the Neptune statue was also born of rivalry. Both Benvenuto Cellini and Baccio Bandinelli wanted this commission from Duke Cosimo, but it was finally given to Bartolommeo Ammannati – and Vasari was instrumental in this award (Rubin 1995, 53). It was constructed from 1563 to 1575. The results were far from felicitous and the statue became known as *Biancone*, the white one.

It is not sufficient, however, to ascertain the presence of the main statues from the Piazza in the prologue to *Don Quixote*. The reader must wonder – why include these sculptures through allusive and veiled ekphrases? There is of course the question of rivalry. Does it simply have to do with literary and artistic rivalries and with the sculpting of giants? There is yet another context that should be foregrounded. Giorgio Vasari cryptically stated: 'David and Hercules were emblems of the palace' (1996, 2.274–5). Indeed, there is a proliferation of images of David and of Hercules around the Palazzo della Signoria. These two figures seem to have had very different political connotations. Donatello's *David*, for example, was placed in the centre of the first courtyard in the Palazzo soon after the fall of the Medici: 'The statue, symbol of regained liberty, was placed on a column, where originally there had probably been a well. About sixty years later, Giorgio Vasari moved the David' (Muccini 1997, 32). At this time, Cosimo was the new Medici duke and may not have prized this symbol of republicanism. And yet, the statue was not removed; it was just moved to a less conspicuous place with the duke's approval (Muccini 1997, 44; Rubin 1995, 328). This move may speak as much of the figure's republicanism as of its polyvalence.

Just as Donatello's bronze *David* stood for liberty, so did Michelangelo's giant marble statue. Howard Hibbard has shown that Michelangelo's statue of the David was considered 'potent in its references to republican anti-Mediciean, civic spirit ... placed as it was before the seat of republican liberty, the gaze of the *David*, facing South, was a warning to hostile Rome and, most particularly in 1504 to the Medici, who were gathering forces for the eventual re-conquest of the city in 1512' (1974, 58). The statue then, is political and antityrannical in nature. David, paradoxically represented as a boy-giant, pauses before his attack on Goliath, the giant of absolute rule. This political dimension of the Florentine David myth also sheds light on the rivalry between Raphael and Michelangelo. The former was constantly associated with the papacy, which was often Medicean during this period. Michelangelo, on the other hand, stood for republicanism, and when executing commissions for the popes often engaged in violent conflicts with his patrons.

The commission for the second statue, the *Hercules and Cacus*, however, followed an opposite political plan. Clement VII gave it to Bandinelli so that his work 'became a symbol of pro-Medician favoritism, despised by the Florentines' (Hibbard 1974, 208). When it was finished in 1534, the Medicis were permanently back in power, and their Herculean symbol, as crafted by Bandinelli, could well vie with Michelangelo's *David* for political ascendancy. Indeed, the Palazzo Vecchio was replete with images of Hercules as Muccini acknowledges: 'The myth of Hercules, a figure associated with Florence in antiquity, frequently recurs in the decoration of Palazzo Vecchio in connection with Cosimo, who like the legendary hero, knew how to triumph over his enemies' (1997, 124). There is a whole room dedicated to Hercules, with a ceiling painted by Vasari, depicting *The Infant Hercules Strangles the Snakes*, a symbol of Medici 'invincible strength' (Muccini 1997, 58). On the walls Marco de Faenza adds a series of paintings of Hercules defeating his rivals, including a *Hercules and Cacus* (Muccini 1997, 61). And a pupil of Bandinelli, Vincenzo de' Rossi sculpts seven of Hercules' labours which are placed in the Salone dei Cinquecento in the late 1500s. They include a *Hercules and Cacus* which both emulates and rivals Bandinelli's sculpture.

Are the political contexts of David/Goliath and Hercules/Cacus at play in *Don Quixote*? Or should they be translated into Spanish political readings, where Hercules stands for the Habsburgs? Is it valid to read the knight's association with the inkeeper/Cacus in the second chapter as a rejection of the power of the Habsburgs or Medicis? It certainly is curious that Don Quixote is armed as a knight by a figure maligned in both mythology and Medicean art. It may be that Don Quixote's failure to take on the role of Hercules in this particular instance points to his desire for a freedom from both political and artistic strictures. But Cervantes' textual image is as mute as the visual arts were said to be. And there seems to be deliberate confusion as Don Quixote also assumes the role of Hercules, as early as the first chapter of the novel

(1978, 1.1.74).[5] And, it may be asked, when he kills Pandafilando, is he taking on the liberating role of a new David or the imperial mantle of a new Hercules? The 'mute' yet eloquent images of Cacus in the art of the Italian Renaissance serve to trigger an active reading of the Cervantine text, one where Renaissance rivalries are made to impinge upon Don Quixote's visions.

Cervantes' prologue, then, is replete with rivalries, either artistic or political – rivalries that impinge upon the text. While Michelangelo's giant *David* towers over Raphael's classical frescoes, Bandinelli's *Hercules and Cacus* proposes a new political context and brings into question Don Quixote's reactions to the innkeeper/Cacus in chapter 2 of the novel – and to a host of giants throughout the text. Vasari condemns Bandinelli, while Michelangelo attempts to surpass Raphael in much the same way as a new Cervantine style counters Raphael's classicism. Papal commissions are contrasted with works representing liberty. Republicanism vies with Medicean patronage and written texts by Vasari and Cellini find fault in their artistic rivals. Thus, the prologue to *Don Quixote* is not just a parody of excessive classical erudition as seen in the friend, a figure akin to Lope de Vega. It also foregrounds literary, artistic, and political competition as the basis for the novel.

We have already seen how Michelangelo's sculpture *David* is a way of muting the impact of Raphael's frescoes in the Cervantine prologue. But there is yet one more portrait that is relevant to this contest. Could references to St Matthew in the prologue point to both Raphael's *Disputa* and Michelangelo's famous statue? (Hersey 1993, 136, 253). Let us recall that Matthew is one of the figures included in the *Disputa*. In addition, Raphael includes the four Gospels as books in his fresco. They are open and the first lines can be read. In Matthew's book, the first of the Gospels, the viewer can clearly read the last word, 'David' – Christ is said to be his son or progeny. This David immediately recalls the earlier *David* of Michelangelo, a work also of significance for the prologue. Thus, Cervantes' references in the prologue create a series of links with Renaissance paintings and sculptures.

Let us see how the rivalries between Raphael and Michelangelo are inscribed through the reference to Matthew. The two sentences cited by Cervantes from his Gospel are rather telling. The first deals with 'la amistad y amor que Dios manda que se tenga al enemigo' (the friendship and love that God tells us to feel for our enemies) (1978, 1.55; 14), while the second deals with evil thoughts. The composition of *Saint*

Matthew (fig. 5.4) was surrounded by thoughts of enemies and rivalries. Michelangelo, in Rome to work on Pope Julius II's future tomb, had to leave the city hurriedly. In a letter, he writes: 'If I stayed in Rome my tomb would be built before the Pope's' (Hibbard 1974, 91). Not only did he think that the pope had turned against him, but 'Michelangelo imagined that there were all kinds of schemes against him instigated by Bramante, by his 'nephew' Raphael, and by the courtiers around them' (Hibbard 1974, 92). His fear of rivalry and of Rome kept him in Florence in spite of a series of entreaties by the pope that he should return to the Vatican. His *Saint Matthew* was one of twelve apostles that the Florentine cathedral commissioned him to sculpt. They asked for one per year starting in 1503. But the *Saint Matthew* was the only one he even began.

The emotions expressed in this statue may well have been those of earthly enmities. The results were revolutionary in the history of art: 'No post-antique work of sculpture is so seized with visible emotion which is expressed with the awesome power that contemporaries called *terribilitá*' (Hibbard 1974, 94). This *terribilitá* went beyond the twists, turns, and contortions that Michelangelo may have imitated from the ancient statue of *Laocöon*, which had been recently unearthed in Rome. The rash movements serve to point to 'his restless imagination and fierce passions working themselves out in the chiseled stone' (Hibbard 1974, 94). The ability to provide such outpourings of emotion and movement to inanimate stone would transform Renaissance classicism. One may thus superimpose Michelangelo's *Saint Matthew* upon the apostle of Raphael's *Disputa*, thus inscribing the artistic rivalries between the two artists and between two styles into the prologue. This double vision points to the prologue's comic rejection of Raphael and the triumph of Michelangelo, whom Cervantes emulates in his break with so many of the genres and techniques of his time.

The *terribilitá* of Michelangelo's *Saint Matthew* is taken to an extreme in the artist's most famous fresco, *The Last Judgment* (fig. 5.5). The work is inspired in part by Matthew's evocation of the Last Days as the Son of Man comes forth among the clouds sending angels with trumpets to gather the chosen from the heavens and from the depths of the earth (Hibbard 1974, 246–7; Hartt 1984, 41; Hersey 1993, 221). But the work goes far beyond the Gospel of Matthew, of the evangelist classically represented by Raphael in his *Disputa*. Here, the apostles, standing in agitated poses behind St Peter and St John, bear the weight of that *terribilitá* which Michelangelo had given the marble St Matthew. Indeed, the work as a whole is even more iconoclastic than the earlier sculpture. As Pierluigi de Vecchi asserts, the fresco calls forth 'the dissolution of order and the formal balance that reflected the notion of an immutable structure' (1996, 216). Its impression upon the viewer is 'genuinely catastrophic,' imposing 'an overarching emotional fervor on the individual elements of the painting, which may collectively even appear incoherent and contradictory ...' (1996, 217). Foreshortening, opposing movements, and chiaroscuro serve to emphasize the frenzied emotions and the cracks in the order and balance of the cosmos. Among the individual flickers that arouse the spectator's emotions, the viewer may perceive, under the shining Christ, diagonally below and to the right, 'the memorably desperate figure who hugs himself and stares out, eyes blazing with horror, having realized only now that he is doomed' (Hersey 1993, 217). Thus, more than anything, the work evokes 'a new and lacerating awareness of the individual's responsibility of choice, and his anguished uncertainty regarding the ultimate destiny' (Vecchi 1996, 217).

It is this flicker of many faces, of clearly delineated individuals who rise and fall that recalls the throng of humanity, the variety of human figures that appear and disappear, triumph or are forgotten or defeated in the novelistic plains of La Mancha. They provide Cervantes' novel its human texture which, when taken together may well appear, as Michelangelo's fresco, as 'incoherent and contradictory' (Vecchi 1996, 217). The very notion of order, evoked through Raphael's classical frescoes, is broken down through never-ending conversations of a multitude of topics, through humour and the systematic destabilization of the tetrad. At the centre of all stands Don Quixote, who is resolute in his quest. His aim, like that of Christ, is one of salvation for humankind. And he perceives himself as someone who comes at the end of time, at the end of the Iron Age, to restore a new Golden Age – to restore paradise. Like Christ, Don Quixote appoints himself as judge of others, condemning those who appear as evil giants and freeing from their chains those who can convince him of their innocence. Like the Christ in Michelangelo's fresco, which was derived from the famous *Apollo Belvedere* housed at the Cortile, or Statue Court, at the Vatican,[6] Don Quixote sees himself as a new Apollo, imparting the light of his justice on those in need.[7] The description of this vision becomes a veiled ekphrasis that reveals the classical roots of Michelangelo's hagiographic program. Of course, Don Quixote's actions betray his imagination. Or, perhaps it is his imagination that betrays his actions. At any rate, he is unable to see either the guilt of the galley slaves whom he frees or the innocence of the many apparent foes with whom he does battle.[8] His justice mocks the judgment of Christ, and his madness reflects solar excesses rather than the light of Apollo.

Don Quixote's concern with justice is made evident in his very first adventure, which takes place in chapter 4. This chapter is particularly significant since the number four, as noted before, emphasizes Raphael's Pythagorean quaternity already present through *enumeratio* in the prologue and the first two chapters of the novel. Chapter 4, like the eighth and final chapter of Part 1 of the 1605 *Quixote*, differs from the rest in that it contains two adventures by the knight. Here we encounter the episodes of the flogging of Andrés and of the impious merchants of Toledo. It is the first of the two that interests us here. While flickers of Raphael's art can be seen throughout the first chapters of *Don Quixote*, in particular through the structures of Pythagorean quaternities, the work of Michelangelo enters the text at this early point so as to trigger a movement away from the tetrad through distortion. And yet, the tetrad is not negated. It is merely transformed. In order to emphasize the continuing importance of the foundational number four in the novel, the main character of this episode, Andrés, will reappear in the fourth chapter of the fourth part of the novel.

Don Quixote hears 'voces delicadas, como de una persona que se quejaba' (faint sounds as of someone moaning) (1978, 1.4.95; 42). He realizes that this sound may lead to an adventure; thus comes his first chance to follow the chivalric code to help the needy: 'Estas voces, sin duda, son de algún menesteroso, o menesterosa, que ha menester mi favor y ayuda' (These cries come, no doubt, from some man or woman in distress, who stands in need of my protection and assistance) (1978, 1.4.95; 42). Following the cries into the woods, Don Quixote comes upon a young man, tied to a tree and naked to the waist, who is being flogged by a farmer. Don Quixote does not listen to the farmer's reasons for punishing the boy. He does not care to hear that the boy had not tended well to his master's flock of sheep, losing one every day. The knight immediately takes the boy's side and commands the farmer to release Andrés and to pay him for his labours. It is clear that Don Quixote reacts to visual and aural stimuli (a youth tied to a tree, screaming) rather than to the reasonable explanations of Juan Haldudo. What he views is nothing less than a hagiographic ekphrasis, one which may be the creation of his imagination, but is based on an actual fresco. This mnemonic image, to which we will soon come, propels him to action. In his desire to render justice, visual appearance, swift decision making, quick arithmetic (he must multiply the boy's wages), and chivalric threats are at the core of the knight's response. He is so sure of himself and of his profession that he accepts Haldudo's statement that he will pay Andrés back at the house, even though the youth complains that the farmer will truly torture him once the knight departs.

Don Quixote does threaten Haldudo that if he does not fulfil his promise, he will return to punish him: 'Si no, por el mismo juramento os juro de volver a buscaros y a castigaros, y que os tengo de hallar, aunque os escondáis más que una lagartija' (For otherwise, by that same oath, I swear that I will come back to punish you, and that I will find you, even if you hide yourself away like a lizard) (1978, 1.4.97; 44). The knight believes that such a threat is more than sufficient. But, upon the knight's departure, the hopeful Andrés discovers that his 'reward' is to be tied again to the tree and beaten to the point of death: 'donde le dió tantos azotes, que le dejó por muerto' (and flogged him half dead) (1978, 1.4.98; 44). In this first attempt to render justice, Don Quixote is seen as a failed knight, one who does not understand human motives – only bookish fantasies. He follows the code of ancient knights, the belief in oral commands and promises, regardless of the fact that in an early modern mercantile society, this has been replaced by a written code of law.

But all these events are located on the surface of the text; and so is Andrés's reappearance in the fourth chapter of part 4 of the novel, where he berates the knight while Don Quixote ignores his plight. But I am much more interested in the visual and hagiographic basis for this episode – the hagiographic ekphrasis is not notional, but true or actual, based on *The Last Judgment*. At this moment in the text, Michelangelo's *terribilitá* becomes embodied in the figures of the tormentor and the tormented. The thrust for universal justice, together with the perilous possibility of making the wrong choice as depicted in Michelangelo's *Last Judgment*, are pictorial elements cast into this brief scene. The image of a tender youth, tied to a tree and being flogged by a corpulent man, visually calls out for justice and may well recall the many figures of saints which decorated the churches of the time. Spanish and Italian art of the time abound in depictions of these frail figures, who are seen enduring innumerable punishments as their pagan tormentors attempt to make them renounce their faith. The fact that Andrés is a shepherd further enhances this hagiographic imprint, since a flock of sheep was a prevalent symbol of the followers of Christ the shepherd.

Michelangelo's *Last Judgment*, like the art of his time, is replete with figures of martyrs, triumphantly showing the instruments of their torture to a shining Christ. In his biography of Michelangelo, published in 1553, Ascanio Condivi describes the most prominent saints in the fresco: '... all the saints of God, each one showing to the tremendous Judge the symbol of his martyrdom by which he glorified God: St. Andrew the cross, St. Bartholomew his skin, St. Lawrence the gridiron, St. Sebastian the arrows, San Biagio the combs of iron, St. Catherine the wheel ...' (Hibbart 1974, 245). It is no coincidence that the first saint described by Condivi is the namesake of the youth in Cervantes. More important, the second saint enumerated by Condivi is also a part of Cervantes' narrative.[9]

When Don Quixote tells Andrés to go back home with the farmer Haldudo, the youth replies: 'Irme yo con él ... más? ¡Mal año! No, señor, ni por pienso: ¿porque en viéndose solo me desuelle como a un San Bartolomé?' (Me, go with him, ever again? ... No fear! No sir, I wouldn't even dream of it – so that as soon as we're alone again he can flay me like St Bartholomew') (1978, 1.4.97; 43). Images of St Bartholomew, who was skinned alive and thus became a Christian martyr, are common in Spanish and Italian art of the period. But none is so poignant and revealing as the one found in Michelangelo's *Last Judgment* (fig. 5.6). Immediately to the right and below Christ is a bearded figure that looks up at the light. He carries a knife and in his hand he holds his own skin, having been skinned alive. Critics have puzzled as to why Bartholomew carries his skin. There is one plausible solution. Michelangelo is depicting the day of the resurrection of the flesh. Although Bartholomew exhibits the skin he lost in martyrdom, he will now be clothed in a new undying skin (Hersey 1993, 217). In the Cervantine parody of the *Last Judgment*, Don Quixote turns the pictorial image of Bartholomew's skin into the leather surface of three pairs of shoes, recalling that Michelangelo, in Raphael's *School of Athens*, wore boots as opposed to the other philosophers and thinkers of the fresco who stood barefooted or wearing sandals. When the farmer explains to Don Quixote that Andrés owes him for three pairs of shoes and two bloodlettings, the knight replies: 'Quédense los zapatos y las sangrías por los azotes que sin culpa le habéis dado; que si el rompió el cuero de los zapatos que vos pagastes, vos le habéis rompido el de su cuerpo; y si le sacó el barbero sangre estando enfermo, vos en sanidad se la habéis sacado' (The shoes and the bloodlettings will be set against the flogging you have given him without due cause: for if he has done some damage to the hide of the shoes that you bought him, you have damaged his own hide, and if the barber bled him when he was ill, you have done the same to him in good health) (1978, 1.4.96–7; 43). As in the fresco, human skin acquires a new dimension. The broken leather of the shoes becomes a symbol of torn human flesh, while the bloodletting recalls the blood that issues from the flogged or flayed skin of the would-be martyr.

In spite of Don Quixote's and Andrés's desire to transform the scene into a hagiographic narrative akin to a moment in Michelangelo's fresco, the events portrayed belittle and even belie this connection. Although Andrés wishes to be seen as a new St Bartholomew, it is clear that his master's belt is a less threatening instrument of torture than the knife held by the saint in Michelangelo's *Last Judgment* – it may resemble instead the instrument used by the barber to carry out his bloodletting and cure. More importantly, Bartholomew died for his religion. Andrés is not punished for saving the sheep that stray from the 'Christian' flock, but for losing them: 'Este muchacho que estoy castigando es un mi criado, que me sirve de guardar una manada de ovejas que tengo en estos contornos, el cual es tan descuidado, que cada día me falta una' (This lad I'm punishing ... is one of my servants, and his job is to look after a flock of sheep for me, but he's so careless that every day one of them goes missing) (1978, 1.4.96; 42). In addition, Don Quixote is a dubious figure as saviour since once he departs the boy's torments will recommence and will be doubled. Instead of welcoming the martyr to the heavenly kingdom (as seen by the rising figures at the right of the fresco), this 'Christian' knight seems to condemn the boy to hellish torments. Very much like the figures on the lower left side of the fresco, Andrés is propelled downward, finding himself among those who are beaten by the boatman Charon. Curiously, Bartholomew in the fresco forms part of that diagonal line emerging from Christ's left hand that ends in hellish torment. Thus Don Quixote, in this scene, replicates the condemning left hand of Christ. It may be that Andrés's fate is called forth by his crime. It is telling that when Andrés reappears in the fourth chapter of part 4 of the 1605 novel, blaming Don Quixote for his plight, the knight fails to help him. It may be that Andrés is beyond redemption for having acquiesced to the loss of the 'Christian' sheep. While Don Quixote demonstrates the severity of justice in this second encounter, Sancho evinces Christian charity, giving food to the starving Andrés.

Both Andrés and Don Quixote seem to have a penchant for disguise and heterodoxy. And both see themselves as more than they are. Andrés, like Don Quixote, envisions himself as a Christ figure. When he exclaims, 'Por la pasión de Dios no lo haré otra vez' (By Christ who died on the Cross I swear I won't [do it again]) (1978, 1.4.95; 42), he is actually inviting comparison between the passion of Christ and his own punishment. But Andrés is a false Bartholomew and a false Christ since he is tormented and crucified for leading the flock astray. Don Quixote's first unwitting condemnation of Andrés and his later indifference to the boy's plight shows him as judgmental, mercurial, and unable to judge with equanimity. While at times he becomes the stern judge reflecting traditional ideologies, at other times his eccentricities place him outside the norm of his society. Thus, he comes to represent opposing extremes of orthodoxy and heterodoxy – very much like the circulating figures in Michelangelo's *Last Judgment*.

There are three other possible links between the fresco and the Cervantine narrative: hierarchy, nudity, and self-representation. As Frederick Hartt reminds us, Michelangelo's fresco breaks with tradition: 'Instead of the solid hierarchical structures of medieval Last Judgments ... in which all figures but the damned are customarily dressed according to their social position, and Christ, the Virgin, and the Apostles are suitably enthroned in Heaven, Michelangelo has represented a unified scene without any break, without thrones, without insignia of rank, generally even without clothes' (1984, 41). The nudity of his figures breaks with both hierarchy and the prudery of the Counter-Reformation. In *Don Quixote*, the break with hierarchy takes on a more subtle and insidious form. To start with, the knight is no knight at all since he was knighted by an innkeeper. Consequently he cannot battle members of high rank nor command others. Indeed, the very figure of a knight was obsolete by the time Cervantes wrote his novel. The scene with Andrés is just one more break with hierarchy since Don Quixote has no power over Juan Haldudo. The farmer may feel threatened by Don Quixote's strange guise and weapons, but he may not hold to the ancient and perhaps fictive belief in the positive power of the chivalric knight. The text's inconsistencies regarding hierarchy go far beyond Don Quixote's knighthood and point to the problematics of rank in an age of rapid change. Although always conscious of the difference in rank between himself and his squire, Don Quixote, when envisioning a Golden Age, believes he can do away with hierarchy and asks Sancho to sit by his side, instead of serving him, at a meager banquet hosted by rustic goatherds in chapter 11. When Sancho refuses, Don Quixote pulls rank and orders him to sit with him. Even though he wants to bring back a Golden Age of human justice and equality, Don Quixote cannot behave as an equal. As noted, the problematics of justice is key to the Andrés episode.

While Michelangelo and Cervantes break with hierarchy in different ways, both introduce the notion of nudity and censorship in their texts. In contradistinction to general religious representations where saints, no matter what their punishment, most often hold on to some of their garments, Michelangelo portrays them as nude in *The Last Judgment*. For George Hersey, 'it is the nudity of desolation, of renunciation, of Christ's own body during the Passion, of the desert saint who hates his own human flesh' (1993, 221). For others, the fresco's nudes are a glorification of the pagan past and are intended to 'rival the classical models of the heroic nude' (Vecchio 1996, 226). In the artist's own time, disagreement over the figures took on a much more intense form. Vasari, setting Michelangelo at the pinnacle of Renaissance art, explained how this Renaissance artist disdained 'the charms of color' (1991, 461), a feminine pursuit, to concentrate on the highly noble and masculine technique of design. For Vasari, the *Last Judgment* shows this amazing ability in design through the 'depiction of the human figure' (461), bodies that reveal 'thoughts and emotions which were never depicted by anyone else' (464). While Vasari, in his hierarchical and misogynistic gendering of art, praised the 'manly' design of the nudes, others harshly criticized Michelangelo's *Last Judgment* for its 'obscenity, lewdness, and disrespect for the established historical and doctrinal truth' (Vecchio 1996, 216).[10] Biagio da Casena, master of ceremonies at the Vatican, declared, for example, that 'it was a most unseemly thing in such a venerable place to have painted so many nudes that so indecently display their shame and that it was not a work for a pope's chapel but rather one for baths and taverns' (Vasari 1991, 461).

In 1564, five years before Cervantes' arrival in Italy, the Council of Trent decreed the 'correction' of the parts of the fresco deemed indecent. Daniele da Volterra was commissioned to cover the nude bodies, adding countless 'braghe' (trousers) – in reality only small drapes to the naked figures. Thus, Cervantes would have seen a Counter-Reformation version of the *Last Judgment*, one censored and corrected by the church. Borrowing from Counter-Reformation censorship, Cervantes adds 'braghe' or trousers to the figure of Andrés in *Don Quixote*. He is described as partially clothed: 'desnudo de medio cuerpo arriba' (naked from the waist up) (1978, 1.4.94; 42). In order to foreground the notion of censorship, Juan Haldudo orders Andrés to hold his tongue ('La lengua queda' [Keep your mouth shut] [1978, 1.4.95; 42]). The silence of the lambs is replicated in Andrés's flaying and forced silence. While it is clear that the *Last Judgment* was censored so as to hide the sensuality and paganism of Michelangelo's figures, it is far from obvious why the body of Andrés is censored and why he is asked to remain silent. The reader is left to wonder what is being hidden in this Cervantine portrait. Although the notion of self-censorship, used by Cervantes, may have been triggered by the blatant censorship of the Counter-Reformation, it may also derive from the Spanish writer's knowledge of Michelangelo's stance. Frederick Hartt explains: 'He was a courageous republican and challenged even his papal patrons with scant respect, yet when the chips were down he fled or hid, and in political danger recommended the strictest concealment of political opinion' (1984, 7).

Very much like Michelangelo, Cervantes conceals any overt ideology in his text. And yet, both the artist and the writer hint at possible answers concealed within their works. The answers to the puzzling silence of Andrés may not be clear, but what is revealed is that the visual image of Michelangelo's *Last Judgment* serves to problematize the textual representation of this episode. It may well be that, instead of a Christian Bartholomew, Andrés replicates pagan figures that should be judged and condemned according to the Counter-Reformation. As mentioned above, he is accused of losing sheep, of allowing members of the Christian flock to go astray. Thus, Andrés is no Bartholomew, but can be found among the figures at the lower right-hand side of the *Last Judgment*. Here are those condemned to everlasting damnation. If this is the case, then Juan Haldudo's/Charon's cruel beatings should be seen in terms of the tortures inflicted by orthodoxy on those who do not conform. If Andrés can be associated with one of the damned, then the text is also foregrounding Don Quixote's ability to defend those who, according to the ideology of the times, should be punished. Let us recall once again that the country gentleman had been knighted by the wrong person – the thief Cacus rather than a Herculean lord. Later he will free galley slaves, taking their exculpating statements literally and not understanding their pun on words.[11] Thus, Don Quixote often seems to mistake the signs of orthodoxy or heterodoxy presented to him. Don Quixote's inability to pick the 'official' ideology is coupled with some characters' ability to mask themselves as figures other than what they are (Andrés as Bartholomew). This confusion in both self-representation and ideology induces the reader to probe the boundaries of orthodoxy and self-definition.

There is one last puzzling element that connects Michelangelo's hagiographic depiction and Cervantes' text. In the fresco, St Bartholomew holds his own skin in his hand. This skin becomes a canvas where a spectator can view a tortured countenance. What is puzzling here is that the tortured visage does not replicate Bartholomew's facial features. Pierluigi de Vecchi echoes the commonly accepted interpretation of this portrayal: 'The face on the skin held by Saint Bartholomew is alleged to be an anguished portrait of the artist Michelangelo himself, who thus contrived to leave a somewhat contradictory personal token, testifying on the one hand to ... his profound dread of the "flesh" and carnal weakness' (1996, 232). While in the *School of Athens*, Raphael had portrayed a melancholy and rebellious Michelangelo, some forty years later Michelangelo goes beyond this depiction and reveals a deeper anguish. He is no longer the Renaissance Michelangelo whose *David* challenges both political and religious hierarchies. Instead, he shows the anguish of one who is about to be judged (or has been judged and found wanting). But this anguish exhibited during a time of religious and political repression did not prevent Michelangelo from exhibiting some of his rebelliousness. Pietro Aretino saw this clearly and demonstrated how Michelangelo's 'cult of the enigmatic' was nothing more than 'a detestable spirit of evasion' (Wind 1968, 188). For Aretino, Michelangelo is concealing pagan allegories in the fresco: St Lawrence may be concealing Hercules while St Bartholomew may be a disguise for Marsyas (Wind 1968, 188). Clearly, Michelangelo's saints in the *Last Judgment* are as naked as his sinners, both groups revealing to some extent the pagan appreciation of the nude human body. As Frederick Hartt states: 'He was always a pious Christian ... yet no artist has ever celebrated more movingly either the heroic grandeur or the melodious sensuality of the nude human body' (1984, 8).[12] Michelangelo may have judged himself as unable to accept fully the tenets of the Counter-Reformation.

Turning to Cervantes' novel, the reader will also discover an anguished figure, a woeful countenance. In chapter 19, Sancho calls Don Quixote 'el Caballero de la Triste Figura' (the Knight of the Sorry Face) (1978, 1.19.234; 151). Sancho's pronouncement goes hand in hand with the wonderment experienced by others on seeing Don Quixote's face. Don Fernando and other newcomers to the inn are shocked to see the knight's countenance: 'Suspendió a don Fernando y a los demás la estraña presencia de don Quixote, viendo su rostro de media legua de andadura, seco y amarillo' (Don Fernando and his party were astounded at the extraordinary figure he presented: his face gaunt and pale and as long as a wet week, his ill-matching arms and armour, his sober demeanour) (1978, 1.37.458; 348). This shrivelled and sallow face recalls the portrait held by Bartholomew. Sancho names Don Quixote precisely at the moment when a cleric, angered by the knight's assault on his person, excomunicates him from the church: 'Olvidábaseme de decir que advierta vuestra merced que queda descomulgado, por haber puesto las manos violentamente en cosa sagrada' (I almost forgot to tell you that you're excommunicated for laying violent hands on what is sacred) (1978, 1.19.235; 152). The words quoted by the cleric refer to a decree from the Council of Trent.[13] Thus, the anguished figure of Don Quixote emerges at the moment when he is removed from the church by excommunication.[14] This parallels Michelangelo, who portrays himself in anguish as he realizes that he cannot fully comply with the Counter-Reformation. Thus, while Cervantes, at the beginning of the novel, portrays himself as the youthful and rebellious Michelangelo from Raphael's fresco, Don Quixote is depicted as the aging and anguished artist who, in the grips of the Counter-Reformation, cannot fully comply with their vision of the ideal Christian. It is no wonder, then, that Don Quixote will adopt this woeful (and for some, risible) figure as his chivalric device. The metaphorical white ermine of his shield will be replaced (albeit only in his mind) by this woeful figure that arises from Michelangelo's *Last Judgment*. This fragmented heraldic ekphrasis transforms the triumphant knight of chapter 2 into the more anguished figure of chapter 19 who battles priests and later seeks to give freedom to galley slaves.

The museum of the mind as depicted in *Don Quixote* includes allusive and fragmented ekphrases of statues and frescoes by Michelangelo in order to disrupt the structure and ideology of the novelistic cosmos and, through contextualization, to problematize the ideological landscape of Counter-Reformation Italy and Spain. While Raphael's optimistic and classicist vision had led to the construction of a series of harmonious tetrads, these are questioned and parodied since they belong to an earlier, more optimistic age. Parody also extends to the elegance of classical allusion and to Renaissance syncretism. Michelangelo's *terribilitá* darkens the optimistic environment of an earlier age and brings up a conflictive present in which artistic rivalries reflect the political moral and religious dilemmas of the epoch. The Cervantine text fleshes out the portrayal of Don Quixote with Michelangelo's anguished self-portrait, while the hagiographic mantle falls upon Andrés in order to foreground the duplicitous nature of self-representation. The covered bodies of *The Last Judgment* point to censorship and their presence in the Cervantine museum prompts the reader to listen ever more carefully to the faint murmur of heterodox voices. The partial nudity and the silence of Andrés serves to both reveal and censor the continuing presence of the counterreligion of paganism in the landscape of La Mancha. And, the *David* pose, adopted by the fictive author and cloaked in the mantle of biblical authority, challenges that very authority while silently pointing to a new political, religious, and textual freedom.

6 The Merchants of Trebizond: Luca Cambiaso

In spite of the fact that the growing prosperity of Spain, as of the other European nations, depended on vigorous and heterogeneous trade throughout the known world, and in spite of the fact that the artisanal skills which supported lucrative industries ... were tightly associated with specific ethnic and religious groupings, the victorious Spanish regime declared ethnic and doctrinal purity as the foundations of the stability of the new state.

Lisa Jardine, *Wordly Goods: A New History of the Renaissance*

Cervantes' initial encounter with Renaissance painting when he travelled to Italy did not include the works of Raphael and Michelangelo, of whose rivalries he would later read in Vasari's *Lives*. The Spanish writer's first glimpse at art in Italy took place in a city less known for its artistic accomplishments than for its mercantile pursuits. It is quite certain that Cervantes went to Italy by ship, arriving first at the port of Genoa around December of 1569. We may assume this from the fact that in two of his fictional voyages to Italy, the one found in the *Captive's Tale* in *Don Quixote* and the one undertaken by Tomás Rodaja in *El licenciado vidriera*, the protagonists enter Italy through the port of Genoa. The impression this city must have made on Cervantes can be gleaned by Rodaja's doubling of the term 'beautiful' to describe this city: 'la hermosa y bellísima ciudad de Génova' (the beautiful and most lovely city of Genoa) (Cervantes 1982, 2.109).

One of the beauties of the city was to be found in its architectural and decorative arts. Most histories of Renaissance art seem to ignore Genoa, even though it produced a staggering number of fine frescoes and paintings. At the time Cervantes arrived in Genoa, the leading artist was Luca Cambiaso (1527–85), also called Luchetto.[1] In fact, Lope de Vega refers to him by this second name in the *Égloga a Claudio*, extolling his ability to paint with both hands. Indeed, this feat was often associated with Luca Cambiaso, as well as the fact that he started accepting commissions to paint when he was seventeen years old. Cervantes, intent on becoming a poet, must have avidly sought the images of this popular artist, whose frescoes were everywhere in Genoa. This chapter will show how Luca Cambiaso's subjects and styles prepared Cervantes to view a number of works by more famous artists. Although I will refer to numerous works by Cambiaso, I am not suggesting that Cervantes saw all of them, but that his experience with some would have further embedded these images in his memory, particularly after seeing in Rome and other cities how this Genoese Luchetto had imitated works by Raphael and Michelangelo. It will be argued that in addition to seeing works by Cambiaso, Cervantes also viewed and made use of one of the masterpieces of Giulio Romano located in this city. This fresco will point to the art of Renaissance Rome, which the Spanish poet will soon encounter.

The son of a painter, Luca Cambiaso was much influenced in his youth by the works of Michelangelo (Suida Manning and Suida 1958, 15). Some art historians label his early work as extravagant and even grotesque, taking Michelangelo's *terribilitá* to an extreme. The vision of Michelangelo's *The Last Judgment* appears in at least two of Cambiaso's works. Around 1550, when Luca was twenty-three years old, he painted a *Guidizio finale* for the Sanctuary of Santa Maria delle Grazie in Zoagli, close to Chiavari. Michelangelo had completed his his last pictorial masterpiece, the *Last Judgment* in 1541, some ten years before Cambiaso's fresco. As Frederick Hartt reminds us, Michelangeo broke from medieval representations of Last Judgments by depicting his as a unified and non-hierarchical scene (Hartt 1984, 41). In Cambiaso's fresco, the lack of strict hierarchies, the flowing sense of the scene, and the absence of clothing recalls Michelangelo's work at the Sistine Chapel. Some of the female nudes in Cambiaso, like those of Michelangelo, suffer the same defect of resembling the male body. Luchetto's Christ, like that of Michelangelo, is nude except for a flowing cloth that conceals his genitals. And, like Michelangelo's figure, Cambiaso's Christ stands in contrapposto, creating the illusion of movement. Both figures have their right hand upraised. Although not as thickly populated with human bodies that rise and/or fall, Cambiaso's painting preserves the sense of movement and impending doom. His *terribilitá* vies with that of Michelangelo as people, long dead, crawl out of their graves, some as mere skeletons. Empty skulls appear in both works (at least three in Michelangelo and two in Luchetto), but Cambiaso increases the sense of death by the proliferation of single human bones. At the bottom of both frescoes, terrifying demons seek to take their prey to hell.

Another intimation of Michelangelo's *Last Judgment* can be found in the Church of the Annunciation (Chiesa di SS. Annunziata di Portoria) in Genoa. This church has been called a seventeenth-century Genoese gallery because of its lavish interiors replete with marble, gilt stucco, and frescoes illustrating the mysteries of the Annunciation, created by more than twenty Genoese artists and numerous sculptors. It is in this church that Bergamasco (Giovanni Battista Castello) completed a fresco of the apparition of Christ during the Last Judgment. Since this painter had to leave for Spain in 1567, Luca Cambiaso took over the commission, and depicted the chosen and the damned on either side of Christ (Suida Manning and Manning 1974, 39–40). Thus, in 1569, the year that Cervantes arrived in Genoa, Luca Cambiaso was at work or may have already finished these canvases for the Church of the Annunciation. These works, more than the 1550 *Guidizio finale*, exhibit a mass of humanity. They move upwards in *The Chosen* (*Gli eletti*) and downwards in *The Damned* (*I reprobi*). In the latter, we witness demons dragging bodies downward as well as snakes that encircle the damned – motifs that are also present in Michelangelo.

What is missing in Luca Cambiaso's works on the Last Judgment and is so prominent in Michelangelo is the presence of the many saints and martyrs that surround Christ. Thus, Michelangelo's St Bartholomew, whose presence in *Don Quixote* has been discussed in the previous chapter, is absent from Luchetto. This is not to say that he failed to draw this figure or that Cervantes may not have had Cambiaso in mind when he finally glanced at this martyr in Michelangelo's *Last Judgment*. In fact, Cambiaso, like Michelangelo, was most interested in this Saint. Luchetto did two canvases and a couple of sketches of his martyrdom. He first painted Saint Bartholomew in 1564 for the Church of San Bartolomeo dell'Olivella, but this painting was destroyed during the Second World War (Suida Manning and Suida 1958, 44, 61). There seems little in the reproduction of this work that recalls Michelangelo. However, a second St Bartholomew certainly stands out for its *terribilitá*. Here, the saint is in the process of being skinned alive. The executioner, with his knife has already removed the skin of his right shoulder and arm. This horrific vision of torture certainly recalls Andrés's complaints in *Don Quixote* that Juan Haldudo is in the process of flaying him alive. However, if the date of this second painting is correct (1575), it is doubtful that Cervantes would have seen it, since he left Naples in September of 1575 to return to Spain, only to be soon captured by corsairs (Canavaggio 1990, 76).

While in his earlier years – and even in late works such as the *Martyrdom of St Bartholomew* – Luchetto imitated Michelangelo, in other works, he was closer to Raphael. For example, in his youth he did a *Triumph of Galatea* which closely imitates Raphael's fresco at the Villa Farnesina, which Cervantes used to portray the eponymous heroine of his pastoral romance *La Galatea*. Luchetto's fresco, of which we preserve only a number of variant drawings, was placed on the façade of the Palazzo del Sig. Sivoli, where Cervantes could have easily seen it (Suida Manning and Manning 1974, 95–6). Thus, Cervantes would have witnessed a version of a work that was key to his fiction months before he saw the actual fresco. The doubling of Raphael's fresco serves to imprint further in the mind of the poet an image that he will cherish. In addition, the opposition Michelangelo – Raphael, so pervasive in Cervantes, is to be found in one artist from Genoa. This further reinforces the notion of Luchetto as a painter who pointed Cervantes towards certain rivalries and tensions in Renaissance art.

As Mario Damonte explains, in Cervantes' *Licenciado Vidriera*, Tomás Rodaja admires not only the beautiful women, the handsome and noble qualities of the men, but also the natural and architectural beauties of Genoa (1991, 202–3). He paints the city as a golden paradise: 'La admirable belleza de la ciudad, que en aquellas peñas parece que tiene las casas engastadas, como diamantes en oro' (The city's admirable beauty, that it seems to have houses set in those cliffs, like diamonds in gold) (1982, 2.110). Joseph Turner actually captured in paint this inimitable mixture of nature and architecture when he arrived for the first time in Genoa at the beginning of the summer of 1828. Tomás Rodaja, on arriving in Genoa, goes to a church, much like Cervantes would have done (1982, 2.109). In the same manner, James Hakewill recommended that Turner visit the Church of Santo Stefano, where he should gaze at one of the most famous oil paintings by Raphael's disciple Giulio Romano. Indeed, some even attributed the *Stoning of St Stephen* to Raphael himself (Hartt 1958, 1.55). And, following these models, Luca Cambiaso did a drawing, *The Stoning of St Stephen*, which was later engraved by Raffaele Schiaminossi (Suida Manning and Suida 1958, 172 and 186).

However, I believe that in this case, it is Giulio Romano who serves as prelude to Raphael rather than Luca Cambiaso (although Luchetto's drawing might have been available in Genoa). If Cervantes visited Genoese churches, as Tomás Rodaja had done in his fictive novela, then it is quite likely that he visited not only the Church of the Annunciation as stated above, but also Santo Stefano, reputedly the place where Christopher Columbus was baptized. Here he would have viewed Giulio Romano's masterpiece of the *Stoning of St Stephen*. In this work, the pagan past serves to present an ominous background to the Christian martyr's death, something that contrasts with many of Giulio's other works in which the ancient past is glorified. As Frederick Hartt states: 'It is as if demonic forces inherent in the building were converting the Roman ruin into the instruments of martyrdom' (1958, 1.6). Cervantes' encounter with this ominous picture is replicated in Don Quixote's first encounter with the menacing figures of his imagination. Chapters 2 and 3 record the knight's first transmutation of reality. Here, a country inn becomes a castle and the innkeeper a *castellano*. The lord of the castle, attuned to Don Quixote's madness, agrees to knight him. It is while Don Quixote keeps a vigil watching his arms in the 'castle's' courtyard that the knight's chivalric imagination turns violent. The attempt by some muleteers to move the arms he is so fanatically guarding, so that they can water their animals, affords Don Quixote the opportunity to show his prowess. Even though the knight fights with his lance, the muleteers find a more ancient and effective weapon: they begin to stone Don Quixote. Stoning is not only the first hostile act experienced by Don Quixote. It is foregrounded through repetition. This will be one of many such instances.

Later, Don Quixote loses some of his teeth when he is once again stoned after he attacks the herds of sheep he believes to be armies (1978, 1.18.224). The helmet of Mambrino, he hopes will deflect future attacks, but it proves ineffective.[2] Not only does the act of stoning typify Don Quixote's 'enemies'; it is also replicated by those he saves. When he frees the galley slaves, they refuse to accept his order to visit Dulcinea and throw stones at the knight and his squire. Why the repetition of this hostile gesture? Stoning was often reserved for those who went against the dictates of society; it was reserved for the Other. This hostile act is found not only in the Bible but also in the many hagiographic legends that point to the hostility of pagan peoples against Christian saints. When viewing Giulio Romano's painting in Genoa, Cervantes would be reminded that the first Christian martyr, Saint Stephen, was killed in this manner. What better way to begin his knight's career than to depict himself as the first martyr, using one of the first paintings Cervantes could have seen on reaching Italy? He would thus create a transformative, fragmented, and narrative ekphasis or picture of himself. The text goes beyond the painting to fashion a highly transgressive dramatic ekphrasis, where the saint becomes a deluded gentleman attempting to live out a fantasy.

Cervantes' understanding of Giulio Romano's painting would be enriched as he experienced the artwork at the Vatican. Indeed, his knowledge of Raphael's Stanze may well have triggered a series of associations which led to the reconstruction of his first encounter with Italian art. While Michelangelo may have provided a model for the Andrés episode in chapter 4, Raphael's *Disputa* in the Stanza della segnatura provides a hagiographic frame for the stoning at the inn in chapter 3. In the *Disputa,* Raphael inscribes a moment in the history of painting. The figure of Fra Angelico to the far left recalls that this artist had painted the frescoes in the Chapel of Nicholas V, a room adjacent to Raphael's Stanze. Fra Angelico's frescoes tell two hagiographic tales: the life of St Stephen and that of St Lawrence (a figure whom Luca Cambiaso often painted). Raphael paid homage to Fra Angelico by including not only his picture, but also that of the two saints which so much interested him in the *Disputa* (Hersey 1993, 136). St Stephen, pointing forwards, is seen on the second level of the painting, the second figure to the left of the main group; St Lawrence is the second figure on the right side, looking upwards and to the right. This parallelism seen in both Fra Angelico and Raphael serves to underline their kinship. In the sixth century, when Stephen's body was brought to Rome, he was buried together with St Lawrence. They represent the East and the West, and the opposing elements earth and fire by which they died.

One of the main purposes of the Stanze is to show the validity of papal claims and their undisputed authority in the church. Fra Angelico's frescoes followed a similar program. A number of parallels are shown between these two saints' lives, including St Stephen's ordination as deacon by Saint Peter in Jerusalem and St Lawrence's ordination by Pope Sixtus in the third century. According to John T. Spike, these parallels 'have been carefully drawn in order to demonstrate the continuity between the early Church of Jerusalem led by Saint Peter and the early Church of Rome guided by the popes' (1996, 176). A careful examination of Fra Angelico's *Expulsion and Stoning of St Stephen* shows few if any parallels with Cervantes' text. The majestic walls of Jerusalem are carefully depicted and the victimizers have little in common with the muleteers of the novel.

Indeed, if we move from Fra Angelico's fresco to Giulio Romano's *Stoning of Saint Stephen* (fig. 6.1), we can perceive an enormous gap between the early Renaissance and the mannerist mode of Raphael's disciple. The formalism of the former gives way to the ruinous, chaotic, and ominous majesty of the latter. The uniform illumination of Fra Angelico turns into the 'spasmodic chiaroscuro' (Hartt 1958, 6) of Giulio Romano. Fra Angelico's stylized wall of the city of Jersusalem is razed by Romano's painting. In its place, there are countless ruins, replicated from the remnants of ancient Rome, thus altering the historical location and even the chronology of events. In Cervantes' novel, ruins are also evoked. The unreliable innkeeper tells Don Quixote that the chapel 'estaba derribada para hacerla de nuevo' (had been demolished to build a new one) (1978, 1.3.89; 37). Although the supposedly destroyed chapel was not likely to be of Roman origin, what is significant is the transformation of time and place, for this is precisely what Don Quixote seeks to achieve through his imagination. The landscape of La Mancha disappears in order that the knight's imagination may display the locale of a chivalric romance. Time also shifts as modern Spain is replaced by a more ancient period. In addition to the manneristic shifts in time and space, Cervantes could well have imitated Giulio Romano's painting in its architectural innovations. The location of the stoning at a country inn could have been suggested by Giulio's *architettura rustica*, where the market of Trajan 'with its precarious vaulting shot with holes to admit stabs of light and its violently rusticated doorway' (Hartt 1958, 56) could well be at home in La Mancha. The rusticated landscape of Don Quixote's travels contrasts with the grandiose edifices constructed by his mind. The contrast, which will be repeated throughout the novel, could well have as its model the rusticated architecture of Romano's *Stoning of Saint Stephen*.

In Giulio's painting, the Milvian bridge, spanning the Tiber, is seen in back of and to the right of the mob, while above it all stands a towered castle on a hill. This castle recalls Don Quixote's imagined locale: 'castillo con sus cuatro torres y chapiteles de luciente plata' (castle with its four towers and their spires of shining silver) (1978, 1.2.82; 32). The shining silver of Cervantes' description meshes with the bright radiance of Giulio's castle standing in back of the darkness that surrounds the violent foreground. As for the Milvian bridge, it can be interpreted as the bridge over the castle's moat: 'puente levadiza y honda cava, con todos aquellos adherentes que semejantes castillos se *pintan*' (drawbridge and its deep moat and all the other accessories that such castles commonly boast [are painted]) (1978, 1.2.82; 32). The verb *pintar* (missing from Rutherford's translation) gives the scene imagined by Don Quixote a painterly flavour. While the castle is seen in the background of the painting, closer to the stoning is a rusticated replica of Trajan's market. While the castle is part of the knight's imagination, this market can represent the realities of La Mancha, the Cervantine inn. In the novel, Don Quixote notices 'dos graciosas damas que delante de la puerta del castillo se estaban solozando' (Sitting by the inn door there happened to be two young women) (1978, 1.2.82; 32) – who turn out to be two prostitutes. The 'rusticated doorway' to Trajan's market in the painting also depicts two women. In front of them, with arms outstretched is an older man whose gesture of pleading could be the model for the Cervantine innkeeper who pleads with the muleteers to stop stoning Don Quixote. More importantly, the 'calculated horror of the grimacing mob' (Hartt 1958, 1.56) in the mannerist painting could have served as models for the muleteers who pummel Don Quixote with stones. And the image 'llover piedras' (to rain stones) (1978, 1.3.91; 39) may have its source in the black clouds above the stone throwers and their victim. Indeed it almost seems as if the raised stones are coming from the darkened heavens – although there the Christian God looks with benevolence towards St Stephen. The accumulation of so many parallels between Giulio's painting and Cervantes' episode provides circumstantial evidence that this painting by Giulio Romano is part of the Cervantine museum of words.

Only the figure of Don Quixote seems to be at odds with the tenor of Giulio's painting. The choleric gentleman in no way seems to resemble the patient and youthful St Stephen. And yet, the angelic face we see today is not the one that was drawn by Giulio Romano. The original head 'damaged by a bullet fired by a French soldier in the Armée d'Italie, is in its present condition entirely a neoclassic performance, executed in the Musée Napoléon by Girodet who had neither seen the cartoon nor the picture before it was damaged.' Frederick Hartt adds: 'The cartoon gives us a frantic version of the tortured martyr reminiscent of the demoniac boy in the *Transfiguration*' (1958, 1.56). Although the full face is still a long way from the emaciated countenance of Don Quixote, its tortured and visionary expression is akin to the face of the 'Caballero de la Triste Figura' (Knight of the Sorry Face) (1978, 1.19.234;

151). Thus, the knight's emblematic title and countenance may derive not only from the tortured visage in Michelangelo's *Last Judgment*, but also from the tortured martyr depicted by Giulio Romano.

More important, a careful look at Cervantes' text provides some curious links between the saint and the knight in the stoning episode at the inn. St Stephen kneels as he is being stoned. Don Quixote twice repeats this movement in the adventure of the muleteers. First he kneels before the innkeeper/lord of the castle in order to ask him to knight him ('se incó de rodillas' [fell upon his knees] [1978, 1.3.87; 36]); and second he must kneel once again in front of the innkeeper in order to be knighted (1978, 1.3.93). In the painting, St Stephen has his eyes on the heavens, looking upwards to the clouds where Christ with God the Father and a number of angels await him. Don Quixote's adventure begins with a similar gesture. He glances upwards in order to implore the aid of his goddess Dulcinea: 'Alzó los ojos al cielo, y puesto el pensamiento – a lo que pareció – en su señora Dulcinea' (He raised his eyes to heaven, and fixing his thoughts, as it seemed, on his lady Dulcinea) (1978, 1.3.91; 38). The transformation in Cervantes' novel of a Christian prayer into a plea to his imagined beloved can also be linked with the art of Giulio Romano. Syncretism, the combination of pagan ideology and Christian theology is central to many of the artistic programs of the Renaissance. In Raphael's Stanze we witness ancient philosophers and Christian church fathers both lending authority to the papacy. But this ideal crumbles in the Counter-Reformation. It is already being replaced in some mannerist art.

In Giulio's *Stoning of Saint Stephen*, the syncretic ideal gives way to the impetus to imbue the painting with menace and violence. Here, two religions and two cultures vie with each other, not reaching the Renaissance syncretic ideal, but clashing instead. Although St Stephen is viewed from above by the Christian God and his angels, the locale that surrounds him cries out for his banishment. As statues of ancient gods and heroes watch impassively, the inhabitants of the place move in a frenzied pace to gather stones. As Hartt explains: 'The upper levels of the architecture are peopled with figures who are dismantling it block by block to provide further missiles' (1958, 1.56). The 'demonic forces' of Roman architecture vie even in their ruin with the rising cultural architecture of Christianity. A similar battle is fought over and over again in Cervantes' novel, albeit in a parodic and displaced manner. The knight's ancient ways, his cult of the goddess Dulcinea, seem to clash with Christian concepts, as Don Quixote is told in a later episode. There,

Vivaldo notes that in many of the romances, knights like Don Quixote fail to pray to God before a battle: 'Nunca en aquel instante de acometella se acuerdan de encomendarse a Dios, como cada cristiano está obligado a hacer en peligros semejantes; antes se encomiendan a sus damas, con tanta gana y devoción como si ellas fueran su Dios: cosa que me parece que huele algo a gentilidad' (It never occurs to them to command themselves to God, as every Christian's meant to do in such moments of danger, but instead they go and commend themselves to their ladies, with as much spirit and devotion as if their ladies were God himself – which seems to me to have a smack of the pagan about it) (1978, 1.13.174; 98). Not only does Don Quixote pray in a manner that suggests his paganism; his very vision of his quest derives from a pagan myth, since he wishes to restore the 'Golden Age,' a prevalent myth of classical origin. Thus, the clash between ancient paganism and modern Christianity, so clearly expressed in Giulio's painting, informs many of Don Quixote's adventures. While the stones that hit St Stephen seem to be pagan demonic missiles seeking to crush Christianity, those aimed at Don Quixote come from purportedly Christian characters who reject his chivalric and quasi-pagan vision.

But Don Quixote's uncompromising vision is permanently altered by the innkeeper. Although the innkeeper is willing to go along with Don Quixote and knight him, he does so using an account book. Carroll Johnson astutely states: 'This account book replaces the Bible or any other authoritative chivalric text as the scriptural basis of the character's transformation. By grounding Don Quixote's knighthood in the details of the fodder consumed by the mule trains crisscrossing the country, the text subordinates chivalry itself to peninsular and international commerce' (2000, 6). Furthermore, the innkeeper teaches the knight some common-sense ways to survive adventures in a modern world. He tells him he must always carry with him clean clothes, medicines for his wounds, a squire to carry the knight's necessities and, most important, money. For in a modern world, as David Quint reminds us, a 'knight' has to pay for his room and board.[3] The innkeeper's mercantile concerns affect the knight who eventually returns to his village to collect these items. It should come as no surprise that Don Quixote's small lesson on trade and currency should come from an inn that is modelled after a painting from Genoa. This city together with Venice, were known during the Renaissance for their mercantile empires. Its merchants did business throughout the known world. In Don Quixote's imagination, mercantile concerns seem alien to his pursuits. Indeed, the innkeeper's telling of his own adventures partakes of the picaresque narrative, a type of fiction that contrasts with the chivalric (1978, 1.3.88–9).[4] Thus, Giulio Romano's painting serves to imbue Cervantes' novel with a series of contrasts akin to the chiaroscuro of the painting. Christian hagiography vies with pagan values; majestic architecture contrasts with rusticity and ruins; and castles and markets commingle to establish a contrast between two ways of living.

There is another painting that can also be related to the beginnings of the novel and to Cervantes' arrival in Italy at the port of Genoa. While so far in this chapter we have dealt mainly with paintings associated with the Bible and with hagiography (one exception being Cambiaso's *Galatea*), another work by Luchetto will take up questions of money and empire. As soon as Don Quixote's madness is declared in chapter 1, the narrator tells of the country gentleman's mad visions and aspirations. Not only does he want to become a knight of old, but he aspires to the highest glory attained by the protagonists of the chivalric romances: 'Imaginábase el pobre ya coronado por el valor de su brazo, por lo menos, del imperio de Trapisonda' (The poor man could already see himself being crowned Emperor of Trebizond, at the very least, through the might of his arm) (1978, 1.1.75; 27). The contrast between Don Quixote's mad imaginings and his everyday reality could not be greater. As a poor *hidalgo* of mature age, it would be almost inconceivable for him to become a knight, much less an emperor, through his prowess in battle. This would be ever more difficult at a time when gunpowder had come to replace the sword and where the knight had become an object of fiction. Thus, the narrator refers to him as 'el pobre' (the poor man) a term that serves to ironically commiserate with this mad gentleman and also to show the gap in rank, income, and ability between him and what he wants to become. To imagine himself as an emperor is simply absurd. And yet, such madness does not belong only to Don Quixote. As Diego Clemencín reminds us, Pedro de Vidal, a twelfth-century troubadour, came to imagine that his wife was the cousin of the Byzantine emperor. Carrying a throne with him, he dreamt of becoming an imperial ruler (Cervantes 1833, 14–15).

As mentioned previously, two authors of books of chivalry were particularly responsible for Don Quixote's madness. By reading one, the gentleman's melancholy was increased, and by reading the second, his choler was exacerbated. Both of these authors discuss Trapisonda, one of the three new empires that arose when Constantinople was conquered in 1204 (Miller 1969, 14). The best known of the three, the

Byzantine Empire, was restored in 1261 at Constantinople. The Empire of Trebrizond (Trapisonda), whose capital was on the Black Sea, remained in Christian hands from its inception until 1461. It survived the fall of Constantinople to the Ottoman Turks by eight years. In Feliciano de Silva's continuations of the *Amadís*, we discover that Amadís de Grecia became emperor of Trapisonda, while in Jerónimo de Fernández's *Belianís de Grecia* its emperor together with Belianís helped in the siege of Babylon (Cervantes 1833, 14–15).[5]

This mention of Trapisonda or Trebizond serves to underline Quixote's reading of the romances. Its importance had already been established in the prologue, in which the author's friend counsels the fictional Cervantes to write his own laudatory poems for inclusion at the beginning of his novel, and to attribute them to famous personages such as the emperor of Trebrizond (1978, 1.54). Since the name of this empire is included in the pictorially dense prologue and is repeated in chapter 1, a reader alert to the visual triggers in the text may search for a possible artistic allusion. And yet, Raphael never depicted the place and Michelangelo never sculpted its people. It was in Genoa that Cervantes became acquainted with this exotic land.

Cervantes' interest in Italian art, as stated above, did not need to await the magnificence of Rome to be awakened;[6] he surely witnessed in Genoa the works of Luca Cambiaso (1527–85). Accustomed to the almost exclusive religious subject matter of Spanish paintings, Cervantes must have immediately noticed how the Italians combined religious with mythological and classical topics. And he would retrospectively notice how Cambiaso also combined traits from Michelangelo and Raphael. The future writer, imbued with a humanistic outlook of his teacher López de Hoyos, would have revelled in the many frescoes of antique subjects executed by Cambiaso, including the *Combat between Aeneas and Turnus*, the *Episode of Ulysses and Poliphemus*, and the *Return of Ulysses*, all at the Palazzo Grimaldi (now della Meridiana). When Cervantes turned to epic models for both his *Numancia* and *Don Quixote*, he could well have recalled these images from the Homeric and Virgilian epics.[7] Indeed, Cambiaso's interest in Roman history, from the *Rape of the Sabines* to *Marco Curzio*, is also reflected in Cervantes. Under the name of Mettius Curtius, this Roman hero sung by Livy appears in the 1615 *Don Quixote* (1978, 2.8.96) as well as in the *Viaje del Parnaso* (6.93–5). During Cervantes' Italian sojourn, Luca Cambiaso was at work not only on images of the Last Judgment such as *The Damned*, as shown above, but also on a fresco for the Palazzo Lercari Parodi in Genoa entitled *The Emperor of Trebisonda Constructing a Fondaco for Megollo Lercari* (Suida Manning and Suida 1958, 90). Whether the fresco was completed before Cervantes' departure from Italy or whether he was even allowed to view it at the Palazzo may not be of necessary concern. After all, the subject of the work must have been known to all those interested in art in Genoa, and preliminary drawings were certainly available to the interested art student.[8] Indeed, there are some who claim that Luca Cambiaso's drawings are often superior to his frescoes.[9]

Cambiaso's fresco serves to foreground the connection between Genoa and the eastern empires of Byzantium and Trebizond. According to William Miller: 'As early as about 1250 Genoa had founded her first colony Caffa, on the Black Sea ... of which Michael VIII by the treaty of Nymphaeum in 1261, had given Genoa a practical monopoly' (1969, 34). Gerald W. Day further explains that this treaty 'granted the Genoese merchants an extremely advantageous commercial concession on which Genoa built an extensive Black Sea trade supervised from the Genoese base at Pera, across the Golden Horn from Constantinople' (1988, 8). In addition to having settlements within the Byzantine Empire, the Genoese also abided in the adjacent Empire of Trebizond where they had 'long established settlement at Daphnous, the marine suburb to the east of Trebizond' (Miller 1969, 34). Cambiaso's fresco contains a laudatory representation of one of the early members of the Lercari family who owned the Genoese Palazzo for which the painting was commissioned. The painting also depicts the profitable yet problematic relationship between Trebizond and Genoa. Sometime between 1314 and 1316,[10] it is said that Megollo Lercari, a Genoese merchant, was playing chess with Andronicus, the favourite of Emperor Alexios, who slapped him in the face. Lercari kept this grudge to himself. Then he returned to Genoa to get ready to embark on a mission to exact satisfaction from the Empire of Trebizond. Among his avenging deeds was cutting off noses and ears of prisoners taken from coastal towns of the empire (and preserving them in salt so as to present them to the emperor) and destroying a number of Greek ships through a stratagem. In the end, the emperor had to concede defeat and provided a number of concessions to the Genoese living in Trebizond, including the building of a large 'Fondaco' or place for merchants to lodge. This would be where the Genoese would live and store their merchandise (Suida Manning and Suida 1958, 90).[11]

The emperor of Trebizond ordered a painting to be done commemorating these events. Indeed such a picture was known and described as late as 1480 (Miller 1969, 36). Luca Cambiaso's fresco is then a second commemorative depiction of the event, done more than two hundred years later. This Renaissance fresco shows not only the building of the 'fondaco,' but also the fashioning of a mercantile structure that made Genoa into an economic 'empire.' While the fresco praises the Genoese mercantile domain, which began its expansion in the thirteenth century, it also provides the spectator with a vision of an ancient age in which an emperor rules exotic lands. The image of building within the fresco is related to empire building, be it by Trebizond or by the Genoese. This very much parallels Don Quixote's vision of his quest. The country gentleman wants to construct himself first into a knight and then into an emperor. He wants to quickly build his own imperial power.

And yet, mercantile ventures are often at odds with the enmities created by traditional (warlike) empires. While Venice, Genoa, and Rhodes viewed with equanimity the expansion of the Ottoman Empire and its threat to the Empires of Byzantium and Trebizond, the papacy and the Habsburg Empire reacted to these expansionist moves with alarm. The mercantile powers, as Lisa Jardine has shown, 'were reluctant to impede the healthy flow of goods across the Ottoman Empire to and from markets of the West. Venice, whose commercial activities, prosperity and power were (after Genoa) most closely enmeshed with those of the Ottoman Empire, tended to be in the forefront of those prepared to tolerate the growing power of the Islamic Empire rather than show open hostility to a lucrative trading partner' (1996, 41). Even the fall of Constantinople to the Ottomans failed to slow the flow of merchandise: within days of its fall 'the Genoese had sent two ambassadors ... to renegotiate their own peaceful coexistence with the new power in the land ... Their neutrality during the siege and the alacrity with which they showed their willingness to submit to Ottoman rule paid off. They were granted an imperial *firman*, a solemn undertaking, which gave them the right to trade within the Ottoman Empire, and freedom to continue to practice the Catholic faith' (Jardine 1996, 45). This ability to coexist with other cultures and religions in order to further trade alienated the Habsburg Empire, and particularly its Spanish side. Indeed, the Genoese merchants came to control the Spanish economy during Cervantes' time, and many migrated to Spain, particularly to Seville. As Anne J. Cruz states: 'The resentment against the Genoese by the Spaniards revealed itself in the latter's search for a means to denigrate and segregate the group, as it had become increasingly assimilated and difficult to distinguish from the Sevillian nobility' (1999, 102–3). Very much like those who objected to the conflation of nobility and commerce, and consequent attempts to make the Genoese into Others, Don Quixote deeply resents the merchants who seem to control an empire that in his mind should be ruled by the aristocracy and by the force of arms and knighthood. The Genoese mercantile empire certainly conflicts with Don Quixote's vision of the world. His chivalric code could not tolerate the mercantile code. Indeed, for David Quint, Cervantes' novel is predicated on this kind of opposition and exhibits a 'movement from an earlier feudal social formation to the modern, money-driven society of Cervantes' age' (2003, 8).

Even before Spain became part of the empire with Charles V, Ferdinand and Isabella, through the expulsion of the Jews and non-tolerance for the Muslims, demonstrated 'a non-reliance on that colourful traffic in goods and commodities which we have seen animating the cultural life of Europe in the second half of the fifteenth century ... In spite of the fact that the growing property of Spain, as of the other European nations, depended on vigorous and heterogeneous trade throughout the known world, and in spite of the fact that the artisanal skills which supported lucrative industries ... were tightly associated with specific ethnic and religious groupings, the victorious Spanish regime declared ethnic and doctrinal purity as the foundations of the stability of the new state' (Jardine 1996, 86–7). This view of Spanish early modern history, which shows how it is opposed to the more prevalent mercantile movement, helps to contextualize a hidden struggle within Cervantes' novel. The very first line of *Don Quixote* both hides and reveals this struggle between the 'amoral' merchant and the ideal imperial knight. The first words of the text, 'En un lugar de la Mancha ...' (In a village in La Mancha ...) (1978, 1.1.69; 25), as Luis Murillo notes in his edition, echo the fifth line of a burlesque ballad found in the 1596 *Flores del Parnaso: Octava Parte*, collected by Luis de Medina, and also in the *Romancero general* of 1600. In this ballad, a Portuguese *lencero* or merchant of linen falls in love with a married woman, but it all ends badly as he is beaten. On the one hand, the line is a kledonomantic statement, auguring the defeat of Don Quixote. Like the merchant, he will be repeatedly beaten. But the very fact that Don Quixote's fate is linked to that of a merchant establishes one of the key dichotomies in the novel. The knight would never succumb to mercantile ideology. There is yet a third important link between the ballad and the novel. The merchant deals in linen or *lienços*. Sebastián Covarrubias explains that *lienço* means not only 'tela hecha y texida de lino' (fabric made and woven from flax) but also 'Lienços sinifican muchas veces los quadros pintados en lienço' (*lienços* mean many times pictures painted on canvas) (1987, 766). Thus, the ballad's insertion in the novel announces not only the opposition between the early modern mercantile ethos and the old imperial ideals, but also the painterly texture of Cervantine textuality/textile.

In chapter 4, the knight clearly demonstrates how his own conception of empire is inimical to the multicultural vision and what Lisa Jardine has called 'global mercantilism.'[12] Don Quixote's rage is directed against merchants from Toledo who were on their way to buy silk in Murcia. The journey to Toledo may in itself be significant. As Giancarlo Maiorino has shown, the first Spanish picaresque novel, *Lazarillo de Tormes,* also traces a journey to Toledo 'the city of business' (2003, 6). Cervantes reverses the journey since his merchants have already acquired the riches wanted by Lazarillo. They go from the city of business to a place where they can acquire goods for sale. The production of silk was one of the 'crafts and skills of the Islamic nations' (Jardine 1996, 83). More to the point, Carroll Johnson explains that although Granada was once the primary source for silk, 'following an epidemic that decimated the mulberry and the expatriation of most of the morisco labor force to Castile following the unsuccessful revolt in the Alpujarra in 1568, Grenadine production suffered an abrupt decline and the Toledo merchants had to find another source. Special permission was given for the establishment of a silk industry in the hands of moriscos in Murcia' (2000, 7). Not only were moriscos engaged in the production of silk in this city, but Murcia was often associated during Cervantes' time with 'judaising *conversos*' (Kamen 1997, 84; see also 73 and 235).

Indeed, the very fact that the troop is made up of merchants creates, in a society intent on purity of blood, a suspicion of Jewishness. Don Quixote as an Old Christian *hidalgo* must oppose the mercantile. An anecdote by Benito Remigio Noydens that shows the opposition between the Christian gentleman and the merchant very much mirrors the situation in Cervantes' novel: 'Un hidalgo fue a visitar a un amigo suyo, gran letrado; y hallándose ocupado en una junta de muchos negociantes ... le saludó risueña y amigablemente dicendo "Ave Rabbi" (An hidalgo went to visit a friend of his, a great man of letters and finding himself occupied with a council of many merchants ... he greeted him smiling and saying a friendly 'Hail Rabbi') (cited in Castro 1961, 174). The very notion of mercantilism suggests to Noydens the Jewishness of his friend. The tripling of otherness (Islamic silks, Murcian Jewishness, and Toledan picaresque materialism) and the 'noxiuous' presence of the mercantile craft trigger in Don Quixote a 'Catholic' reaction. He orders the merchants to 'confess' that Dulcinea is the most beautiful woman in the world.[13] When the merchants state that they need to see at least a portrait of the lady, Don Quixote claims: 'La importancia está en que sin verla lo habéis de creer' (The whole point is that, without seeing her, you must believe) (1978, 1.4.100; 46). This totalizing faith is what the knight requires of the multicultural and tolerant mercantile profession. They must confess their 'Christian' belief or be destroyed.[14] Of course, the irony of the situation is that in establishing Dulcinea as the goddess, Don Quixote becomes the proponent of a kind of paganism opposed to the Christianity he ostensibly supports. The clash between Don Quixote and the merchants is then the opposition between mercantile empires, such as the Genoese, and empires based on totalizing faith and purity of blood, such as the Spanish.[15] In Cambiaso's fresco, Genoese mercantilism triumphs over a traditional empire. The same occurs in the Cervantine episode, in which Don Quixote is defeated by the merchants. Indeed, this is what seems to be happening in Cervantes' Spain where the Genoese merchants and bankers seem to run the economy.[16]

The fresco's vision of economic power and conquest stands in contradistinction to Genoa's political influence at the time of Cervantes' visit. By then, this Italian city had lost its independence and its many Mediterranean possessions (except for Corsica), becoming a de facto possession of Spain. As for Trebizond, it had disappeared as an independent region to become part of the Ottoman Empire. Historical circumstances thus impart Cambiaso's fresco with a contrastive perspective of past imperial glory versus a declining power (Genoa) and a forgotten empire (Trebizond). This contrast helped Cervantes to fashion a double vision in his own novel – one of past Spanish power and glory and a present that may be pointing to imperial decline. The inscription of Cambiaso's fresco within Cervantes' text can serve as a mnemonic image of empire building and a nostalgic reminder of an imperial past where such structures of power could be swiftly constructed.

As if to emphasize the dependency of Genoa on Spain, the crowning moments of Cambiaso's career occur when he is summoned to Spain by Philip II in 1583 to help with the decoration of the Escorial. But, in many ways, this is an ironic hierarchy and dependency. While Spain fought for its place as an 'imperial' land that had territories in several continents, Genoa continued to rule behind the scenes as a needed site of merchants and bankers. Indeed, Mateo Alemán, the author of the picaresque *Guzmán de Alfarache,* explains that his rogue character, Guzmán de Alfarache, had a father who was a usurer in Genoa. Anne J.

Cruz asserts: 'As a Genoese he is a reminder of the hated foreign bankers enriching themselves from Spanish spoils' (1999, 100). Thus the dependency of Genoa on Spain could be reversed. And many Spaniards viewed the Genoese with suspicion. Of course, to have a Genoese/ Italian artist to decorate the Escorial was quite a different matter. Here, it is Italy's cultural capital that is being called upon and paid for, rather than its needed but more problematic economic force.

Thus, Cambiaso was at first most welcome by Philip at the Escorial. He placed at the monastery a series of seven canvases dealing with the battle of Lepanto, something that would be of great interest to Cervantes as a participant in the battle. If Cervantes saw these art works or heard accounts of them, he would have been able to reenact in his mind the whole expedition, since it starts with a painting of *The Departure of the Armada from the Port of Messina*, culminates with *The Withdrawal of the Turks* together with an allegory of Victory, and ends with *The Return of the Armada*, with the figure of Fame (Checa Cremades 2002, 103–5).

Cambiaso's best-known commission for the Escorial was a fresco, *La Gloria* (1584–5), for the vault of the choir in the basilica (fig. 6.2). He also composed a number of other paintings to be placed both in the basilica and in the monastery.[17] Thus, Cambiaso arrives in Spain three years after Cervantes' return from captivity in Algiers. It could be that the Genoese artist's work at the Escorial triggered Cervantes' remembrance of his earlier *Emperor of Trebizond*. But the fresco at the Escorial was vastly different in ideology. No longer is Cambiaso praising the multicultural mercantile empire. Instead, his fresco is one of religious hierarchy and orthodoxy, one that authorizes the power of Philip II as a Catholic king.[18] Jonathan Brown explains: 'The painting represents a heavenly glory with row after row of saints and angels adoring the Holy Trinity, while along the sidelines are figures in contemporary costume aspiring to join the ranks of the blessed' (1991, 62). Traditional courtly hierarchy is applied to the heavenly abode. The very images of God the Father and the Son (Jesus) seated on thrones and brandishing their symbols of power at the centre of the fresco may recall that the Spanish empire rose to preeminence with Charles V (God the Father) and continued to flourish with Philip II, his son.

But for this fresco to come about, Luca Cambiaso had to make some changes. According to Soprani, who wrote an early biography of Cambiaso in 1674,[19] the painter's design exhibited features that were not attuned to the palace as symbol of hierarchy and 'superiority of the Spanish prince' (von Braghahn 1985, 1.157). He had included extravagant poses typical of Michelangelo as well as airy figures that did not correspond to the majesty required of the work. Philip II rejected this program, objecting to the 'placement' of the saints (Bernini 1985, 49). Philip's 'authority' at the Escorial may have served to counterbalance Genoese financial power and Cambiaso could be seen as both a trophy and a scapegoat for a mercantile culture. The disorder of a mercantile power had to be ordered by a Catholic empire. Fray Antonio de Villacastín helped to revise Cambiaso's program, placing 'order' in his celestial world. This censorship of Cambiaso can well recall the way Michelangelo's *Last Judgment* was changed by Counter-Reformational decrees. The free-spirited Luca Cambiaso, whom Cervantes had encountered through paintings like *The Last Judgment*, *The Martyrdom of St Bartholomew*, and perhaps even *The Damned*, is now subjected to princely desires of praise and hierarchy. Cambiaso may have wanted to paint a *Gloria* reminiscent of Titian's canvas, which was finished in 1554 and taken to Yuste, the monastery to which Charles V retreated after abdicating his earthly possessions. This painting shows Charles V near the Trinity and the Virgin, kneeling in front of some of his relatives, including his son, Philip II. Already in 1574 it had been transferred to the Escorial (Pedrocco 2000, 231), and Cambiaso must have sought to compete with it. But the airy figures and exotic images and poses were denied to him. We do preserve them in a sketch book discovered by Dante Bernini in Palermo. Philip insisted on a most hierarchical composition, where rows and rows of figures sit with great dignity under the Trinity. Gone are the naked people of both Michelangelo's and Cambiaso's *Last Judgment*. The heavenly beings here are heavily cloaked in the robes of their status. Perhaps the only heterodox element in the painting is the strange cube upon which God the Father and Jesus place their feet. And yet, even this may conform to a more esoteric notion of order based on the theories of Lull where it represents both the earth and the 'Supremum Numen' (Checa Cremades 2002, 99–103; Taylor 1976, 5–7). If Cervantes somehow heard of this censorship applied to Cambiaso, he would have once again linked Luchetto to Michelangelo. In an ordered and hierarchical world, the artist, with his uncomfortable imaginings, was at risk. Thus, Cervantes 'painted' Don Quixote and his world as an ostensibly funny book filled with the wild imaginings of a madman. Laughter and madness can hide elements of criticism and *terribilitá*. Beneath this antihierarchical cloak, he could conceal his desire for the Renaissance, a desire that draws artistic freedom and subversive poses.

While the new work by Cambiaso may have triggered Cervantes' recollection of his Genoese fresco, it was not to be exhibited in the Cervantine museum. Its absence points to Philip II's censorship and once again leads to a kind of self-censorship in the Quixotic worlds, where madness and laughter hide other concerns. On the other hand, the two references to the emperor of Trebizond at the beginning of the novel may serve not only to point to some of Don Quixote's favourite chivalric authors, but also to recall the magnificence of Cambiaso's fresco with both its nostalgic view of an imperial past and an ironic perspective on a present of political decline and economic power. Genoa was not only the first Italian city visited by Cervantes; it was also one of the first to provide pictorial models for his *Don Quixote*. Whether borrowing from Giulio Romano a rustic architecture that contrasts with majestic palaces, a clash of pagan and Christian values, and a chiaroscuro in which the darkness of violence gives way to the light of vision; or whether borrowing from the ironic vision of Cambiaso's fresco, Cervantes' text often returns to the mercantilism of Genoa in a modern manner that is in opposition to the knights of old.

7 Drawing Decorum: Titian

The Emperor appears precisely as he did when riding into combat on that fateful April day in 1547, spear in hand, his face deadly pale with illness yet unperturbed and imperturbable, his ungainly mouth set forth in an unshakable resolve ...

Erwin Panofsky, *Problems in Titian: Mostly Iconographic*

From the very start of the novel, Don Quixote dreams of kingship and even of empire. In chapter 1, he sees himself crowned as emperor of Trebizond; much later, he is asked to kill the giant Pandafilando so that he can marry Princess Micomicona and become ruler of her lands. The comic manner in which he 'defeats' the giant and reluctantly turns down Micomicona's hand in favour of Dulcinea does not attenuate his desire for kingship or empire.[1] His wish to revive the ancient chivalric past, the world of Amadís, of King Arthur and his knights, is absolute, as is his desire for empire. Don Quixote's fight to recapture the imperial past, to renew the glories of Trebizond, might be mitigated by an image of the fall of empires. But the would-be knight in the novel pays little heed to such warnings and seems to have little historical consciousness. He lives for his imperial and knightly myths. If he were to emulate an emperor outside of his chivalric fictions, it would certainly be Charles V, who wanted to revive the glories of chivalry and was viewed by many as the universal emperor, the one who would bring back the mythical Golden Age. He is thus represented in one of the more cited books in *Don Quixote* – Ariosto's *Orlando furioso*.

Taking into account the myths surrounding Charles V, and given the setting of Cervantes' novel, it would seem plausible that the empire that Don Quixote wants to revive is the Spanish empire, a land divided after Charles V renounced the throne and gave parts of Italy, Spain, America, and the Low Lands to his son Philip II, while the German lands and the crown of the Holy Roman Empire were deeded to Charles's brother, Ferdinand. Actually, this loss of empire was not totally voluntary on the part of Charles V. While after the triumph at Mühlberg it seemed that Germany would remain his and could be deeded to his son Philip, the battle actually backfired as many German rulers feared his power. In 1552 his fate was sealed when Charles had to flee Innsbruck where he was holding talks with Ferdinand. From that moment on, the only 'true' empire was fated to leave Spanish hands. Even if some were to later think of Philip II as Emperor of the Indies, this was not recognized as a true empire, since it was distinct from the one empire that descended from the ancient Romans. Don Quixote's desire to be a new Charles V is thus as anachronistic as his emulation of the chivalric code or his vision of Trebizond.

Over the centuries, a number of critics have debated whether the *Quixote* is to be viewed as an embodiment of the deeds and imperial conceptions of Charles V or as a satire on this emperor's ideals. Already in 1878 Díaz de Benjumea referred to critics of the previous century who claimed that Don Quixote 'era el retrato del alma española, la pintura de Carlos V' (was the portrait of the Spanish soul, the painting of Charles V) (1878, 124). In 1973 Richard L. Predmore called Charles V's challenge of Francis I to single combat a 'challenge worthy of Don Quixote himself' (1973, 15). Indeed, he added that Charles's ideal to restore Christian unity failed very much like Don Quixote's own ideals were doomed to failure (19). Perhaps the most complete and engaging comparison of Charles and Quixote was elaborated by José Antonio Maravall. In his 1948 version of utopianism in *Don Quixote,* Maravall argued that Cervantes, as well as the protagonist of his novel, partook of the utopian vision prevalent during the times of Charles V: 'Así Cervantes es utopista al par del caballero andante de la Mancha; es un inadaptado como Don Quixote; vive dentro de las ideas que tuvieron curso medio siglo antes, en la época de Carlos V' (Thus Cervantes is an utopian just as the knight-errant of La Mancha; he cannot adapt like Don Quixote; he lives within the ideas that took shape a half century before, in the epoch of Charles V) (1948, ix). In the preface to the first edition of Maravall's book, Menéndez Pidal agrees and promotes this utopian interpretation (1948, x). But years later, Maravall changed his view, demonstrating instead in 1991 how Cervantes' text is actually a critique of Don Quixote's utopianism. With the division of the empire after Charles V, Spain lost its place in the imperial scheme. Charles thus came to represent the last Spanish emperor tied to an ancient ideal: 'The traditional institution of Empire, which had a religious and moral mission dating from its distant Carolingian past, wished to be used by the Spanish people, along with the Church, under the government of the titular head of the Holy Empire in the work of perfection and purification of Christian life' (1991, 25). According to Maravall's revised theory, the novel present us 'with the defeat of that ideal along with the defeat of its protagonist' (25). Maravall contrasts Antonio de Guevara's work as a 'utopian vision of the Empire' with *Don Quixote* which, as a 'genuine anti-Guevara treatise ... is in fact a powerful antidote to the extensive and intellect-stifling utopianism in sixteenth century Spain' (17–18).

It would be impossible, in one chapter, to deal exhaustively with the whole question of Charles V, utopianism, imperialism, and their link to *Don Quixote*. The purpose of this chapter is much more modest. By reviewing the link between Charles V and *Don Quixote* from an ekphrastic perspective, it seeks to show that the text's political contexts can be viewed through one of the key paintings of the Renaissance. This painting as well as the novel's vision of Charles V must be glimpsed from a confusing allusion located at the beginning of chapter 7 in the novel. Let us begin with the allusion and then turn to the central argument that Titian's polychromic art can serve as a future point of departure for studies of the polyvalence of the quixotic narrative. As the priest and barber are performing their 'inquisition' of Don Quixote's library, intending to burn numerous chivalric novels, pastoral romances, and epic poems, they hear Don Quixote, who has just awakened and is crying out as he lashes out against his invisible enemies. Thus, the inquisitors must abandon their job. A number of books are not scrutinized for error and thus 'fueron al fuego sin ser vistos ni oídos' (went to the flames without being seen nor heard) (1978, 1.7.122).[2] Three works are mentioned: '*La Carolea* y *León de España*, con *Los hechos del Emperador* compuestos por Don Luis de Ávila' (*Carolea* and *The Lion of Spain*, together with *The Exploits of the Emperor* by Luis de Ávila) (1978, 1.7.122; 59). Although all three books deal with the feats of Emperor Charles V, the last one by Luis de Ávila does not really belong in this grouping since, as Luis Andrés Murillo notes, 'es obra seria de historia, en prosa, y digna de elogio, y parece estar fuera de lugar citarla en una plática sobre libros de entretenimiento, entre un grupo de obras en verso' (it is a serious work of history, in prose, and worthy of praise, and seems to be out of place to cite it in a discussion about books of entertainment, among a group of works in verse) (1978, 1.7.122, note 1). This curious misplacement of Ávila y Zúñiga's book may well serve as a signal to its importance in the text. As will be shown below, this book was used by Titian to compose his famous painting, *Charles V at Mühlberg*. Both the painting and the book will be important in the portrayal of the knight of La Mancha. In addition, Murillo suggests that Cervantes may have confused Ávila's work with a poem on Charles V by Luis Zapata entitled *Carlo famoso*. The poem does laud 'los hechos, las empresas, las hazañas del Emperador' (the deeds, the enterprises, the feats of the Emperor) (1978, 1.7.122 note 1). I will argue that there is no confusion, but fusion of these two works. While Ávila y Zúñiga praises the emperor, Zapata includes numerous criticisms of Charles V in his laudatory heroic poem.[3] Thus, Cervantes' *Don Quixote* can be viewed as both celebration and criticism of the emperor, his vision, and his followers' vision (or lack of it) through the image of the crazed but determined and valiant knight.

Over Luca Cambiaso's fresco of Trebizond, a new painting could be superimposed (or viceversa – this is a fluid relationship in Cervantes). And indeed, Renaissance artists often painted over works of predecessors to implement the program of their new patron. In many cases, remnants of the old program remained. There are several clues in chapter 1 of Cervantes' novel that allow the reader to visualize this second program, this second imperial image. Perhaps the most important has to do with the uncertainty as to the *hidalgo*'s name. As has been noted previously, three names are given as possibilities (Quijada, Quesada, Quejana [1978, 1.1.71]), only to establish a quaternity with the new name taken by the gentleman when he 'becomes' a knight, Don Quixote de la Mancha.[4] Although most critical interest in naming has been focused on the latter,[5] a number of critics have been concerned with the different onomastic possibilities offered by the three names. Augustin Redondo, for example, relates Quijada to the carnivalesque figure of the Ganassa, arguing that it represents Lent (Don Quixote), who in these festivals battles the opposite figure, Bottarga (Sancho Panza), the revelry and satiety of Carnival (1998, 209–14).[6] Quesada has been related to *queso* (cheese), a product that La Mancha was famous for – and Redondo links cheese to madness (1998, 215–16). Josep M. Sola-Solé foregrounds the third name mentioned, Quejana, and notes its kinship to the verb 'queja' (lament) in order to ponder on 'la posible relación existente entre *marrano* y la idea básica de 'lamentarse gritando''' (the possible existing relationship between *marrano* [Jewish] and the basic idea of 'to lament shouting') (1981, 720). He buttresses his argument of the Jewish origin of the knight's name by then turning to the first name mentioned. Sola-Solé takes as a point of departure a comment by Rodríguez Marín that a possible model for Don Quixote was a certain Alonso Quijada (Rodríguez Marín 1947, 561ff). Since the Quijada family from the town of Esquivias was said to be of Jewish descent, Sola-Solé concludes that the different names given to Don Quixote at the beginning of the novel serve to point to his 'new Christian' ascendancy (1981, 721–2).

This may be the case. If so, what I am about to propose assumes an even greater irony. Quijada, the first name given to Don Quixote, is also the name of one of the knight's ancestors. Towards the end of the 1605 novel, Don Quixote brags that he descends from 'los valientes españoles Pedro Barba y Gutierre Quijada' (those courageous Spaniards Pedro Barba and Gutierre Quixada) (1978, 1.49.581; 454). Although, as James Parr states, Don Quixote 'subsequently reveals his niece's name to be Antonia Quijana and finally settles on Alonso Quijano for himself' (1988, 93), this does not take place until the end of the 1615 novel. But, even Avellaneda's 1614 'false' *Quixote* accepts Quijada as Quixote's true name.[7] It is clear that Quijada has preeminence in Part 1 – it is the first name given to him and it is the name of his ancestors – and it is accepted by Avellaneda. Through this name, as MacCurdy and Rodríguez argue, the knight is showing his 'orgullo genealógico' (genealogical pride) (1978, 453). Indeed, Charles V was particularly fond of a soldier named Don Luis Quijada, who was famous for his valour and heroic deeds.[8] Quijada is thus a name that looks to the past and is appropriately given to this country gentleman who nostalgically recalls the glories of past empires – be they the ancient Trebizond or Spain as part of the Holy Roman Empire. And Quijada is nothing else but the central clue for his association with the greatest of all Spanish emperors, Charles V. It also leads us to one of the most famous portraits of this ruler. In 1530 Titian was commissioned to paint a portrait of Charles V. Giorgio Vasari claims that Titian was summoned to Bologna, where the emperor was at the time. There, 'he painted a truly beautiful portrait of His Majesty in full armour that delighted the emperor so greatly that he made Titian a gift of one thousand *scudi*' (1991, 497). Unfortunately, this portrait has been lost (Panofsky 1969, 7). When Charles returned to Bologna in 1532–3, 'he once again desired to have his portrait done by Titian' (Vasari 1991, 498). For Erwin Panofsky these meetings constituted the beginning of a relationship between artist and patron 'which is almost unique in the annals of art' (1969, 7). The Venetian painter was to become the 'official' portrait artist of the emperor, thus imitating the ancient relationship between Alexander the Great and Apelles.[9]

Titian met the challenge of portraiture in a manner later praised by Carducci and subsequently by Lope de Vega,[10] that is, by his stress on *decorum* as opposed to *imitatio*.[11] The difficulties were clear from the start since 'we know that the ruler's extremely deformed jaw did not permit the upper and lower teeth to meet or the mouth to close' (Wethey 1971, 19). We can see the challenge of the jaw in a number of works by Lucas Cranach, painter and childhood friend of the future emperor (García Simón 103). Titian solved this and other problems to the emperor's satisfaction. Among the portraits perhaps the most famous is the 1548 *Charles V at Mühlberg* (fig. 7.1). Panofsky has called it 'the first self-sufficient, unallegorical and unceremonial equestrian portrait in the history of painting' (1969, 84). Harold Wethey comments on its impact: 'Rubens, Van Dyck and many other painters followed the example of *Charles V at Mühlberg*, a work which can justifiably be called the climactic monument in state portraiture of both the Renaissance and Baroque periods' (1971, 36). It is this portrait, I will argue, that serves as mirror to Don Quixote. As opposed to most of the other paintings and frescoes discussed in this book, Cervantes would have seen Charles's portrait in Spain and not in Italy. The painting was shipped to the Iberian peninsula in 1556 and inherited by Philip II in 1558 (Wethey 1971, 89). It was exhibited by the Habsburg monarchs in the most accessible and conspicuous rooms at both the country house at El Pardo just north of the capital and at the Alcázar in Madrid.[12] Indeed, in 1604, the year before the publication of *Don Quixote*, the portrait had to be moved out of the antechamber of the king's audience room of the Pardo when this country palace 'was damaged by fire' (Brown and Elliott 1980, 151, 272 note 25).[13] It remained at the Pardo until it was transferred to the New Room or Hall of Mirrors at the Alcázar in Madrid around September of 1624.[14]

As noted above, the first clue as to the relationship of Don Quixote and Charles is the first name given to the *hidalgo* in the text, 'Quijada.' *Quijada* or 'jaw' is precisely the anatomical feature that made it particularly difficult to portray Charles V and subsequent Habsburg monarchs.[15] It is also the name of one of Charles V's favourite soldiers (Luis Quijada), thus pointing to the emperor once again. Titian's satisfactory portrayals of the ruler, including his *Charles V at Mühlberg* transforms the misshapen jaw into a sign of determination, 'his ungainly mouth set in an expression of unshakable resolve' (Panofsky 1969, 85). It is this will to move forward and to conquer that shapes this nonallegorical painting. Cervantes' novel also eschews the allegorical to present in familiar terms a knight whose wilfulness and determination are unmitigated by his many failures. As Luis Pérez Botero status: 'Don Quixote lleva a cabo una transformación real del mundo ... por el sólo efecto de su voluntad de que las cosas sean como él quiere que sean' (Don Quixote accomplishes a real transformation of the world ... by the only effect of his will that things should be as he wants them to be) (1981, 517). This notion of wilfulness and determination as key to Don Quixote's heroism is, of course, nothing new. The 'romantic' interpretation of the novel revelled in such statements. Ortega y Gasset, for example, perceived that 'Don Quixote embodies the will to accomplish ideals.' This, he thought, was the basis for heroism (Close 1978, 183). Américo Castro's late existentialist view of the novel also stresses this will or volition, which is central to the heroic transformation of Don Quixote.[16] From each of his defeats, the knight emerges a greater and more 'tragic' hero since he has chosen his own path in life and is determined to see it to the end. Thus, Titian's painting serves as an extended ekphrasis that underscores the links and differences between emperor and knight throughout the novel. The painting is also utilized in terms of fragmented and transformative ekphrasis. Different segments keep being exhibited, such as the lance, the horse, the chivalric pose, the solar qualities of the emperor/knight, his melancholy, etc. But all these elements are repeatedly transformed into something less majestic and ideal. While Charles V, in Titian's painting, is a figure of decorum, heroism, will, and empire, the would-be Charles in Cervantes' novel is 'painted' by the Moorish narrator as impotent against his foes. In spite of his determination, he can be viewed either as an undeterred idealist or as a comic and pathetic fool. Indeed, the jaw of determination that links him to the greatest of Spanish emperors, also relates him, as noted above, to the Ganassa character at carnival. Ganassa, a lean figure with a large jaw, stands for Lent and battles Bottarga or the spirit of Carnival itself. The latter is prone to eating and resting and is thus fat and easily defeated. It is this carnivalesque contest that serves as genesis for Don Quixote and Sancho according to Augustin Redondo (1998, 210–14). While Titian's painting stresses decorum in depicting character, Cervantes' novel will point to Titian in order to both draw idealized majesty and determination, and to break with decorum through laughter the representation of 'unworthy' and carnivalesque situations and actions. Indeed, the text will often foreground the incorporation of certain unseemly descriptions by the knight's biographer and 'enemy,' Cide Hamete Benengeli – referred to as a moor, a group typified for its lies.[17]

Discussing the two main critical perceptions of the character of Don Quixote, the protagonist as hero and as fool, John J. Allen shows that the critics who uphold the former view are convinced of the 'persistent and invincible sublimity of Don Quixote's motivation' (1969, 3). We need only glance at Titian's *Charles V at Mühlberg* to perceive such persistence and such motivation. The painting mirrors the emperor's own convictions. Charles followed Gattinara and Guiccardini in the belief that 'war was an essential instrument for the enlargement of his power' (Kleinschmidt 2004, 93). A key to Don Quixote's never-ending struggles may also be based on this principle. Although he is constantly defeated, his determination leads him from one battle to the next.

In addition to foregrounding the jaw of determination, there are a number of other parallels between the canvas and the novel. One of Titian's innovations in his equestrian painting is to have the commanding general, Charles V, carry neither sword nor baton. Instead, the emperor is seen with a spear, an image that reflects the historical circumstances, since he led the battle with this curious weapon. From the start of Cervantes' novel, it is clear that Don Quixote's lance is his most important weapon.[18] In his first combat, when he battles the muleteers who disturb his vigil before he is knighted by the innkeeper, he fights with this weapon: 'alzó la lanza a dos manos y dio con ella tan gran golpe al arriero en la cabeza, que le derribó en el suelo tan maltrecho ...' (raised his lance with both hands, and dealt the muleteer so powerful a blow to the head that he fell on the ground in such a sorry state) (1978, 1.3.91; 39). Whether attacking the merchants from Toledo or jousting with windmills, the knight, with few exceptions, brandishes his lance or spear. However, the idealized mirror of Don Quixote as Charles V consistently shatters since many times this lance bends or breaks, becoming, in John Cull's view, a symbol of the knight's impotence (1990).

Studying Titian's *Charles V at Mühlberg*, Panofsky explains that the lance or spear carried by the emperor had a double symbolic value. First of all 'the spear was the weapon of such valiant killers of dragons (that is to say, heresies) as St. George, and very often, St. Michael' (1969, 86). On this subject we need only recall two paintings by Raphael, one of St George slaying the dragon and the other of St Michael having squashed a demon (fig. 7.2). In both we can see the spear or lance as the weapon of choice for killing the enemies of Christianity, be they dragon or demon. Don Quixote seems to prefer to do battle with yet another enemy of Christianity, the giant. For example, in jousting with the windmills the knight thinks he is battling against 'desaforados gigantes' (monstrous giants) (1978, 1.8.129; 63). As Eduardo Urbina has noted, Don Quixote, throughout Part 1, keeps encountering imaginary giants.[19] As embodiments of pride, these creatures were linked analogically with the devil and thus often symbolized evil forces that stood against Christianity. Once again, a fragmented ekphrasis has become a transformative one, diminishing the powers of Don Quixote, the man who would be emperor.

Panofsky adds of the spear or lance that 'in a wider application it is the weapon of the "Christian Knight" described by Erasmus of Rotterdam and glorified in Dürer's famous engraving of 1513' (1969, 86). Here, Panofsky is referring to Dürer's *The Knight, Death, and the Devil* (fig. 7.3). In this allegory of Christian salvation, the knight in armour and on horseback 'advances, contemptuous of the lurking threats – a symbol of courage' (Bailey 1995, 15). Don Quixote strives to mirror such an image. In the 1615 novel the knight confronts the devil riding a cart.[20] He also discovers that death is one of the curious figures riding in the cart: 'La primera figura se le ofreció a los ojos de Don Quixote fue la de la misma muerte, con rostro humano' (The first figure that presented itself to Don Quixote's gaze was Death itself, but with a human face) (1978, 2.11.115; 553). Although here Don Quixote does not have to battle these figures since they turn out to be actors dressed to perform a sacramental play, the knight still wishes to engage them in battle since the devilish actor briefly steals Sancho's ass. But, when confronted by all the players who hold stones ready to hurl at the knight, Don Quixote backs down, accepting Sancho's counsel not to attack them since they are not of sufficient social standing.[21] It seems that the knight has learned his lesson from the many stonings he received in the 1605 text, where his 'martyrdom,' as studied in chapter 6, can be related to St Stephen. The astonishingly unquixotic behaviour in the 1615 novel occurs when faced with the very essence of the Christian's knight's foes: death and the devil. While Don Quixote may want to emulate the perfect knight and attain such renown as to become emperor, his behaviour constantly belies his aspirations.

Of course, this is not the only time that the Cervantine knight confronts the devil. This figure is perceived by the knight at many other points in the novel, as both Michael Hasbrouck (1992, 117–26) and

Hilaire Kallendorf (2003, 172) have pointed out. A goatherd, for example, is suspected by Don Quixote of being a demon in disguise: 'Hermano demonio, que no es posible que dejes de serlo, pues has tenido valor y fuerzas para sujetar las mías' (Brother devil, for that is what you must be, since you have found the resolve and the strength to overpower me) (1978, 1.52.598; 469). A prophesying monkey leads the knight to believe that his owner 'debe de tener hecho algún concierto con el demonio, de que infunda esa habilidad en el mono' (must have come to some agreement with the devil, who provides the ape with this skill) (1978, 2.25.237; 660).[22] Don Quixote, then, is consistently representing himself as the Christian knight, battling giants and devils and exhibiting courage when facing death. Of course, actual events often contradict his self-representation. Discussing the episode of the troupe of actors, Percas de Ponseti concludes that 'Don Quixote's moral error and its consequences seem to be a graphic reversal of Dürer's depiction of the unfaltering knight in his famous engraving *The Knight, Death, and the Devil*' (1988, 22).

Dürer's vision of the knight is very much what Titian sought to portray in his *Charles V at Mühlberg*. Since the battle at Mühlberg was fought against the Protestant League, Charles V is shown as a Christian knight defeating those who are guilty of heresy. Don Quixote is well aware of the role of a Christian warrior, affirming: 'Que ésta es buena guerra, y es gran servicio de Dios quitar tan mala simiente de sobre la faz de la tierra' (For this is a just war, and it is a great service to God to wipe such a wicked breed from the face of the earth) (1978, 1.8.129; 63). Charles V's use of the knightly lance or spear may also recall 'Charlemagne's Holy Lance with the nail from the Cross' (Tanner 1993, 128),[23] and can thus be associated with the many romances of chivalry written on the matter of France. Indeed Charles V was often 'identified with Charlemagne in the chivalric sagas which constituted one of the most important genres of Renaissance literature' (Tanner 1993, 128). It may be that Charlemagne's chivalric deeds led Charles V to become increasingly interested in the romances of chivalry. He so delighted in Jerónimo Fernández's *Belianís de Grecia* that books 3 and 4 were written to further please the emperor: 'Auer agradado tanto a la Magestad de Carlos quinto, Inuictisimo Emperador y señor nro, la primera y segunda parte que gustó de oyrlas diuersas vezes dio causa a quel Auctor que fue el Licenciado Fernandez mi hermano escriuiese tambien tercera y quarta' (The first and second parts pleased so much his Majesty Carlos V, the Invincible Emperor and our lord, for he enjoyed listening to the diverse voices, that he gave reason to that author who was my brother the Bachelor Fernandez to also write the third and fourth') (cited in Thomas 1952, 115).[24] Before becoming a knight, the gentleman from La Mancha even considered writing a conclusion to the *Belianís*.[25] Rather than writing the conclusion to one of Charles V's favourite romances of chivalry, Don Quixote would become a knight in the image of the emperor, so as to revive Spanish imperialism.

According to Panofsky, the portrait of a Christian knight, of a chivalric hero, was but one of two reasons for Titian's choice of the spear in his representation of Charles V. The Romans considered it 'the principal symbol, in fact the very embodiment, of supreme power, and it is therefore the spear – *hasta summa Imperii* – which the Roman Emperors, the legal predecessors of Charles V, carried when making their solemn entry into a city ... and, quite particularly when opening a campaign or setting out for an important battle' (1969, 86). While Charles V exhibits his imperial powers, Don Quixote uses the lance to express his will to become an emperor – or at least a king. This is the knight's supreme personal dream. In what is truly a miniature of a romance of chivalry, Don Quixote elaborates upon his knightly and imperial dream telling Sancho how, after many battles, and after winning the love of a princess, the knight marries her and eventually becomes king (1978, 1.21.261). We have seen how in chapter 1, Don Quixote imagines that he has been crowned emperor of Trebizond (1978, 1.1.75). But the battles that Don Quixote fights to win far-away kingdoms and empires, be they the 'gran reino Micomicón' (great kingdom of Micomicón) (1978, 1.30.373; 272) or the Empire of Trapisonda, are actually fought on Spanish soil. It thus seems likely that the knight is fighting to win back the heritage of imperial Spain with courage and determination. Of course, his enemies are not actual foes but imagined ones. And in general, they have no consequence to the acquisition or preservation of empire, being in the main commoners from the area.

The battle at Mühlberg was in many ways a combat akin to those found in the books of chivalry; although fought on German soil, its purpose was to preserve the religious unity of the empire. It would appear a typical chivalric exaggeration to point out that fifty men were lost while approximately two thousand of the enemy had been eliminated and many of their leaders captured. In chivalric fashion a few 'knights' can easily defeat a large army. After all, the *Quixote* reminds us that Felixmarte de Hircania 'arremetió con un grandísimo y poderosísimo ejército, Donde llevó más de un millón y seiscientos mil soldados, todos armados desde el pie hasta la cabeza, y los desbarató a todos' (charged at an enormous powerful army and defeated more than one million six hundred thousand soldiers all in armour from head to foot, and he routed the lot of them) (1978, 1.32.396; 292). Thus, Don Quixote does not worry that many are against him. He holds firm to the chivalric belief that the knight can defeat a large number of enemies, be they thirty or forty giants/windmills or a whole army of pagans. But Titian's portrait shows nothing of the victory or of the troops. His painting delimits the canvas to show the emperor on horseback. It is his knightly determination that will lead to victory.

The painting's tight focus is also found in the colours utilized. This should come as no surprise: 'Ever since Paolo Pino in his *Dialogo della Pittura* of 1548 had equated the names of Michelangelo and Titian with the categories of "design" and "color," Titian has been considered the colorist *par excellence*' (Panofsky 1969, 13). The use of colours will also characterize Cervantes' portrayal of Don Quixote as a figure akin to Titian's *Charles V at Mühlberg*. Thus, Cervantes not only imitates Titian, the quintessential painter of the 'feminine' city of Venice,[26] but also uses his colourist style which was deemed as feminine and thus inferior to Michelangelo's stress on design. This imitative move may appear to be a surprising one, since Cervantes always represents his novel as masculine. In the prologue, for example, the novel is depicted as dry ('hijo seco' [dry ... child] [1978, 1.50; 11]), a quality that often stands in opposition to feminine humidity. It lacks the 'feminine' adornments of a prologue, of preliminary verses, etc.[27] Don Quixote himself is seen as excessively dry/masculine ('seco de carnes' [dried-up flesh] [1978, 1.1.71; 25]), a quality that leads him to madness: 'se le secó el cerebro' (withered his brain) (1978, 1.1.73; 26–7).

If maleness in style, design, and characterization is central to the novel, why turn to Titian's 'feminine' colours to depict the knight? This move has a double design. First, it is a defence of Titian, showing him to be an artist who balances in his works the masculine and the feminine types of style. Rather than describing one of his mythological paintings in which colour accentuates the beauty of the female nude, Cervantes, at this point in the novel, foregrounds the portrait of an imperial ruler, the epitome of male purposefulness and control. In stressing the transformation of the jaw from a grotesque quality to a sign of control, Cervantes shows that Titian was not just concerned with colour, but also with idea and design. Second, in choosing Titian for this crucial and extensive allusive ekphrasis to Italian art, Cervantes shows how his masculine text can achieve balance by the inclusion of certain feminine traits. Colour, like the adornments proposed by the friend in the prologue, should be used sparingly in Cervantes' gendered theory of art. But it should be included so as to prevent an extreme humoural/elemental imbalance stemming from the excessive dryness of a text and a style. Thus, Cervantes' theories of writing reflect Aristotelian and Pythagorean hierarchical opposition of male/female (Sohm 1995, 767), as well as the notion of a gendered style which became common in art criticism during the Renaissance.

In *Charles V at Mühlberg* Titian does not use the whole range of colours. Rather, he selects a discrete number of pigments to create a 'coloristic pattern' on the canvas.[28] Colour was often linked to space, and Titian 'disliked boxed interiors closed on all sides' (Panofsky 1969, 15) even for his portraits. In the Munich *Portrait of Charles V* (fig. 7.4) for example, the emperor is in a loggia 'where the indoors osmotically interpenetrates with the outdoors' (Panofsky 1969, 15). Titian's preference for open space parallels Cervantes' own utilization of the countryside as the backdrop for most of the knight's adventures in the 1605 *Quixote*. Don Quixote is ever eager to leave his home and we seldom catch a glimpse of him there. When we do, his imagination or his books expand the closed environment. The books share this movement towards the outside, not only by providing the knight with imagined adventures but by literally being moved outside to the yard where most of them are burned by the priest and the barber. Even when at the inns of La Mancha, the knight is often seen outside. He is knighted by the innkeeper in the patio; he is left hanging by Maritornes from a window; and even Sancho finds his own adventures in the open air surrounding the inn, as when he is tossed on a blanket.[29]

Charles V at Mühlberg clearly typifies Titian's preference for open air. It also shows him as a supreme colourist. Panofsky explains that in this portrait 'Titian's palatte is almost entirely limited to shades of white, black and red ... only in the landscape and in the trimmings of the armor do we find some golden yellow, blue and green' (1969, 84). I would argue that the three major colours, together with golden yellow, are of particular significance not only to the portrait but to the reflections of the painting upon the novel. Fernando Checa has shown that the colour of the armour worn by Charles V is consistent with the description found in Luis de Ávila y Zúñiga's *Comentario de la guerra de Alemania hecha por Carlos V ... en el año 1546* (*Commentary of the War of Germany Executed by Charles V ... in the Year 1546*). This chronicler points to 'unas armas blancas y doradas' (some white and golden arms) (Ávila y Zúñiga 1876, 441; Checa 1994, 40). These colours are indeed those found in Titian's painting – and we can also locate them in the portrait of Don Quixote. As the knight sets out from home, he realizes that he 'había de llevar las armas blancas' (he would have been obliged to bear white arms) (1978, 1.2.79; 30). By this he means that he can carry no emblem upon his shield since he had yet to have an adventure. But then, he seems to confuse the lack of emblem with the cleanliness of his armour and weapons: 'Pensaba limpiarlas de manera, en teniendo lugar, que lo fuesen mas que un armiño' (He resolved to give his lance and his armour such a scouring, as soon as the opportunity arose, to make them cleaner and whiter than ermine) (1978, 1.2.79–80; 30). Don Quixote is allowing metaphorical language to replace action. The white ermine becomes an appropriate symbol to carry on the shield. Don Quixote has chosen well, for the ermine, as noted previously, was considered 'a suitable emblem for sovereignty' (Rowland 1973, 75) and curiously, it was one of the royal symbols of Elizabeth I of England (Yates 1975, 114). Thus, Cervantes' knight is already thinking regal thoughts and is appropriating for himself the royal symbol of one of the enemies of Spain – under Elizabeth's reign the Armada had been defeated.[30] But the ermine is itself symbolized by the shining whiteness of Don Quixote's armour and weapons. The emphasis on 'armas blancas' (white arms) could thus be a reflection of the regal shining whiteness of Charles V's arms and armour as depicted both in Zúñiga's account of the battle at Mühlberg and in Titian's painting.

But both Zúñiga and Titian emphasize whiteness together with gold. The somewhat darkened sky in the portrait glows with yellow light, a golden colour reflected in Charles V's armour. This golden hue is also captured by Cervantes' novel since Don Quixote is intent on bringing back through his deeds the lost Golden Age of mythical times (1978, 1.11). In a sense, Don Quixote's imperialist vision of a Golden Age is not different from that which poets and chroniclers forged for Charles V. A statue erected in his honour in 1539 'saluted the emperor as the offspring of the gods and the founder of the Golden Age' (Tanner 1993, 115). And, Ariosto 'hailed the Emperor ... as destined to bring back the rule of Astraea, or justice, and the golden age' (Yates 1975, 23). Charles V is often seen as the 'Last World Emperor,' bringing into the fold all nations and peoples and creating an Augustan peace that would last to the end of time. Indeed, the year 1548, the year of Titian's portrait of the emperor, also saw a prophecy: 'Within the year 1548 the whole world

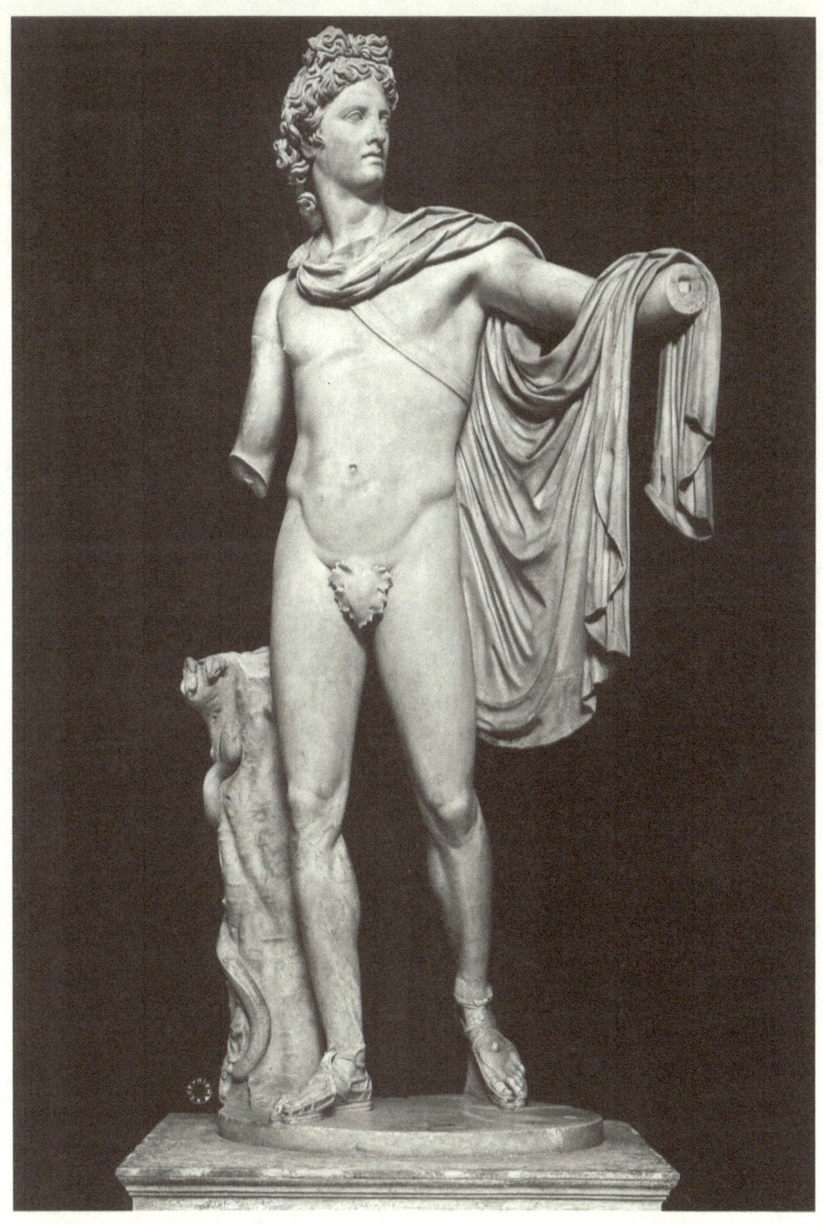

1.1 *Apollo Belvedere*. Roman marble copy of a Greek original, 4th BCE. Palazzo Farnese, Rome, Italy. Alinari / Art Resource, NY.

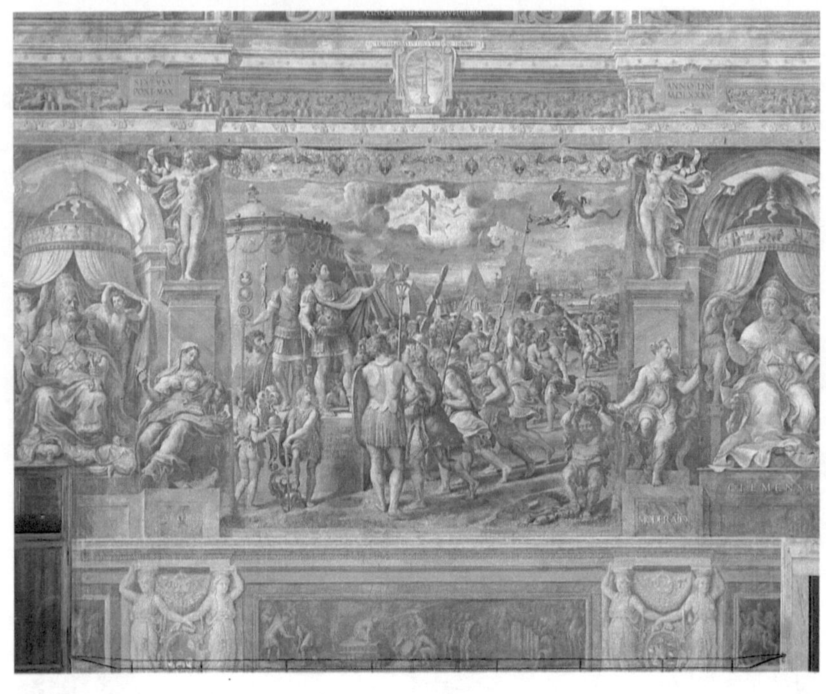

2.1 Raphael / Giulio Romano. *The Cross Appearing to Constantine the Great, flanked by portraits of two popes.* Stanze de Raffaello, Vatican Palace, Vatican State. Scala / Art Resource, NY.

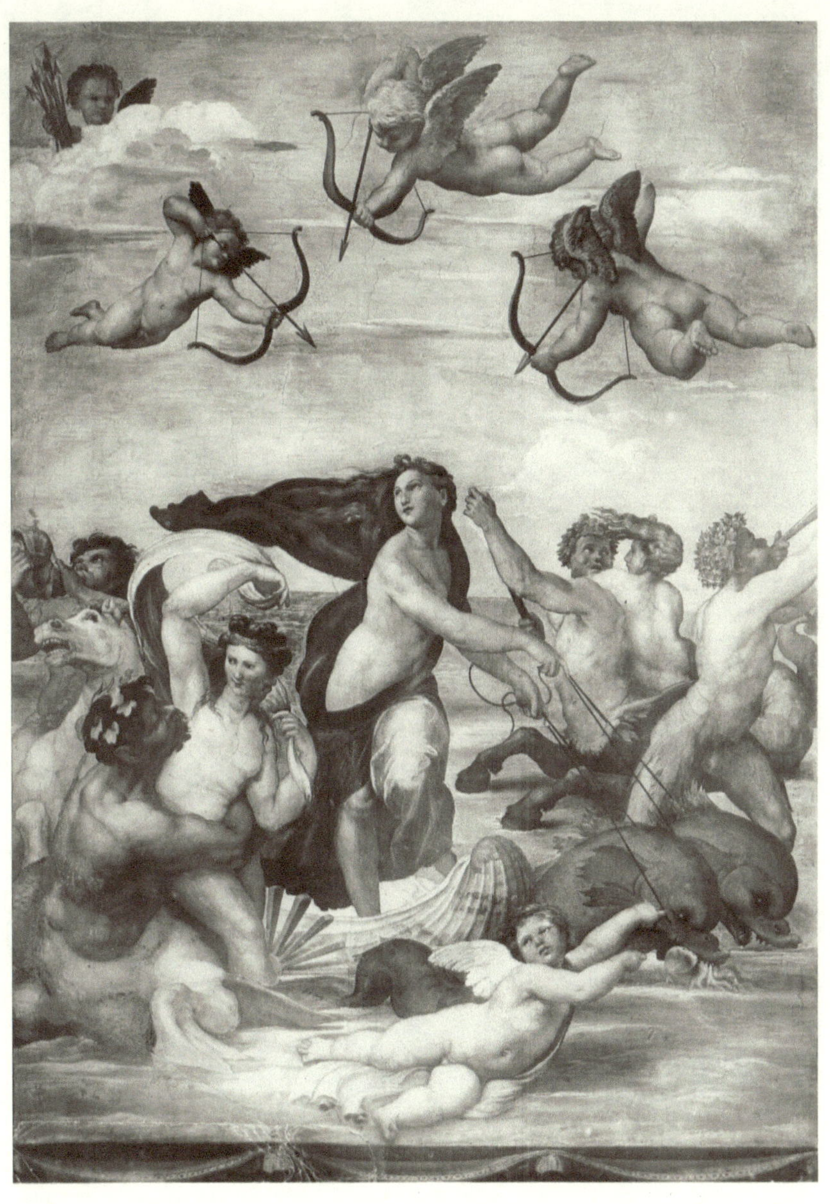

2.2 Raphael. *The Triumph of Galatea*. Palazzo Farnese, Rome, Italy. Alinari / Art Resource, NY.

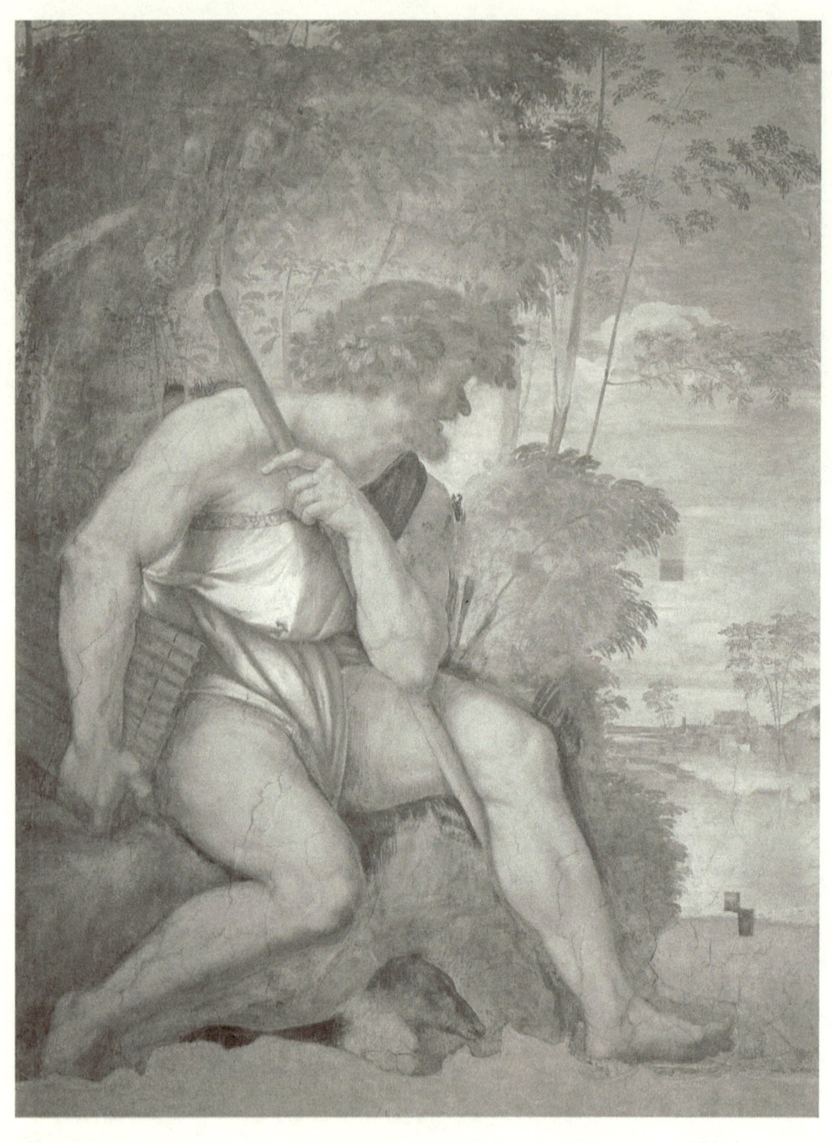

2.3 Sebastiano del Piombo. *Polyphemus*. Palazzo della Farnesina, Rome, Italy. Scala / Art Resource, NY.

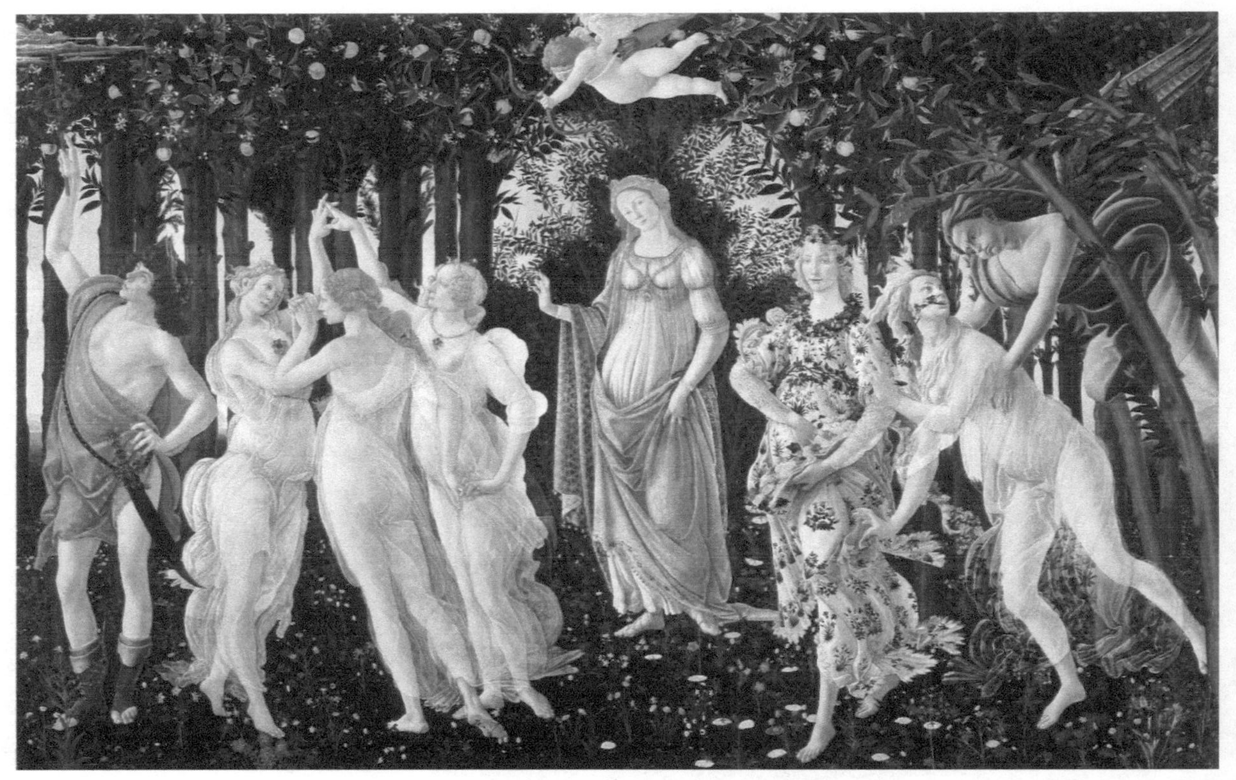

2.4 Botticelli, Sandro. *Primavera*. Uffizi, Florence, Italy. Scala / Art Resource, NY.

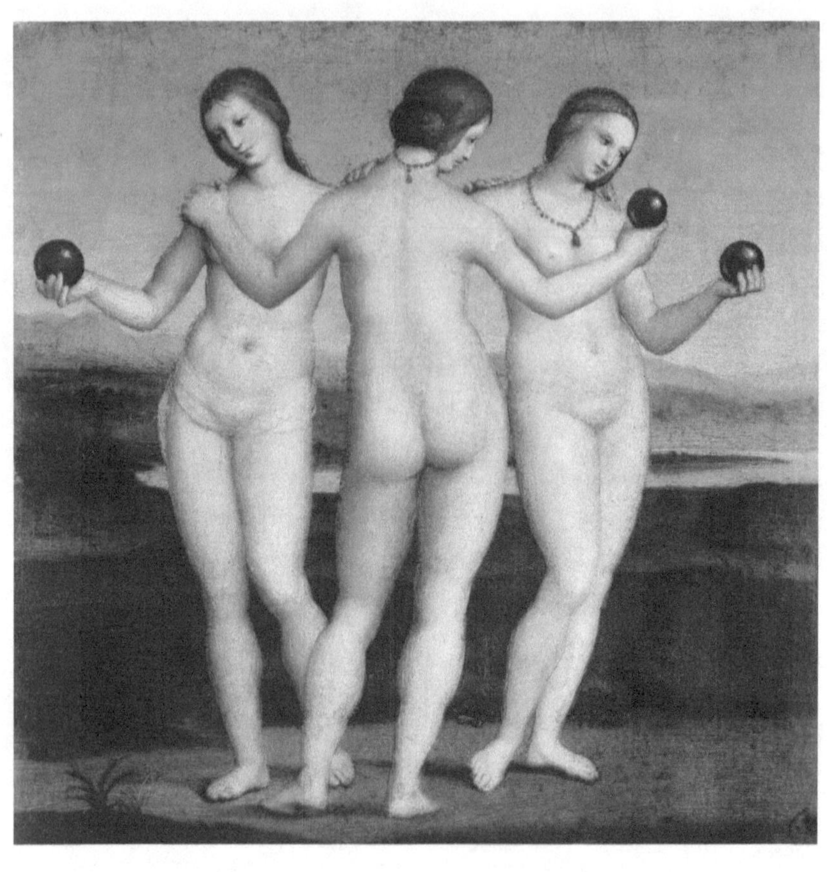

2.5 Raphael. *The Three Graces*. Musée Condé, Chantilly, France. Erich Lessing / Art Resource, NY.

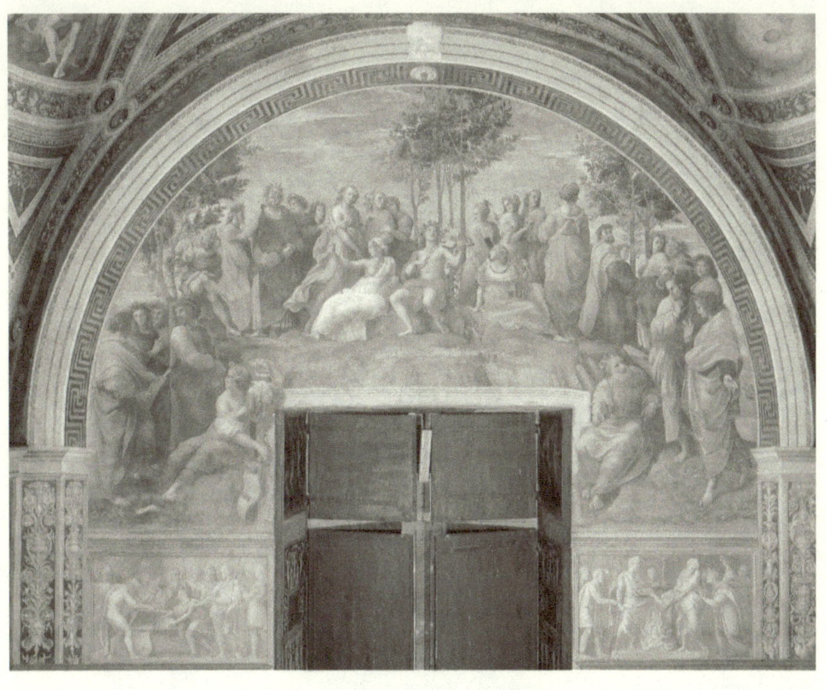

3.1 Raphael. *Parnassus*. Stanza della Segnatura, Vatican Palace, Vatican State. Scala / Art Resource, NY.

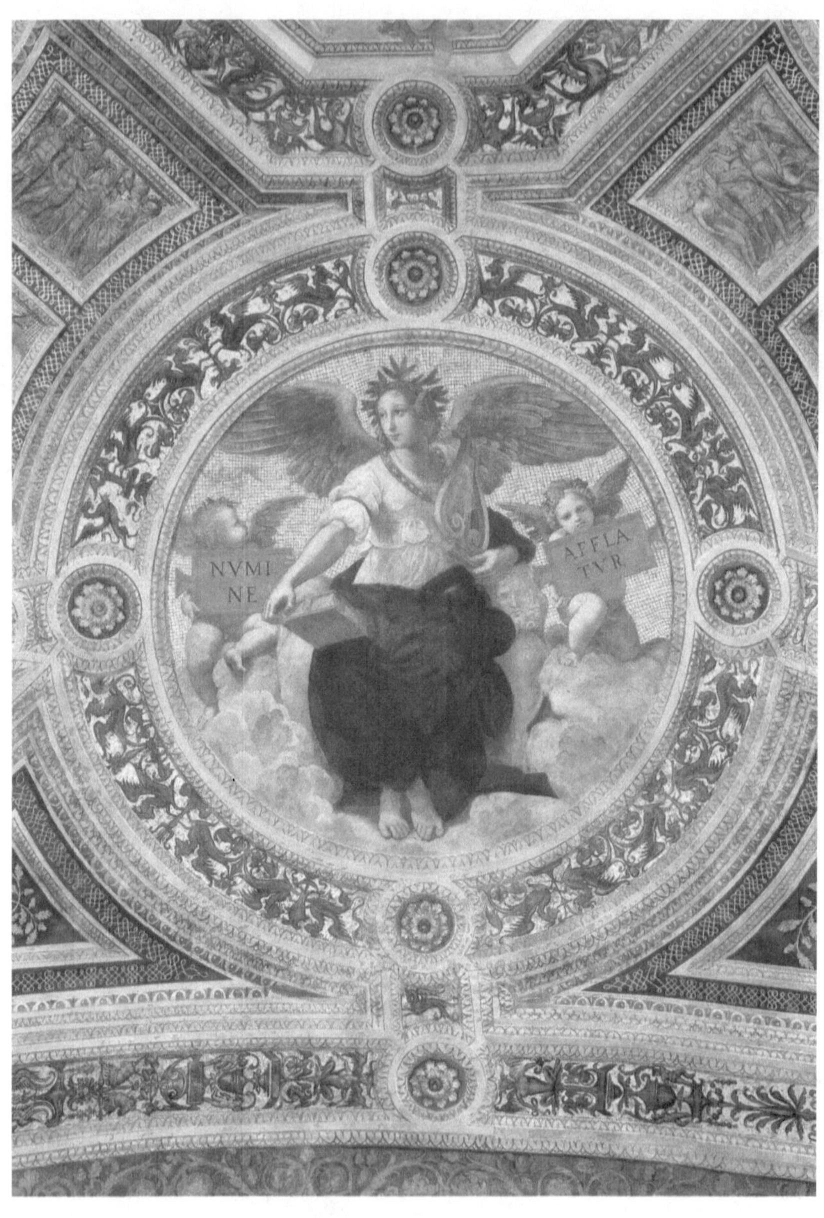

3.2 Raphael. *Poetry*. Detail from the ceiling of the Stanza della Segnatura. Stanza della Segnatura, Vatican Palace, Vatican State. Scala / Art Resource, NY.

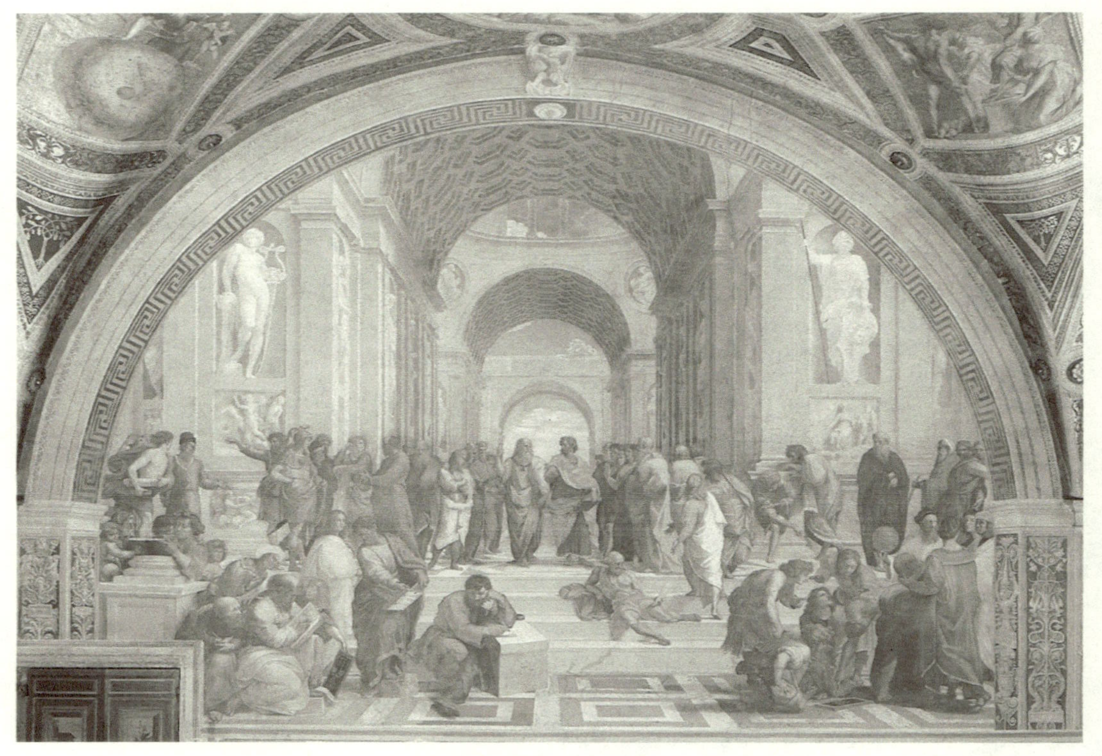

3.3 Raphael. *The School of Athens*. Stanza della Segnatura, Vatican Palace, Vatican State. Scala / Art Resource, NY.

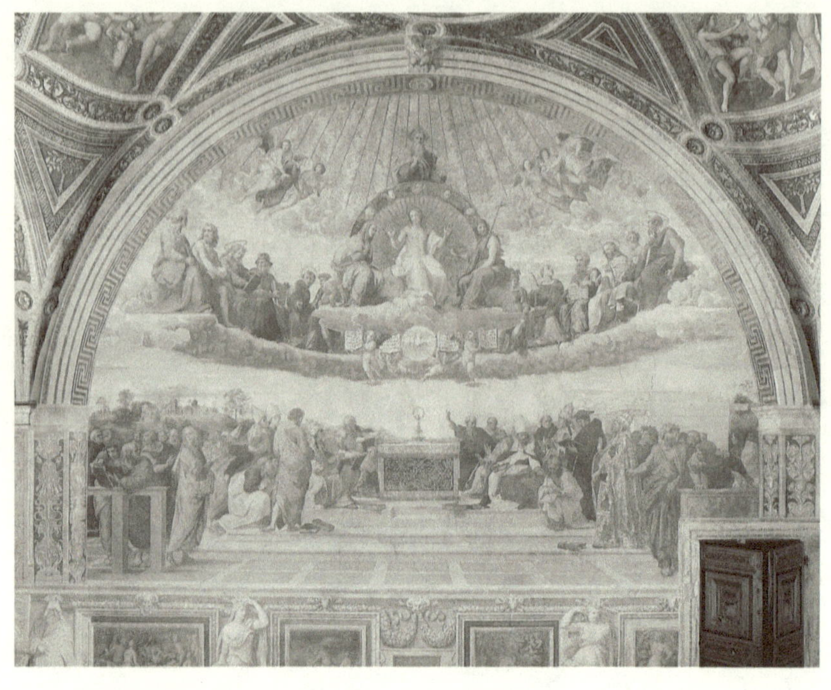

3.4 Raphael. *Disputa* (Disputation over the Blessed Sacrament). Stanza della Segnatura, Vatican Palace, Vatican State. Scala / Art Resource, NY.

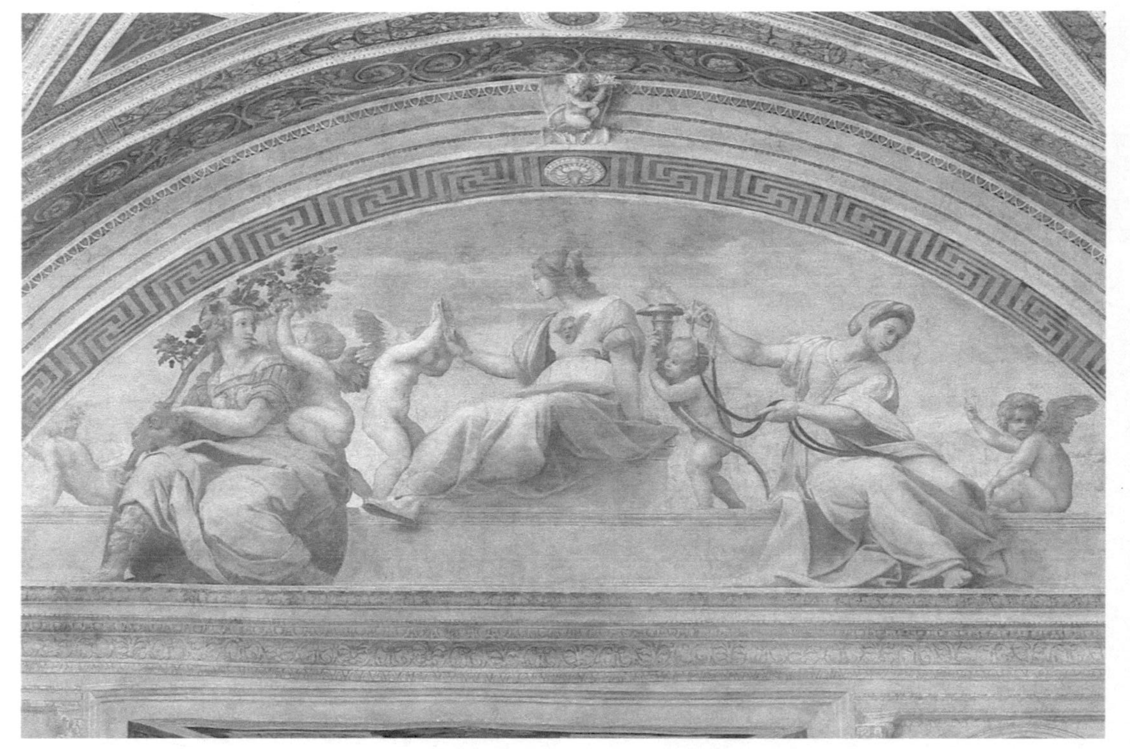

3.5 Raphael. *The Virtues, Fortitude, Prudence (with Janus head) and Temperance*. Stanza della Segnatura, Vatican Palace, Vatican State. Scala / Art Resource, NY.

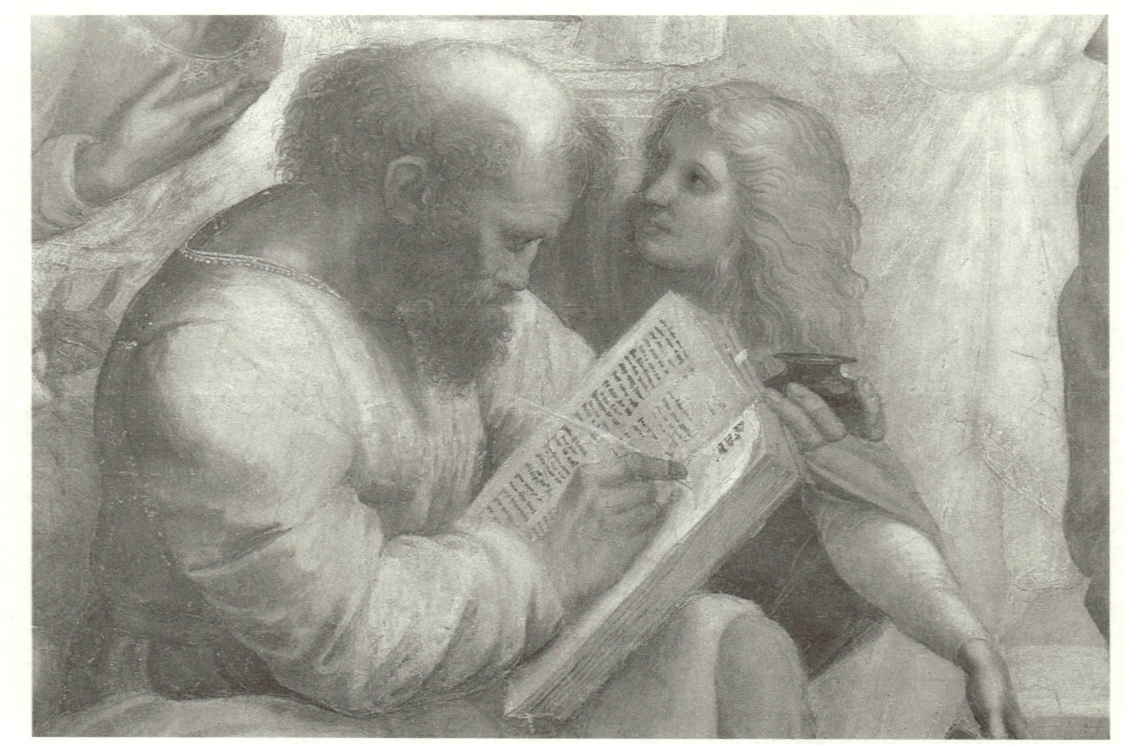

4.1 Raphael. *The School of Athens*, detail of Pythagoras with a boy. Stanza della Segnatura, Vatican Palace, Vatican State. Scala / Art Resource, NY.

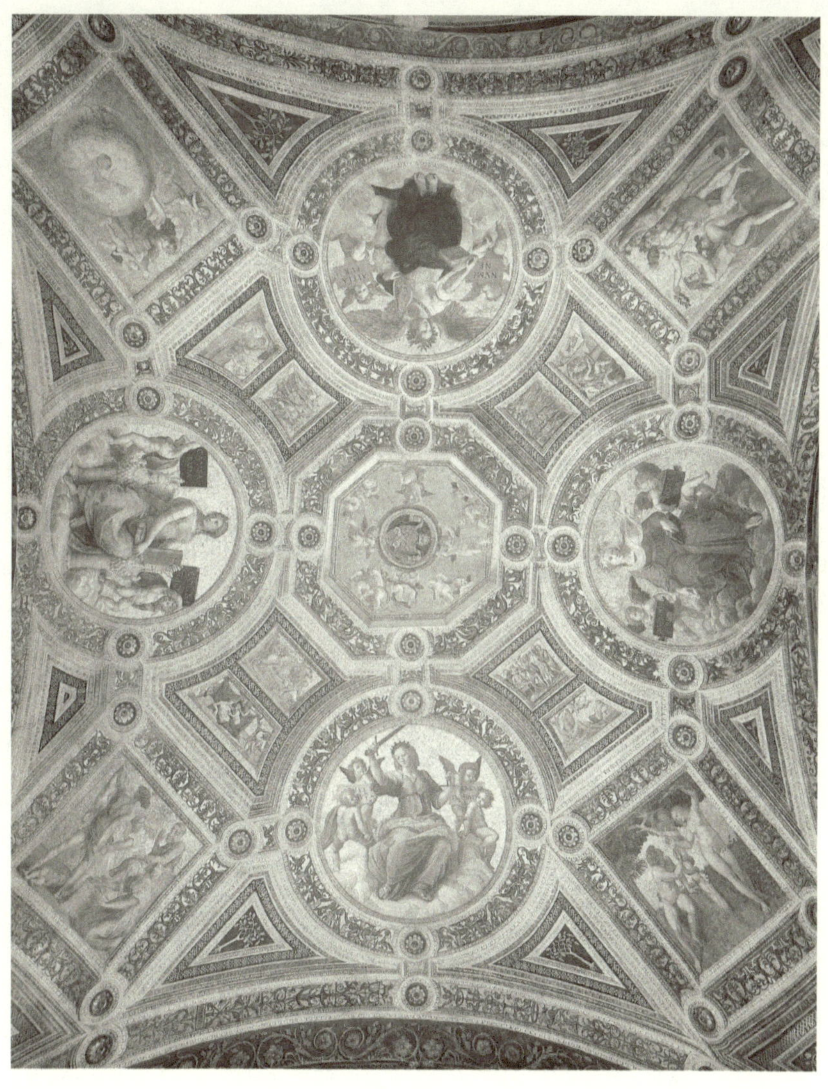

4.2 Raphael. *Ceiling of the Stanza della Segnatura*. Stanza della Segnatura, Vatican Palace, Vatican State. Scala / Art Resource, NY.

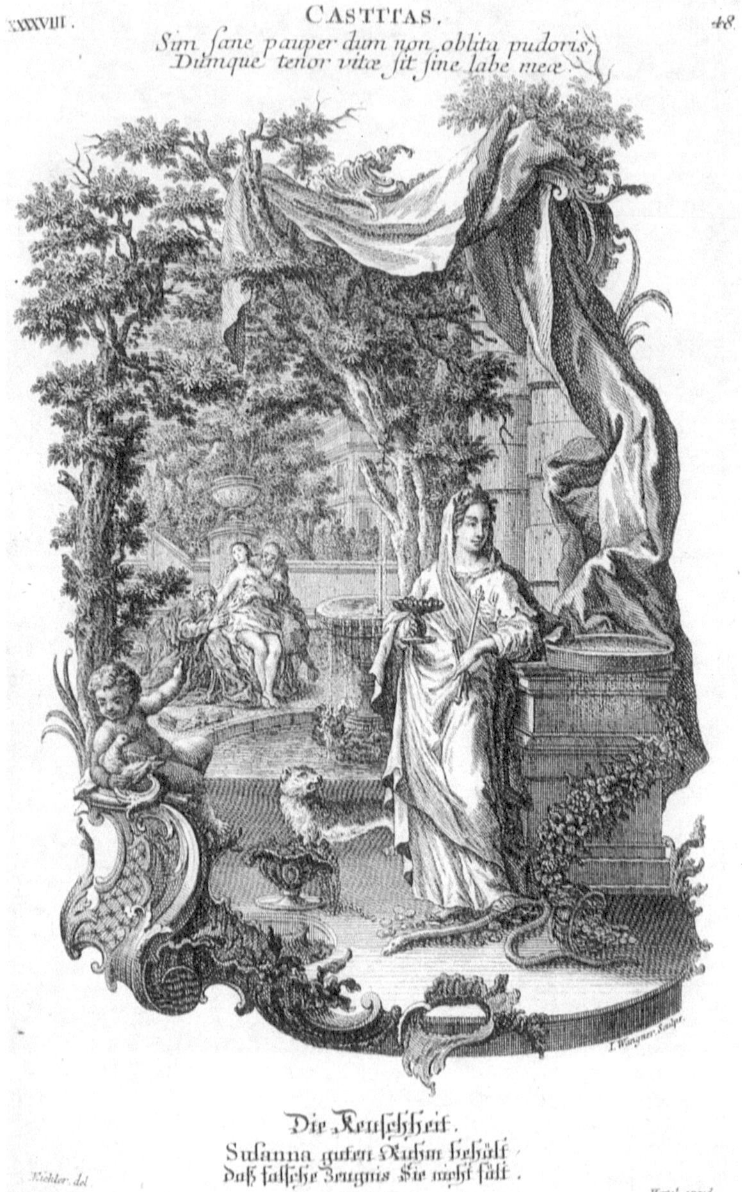

4.3 Ripa, Cesare (edited by J. Georg Hertel). *Castitas*. 1760. Washington University Libraries, Department of Special Collections, Saint Louis.

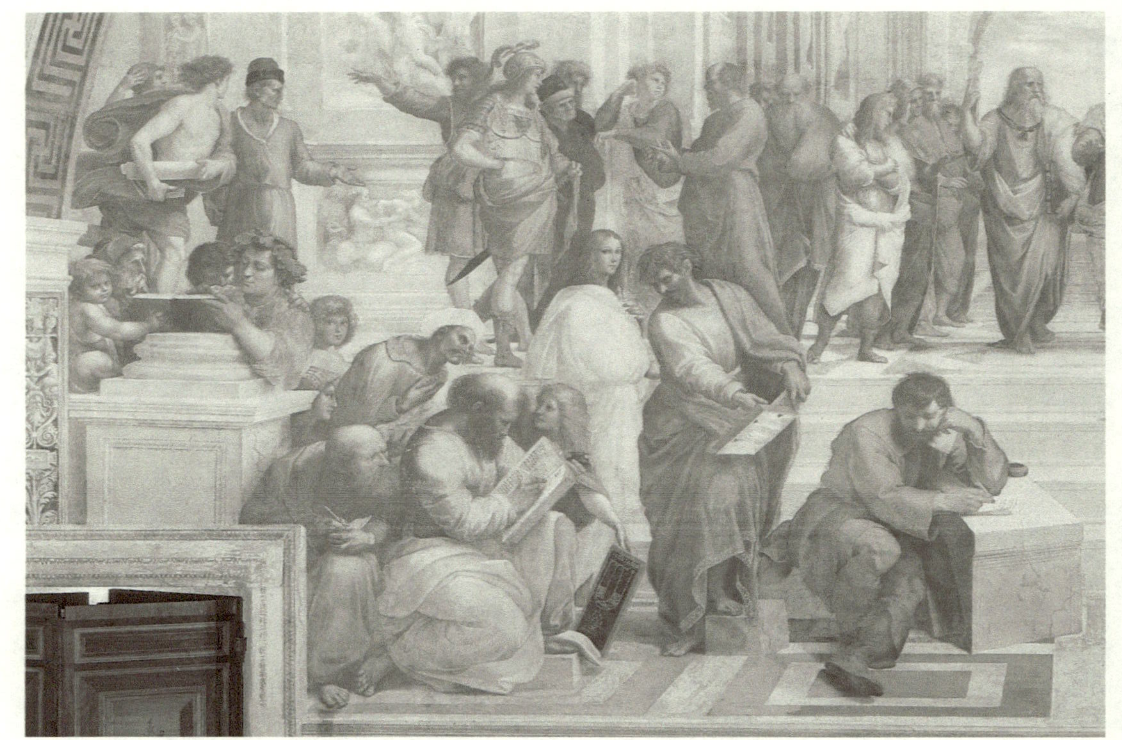

5.1 Raphael. *The School of Athens*, detail of left half. Stanza della Segnatura, Vatican Palace, Vatican State. Scala / Art Resource, NY.

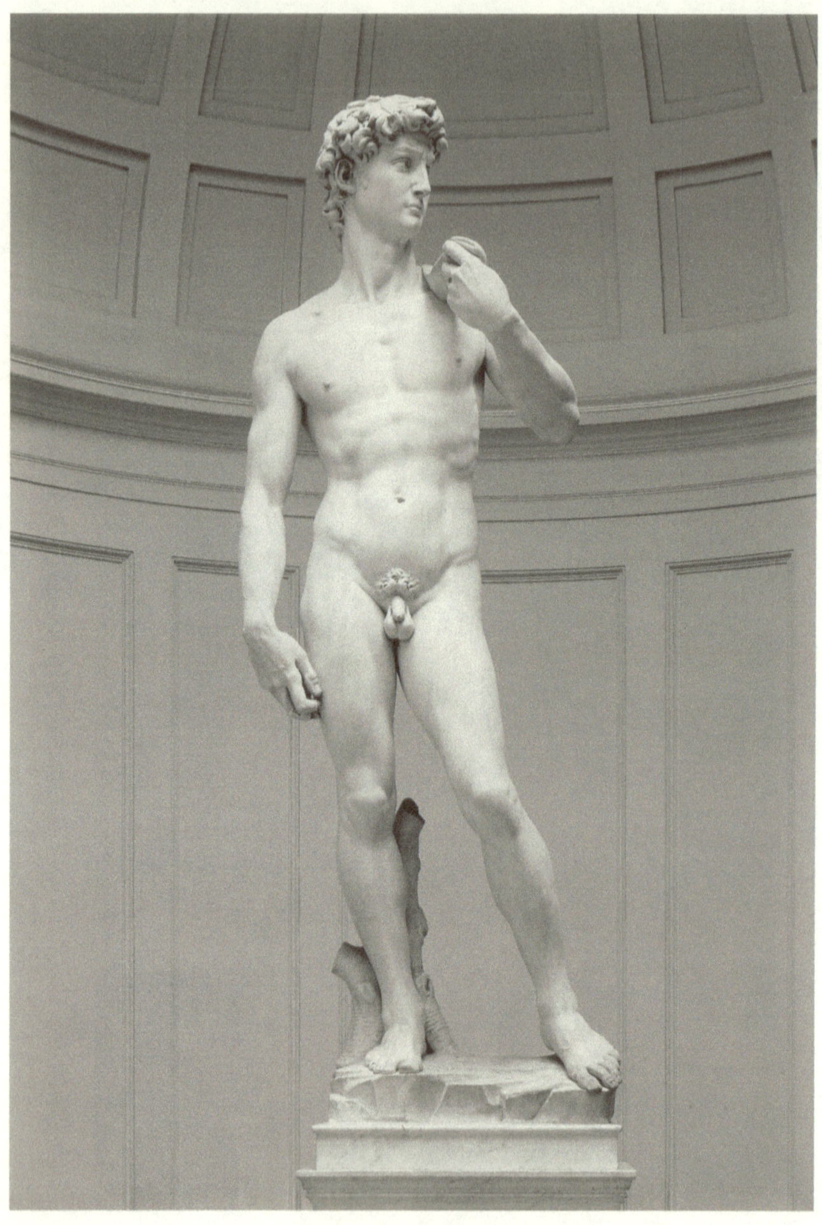

5.2 Michelangelo. *David* (frontal view). Accademia, Florence, Italy. Ufizzi, Florence. Scala / Art Resource, NY.

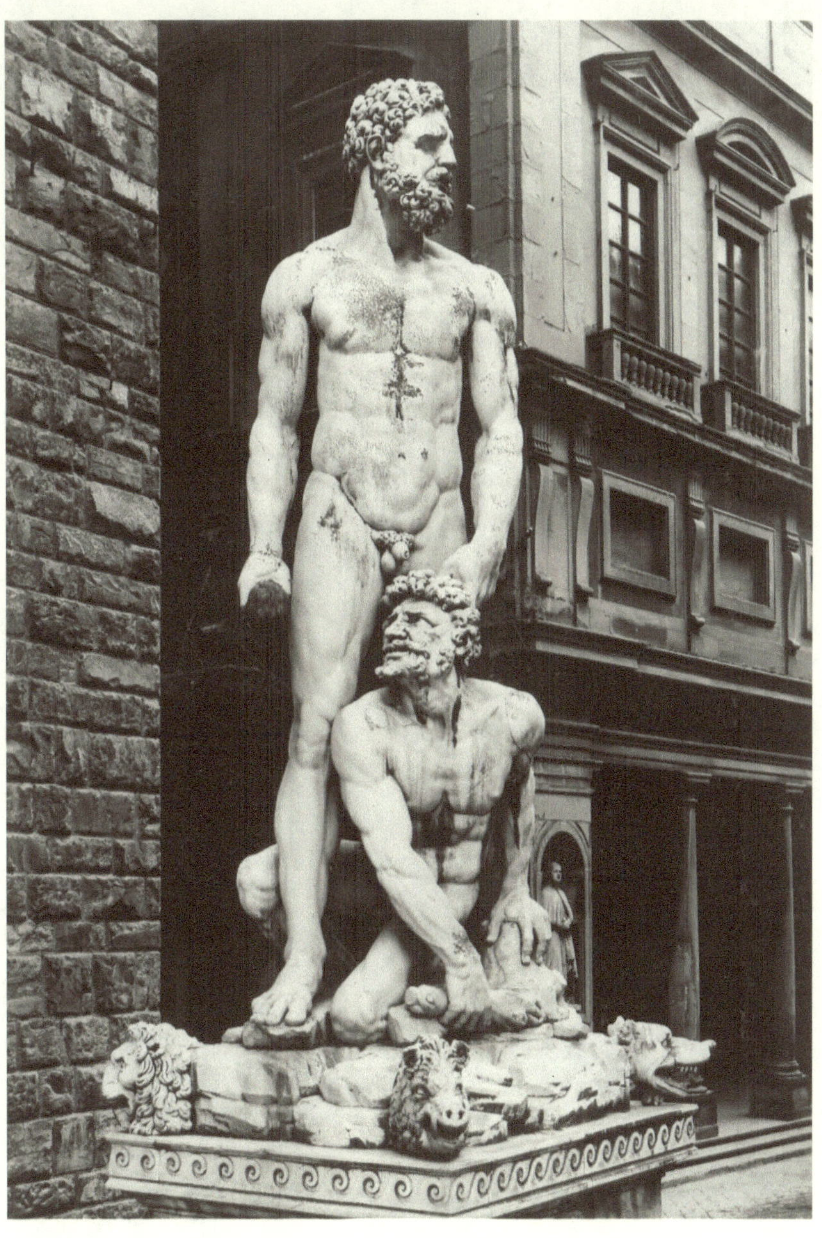

5.3 Bandinelli, Baccio. *Hercules and Cacus*. Piazza della Signoria, Florence, Italy. Alinari / Art Resource, NY.

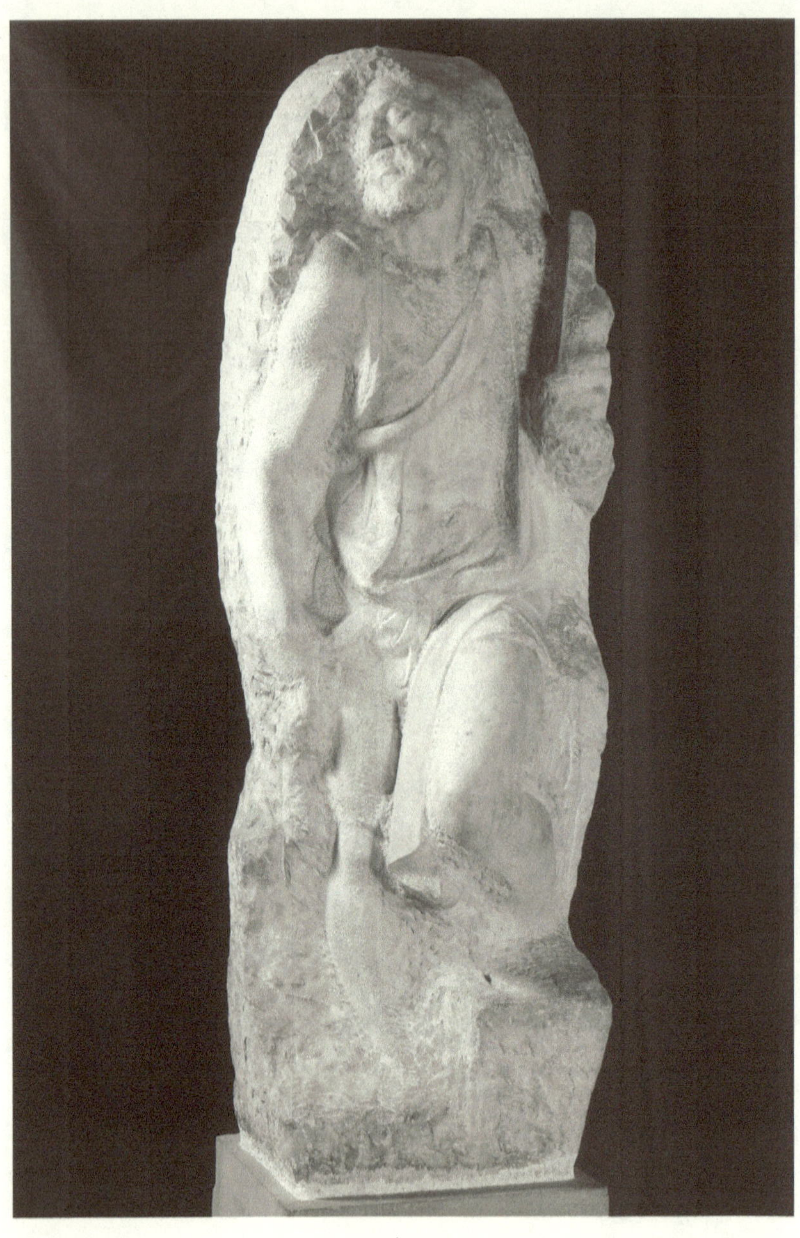

5.4 Michelangelo. *Saint Matthew*. Accademia, Florence, Italy. Nimatallah / Art Resource, NY.

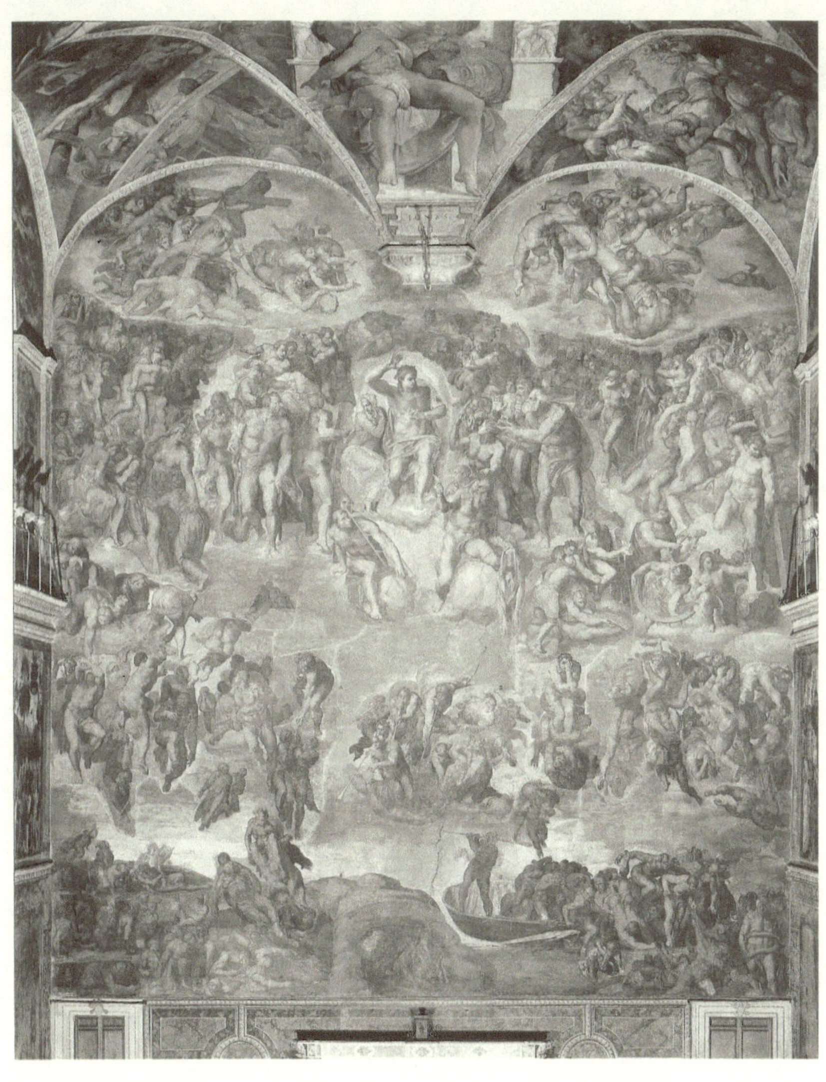

5.5 Michelangelo. *Last Judgment*. Sistine Chapel, Vatican Palace, Vatican State. Scala / Art Resource, NY.

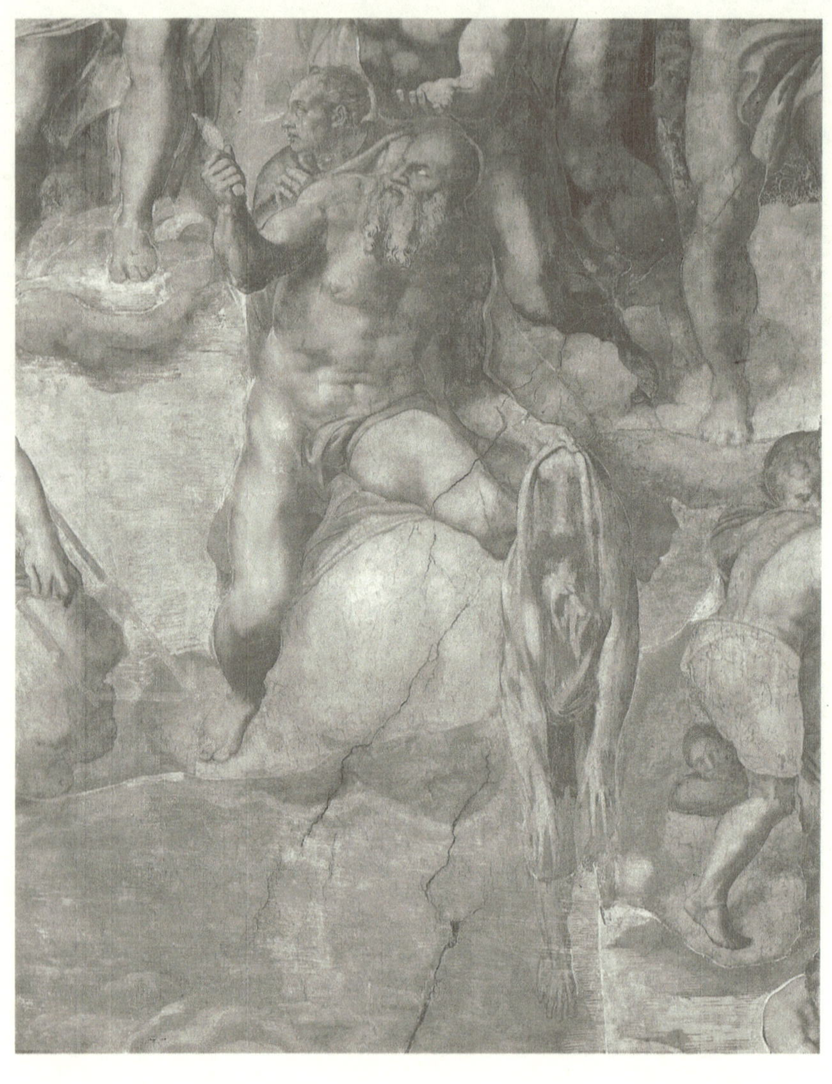

5.6 Michelangelo. *Saint Bartholomew*, detail of *Last Judgment*. Sistine Chapel, Vatican Palace, Vatican State. Scala / Art Resource, NY.

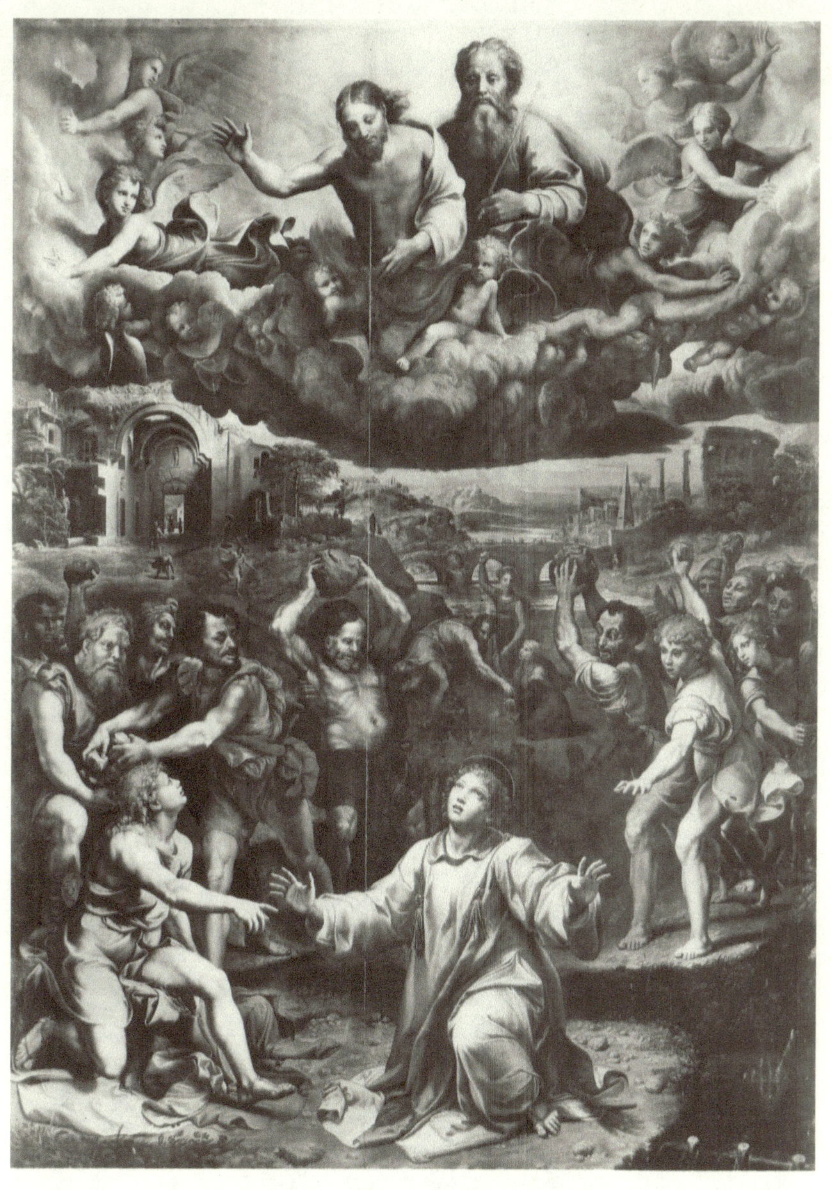

6.1 Romano, Giulio. *The Stoning of Saint Stephen*. S. Stefano, Genoa, Italy. Alinari / Art Resource, NY.

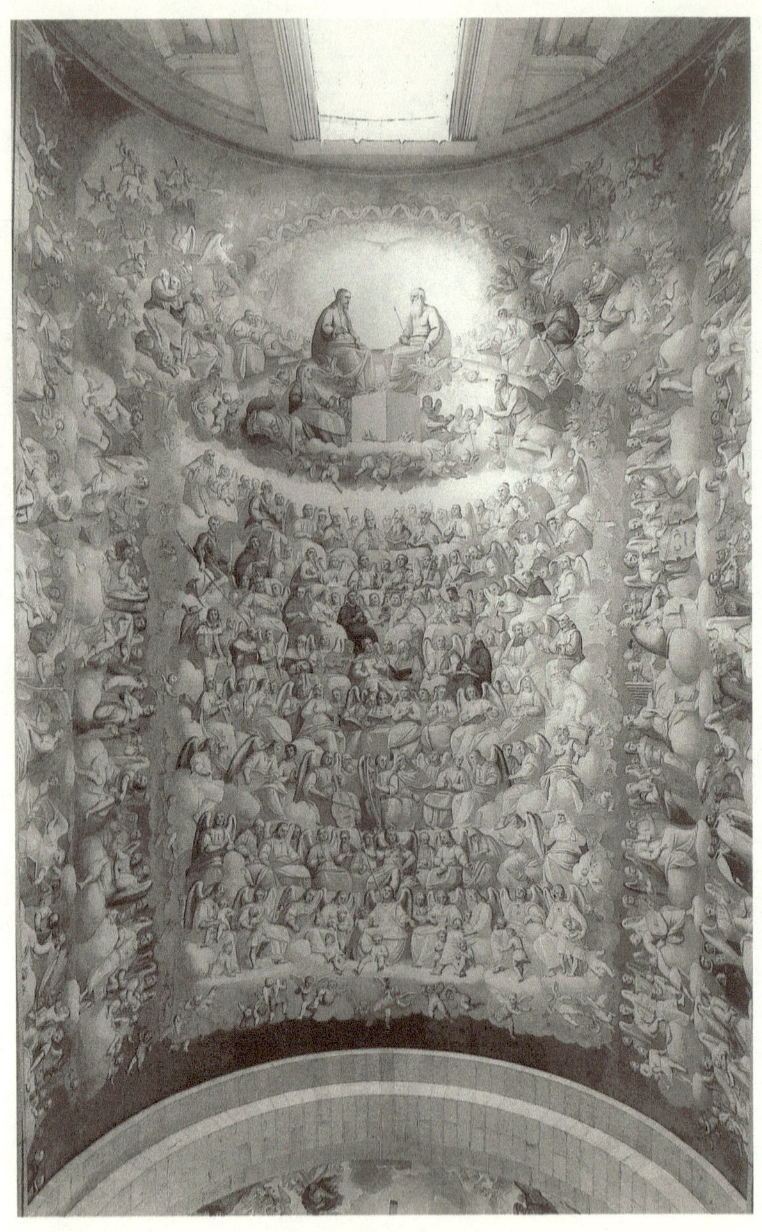

6.2 Cambiaso, Luca. *La Gloria*. Real Monasterio de San Lorenzo de El Escorial, Madrid.

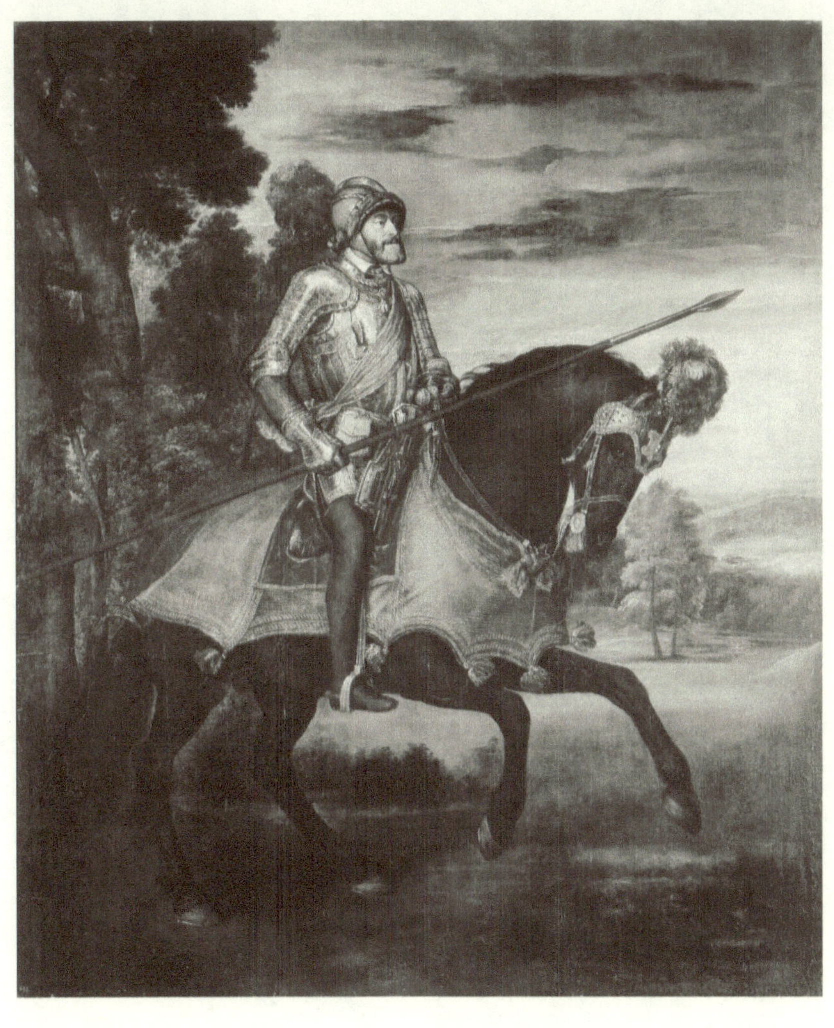

7.1 Titian. *Charles V at Mühlberg*. Museo del Prado, Madrid, Spain. Scala / Art Resource, NY.

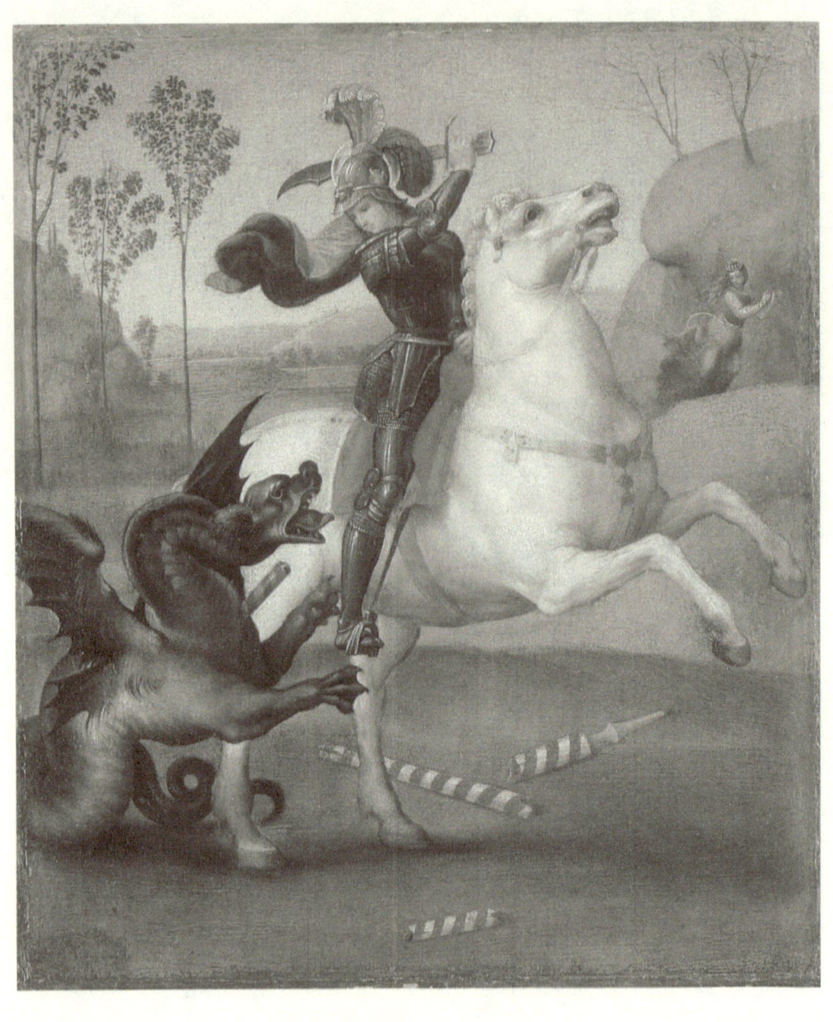

7.2 Raphael. *Saint George fighting the dragon.* Louvre, Paris, France. Réunion des Musées Nationaux / Art Resource, NY.

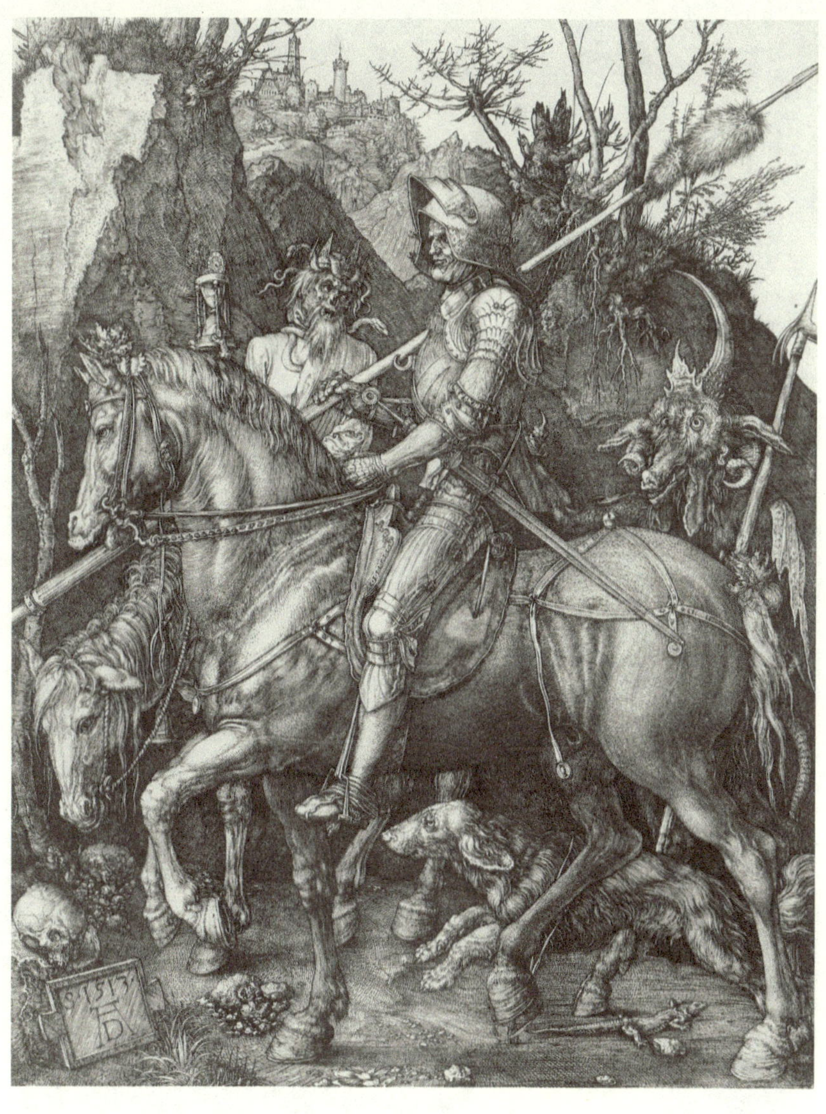

7.3 Dürer, Albrecht. *The Knight, Death and the Devil*. Musée du Petit Palais, Paris, France. Bridgeman-Giraudon / Art Resource, NY.

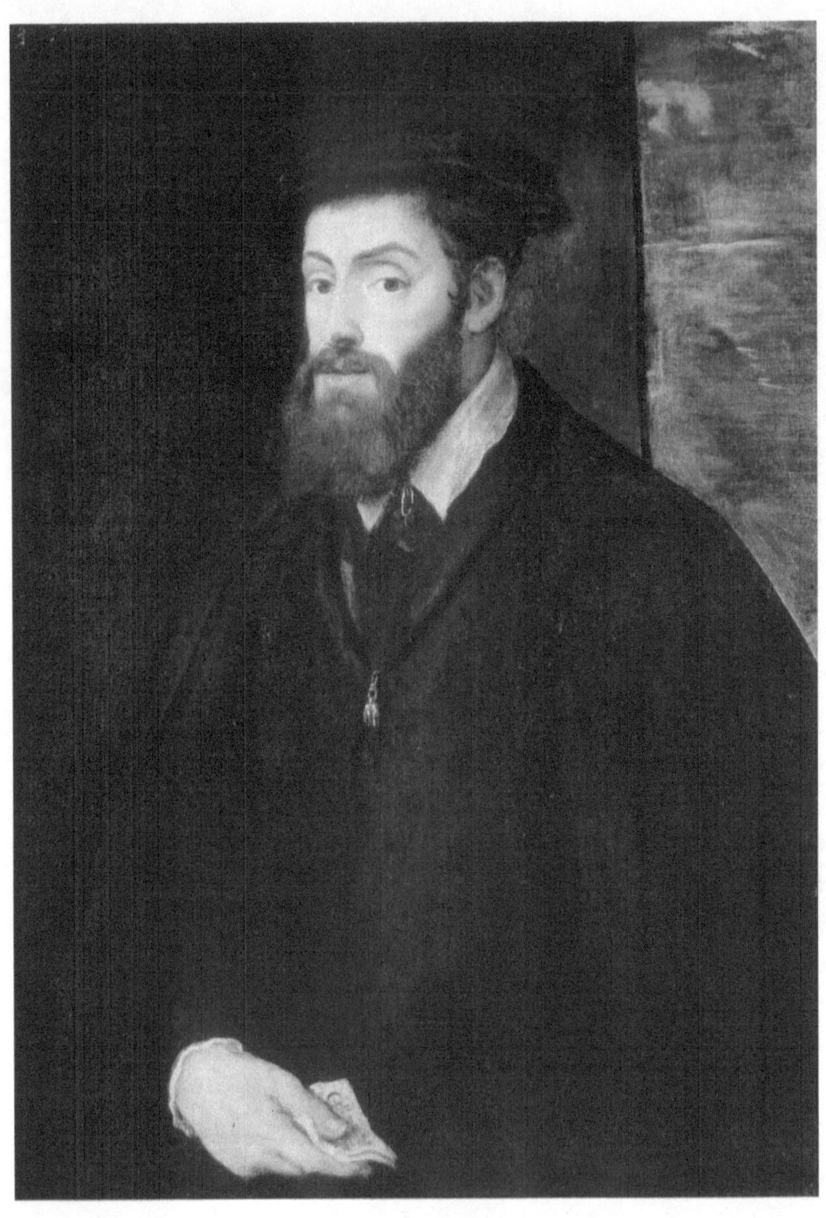

7.4 Titian. *Portrait of Charles V, Holy Roman Emperor*. Museo Nazionale di Capodimonte, Naples, Italy. Scala / Art Resource, NY.

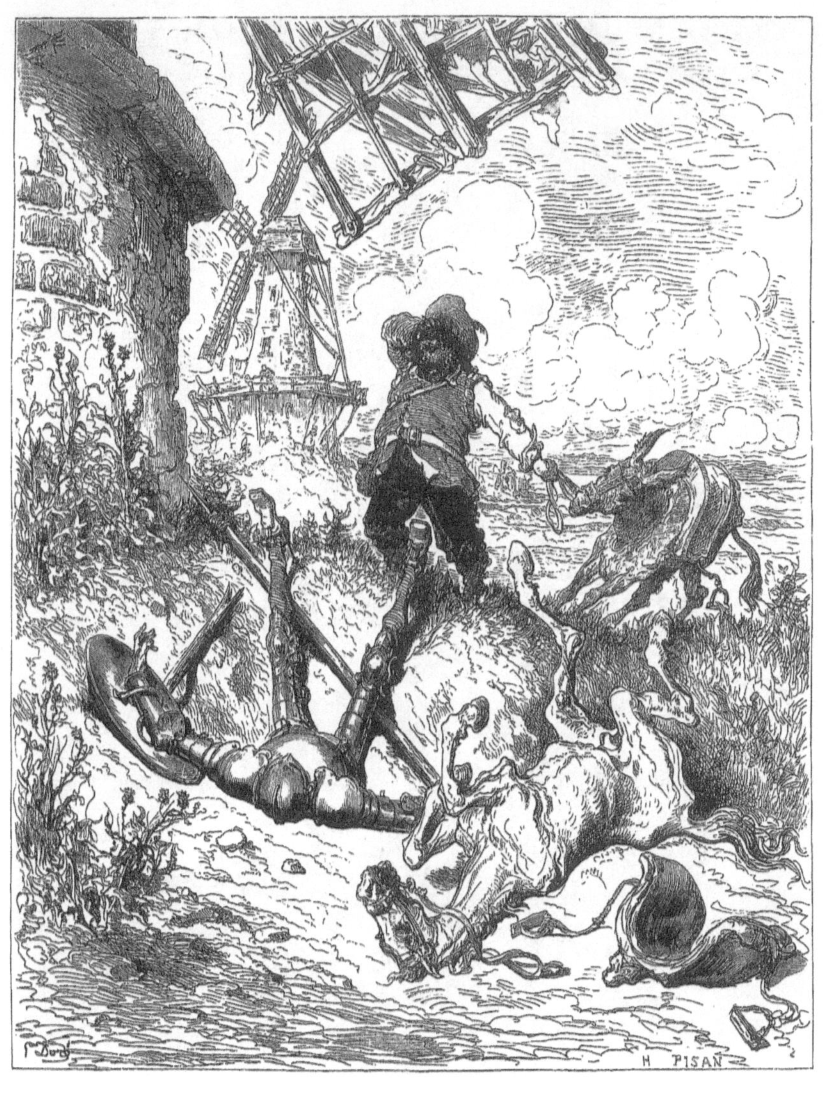

8.1 Doré, Gustave. *Miséricorde! S'Écria Sancho*. 1863. University of Chicago Library, Special Collections Research Center, Chicago.

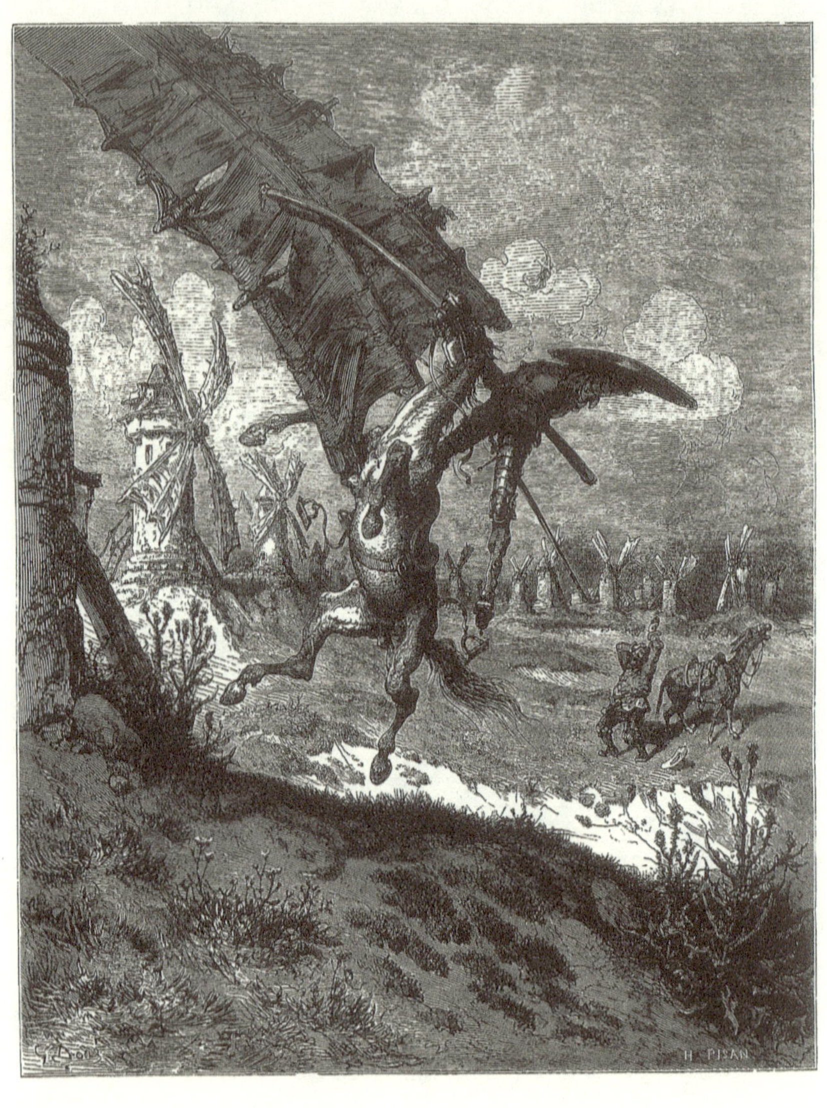

8.2 Doré, Gustave. *L'aile emporte après elle le cheval et le chevalier.* 1863. University of Chicago Library, Special Collections Research Center, Chicago.

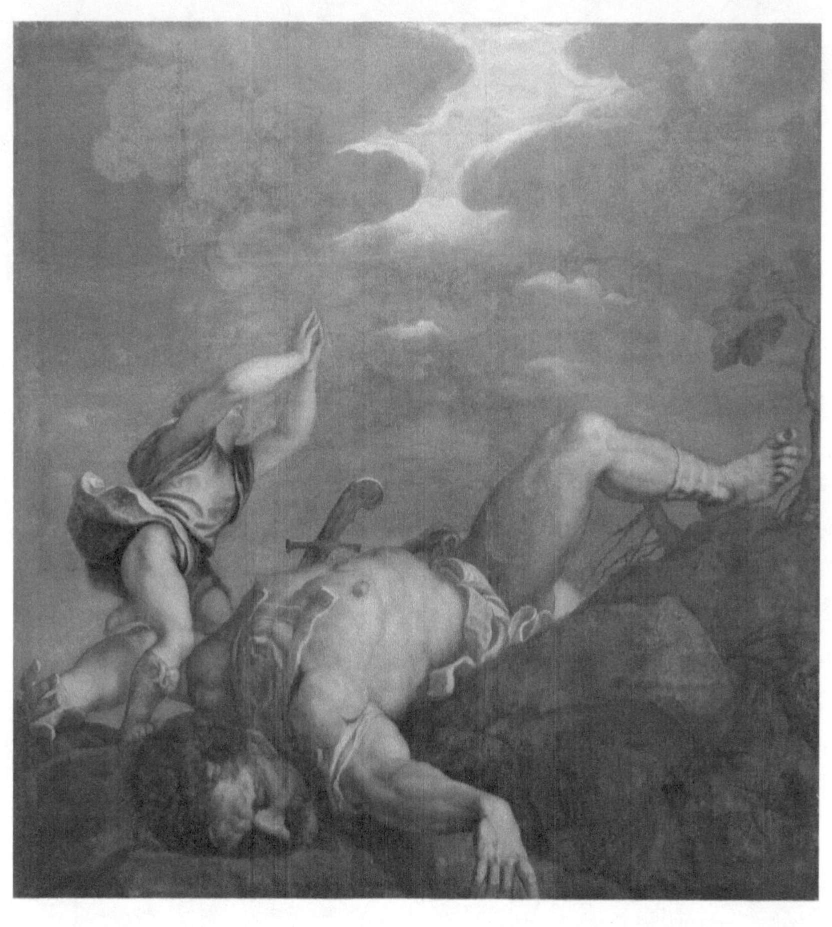

8.3 Titian. *David and Goliath*. S. Maria della Salute, Venice, Italy. Erich Lessing / Art Resource, NY.

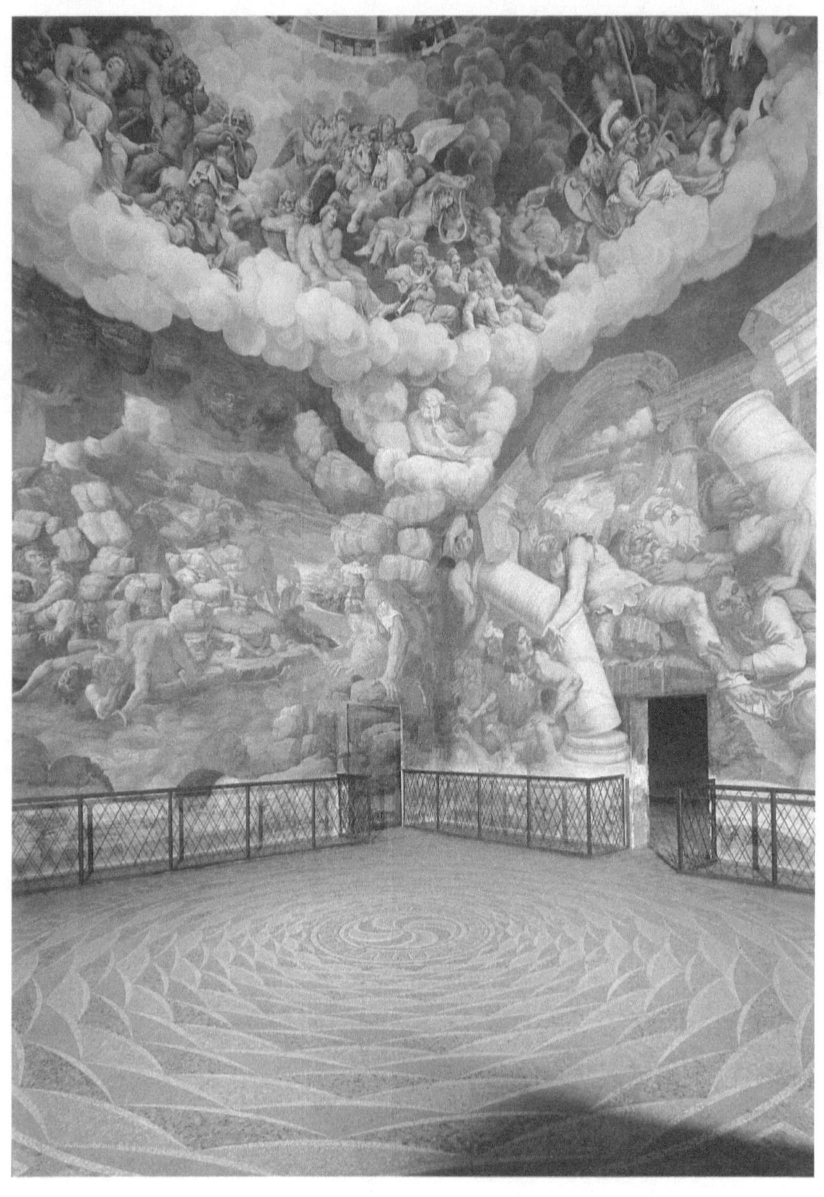

8.4 Romano, Giulio. *Room of the Giants.* Palazzo del Té, Mantua, Italy. Scala / Art Resource, NY.

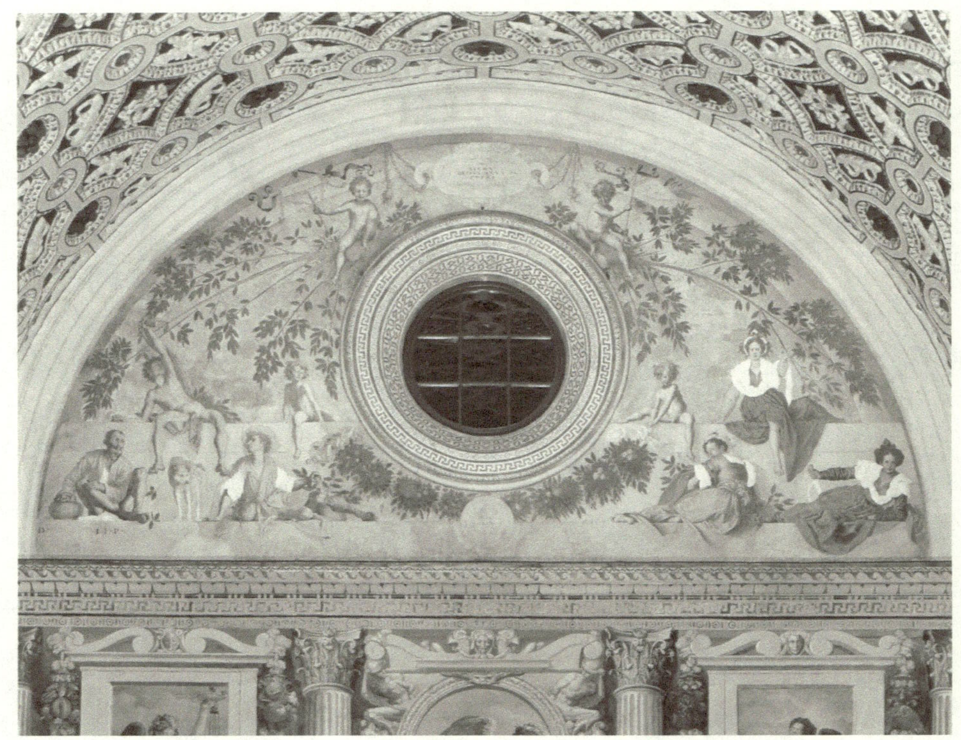

9.1 Pontormo, Jacopo. *Vertumnus and Pomona*. Villa Medici, Poggio a Caiano, Italy. Scala / Art Resource, NY.

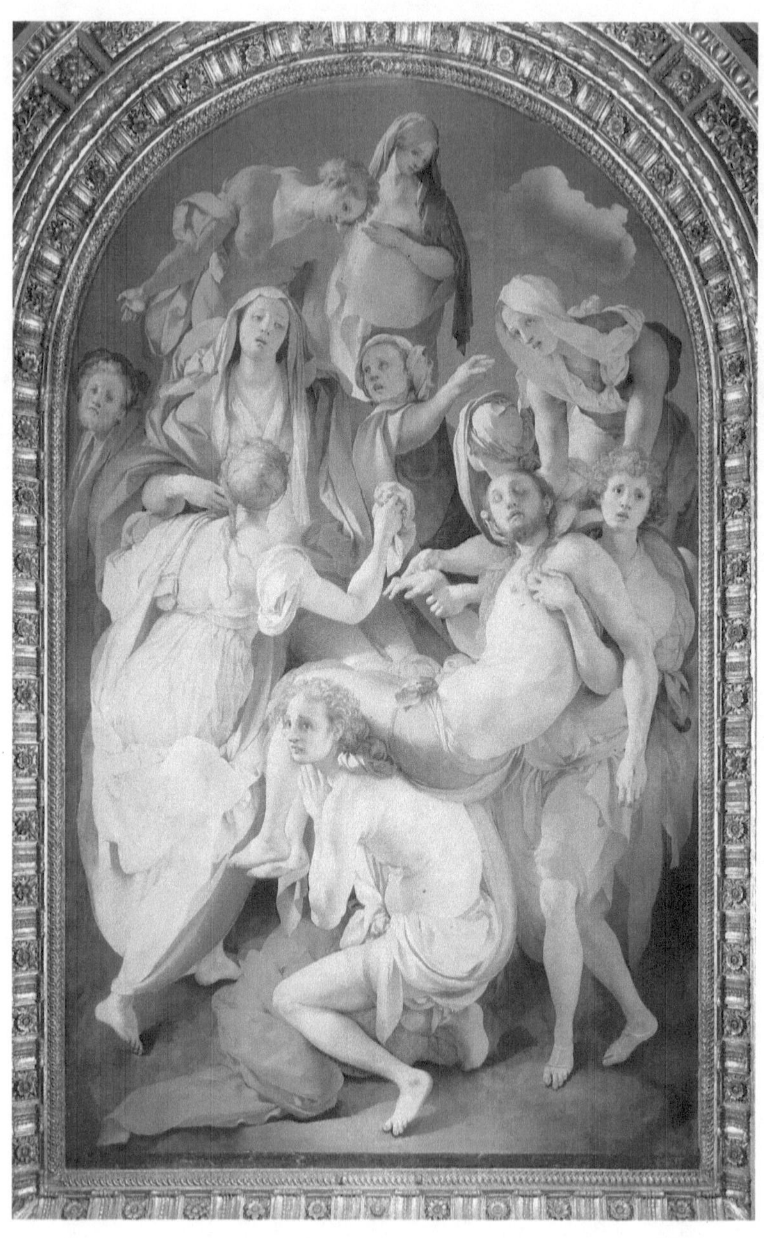

9.2 Pontormo, Jacopo. *The Entombment*. S. Felicita, Florence, Italy. Scala / Art Resource, NY.

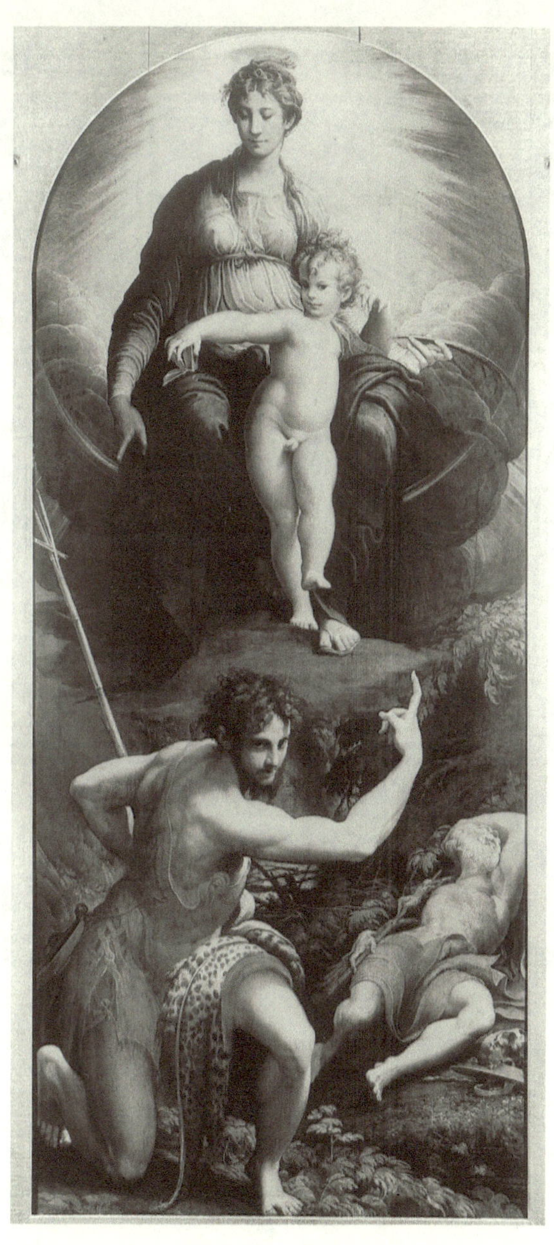

9.3 Parmigianino. *Altarpiece: The Madonna and Child with Saints John the Baptist and Jerome*. 1527. National Gallery, London.

grãdes señores y señoras y lo q̃ en llo se hizo.

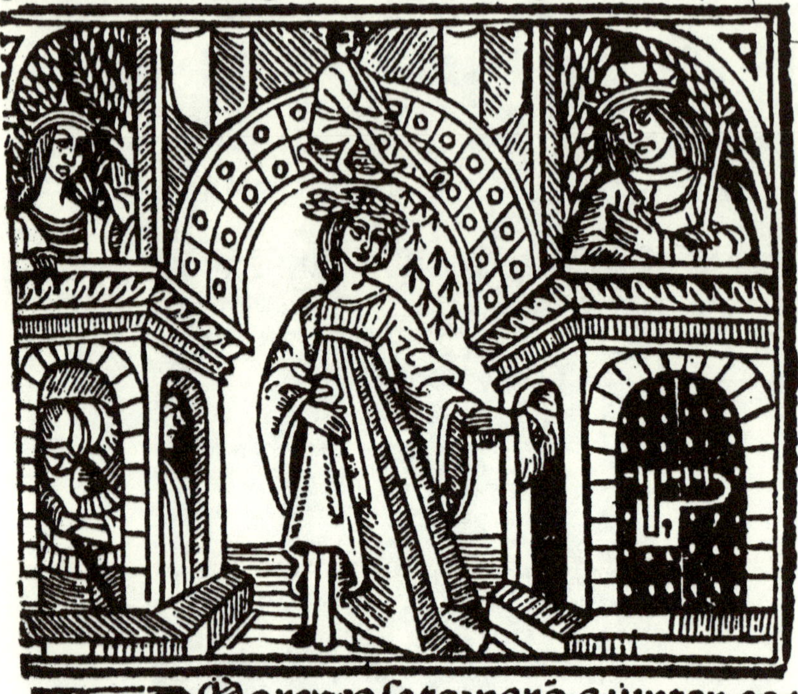

LOs reyes se tornarõ a juntar como de ante ⁊ concertarõ las bodas pa el q̃rto dia: y q̃ durassen
las fiestas q̃nze dias: en cabo de-

10.1 Cromberger, Iacobo, and Iuan Cromberger, eds, *Amadis de Gaula. Oriana*. Biblioteca Nacional de Portugal, Lisboa, Portugal.

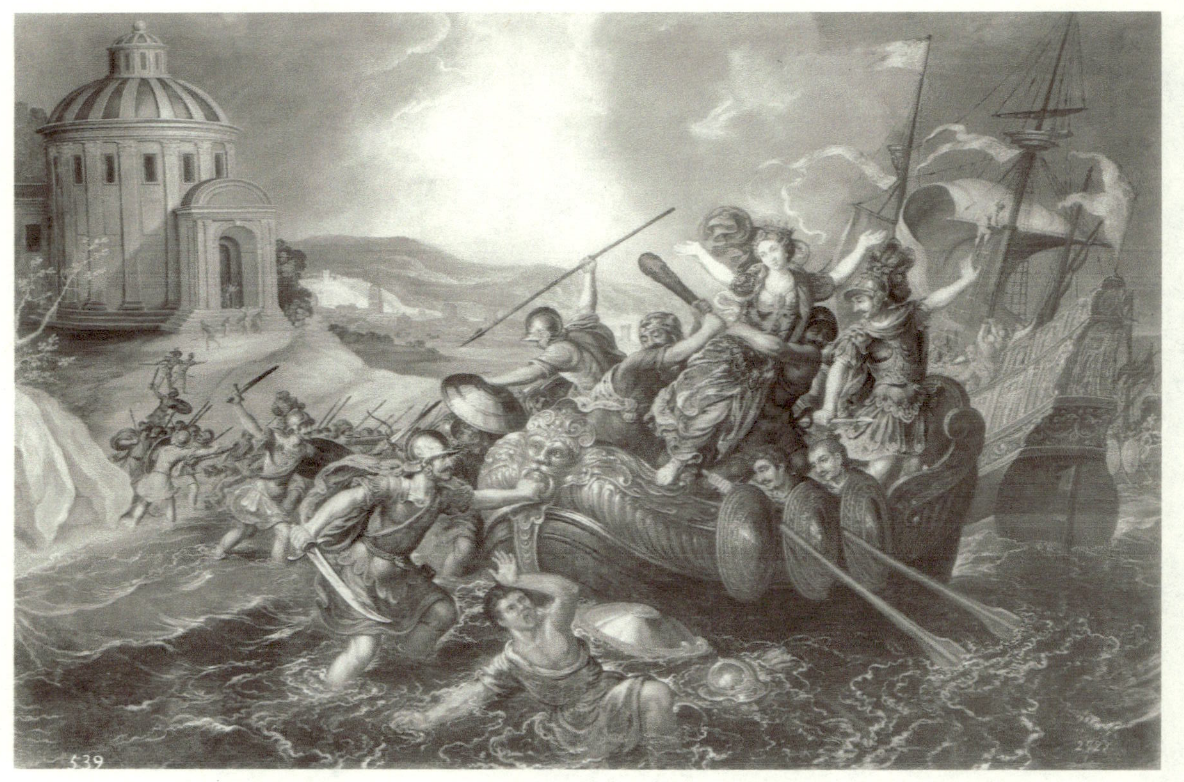

10.2 Juan de la Corte. *El rapto de Helena*. 1631. Museo Nacional del Prado, Madrid, Spain.

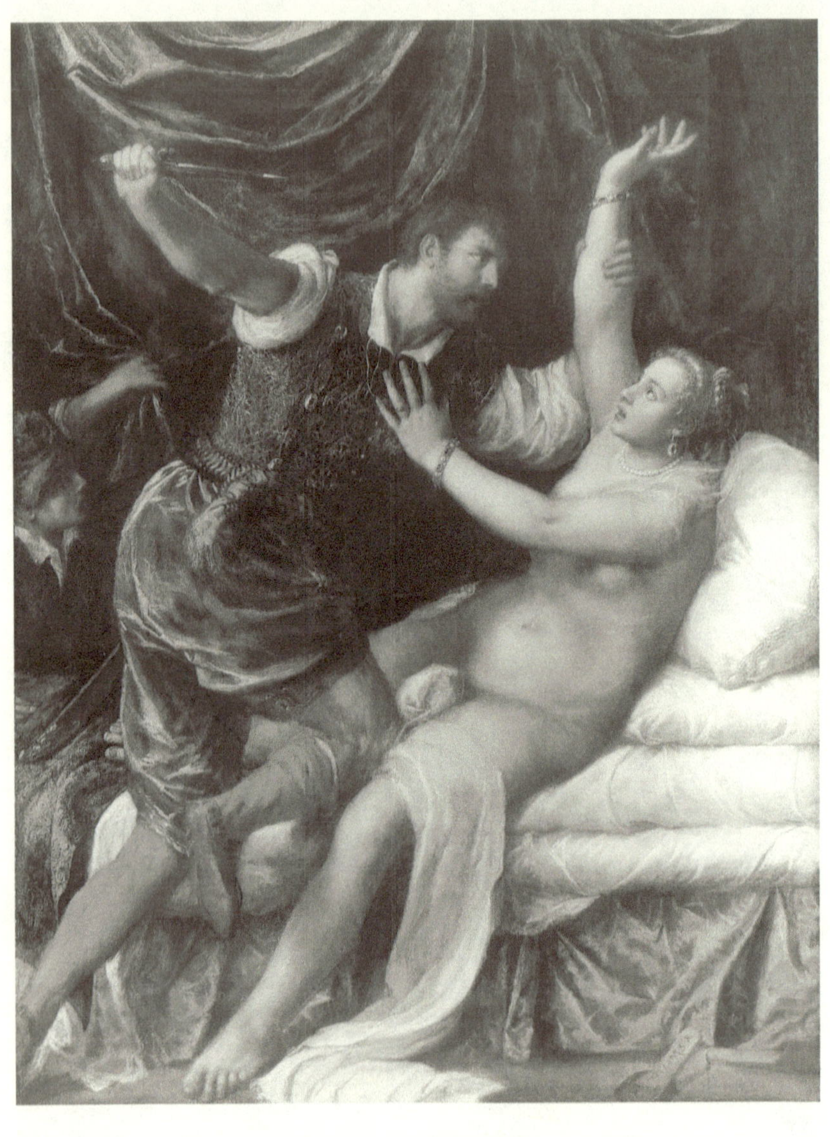

10.3 Titian. *Tarquin and Lucrecia*. 1571. Fitzwilliam Museum of Cambridge, Cambridge.

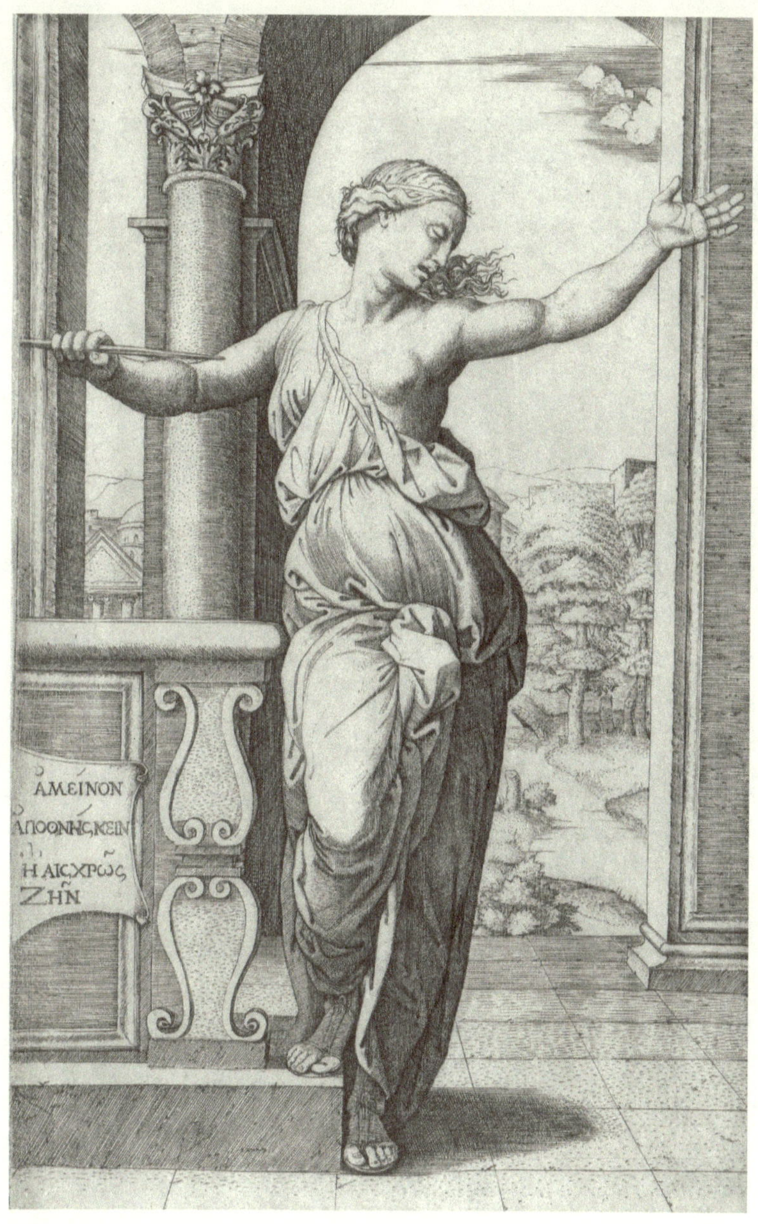

10.4 Raimondi, Marcantonio. *The Death of Lucretia.* Bildarchiv Preussischer Kulturbesitz / Art Resource, NY.

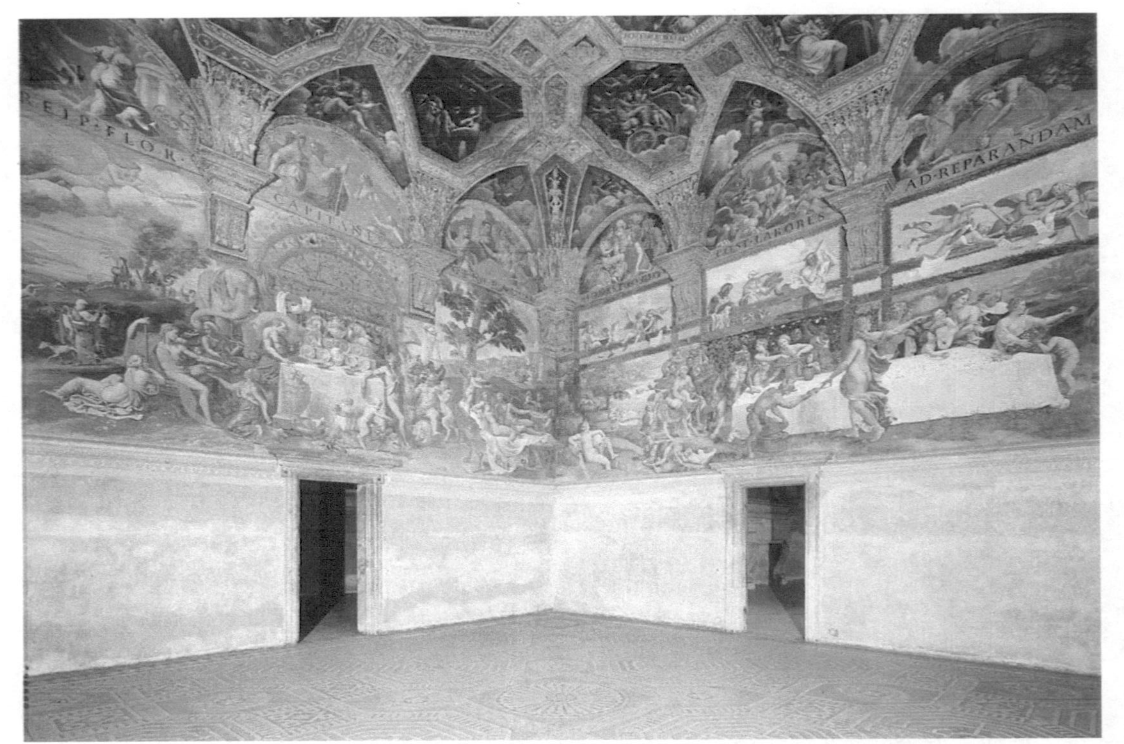

11.1 Romano, Giulio. *The Wedding Banquet of Psyche and Cupid*. Palazzo del Té, Mantua, Italy. Scala / Art Resource, NY.

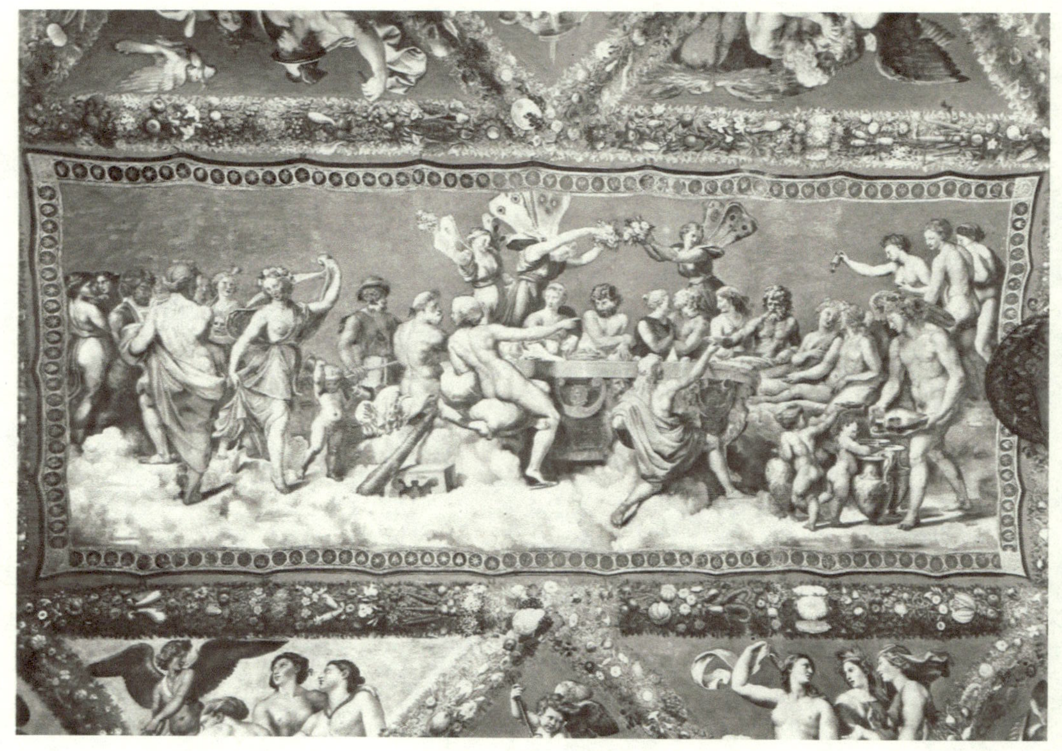

11.2 Raphael. *The Banquet of the Gods*. Palazzo della Farnesina, Rome, Italy. Alinari / Art Resource, NY.

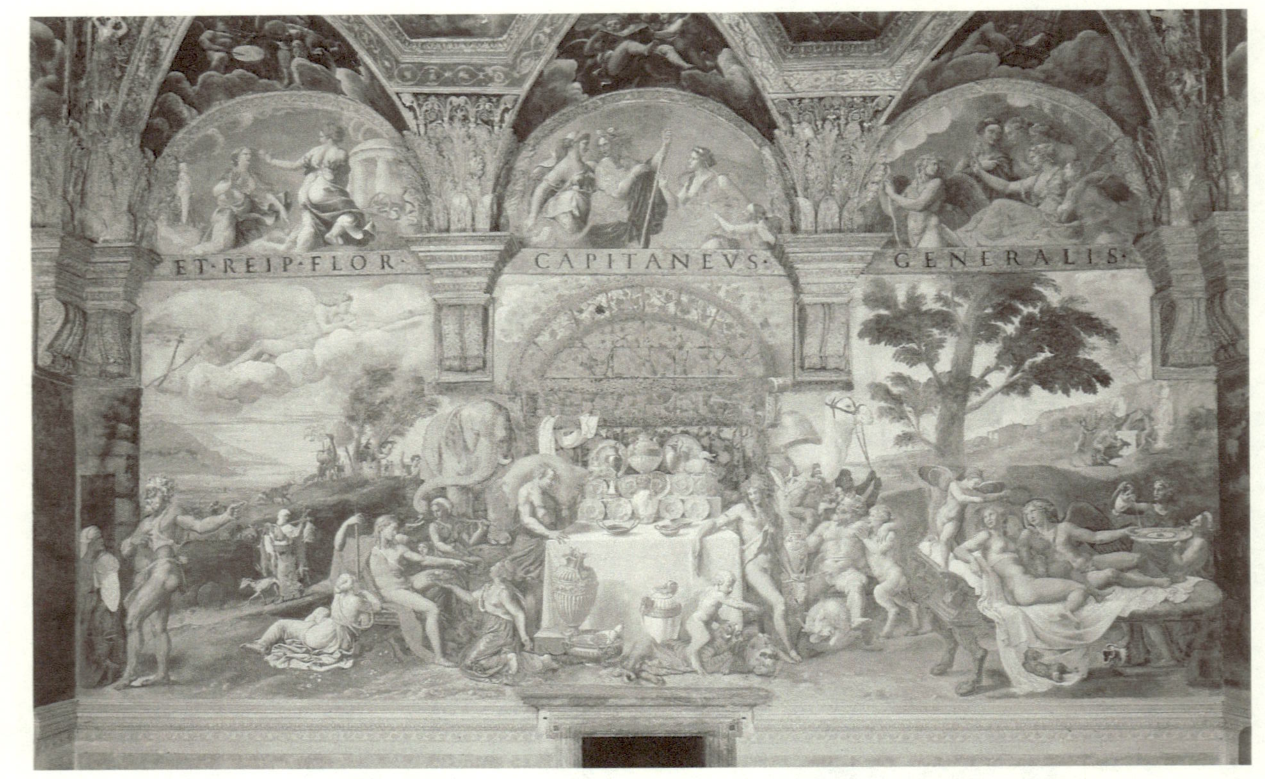

11.3 Romano, Giulio. *Wedding Banquet of Amor and Psyche*. Palazzo del Té, Mantua, Italy. Scala / Art Resource, NY.

will be gathered in one flock with one shepherd.'[31] It is no coincidence that Don Quixote declaims his speech on the Golden Age in the presence of goatherds. He is the shepherd who will gather them all together. He is the Christian knight and the future king who will create a world empire where peace and justice will reign. Thus, Don Quixote wants to bring about an imperial *renovatio* that will continue and bring to fulfilment Charles V's imperial vision.[32] The knight's triumphant vision, however, has little to do with reality, pointing to either the decline of Spanish power or a certain suspicion as to the use of power to promote through war the imperial myth.

The gold of the painting is also a reflection of sunlight. And solar imagery is also key to the portrayal of Charles V's empire. Virgil's *Fourth Eclogue* foretells the return of Astraea and of the Golden Age under Augustus's rule. In addition, 'Apollo is the prophesied king of a reborn universe' (Tanner 1993, 225). Myth is conflated with history when Augustus's victory at Actium 'was attributed to the god's intervention and Augustus erected a temple in Apollo's honor on the spot ... Following the victory at Actium, Augustus claimed Apollo as his special patron' (Tanner 1993, 226). Apollo, then, became a god of empire, and more particularly of the *Pax Romana* brought about by Augustus, a peace equated with the mythical Golden Age. These associations were not lost on the Habsburg image-makers: 'As heir to the Spanish discovery of the New World, Charles V was able to inject a powerful new element into imperial solar pretensions; he was acclaimed for bringing the light of the sun to the dark hemisphere' (Tanner 1993, 233). Following in the emperor's footsteps, Don Quixote sallies forth while imagining Apollo: 'Apenas había el rubicundo Apolo tendido por la faz de la ancha y espaciosa tierra las doradas hebras de sus hermosos cabellos ... cuando el famoso caballero don Quijote de la Mancha, dejando las ociosas plumas, subió sobre su famoso caballo Rocinante, y comenzó a caminar por el antiguo y conocido campo de Montiel' (Scarce had ruddy Apollo spread over the face of the wide and spacious earth the golden tresses of his beauteous hair ... when the famous knight Don Quixote de la Mancha, quitting the slothful feathers of his bed, mounted his famous steed Rocinante and began to ride over the ancient and farfamed Plain of Montiel) (1978, 1.2.80; 30–1). Apollo's golden locks, his solar light, is thus as important to the initial portrait of Don Quixote as it is to Titian's portrayal of a solar emperor. Indeed, Don Quixote is associated with the rising sun at key moments in the novel, as when he sets out from the inn/castle after being knighted (1978, 1.4.94) and when he abides with the goatherds and is impelled to give his speech on the Golden Age (1978, 1.12.167).

The sun that shines upon Charles V at the battle of Mühlberg is not just golden. Ávila y Zúñiga points this out: 'Aquel dia fué de harto calor, y el sol tenía un color que claramente parecía sangriento' (That day was quite hot, and the sun had a color that it clearly seemed bloody) (Ávila y Zúñiga 1876, 444; Checa 1994, 44). For Checa, this explains the startling redness of Titian's canvas. Apollo is tainted with the redness of Mars as a bloody battle is about to take place. The sun god reflects this martial aspect through the red heat of the day. In Titian's portrait, this element is reflected in the red worn by the emperor and found on his horse.[33] In Cervantes' novel, the sun is equally fierce as the knight sets out on his first adventure: 'Con esto, caminaba tan despacio, y el sol entraba tan apriesa y con tanto ardor, que fuera bastante a derretirle los sesos, si algunos tuviera' (This made his progress so slow, and the sun was rising so fast and becoming so hot, that his brains would have melted, if he'd had any) (1978, 1.2.81; 31). Thus, the sun is not a particularly benefic Ptolemaic planet when it comes to Don Quixote – it is the sun that further dries his brain, increasing his madness. The heat from the sun also increments the knight's choleric disposition.

While in back of Charles V, the viewer can detect traces of green in the landscape, the advancing emperor steps into a parched, red, and dry land. The green of the background reflects the humidity and femininity that is being left behind. In Francesco da Hollanda's *Tractado de Pintura Antigua*, one of the speakers, Michelangelo, inveighs against the sensual vision of paintings that simply represent 'the green grass of the fields, the shadows of the trees ...' (Sohm 1995, 776). Charles V, however, is carefully depicted as leaving behind the cares of feminine nature (green fields and trees) as he moves forward into the epic and martial fields of battle. Don Quixote also moves from the feminine to the masculine as he seeks to become a famed knight. Ruth El Saffar has noted: 'The chivalric approach to the feminine is to put the woman out of sight and to engage in her name in a fascinating game of warfare with men' (1984, 53). Don Quixote leaves behind the fields he possesses as well as a home where abide his unmarried niece and a middle-aged housekeeper, women who, according to Carroll Johnson, may be the source of anxiety for the unmarried gentleman.[34] Like Charles V in Titian's portrait, Don Quixote leaves behind the feminine in order to engage in solar and martial pursuits. The martial fields of Mühlberg are transformed into the parched fields of La Mancha. Only after the adventure of the galley slaves do Sancho and Don Quixote leave the solar plains. Going to Sierra Morena, Don Quixote seeks to do penance for Dulcinea in a green and grassy area, thus bringing back the feminine into the novel.[35]

While the battle at Mühlberg takes place during the month of April, Cervantes' knight sets forth on a day that was 'uno de los calurosos del mes de julio' (one of those sweltering July days) (1978, 1.2.81; 30). The difference in month may serve as one more parallel between Titian's Charles V and Cervantes' Don Quixote. Cervantes' change of month from April to July may again reflect Ávila y Zúñiga's narrative and Titian's painting. This chronicler describes the moments before the battle in terms of classical antiquity: 'Fué como la que escriben de Julio César cuando pasó el Rubicón y dijo aquellas palabras tan señaladas; y sin duda ninguna cosa más al propio no se podía representar á los ojos de los que allí estábamos, porque allí vimos a César que pasaba un río, él armado y con ejército armado, y que de la otra parte no había que tratar sino de vencer, y que el pasar del río había de ser con esta determinación y con esta esperanza' (It was like the events written about Julius Caesar when he crossed the Rubicon and said those well-known words; and without a doubt nothing more appropriate could be represented to the eyes of those who were there, because there we saw Caesar who crossed the river, armed and with an army, and who only had to try to conquer those on the other side, and that crossing the river had to be with this determination and this hope) (Ávila y Zúñiga 1876, 441).[36] The month of July was named after Julius Caesar. If, then, Charles V, crossing the river Elba (Albis) at the battle of Mühlberg, is imitating Julius Caesar's crossing of the Rubicon,[37] then Don Quixote must in some way also follow this model. And he does so by sallying forth during the month named after Julius Caesar, July. The novel first alerts us to possible parallels between the knight and the Roman Caesar by alluding to Julius's writings in the prologue: 'Si tratáredes ... de capitanes valerosos, el mesmo Julio César os prestará a sí mismo en sus *Comentarios*' (If you deal with ... valiant captains, Julius Caesar will lend you himself in his *Commentaries*) (1978, 1.56; 15). At the end of Ávila y Zúñiga's *Comentario*, we encounter a comparison between the German wars he chronicles and Julius Caesar's Gallic wars: 'Sólo esto diré, que César, de cuyos comentarios el mundo está lleno, tardó en sojuzgar a Francia diez años, y con solo haber pasado el Rin y estado diez y ocho días en Alemania, Roma hacia suplicaciones a los dioses, y le pareció que bastaba aquello para la autoridad y dignidad del pueblo que señoreaba el mundo. El emperador en menos de un año sojuzgó esta provincia, bravísima por testimonio de los romanos y de los de nuestros tiempos' (I only will say this, that Caesar, of whose commentaries the world is full, delayed ten days in subjugating France, and with only having crossed the Rhine and being in Germany eighteen days, Rome made supplications to the gods, and it seemed to him that all that was sufficient for the authority and dignity of the people who ruled the world. In less than a year, the emperor subjugated this province whose inhabitants the Romans and those of our time attested to be extremely brave) (1876, 449). Thus, Charles V is superior to Julius Caesar and can truly be seen as *Dominus mundi*. Don Quixote as an imagined warrior and emperor also attempts to follow Caesar. Indeed, at several points in the novel, Don Quixote's character and feats are discussed in terms of Caesar.[38] It may be no coincidence that an allusion to the crossing of the Rubicon takes place right before Don Quixote is to see the princess Dulcinea for the first time (1978, 2.8.96). This is indeed a fateful moment in the 1615 novel, one that shifts the course of the action since Dulcinea will be enchanted. While in Titian's painting the only trace of Ávila y Zúñiga's evocation of Caesar may be seen in the determination[39] found in the emperor's features, in *Don Quixote* the traces of Caesar's presence include the month bearing his name, an allusion to his *Comentarios*, parallels in action and characterization, and most important the knight's amazing determination.

Cervantes was well aware that Titian's equestrian portrait of the emperor included a number of elements from the chronicle by Ávila y Zúñiga. The novel not only uses elements from the painting, but adds others from the *Comentarios*. Indeed, Cervantes' text clearly points to this historical model. As noted above, the misplacement of a historical work among texts of fiction following the 'inquisition' of Don Quixote's books points to its importance. A work on the feats of Charles V in Germany may have been a more important model for Don Quixote's mad deeds than the books of chivalry. Thus, history and fiction are intertwined in the mind of a protagonist whose imitative furor will just as easily follow Amadís as Charles V. This in itself signals the deep intrusion of historical contexts within the seemingly metafictional text. Ávila y Zúñiga's history and Titian's portrait of Charles V serve as two of the bases for Don Quixote's actions. The latter's crazed adventures reflect through a distorted mirror the famous deeds of the former emperor. Furthermore, both the emperor and the knight consciously follow Julius Caesar. It is no coincidence that Charles V was particularly fond of Caesar's *Commentaries* and wrote his own to rival his model. Indeed this is one of the few books Charles took with him to Yuste when he abdicated (Kleinschmidt 2004, 225). Thus, it makes sense that Cervantes refers to Caesar's *Commentaries* in the prologue to his novel. Are we to envision both Caesar's and Charles's works as models for the writing of Don Quixote's exploits? If we add to this Ávila y Zúñiga's text with its many references to Charles as Caesar, we see that a series of reflections is thus created between knight, emperor, and Caesar placing all three under greater scrutiny and problematizing their "historical" narratives, their bellicose behaviour and its results.

For Fernando Checa, the emperor's determination in Titian's painting signals his imperial *maiestas*, or what he calls the 'vencimiento de sí mismo' (conquering of himself) (1994, 44). By the time Titian was painting both the Munich *Portrait of Charles V* and *Charles V at Mühlberg*, the emperor was suffering from ill health. Already in 1545, 'his health was beginning to break down and he was frequently bedridden with gout' (Fernández Alvarez 1975, 133).[40] The 1548 seated portrait shows him with a cane 'characterizing him as a very human sufferer from gout – then a most formidable disease' (Panofsky 1969, 83). Although his face is sickly pale, he is 'yet unperturbed and imperturbable' (Panofsky 1969, 85). The golden hue of the sun, symbolic of the Golden Age in *Charles V at Mühlberg*, also reflects upon the pale skin of the sickly yet determined emperor, imbuing him with a slight yellowish tint, what Covarrubias calls 'oro amortiguado' (pale gold) (1987, 110) which, for the period was emblematic of illness and melancholy. Paleness[41] and illness also characterize Don Quixote's body and countenance. When Sancho comes to report as to his master's fitness during the penance in the Sierra Morena, he tells his listeners 'como le había hallado desnudo en camisa, flaco, amarillo y muerto de hambre' (he'd found him ... dressed only in his shirt, skinny, pale and half dead with hunger) (1978, 1.29.361; 262). He is certainly not much better when he turns up at his village at the end of part 1, led there in an enchanted cart: 'Su tío y su señor venía flaco y amarillo, y tendido sobre un montón de heno' (Their master and uncle had come back, thin and pale, and lying on top of a pile of hay) (1978, 1.52.602; 472–3). Both descriptions foreground Don Quixote's yellow complexion. This is clearly a sign of serious illness and even of approaching death as Sebastián de Covarrubias explains: 'Entre las colores se tiene por la más infelice, por ser la de la muerte, y de la larga y peligrosa enfermedad y la color de los enamorados' (Among the colors this one is held among the most unhappy, being the color of death, and of a protracted and dangerous illness and the color of lovesickness) (1987, 110). Covarrubias relates it to lovers because in its most extreme form, passion is associated with melancholy. Both W.L. Fichter (1927, 223) and Teresa Soufas (1990, 81–2) have provided many examples of literary texts of the Spanish Golden Age where yellow stands for sadness, grief, and melancholy.[42] It is thus not surprising that the golden hue of a perfect age is also translated in the 'oro amortiguado' (pale gold) (Covarrubias 1987, 110) of the ill idealists, Don Quixote and Emperor Charles V.

Only one of Titian's colours is left to mention. The prominence of black in the painting further underlines determination in the face of mighty odds. Indeed, black (and yellow) are the colours of melancholy, and Charles V suffered from this humoral imbalance (Panofsky 1969, 7). Fernández Alvarez, disputing any triumphal interpretations of the painting, claims that Titian's portrait 'conveys no air of triumph: the bloodshot eyes have a sad and defeated look' (1975, fig. 36). There may be sadness, but there is no defeatist look in this portrait of the emperor. Paleness, sadness, and melancholy are certainly traits that the emperor shares with Don Quixote. While the emperor carried on with his mission, so did Don Quixote. And both were eventually defeated in their quest for empire. Charles had to hastily leave the meeting with Ferdinand at Innsbruck, knowing that the empire would be divided,[43] while Don Quixote would be taken home 'enchanted' and yellow at the end of the 1605 novel, and totally defeated by the disguised Sansón Carrasco at the end of the 1615 text. Charles could indulge his melancholy when he abdicated the throne in favour of Philip II and retreated to the monastery of Yuste (taking with him a number of paintings by Titian). For an emperor who saw his imperial quest in terms of chivalric pursuits, this was both a defeat and a blessing since he could attempt to reconcile his life with God's dictates before death. Don Quixote's monastery was simply his home, to which he returned at the end of both the 1605 and 1615 texts. Like Charles, he turned away from the world in the final episode, and in a melancholy mood, proclaimed that he was now Alonso Quijano the Good rather than Don Quixote. Imperial biography and fictional text both end with a turning away from chivalry and a desire to make peace with eternity.

An imperial portrait, then, seems to inform the action of a novel establishing detailed and intriguing parallels between Charles V and Don Quixote. While many of these links shatter through parody (like the broken lance), others infuse the knight with a certain air of decorum that even his enemy and biographer, Cide Hamete Benengeli, cannot fully dispel. The ability of a painting to keep reappearing in different guises throughout the novel goes far beyond the technique of ekphrasis. Cervantes may well be using anamorphosis, a technique that goes back to the beginnings of the sixteenth century. In these works of art, the observer can discover new objects, figures or perspectives when looking at the work from different points of view. One such composition may be particularly apt for our discussion. Erhard Schön, a Nuremberg engraver and disciple of Dürer, presents the observer with what appears to be a jumbled set of lines and meaningless drawings. Only at the very top and bottom can we make out a meaningful sketch: a castle or palace on a hillside and a landscape with camels. However, the meaningless lines, when viewed laterally, show portraits of Charles V, Ferdinand I, Pope Paul III, and the French king Francis I (Jeanneret 2001, 258–61). These are, of course, key figures for Cervantes' novel. Francis I allowed Charles to display his chivalric spirit by first imprisoning him after the battle of Pavia and then releasing him on his word. Ferdinand is to obtain the Holy Roman Empire after Charles's meeting with him at Innsbruck. And Paul III is both the pope that ushers in the Counter-Reformation and a patron of the arts who impels Michelangelo to decorate the Sistine Chapel. All these figures, then, are folded into Cervantes's novel. It takes a way of looking, an active reader, to bring out the images of an anamorphic text that hides historical figures and paintings from the Italian Renaissance in surprising and revealing ways.

8 Dancing with Giants: Philostratus

But as they move in a circle, behold the result – you see in imagination the whirling of a wheel ...

Philostratus the Younger, *Imagines*

Considering the length of *Don Quixote*, it is surprising that the adventure of the windmills, taking up a few paragraphs in the text, can come to represent the substance of it. In many ways, the episode is not unique, following what, for Ian Watt, is the pattern of the knight's adventures: 'a visual stimulus, a misinterpretation of the stimulus by Quixote in terms of his chivalric compulsions; a realistic correction by Sancho Panza ...' (1996, 64).[1] Perhaps one of the reasons it has captured the imagination of readers and artists has to do with the scene's amazing pictorialism, the ease with which the visual imagination can recreate not only the objects described (the visual stimulus), but also the transformation of objects into threatening animate beings (Don Quixote's misinterpretation). In fact, it is the very juxtaposition of the two descriptions, that of windmills and that of giants, that underlines the pictorial amplitude of the scene. Taken by itself, the description of the windmills is minimal: 'En esto, descubrieron treinta o cuarenta molinos de viento que hay en aquel campo' (As he was saying this, they caught sight of thirty or forty windmills standing on the plain) (1978, 1.8.128; 63). But the true discovery is that these objects can be viewed in a different way by the knight who sees 'donde se descubren treinta, o poco más, desaforados gigantes' (where stand thirty or more monstrous giants) (1978, 1.8.129; 63). The link between objects and giants is not new to Cervantes. Augustin Redondo has pointed out that in chivalric romances there is often a connection between towers and towering giants, a link that Cervantes himself includes in his novel.[2] There are even pictorial representations of this; Bosch's *Temptation of St Anthony*, which includes a tower with agitated arms (Redondo 1998, 339). Sancho also alerts the reader to another striking similarity between windmills and giants: 'Y los que en ellos parecen brazos son las aspas que, volteadas del viento, hacen andar la piedra del molino' (And what look to you like arms are sails – when the wind turns them they make the millstones go round) (1978, 1.8.129; 64). And this is precisely what happens in the scene. As the knight spurs his steed towards what for him are threatening enemies, a soft wind begins to blow: 'Levantóse en este momento un poco de viento, y las grandes aspas empezaron a moverse' (A gust of wind arose, and the great sails began to move) (1978, 1.8.129; 64). These turns become, in the knight's imagination, the moving arms of the hundred-handed giants.

This scene, then, seems to fall under what Jean Hagstrum has called 'pictorialism.' To be pictorial 'a description or an image must be, in its essentials, capable of translation into painting or some other visual art. It need not resemble a particular painting or even a school of painting. But its leading details and their manner and order of presentation must be imaginable as a painting or sculpture ... The pictorial implies some limitation of meaning ... Meaning must seem to arise from the *visibilia* present. General didactic statement may appear, but in a pictorial context it must seem, like an inscription on a statue, to be subordinate to the visual presentation' (1958, xxiii). It is the sparse but tangible *visibilia* of the scene that led Gustave Doré, the most famous illustrator of the *Quixote*, to draw this scene not once, but twice (fig. 8.1). Doré first shows Don Quixote as he engages the giants/windmills in battle, and then (fig. 8.2) portrays him as he lies defeated at their feet. Doré concentrates on the actual objects present, and thus, he does not include in his scenes Don Quixote's imaginative leap that links windmills to giants: 'donde se descubren treinta, o poco más, desaforados gigantes' (where stand thirty or more monstrous giants) (1978, 1.8.129; 63). And yet, Gustave Doré is aware that it is the very juxtaposition of the two descriptions, that of windmills and that of giants, that underlines the pictorial amplitude of the scene. Without portraying the imaginative vision of the knight, Doré is able to give his inanimate windmills the illusion of animation and purpose; he is even able to endow these objects with a certain threatening quality. The threatening sky compounds the menacing presence of the mills. Doré even creates the illusion of movement by showing Don Quixote's lance stuck on one of the windmill's arms. Since it appears to be moving upwards, this motion is able to unseat the knight from his horse. The movement of the sails of the mill, together with the suggestion of a coming storm, are key elements in transferring time and movement (narrative) to the stillness of a picture.

Although Doré hints at the transformation of windmills into animate beings, he fails to represent the metamorphosis since this is something that takes place in Don Quixote's mind. But it is precisely this transformation of windmills into giants that gives the scene its imaginative power. By imparting upon the windmills a new dimension, Don Quixote allows for a more complex definition of the pictorial, one in which the viewer within the text or picture transforms the way in which the external viewer of the work sees the scene. Indeed, Don Quixote encourages the inside viewer (in this case, Sancho) to see with his eyes 'aquellos que allí ves ... de los brazos largos' (those giants that you can see over there ... with long arms) (1978, 1.8.129; 63). A work of art that would reproduce this distinctive form of pictorialism must then take into account the process of perception, the way in which different subjects see and interpret *visibilia*. During the sixteenth century, the notion of anamorphosis in artistic representation came into vogue. This technique, as noted in the previous chapter, seeks to produce a different image when an observer looks at it from a different perspective. For example, 'Jerónimo de Alcalá speaks of a skull that, seen from two different oblique angles, would alternately appear as a woman and as a young man' (Castillo 2001, 2). What in painting came to be known as anamorphosis is intimately linked to the well-known perspectivism of Cervantes' *Don Quixote*, as delineated by Leo Spitzer, Américo Castro, and other critics.[3] An illustration by Theodoro Miciano for the 1952 edition of *Don Quixote* takes into account the double perspective of perception as represented by Don Quixote's and Sancho's imaginations. In the foreground, the stone from a windmill intrudes into our perception of the landscape. So large is this windmill that the viewer sees only part of it. Sancho, lamenting his master's madness, faces this gigantic object. Its materiality thus reflects Sancho's imagination. The background includes insubstantial images of threatening gigantic figures that blend with the nebulous sky. Don Quixote is relegated to the background, where he is seen battling the images from his imagination. Thus solidity contrasts with insubstantiality and a vast landscape that beckons the knight to adventure is opposed to the solid wall of materiality against which Sancho leans. This illustration both transforms the text by foregrounding Sancho and captures an essential element of the narrative, the relationship between perceiver and object.

Although narrative pictorialism and an incipient anamorphosis help to explain why the episode of the windmills was so popular with visual artists, it does not fully illuminate the technique utilized in Cervantes' narrative. The narrative itself is based on a certain stillness, the menacing presence of the windmills. Their description calls for ekphrasis, while pointedly denying the reader this pleasure. At the same time, the fury of the winds that set in motion Don Quixote's defeat points to the precarious technology that the knight wishes to destroy. In this chapter, I would like to study the pseudoekphrastic technique of the writer together with the technology of the windmills. Such an *ars combinatoria* has classical precedent since the term *techné* in both Plato[4] and Aristotle refers to both art and technology. Since the latter believes that all made things can be evaluated by their level of *techné* or skill,[5] it is possible to look at the episode in terms of the uses of imitation and the skill in making objects. This double *techné*[6] points to the fact that both the imitation of ekphrasis and the invention of the windmills are linked to classical texts. Their views, as reinterpreted by the Renaissance, will inform Cervantes' episode.

As has been noted previously, in Hellenistic rhetoric, ekphrasis referred simply to an extended verbal description of some object. The purpose of the description was 'to intrude upon the flow of discourse and, for its duration, to suspend the argument' (Krieger 1992, 7). If we look carefully at Cervantes' scene, we discover that the flow of the narrative is hardly ever interrupted. The description of objects is minimal, barely taking into account any of their characteristics. But ekphrasis assumed a more specific meaning in Philostratus: the verbal description of a specific type of object, an art object, a painting.[7] Thus in Philostratus's *Imagines*, the verbal and the visual vie with each other. The ornate rhetoric of this work seeks to surpass the beauty and complexity of the paintings described at a villa in Naples. Philostratus's grandson, also a sophist, continued this tradition with his own *Imagines*. It is here that we encounter the use of the term 'ekphrasis' in reference to works of art (Krieger 1992, 8). His successor, Callistratus, turns from painting to sculpture in his *Descriptions*. These three works were published in Venice by Aldus Manutius, an important humanist whose publishing house, started in 1495, is responsible for an extensive list of Greek texts (Wilson 1992, 127). There were also Latin versions, and they seem to have impacted patrons, writers, and painters of the Renaissance: 'We know that Alfonso d'Este borrowed, and kept too long, his sister Isabella's Latin translation of the *Imagines*' (Kennedy 1964, 163–4). Both Ariosto and Titian may have learned of the text from Alfonso, who decided to create a 'studio' in Ferrara to rival the one at the Neopolitan villa as described by Philostratus. Titian's *The Worship of Venus*, based on Philostratus, was painted for Alfonso's studio. Other works by Titian also rely on descriptions by Philostratus, in particular, the *Bacchanal of the Andrians*.[8]

Philostratus was also read by writers and humanists in England and France, Shakespeare among them.[9] His fame may have been augmented by name confusion since he was the son-in-law of the Philostratus who wrote the *Life of Apollonius of Tyana* and a work on the gymnosophists.[10] I believe that Cervantes forms part of this select European readership. He would certainly have come across Philostratus's name in Della Porta's *L'Arte del ricordare*.[11] And indeed, Cervantes acknowledges the tradition of ekphrasis, incorporating it in the episode following that of the windmills.

The windmill episode is, in a sense, a ludic preface to the more obvious and complete ekphrasis of the following chapter of Cervantes' novel. Here, we come to a break in the action at the very moment in which Don Quixote and the *vizcaíno*, both 'con las espadas altas y desnudas' (with naked swords aloft) (1978, 1.9.139; 73) are ready to engage in battle. The fictional author thus sets out to find the rest of the manuscript in order to continue his tale. When he finds a copy of the work in Toledo's market, the action is further delayed by a description of this manuscript. This is the oldest definition of ekphrasis, a stop in the narrative to describe an object. As the manuscript is being described in Cervantes' novel, the fictive author states: 'Estaba en el primero cartapacio pintada muy al natural la batalla de don Quijote con el vizcaíno' (In the first notebook there was a realistic picture of Don Quixote's battle with the Basque) (1978, 1.9.144; 75). A lengthy narration of this illustration creates a further break in the action and takes us to the second definition of ekphrasis, a description in words of a work of art. Thus, we are in the presence of a metaekphrasis. To further foreground the interaction between the verbal and the visual, we are told that this illustration contains writing, the names of the participants in the battle.

Although this is the most obvious ekphrasis in the novel, one that illustrates the 'partial magic' of the text (Alter 1975, 6–11), one that foregrounds the novel's artifice and thus its self-consciousness (Alter 1975, x), illustrators repeatedly turn away from this in order to focus on the episode of the windmills. Partial magic is dismissed in favour of what I have called 'simple magic.' This is how a modern translator has rendered Ariosto's term for the extended ekphrasis in canto 33 of his *Orlando furioso*, in which Merlin's gallery foretells the future. Cervantes' 'simple magic,' although not about the future, delves into enchanters, and thus links perspectivism, the oscillation of reality, to the magic of a text that is replete with ekphrastic and anamorphic moments. As has been noted above, Cervantes' use of ekphrasis is quirky, almost as deranged as the vision of his knight. In the adventure of the windmills, ekphrasis is almost disabled by quickness,[12] by a refusal to stop the plot, and by the fact that descriptions are often embedded in the dialogue rather than in the primary narrative. The presence of this ancient technique has to do with allusions to previous ekphrasitic literature. We can barely locate traces of the first type of ekphrasis, the description of an object, both in the narrative itself and in Sancho's account of the windmills, while the narrative itself only names, but does not describe: 'En esto, descubrieron treinta o cuarenta molinos de viento que hay en aquel campo' (As he was saying this, they caught sight of thirty or forty windmills standing on the plain) (1978, 1.8.128; 63). Details are left to the viewers, Don Quixote and Sancho. The squire counters Don Quixote's imaginings by describing the windmills: they 'no son gigantes, sino molinos de viento, y lo que en ellos parecen brazos son las aspas, que, volteadas del viento, hacen andar la piedra del molino' (aren't gaints, they're windmills and what look to you like arms are sails – when the wind turns them they make the millstones go round) (1978, 1.8.129; 64). This is actually a description of the technology behind the mill's operations.

While Sancho describes the *techné* of a real object, Don Quixote portrays an art object derived from his imagination. He cannot perceive the windmills' actual shape even when he gets close, 'ni echaba de ver, aunque estaba ya bien cerca, lo que eran [molinos]' (nor saw what stood in front of him, even though he was by now upon them) (1978, 1.8.129; 64). This misperception is based on personification, on figurative thinking. The knight sees stones and gives them the appearance of giants. Very much like Michelangelo, the knight configures stone into gigantic statues.[13] Don Quixote, then, is an artist who reinvents the reality around him. The reader gathers that he is interpreting since he does not say that he sees giants but they 'se descubren' (are discovered) (1978, 1.8.129).[14]

As Sebastián de Covarrubias explains: 'Descubrir. Manifestar lo que estava cubierto ... hallar cosas nuevas' (To disover. To manifest what was covered ... to find new things) (1987, 457). What the stones are covering are the shapes of giants.[15] The windmills, in a sense, are statues so artfully wrought in the mind of the knight-artist that they are giants, such as those sculpted by Michelangelo. The reader is thus in the presence of an ur-ekphrasis, a technique that reveals the inception of a work of art in the mind of its creator. But technology has also been described as a mode of revealing (Maiorino 1992, 152). There may be a doubling of meaning here, referring to both art and technology. Don Quixote is transforming technology into art, incorporating the two meanings of *techné*.

Discussing a painting of Pasiphae and the Bull, Philostratus tells of the greatness of the ancient artificer Daedalus in sculpting statues (1931, 65; 1.16) – never mind that he also 'designed the equipment ... for Pasiphae to couple with a bull' (Maiorino 1992, 144). Philostratus is alluding here to an ancient Greek legend, where Daedalus is said to have made statues that could move and even walk, where stone acquires life.[16] Thus, Daedalus was interested in a double *techné*, the art of sculpting and the technology of making objects move. In Cervantes' text, the statues of giants seem to move, to come to life, as they had with Daedalus, and, like Daedalus's works, they do not speak, although the knight addresses himself to them. Cervantes, then, may be borrowing from the tradition of ekphrasis and from the ancient legend of Daedalus, in order to fashion this pictorial episode. But his ekphrasis exists only in allusion and imagination. It barely spills into the text. As opposed to the scene of the *Vizcaíno*, the art objects exist only in the mind of the perceiver, Don Quixote. The narrative, then, does not describe a sculpture made by an artist, but the process through which an artist (Don Quixote – a new Daedalus and a pseudo-Michelangelo) artfully reenvisions reality. The reader is led to imagine what is present in the knight's visual imagination, and thus becomes cocreator of this ur-ekphrasis. It is Don Quixote's imaginary art that draws the reader and a whole succession of artists to draw these menacing windmills. Don Quixote's *techné* is pure art since the statues move only in his imagination.

Philostratus the Younger also refers to Daedalus in a scene that is a tour de force, containing several layers of competition between the verbal and the visual. He describes a painting which depicts the battle between Eurypylus and Neoptolemus during the Trojan War. In this battle, the latter, being the son of Achilles, carries his famous shield.

Philostratus describes the cities, the celestial constellations, and the battles that are found in this painting of the shield. Thus, we move towards origins, to the locus classicus of ekphrasis, the description of Achilles' shield in the *Iliad* (1988, 2.323–33; 18.478–608). This epic ekphrasis represents a turning point in the Homeric poem. Thetis asks Hephaestus to make Achilles new armour; this beautiful and complex work of art deflects Achilles' wrath towards Agamemnon. He now decides to avenge the slaying of Patroclus. The shield contains five layers, fashioned from different metals such as tin, gold, bronze, and silver. As James Heffernan asserts: 'The shield is shielded by the very language that purports to reveal it to us ... Exactly what Hephaestus wrought on the shield is ultimately impossible to visualize ... All we can see ... is Homer's language which not only rivals but actually displaces the work of art it ostensibly describes and salutes' (1993, 14). But Philostratus points to a painting that depicts this impossible scene, and then proceeds to describe it. Most of his prose is devoted to a recounting of the images on the shield. When he comes to a scene of dancers, he alludes to a 'chorus which Daedalus is said to have given to Ariadne' (1931, 341; 10). Hepahaestus the lame can depict a floor on which dancers dance nimbly, just as the mythical 'blind Homer' can compose an ekphrasis where one can see with the mind's eye what may be impossible to depict. Before them is Daedalus who wrought this dance floor. The whirling figures of Daedalus, Hephaestus, and Homer are described by Philostratus: 'But as they move in a circle, behold the result – you see in imagination the whirling of a wheel' (1931, 341; 10). Don Quixote, as a new Daedalus, also imagines a whirling of a wheel. As the wind turns the sails of the mill, he asks us to view them as the whirling limbs of giants. As with Philostratus the Younger, the reader is inclined to ask: Who paints, who sculpts, and who writes? And who wins the forever ongoing battle between the visual and the verbal?

In spite of the many questions raised, Philostratus makes it clear that Daedalus's art of making moving statues is inextricably interrelated to Hephaestus's fashioning of a shield. And we may ask: What of Don Quixote's shield? This question has already been discussed in a previous chapter. Suffice it to say that its description in chapter 2 of Cervantes' novel may contain reminiscences from Philostratus. As has been previously noted, when Don Quixote first sallies forth, he has no device since he has no great feat to commemorate. His 'armas blancas' (white arms) recall that Eurypylus wore 'no device' (Philostratus 1931, 327; 10). Don Quixote wants to polish his shield and arms to make them shine and, indeed, Eurypylus's shield 'gives forth like a rainbow, a light that varies with his position and movement' (Philostratus 1931, 327; 10).

But let us return to the adventure of the windmills. Here, the sails of the mill, the arms of the giants, defeat Don Quixote. To what *techné* is this failure due, to art or technology? Daedalus too is remembered for many dubious and failed technologies. The wings he crafted for his son Icarus led to tragedy. The youth flew too close to the sun and the wax on the wings melted, causing his fall. Like Icarus, Don Quixote is lifted up to the heavens. Instead of wings he flies on the sails of the mill. And also like him, he is precipitously brought down. A number of illustrations of the windmill episode, including Doré's, show a shining sun in the background. Pilar Coomonte draws a huge sun whose lines are intermingled and confused with the sails of the mill.[17] Such illustrations recall that Don Quixote's imaginings are brought about, in part, by the heat of the sun: 'Y el sol entraba tan apriesa y con tanto ardor que fuera bastante a derretirle los sesos, si alguno tuviera' (And the sun was rising so fast and becoming so hot, that his brains would have melted, if he'd had any) (1978, 1.2.81; 31). The sun seemingly causes the downfall of both Icarus and Don Quixote. They seem victims of solar power and of technology.

There are other Daedalian *technai* in Cervantes' novel,[18] but let us continue with giants and return to Daedalus later. Giants, of course, are a fundamental element in any chivalric narrative and Cervantes' novel is constantly alluding to these beings. There is the gigantic moor Fierabrás who robbed the precious liquid in which Christ was embalmed (1978, 1.10.149); the 'descomunal gigante' (enormous giant) who bloodies Don Quixote's jaw in the inn/castle (1978, 1.17.207; 130) as the knight is wooed by the princess/Maritornes. There are also those giants who, in the imagination of Don Quixote, go down in defeat, such as Brocabruno de la Gran Fuerza (1978, 1.21.258), Caraculiambro (1978, 1.1.77) and Pandafilando de la Fosca Vista (1978, 1.30.373–5; 1.35.438). Stressing the importance of giants in the romances of chivalry, Augustin Redondo argues that from the very first chapter of *Don Quixote*, the knight wishes to triumph over one of these creatures (1998, 325ff). And yet, the first giants found in the novel seem to have little to do with these chivalric spawns. The prologue mentions two giants: Goliath and Cacus. Both reappear in the novel. While the height of Goliath is discussed in the 1615 novel (1978, 2.1.50), several figures in the 1605 text are linked to Cacus.[19] As noted in chapter 5, neither of these two figures belongs to the chivalric tradition, being biblical and Virgilian in origin. Cervantes' giants, and particularly the windmill giants, I would argue, are a mixed breed. Certainly, there is a chivalric surface on which they tread. But if we investigate further, we discover biblical echoes and clear classical models. And, of course, such models will lead to examples from the ekphrastic tradition and from Italian Renaissance art. It is their mixed ancestry that makes these giants paragons of the monstrous, vivid examples of the excesses and the virtuosity of imitation.

Both the biblical and the Virgilian giants of the prologue are part of the Cervantine construction of the windmill-giants. In a suggestive although flawed discussion of the episode, George Camamis argues that the windmill 'is a perfect figure of the cross of Christianity,' a Christianity that had split into numerous sects, perhaps thirty-four, a number which would correspond to the thirty-some windmills seen by don Quixote' (1991, 238). Don Quixote's battle represents the Catholic Church's and specifically the pope's battle against heretics.[20] Even if we are to reject Camamis's interpretation, the image of Don Quixote as a new David battling the mighty Goliath had already been suggested in the prologue by the friend's advice to transform a giant in the text into a Goliath. Indeed, the thirty or forty windmills in the Cervantine episode can recall the forty days the Philistines threatened the army of Israel (Samuel 1:17). Like a new David, Don Quixote appears to be at a disadvantage. His emaciated body, like David's frail youthfulness, contrasts with the giant's bulk and size. The knight's one lance, like David's sling, is but little comfort against the might of the foe. And yet, the knight, like David, believes that although the enemy appears to be much more powerful, he will win since he has God on his side. Don Quixote asks Sancho to pray while he does battle and explicitly states that he is fighting a 'buena guerra' (just war), one that is a 'gran servicio de Dios' (great service to God) (1978, 1.8.129; 63). Don Quixote's attitude may recall Titian's famous painting of *David and Goliath* (fig. 8.3), in which David takes on the pose of a Christian saint, 'his arms ecstatically raised and joined above his head' in prayer (Panofsky 1969, 35).[21] But Don Quixote is not a new David. His battle against the monstrous giants, be they Philistines or Protestants, ends in disaster. God does not appear to sanction his holy war.

Although Don Quixote may be viewing himself as a Christian exemplar who battles the monstrous Other in this episode, he is also comparing his feats to those of ancient epic heroes. Even though he does not bring up the figure of Cacus, Don Quixote does allude to another ancient giant. When the wind moves the sails of the windmills, the knight sees them as gigantic arms, and challenges the nearest giant/edifice: 'Pues aunque mováis más brazos que los del gigante Briareo, me lo habéis de pagar' (Though you flourish more arms than the giant Briareus, I will make you pay for it) (1978, 1.8.130; 64). In substituting Briareus for Cacus, the text is granting greater power and invincibility to the windmills/giants. While Cacus was a three-headed fire-breathing giant, Briareus was one of the three hundred-handed (or hundred-armed) giants, born close to the beginning of time, offspring of Sky and Earth. Due to his great might, Briareus was given the task of guarding the Titans in Tartarus. The substitution of Cacus for Briareus, then, renders the windmills more powerful while at the same time pointing to a classical text, a famous illustration, and an epic ekphrasis.

In Plutarch's *Life of Marcellus*, we read that this Roman consul was for the longest time unable to take Syracuse because its inhabitants were utilizing a number of engines designed by Archimedes 'against which no man could stand' (1996, 377). These machines would fire all sorts of missile weapons and immense masses of stone. Some contraptions would even lift a ship up in the air and shake all the mariners from its deck. In an often quoted speech, Marcellus asks his soldiers: 'What ... must we give up fighting with this geometrical Briareus, who plays pitch-and-toss with our ships, and with the multitude of darts which he showers at a single moment upon us, really outdoes the hundred-handed giants of mythology?' (1996, 378). Like Marcellus, Don Quixote is battling such a monstrous machine. In calling a windmill Briareus, he foreshadows his own fate. The windmill lifts him up into the air and shakes him off his horse, just like Archimedes' engines removed sailors from a ship. Like Marcellus, Don Quixote views a technical invention in terms of a giant of old. Iván Jaksic has argued: 'Cervantes dramatizes the tensions between past and present by making use of such technologies as windmills, water-powered grain mills, fulling hammers and firearms, among others. He associates these technologies with modernity, and uses the anachronistic Don Quixote as a vehicle for illustrating the impact of technology on human sensibility ... the battered knight demonstrates how prosaic and removed from human values technology can be' (1994, 77).

Although Jaksic's summary represents a good starting point, the question of technology in the novel is much more complex, for Don Quixote at times embraces it. Jaksic mentions the water-powered mills, but the knight does not attack them.[22] He only vents his fury at the windmills. The allusion to Briareus in Cervantes foregrounds the notion that the battle over technology was fought as much in classical times as in the days when *Don Quixote* came to light. Plutarch makes it clear that Archimedes was much more interested in the study of geometry than in mechanics. He created the machines that almost save his city as mere 'amusement' (1996, 376). Otherwise, he was totally devoted to abstract geometry and believed that mechanics were a 'corruption and annihilation of the one good of geometry, which was thus shamefully turning its back upon the unembodied objects of pure intelligence to recur to sensation' (376). As Giancarlo Maiorino asserts: 'Euclid and Archimedes did not promote progress in a modern sense, and the secondary role that technology was allowed to play in Greek culture was a factor in its decline' (1992, 142). The Platonic rejection of technology is also present in Cervantes' novel.[23] Don Quixote battles against a Briarean giant who destroys the 'human' values of chivalry. The sixteenth century in Spain had been a period of significant advances in technology, including engines of war. During this era, humanists such as Juan Luis Vives, Fernán Pérez de Oliva, and Pedro Mexía praise and disseminate such 'progress' (López Piñero 1979, 154–63).[24] By the beginning of the seventeenth century, however, we see, in López Piñero's words, both the 'repression' and the 'collapse' of science and technology resulting from religious and political imperatives (1979, 372–3). In Cervantes' *Don Quixote*, the knight battles certain forms of technology, validating his stance through a desire to return to a simpler age, be it a Golden Age or an age of chivalry. For example, Don Quixote rails against firearms, while praising their absence from the Golden Age: 'Bien hayan aquellos benditos siglos que carecieron de la espantable furia de aquestos endemoniados instrumentos de artillería, a cuyo inventor tengo para mi que en el infierno se le está dando premio de su diabólica invención' (A blessing on those happy ages that did not know the dreadful fury of these devilish instruments of artillery, whose inventor is, I feel sure, being rewarded in hell for his diabolical creation) (1978, 1.38.470–1; 358). He adds that these weapons are inimical to the chivalric art. In many ways, Don Quixote seems to want to imitate Charles V, and become a *dominus mundi* who espouses the ideals of chivalry. But Charles was very interested in technology. The knight's opposition to certain advances may seem to establish a tension between the two figures. But, let us reconsider.

Charles so much admired the inventions and machines of Juanelo Turriano that he invited him to join him at Yuste. Cervantes certainly knew of his inventions, alluding to the 'artificio de Juanelo' (craftsmanship of Juanelo) in *La ilustre fregona* (*The Illustrious Kitchenmaid*). This refers to the strange and wondrous device used by Juanelo to bring up water from the Tajo into the city of Toledo.[25] This contraption is praised in a 1616 poem by José de Valdivielso (1616, 427).

Praise of Juanelo also connected him to antiquity. Ambrosio de Morales, a historian read by Cervantes, called Turriano a new Archimedes (López Piñero 1979, 156). It may well be that the Briarean windmills not only allude to ancient technology, but to its advances in Cervantes' Spain. In the *Veintiún libros de los ingenios y máquinas de Juanelo Turriano* (*Twenty-one Books of the Devices and Machines of Juanelo Turriano*), a treatise attributed to Turriano,[26] this technician from Cremona, Italy, describes in his eleventh book the various types of mills. He devotes a great deal of attention to water mills, but also discusses those run by animals ('de sangre' [of blood] [1983, 341]), by humans, by weights, etc.[27] Thus, Don Quixote's mills seem to fuse both the Briarean inventions of Archimedes and Turriano's creations. However, a careful reading of Turriano's chapter on mills shows that he, like Don Quixote, disliked the 'molinos de viento' (windmills). Turriano complains that windmills 'no sirven en España y menos en Italia por causa que los vientos no son ordinarios' (are not useful in Spain and less in Italy because the winds are not ordinary) (1983, 342).[28] Don Quixote assails these inventions as 'viles criaturas' (vile creatures) since they do not belong in the Spanish landscape. Turriano explains that windmills are suited to Germany, Flanders, and France since the winds in these countries are moderate. In Spain, however, windmills are useless because of the very great fury of the winds: they 'no se pueden conservar por causa del gradissimo furor que llevaría que todo lo rompería' (cannot be conserved due to the great frenzy [of the winds] that would destroy everything) (1983, 342). Following Turriano, then, Don Quixote is right in trying to extirpate such giants/windmills from Spain. But as he gallops forth and attacks the mill, he is defeated precisely by that element that Turriano warns against: 'La volvió el viento con tanta furia que hizo la lanza pedazos' (The wind turned it with so much fury that it shattered the lance into pieces) (1978, 1.8.130). Thus, the furious wind that is supposed to make the windmills useless in Spain becomes the wind that defeats Don Quixote. In this example, the knight's attack is not against technology, but against what Juanelo deems to be inventions that are inappropriate for Spain. In this sense, there is no tension between the chivalric and inventive Charles V and the crazed knight from La Mancha. Indeed, Charles V revelled in spectacles that resurrected the chivalric world of old. In these spectacles, mechanical machines, inventions of a modern world, helped to enhance the allure of the medieval past. At a feast for Princess María de Portugal in 1543, for example, the scenery included not only a castle but also a moving and fire-breathing dragon or 'sierpe.' To further astound the audience, twelve knights emerged from the body of the dragon (Ferrer Valls 1990, 23; López 2002, 190).[29]

While Archimedes practised technology only for amusement, Daedalus was most serious in its pursuit, building Pasiphae's contraption; constructing the labyrinth that was to hold and hide the offspring, made possible by technology; and designing the wings that lead to Icarus's fatal fall. In conceiving his giants, Don Quixote clothes technology with transgression and hubris. This figuration makes his attack much easier. And yet, his ability to see whirling giants links him to Daedalus. Don Quixote's machines, then, reflect both the warrior who is inspired to destroy the material evils of certain technology and the artist who partakes of transgression and hubris to demonstrate his talents.

Cervantes' Briareus, then, as a fallen giant and an emblem of fallen inventions akin to diabolical firearms, must be studied as part of Dante's infernal geography. In the *Inferno*, the poet asks Virgil to show him 'the enormous one, Briareus' (1980, 31.99). But he is only allowed to see Anteus who is unfettered and can speak. The other is further down in the pit and 'is bound up and just as huge as this one / and even more ferocious in his gaze' (31.104–5). This inability to view the ferocious Briareus is remedied in the *Purgatorio* where there is an effigy of him on the mountainside 'carved more skillfully, with greater sense of likeness' than those on tombstones. Exhibited here are thirteen sculptures, examples of pride. Immediately following the first, Satan, Dante relates: 'I saw, upon the other side, Briareus / transfixed by the celestial shaft: he lay, / ponderous, on the ground, in fatal cold' (1982, 12.28–30).[30] By naming the giant Briareus, Cervantes points to a pagan figure associated with technology and to an infernal example of ekphrasis. Here, Briareus is placed next to other nameless giants and is equated with Satan and pride.[31] The windmills of technology thus acquire a vicious and infernal texture.

Virgil, who guided Dante through the Inferno and the Purgatorio, also wrote of Briareus. The passage in the *Aeneid* in which this giant appears may be considered as yet one more model for the composition of the windmill episode.[32] In the sixth book of the epic, Aeneas descends to the underworld in order to seek his father's advice. In the entrance court or threshold to the realm of Pluto, the Virgilian hero encounters an immense and foreboding tree. 'In the midst an elm, shadowy and vast, spreads her boughs and aged arms, the home which, men say, false Dreams hold in throngs, clinging under every leaf' (1978, 1.527; 6.282–4). The description of the tree is followed immediately by the portrayal of 'many monstrous forms' by the doors of Hades. Together with the Hydra, the Chimerae, Gorgons, and Harpies is Briareus. The aged arms of the elm are replicated in Briareus's hundred arms, thus verbally linking tree and giant. This link may reflect Don Quixote's vision. The knight's perception is nothing more than a false dream, an epic nightmare experienced in the plains of La Mancha. Even Aeneas has difficulty separating the embodied from the disembodied, reality from illusion. As Briareus and other monsters approach, he finds them so threatening that he responds with terror and grasps his sword. Like Don Quixote, the Virgilian hero is about to attack creatures of the imagination. While Aeneas finally heeds the Sybil's warning that these are disembodied spirits who cannot harm him, Don Quixote will not listen to Sancho's reasons. He attacks and is defeated. But then the knight decides to fashion a lance out of the branches of a tree (1978, 1.8.131). The Virgilian elm of illusion becomes for Don Quixote a tree of future hope, from which a new weapon can be forged to fight these creatures of the imagination.

The Virgilian poem with all its ekphrases calls out for artistic imitation in an age where the ancients are revered as authorities, as subjects of imitation, and where the struggle between the verbal and the visual often finds its way into art through pictoric representations of the written. We have seen Raphael's constant allusions to written texts in the figures portrayed in the Stanza della Segnatura. His disciple, Giulio Romano, who took over work at the Stanza and decorated the Sala di Constantino after Raphael's demise, not only echoed this interest in portraying the written, but carried it even further than his teacher. Having moved to Mantua to serve Federigo Gonzaga, he decorated portions of the Palazzo Ducale with rooms for horses, falcons, and emperors. His Sala di Troia has been called by Frederick Hartt 'one of Giulio's most brilliant inventions and one of his worst failures' (1958, 1.179). It is here that we discover *Thetis Buckling on Achilles' Shield*, an audacious attempt to outdo Homer's ekphrasis, on which Virgil based his own pictorial recounting of Aeneas's shield. But let us finish with giants and leave shields for another moment.

Far more audacious are Giulio Romano's decorations for the famed Palazzo del Te. Here, we can discover the Sala dei Giganti, which Hartt calls 'the most fantastic and frightening creation of the entire Italian Renaissance in any medium' (1958, 1.153).[33] Even if Cervantes had been unable to see this Sala he certainly would have read Giorgio Vasari's description of it. And of course, Vasari's detailed narrative is certainly akin to ekphrasis.[34] As Patricia Lee Rubin states: 'Starting from extant works, he [Vasari] placed them in the mind's eye, seizing on and expounding upon details and episodes that made them compelling and lifelike' (1995, 275). Viewing the Room of the Giants (fig. 8.4), Vasari states: 'Wherefore let no one ever think to see a work of the brush more horrible and terrifying' (1996, 2.132). Visitors came from all over the world to see the wonders of this room. Here, the gods watch in horror as Jupiter destroys the giants who have rebelled against the Olympian deities and are ascending the heavens.[35] Some giants are still attacking and 'have upon their backs mountains and immense rocks which they support with their stout shoulders, in order to pile them up and thus ascend to Heaven' (Vasari 1996, 2.131). But most have fallen to Jupiter's thunderbolts, 'upon whom are falling temples, columns, and other pieces of buildings, making a vast slaughter and havoc of those proud beings' (Vasari 1996, 2.131). Indeed, the Sala itself is built as if it is about to fall upon the visitor. A pen and ink drawing of a giant being buried by stone clearly shows that the dangers are brought close to the spectator: 'His bulging forearms and straining back alert the viewer that his bare-knuckled, brute strength alone prevents an inevitable avalanche of boulders into the room' (Taylor 1999, 112). The many pieces and fragments point to the many models used by the artist and can also reflect the allusive power of Cervantes' text, where, through *contaminatio*,[36] chivalric giants can also be glimpsed as figures of ancient and Christian epics, as whirling statues, and as infernal machines. The arms and heads floating amongst rocks could well have provided a model for the conflation of giant with stone (windmills) in Cervantes' novel. The windmill's many arms are reflected in the disembodied limbs and the arms that fight the falling rock in the fresco. The strong winds that are pictured as blowing across the painting may also indicate how the giant/windmill is activated: 'Levantose en esto un poco de viento, y las grandes aspas comenzaron a moverse' (A gust of wind arose, the great sails began to move) (1978, 8.129; 64). Amidst all these giants, 'Giulio painted Briareus in a dark cavern, almost covered with vast fragments of mountains' (Vasari 1996, 1.31). Perhaps this is how Don Quixote viewed the result of his 'buena guerra' (just war) (1978, 1.8.129; 63) against the giants. But he is no Jupiter and his lance does not have the power of the thunderbolt. Indeed, technology is on the side of the giants.

The power of the windmill is delineated in Giulio Romano's hall. Frederick Hartt asserts that 'the very floor participates in the cosmic catastrophe. The center of the design is formed by a sort of pinwheel within a meander ...' (1958, 155). This mill at the very pit of Giulio's room of giants, which also seems to rise to celestial heights, may serve to indicate the infernal site into which the doomed are falling. The menacing and even infernal qualities of Giulio's and Cervantes' mills derive from Dante's description of the deepest circle in hell where Satan's three mouths are likened to the grinding stones of a mill.[37] It is upon Satan that the poet reverses the 'upside down logic of the universe in order to proceed' (Graf 1999, 74–5; Fajardo-Acosta 1989, 15–25; Avery 1961–2, 3). And, as we have seen, this ninth circle or central pit of hell is the infernal home of Briareus. It is quite possible then that Giulio Romano's painting, with echoes of Dante's *Inferno* and with the presence of a Briareus once drawn by Botticelli, evoked by Virgil but rejected by Dante, may have served as the initial trigger for Cervantes' episode of the windmills. The complex iconography of Giulio's giants could also serve as a map for Cervantes' textual and pictorial models. All of these works share a common link, the battle between the verbal and the visual. They seek to represent the amazing and the terrifying in the figure of giants. While for Dante this terror is an absence or a statue, and for Virgil it is a nightmarish apparition, for Botticelli it becomes a trigger for representation, a challenge that is taken up by Giulio Romano. Cervantes cannot allow these whirling stones to stand still. Virgil, Dante, Botticelli, and Giulio Romano have led us to the Cervantine Briareus, a being who in Don Quixote's mind is evil, disembodied, towering, and related to rock. He rises out of the windmills of Don Quixote's mind and becomes the devil's hellish mill. While passing through the windmill in Dante will lead to reverse the upside-down logic of the descent into the Inferno, Don Quixote cannot pass. He is stuck in his hellish imaginings and is defeated by them. He is thus condemned by the mechanics of Archimedes and by the inventions criticized by Juanelo.

But Don Quixote's brief adventure is not just about epic and ekphrasis, about the battle between the verbal and the visual, about the artist and the scientists, about the horrors of technology. There is also the politics of imitation, which serves to further ground the *contaminatio* of fresco and quixotic text. Federico Gonzaga ordered the Sala dei Giganti to be completed in a hurry so that Emperor Charles V could view it on his return to Mantua in 1532. Having witnessed the many wars, battles, and rebellions which plagued the states of northern Italy and having just gone through the famous sack of Rome of 1527, many thought that it was time for a restoration of order through the image of a powerful imperial figure. Thus, the Sala dei Giganti can be seen to represent Charles V as a new Jupiter who subdues the giants of rebellion in Italy – and throughout the empire.[38] The notion of giants brings up not only the mythological context, but also Charles V's fascination with the chivalric, where giants (images of pride, heresy, and paganism) are forever menacing the innocent and are vanquished by Christian knights. To destroy the giants of rebellion, heresy, and paganism, Charles makes use of infernal inventions. He is interested in Juanelo's inventions to make defences for harbours. Indeed, his chancellor decided how many canons were sufficient to protect Milan from the French (Maiorino 1992, 125). Jupiter's thunderbolt is now a proliferation of weapons and engines, of mills and fortified ports.

Cervantes' brief episode of the windmills outshines with its quickness the labours of many who came before. Don Quixote is indeed dancing with giants as he evokes the turning pit of hell, the floor of Giulio's palace, and the gyrating hundred arms of the giants. He dances as he gallops to meet the moving sails of the demonic mill. But his dance breaks the circle of perfection. He is caught in Archimedes' infernal machine. This Briareus lifts him up and shakes him from his horse. Even though Don Quixote is represented as a mock-heroic descendant of Charles V, he will reject the very technology that so much interested the emperor. But in this he is partially justified since Juanelo had objected to the establishment of windmills in Spain. As an imperial figure, the knight fans the winds of war in order to exhibit his might. But Don Quixote's lance no longer has the power of Jupiter's thunderbolt. His imaginings may call upon Daedalus, or his modern successor, Leonardo da Vinci, who drew a giant crossbow (Maiorino 1992, 158–9). But unlike these artists, Don Quixote will not enter the mechanical world, will not soil his hands to fashion weapons of war. Rather, he would return to an age where these were not available. His desire to bring back a fabled Golden Age, an age of innocence, is foiled by a menacing present. It is also foiled by the past, for even his most ancient models, the Greeks, had to deal with the question of technology. While the imagination of Don Quixote can conceive of Daedalian feats, his pictorial designs are always erased by his inability to sculpt victory upon Spanish soil. He dances in the arms of giants only to fall ignominiously at the slightest wind. His artistry is unstable, partaking of Daedalus's hubris, of Marcellus's wrath, of Archimedes' contempt, of Juanelo's objections, of Dante's demonizations, and of Giulio's illusions. But the complex genealogy of his fall foregrounds the *techné* of the text, one where the illusion of simplicity conceals the craft of a new Daedalus.

9 A Mannerist Theophany / A Cruel *Teichoskopia*: Pontormo and Parmigianino

Even in such wise sat the leaders of the Trojans upon the wall. Now when they saw Helen coming upon the wall, softly they spake winged words one to another: 'Small blame that Trojans and well-greaved Achaeans should for such a woman long time suffer woes; wondrously like is she to the immortal goddesses to look upon.'

Iliad, Book III

The pastoral tale of Grisóstomo and Marcela, which takes up the bulk of Part 2 of the 1605 *Quixote*, seems almost as out of place as the interpolated tale of the *Curioso impertinente*. Indeed, it was Cervantes who began the debate on the latter, having his character, Sansón Carrasco, complain that readers have objected to the *Curioso*'s inclusion: 'Por no ser de aquel lugar' (But it's out of place) (1978, 2.3.63; 506). The 1615 novel also affirms that *novelas* and other digressions will no longer be included since readers 'llevados de la atención que piden las hazañas de don Quijote no la darían atención' (with all their attention engrossed by the deeds of Don Quixote, might not have any attention left for the tales) (1978, 2.44.366; 776). But, the critical attention lavished by the author on this interpolation directs the readers' attention to its presence in the narrative rather than deflecting their gaze. This may well have been the function of Cervantes' criticisms, to increase the visibility of the *novelas* and their function, and to arouse curiosity at their placement. Indeed, why place the tale of Marcela and Grisóstomo at the moment when, having discovered the manuscript, the reader is eager to move forward with other adventures like that of the Basque? Although the intrusion of pastoral in chivalric novels was a common element, in the case of *Don Quixote* it seems to clash with expectations. The first part of the 1605 novel had provided a very carefully balanced text that included two adventures each in the fourth and eighth chapters, culminating in the windmills and the conflict with the Basque. Part 2 fails to include any new adventures. Instead, we are subjected to a speech on the mythical Golden Age, to a description of goatherds, and to the amorous misadventures of Grisóstomo and Marcela.

I will argue that this misplacement serves to foreground at least two important concerns in the novel: first, I believe that one of the reasons for the insertion of this episode at this early point in the work is to foreground the notion of a Virgilian literary career, one that moves from pastoral to epic (De Armas 2002: 274–9); and second, to exhibit epic devices that will be utilized later in the novel: theophany and *teichoskopia*. These two epic elements focus on women, thus attempting an uneasy balance between a male-dominated epic and woman's role. Although *Don Quixote* had commenced as a parody of romances of chivalry, it seeks to point to its affiliations with epic. And it does this, paradoxically, using the lowest genre, that of eclogue or pastoral.

The links between *Don Quixote* and the ancient epics of Homer and Virgil were part of the process which led to the canonization of the text in the eighteenth-century. For Rachel Schmidt, this process began with the London 1738 deluxe edition of *Don Quixote*. Here, a frontispiece by John Vanderbank showing Cervantes as a new Hercules who liberates Parnassus from the fantastic romances of chivalry[1] goes hand in hand with Gregorio Mayans y Sicar's biography in which Cervantes becomes 'a champion of European neoclassical values ... with the clear values of reason and proportion' (Schmidt 1999, 48). By the end of the eighteenth century, the repeated references to *Don Quixote* as a work akin to the classical epic culminated in the work of Vicente de los Ríos, who dealt extensively with the similarities between Cervantes and Homer. De los Ríos, who in his 1780 edition of *Don Quixote* never doubted the existence of a historical Homer, displays a series of biographical parallels: 'Ambos fueron poco estimados en sus patrias, anduvieron errantes y miserables toda su vida, y después han sido objeto de la admiración y del aplauso de los hombres sabios en todas las edades, países y naciones' (Both were not very esteemed in their homelands, they roamed errant and miserable all their life, but afterwards have been the object of admiration and applause from wise men in every age, country and nation) (1819, 14). But he goes well beyond such platitudes to discover compelling comparisons between the Greek epics and *Don Quixote*. Of course, de los Ríos goes on to stress that whereas Homer narrates a heroic action, Cervantes composes a ridiculous one (1819, 24–5). Whereas the epic poet 'presentó a los hombres toda la magestad de sus dioses, toda la grandeza de sus héroes' (presented to men all the majesty of their gods, all the grandeur of their heroes), the Spanish writer, 'menos atrevido' (less daring), decided to only represent everyday human beings and 'retratarles al natural sus defectos' (portray their true to life defects) (1819, 15). Contemporary critics would certainly reject the notion that Cervantes is 'menos atrevido.' They may also, as Anthony Close asserts, find the neoclassicist approach which focuses on reason and good taste 'off-putting' (1977, 15). De los Ríos' influence, however, was unquestioned: In Spain, his analysis 'was to remain the most authoritative guide to *Don Quixote* until the mid-nineteenth century' (Close 1978, 15).

Although many came to reject these parallels,[2] the link between Cervantes and the epic or at least his utilization of the mock-epic, or of epic to create a mock-epic, came to represent a continuing aspect of criticism. In the twentieth century, the most important continuator of Vicente de los Ríos was Arturo Marasso who, turning away from the link with Homer,[3] explored in more detail the relations between Cervantes and Virgil. It is surprising that this book did not trigger further investigations, given Georg Lukács's theories concerning the emergence of the modern novel from the epic.[4] Even Michael McGaha's important article on the subject in 1980 as well as Susanne Wofford's book failed to arouse much comment.[5]

In this chapter, I would like to return to the subject by briefly discussing Grisóstomo's literary career in terms of epic and then turning to two epic devices used by both Homer and Virgil, theophany and *teichoskopia*. I believe that Cervantes chose these two devices since they further his interest in both epic devices and in the pictorial nature of his fiction – both have to do with the sense of sight: seeing a divine apparition, or looking out from a high place. After all, the Grisóstomo/Marcela episode comes right after the discovery of the Toledo manuscript which contains a drawing of the battle with the Basque. The double ekphrasis of this chapter (and ekphrasis is a common epic device) leads very clearly to the visual nature of theophany and *teichoskopia* in the pastoral digression. Finally, I will connect these devices with Renaissance art, showing how theophany not only derives from a Virgilian episode but also from the mannerist art of Jacopo Pontorno and Parmaginiano.

From the beginnings of his literary career, Cervantes was concerned with Italian Renaissance art and with the classical world that often emerged in these paintings. One of Raphael's last projects was 'that of drawing up, on the basis of excavation and the evidence of ancient writers, a scientific reconstruction of the original appearance of the whole of ancient Rome' (Jones and Penny 1983, 199). It is this interest in the archaeology of the ancients coupled with a strong admiration for what Renaissance artists were doing that led Cervantes to his own initial archaeological project – the recreation of the ancient Celtiberian city of Numancia, a city he modelled after Troy and Rome.[6] The tragedy of *Numancia*, an epic recreation of a city based on Virgil's *Aeneid*, may have led him to consider yet another great Virgilian myth, that of the origins of a great poet. Throughout the early modern period, European poets sought to emulate the career patterns of the ancients. Cervantes' literary career may be studied in terms of the Virgilian *cursus*, redefined in the Middle Ages as the Virgilian Wheel. As Ernst Curtius has pointed out, the *Rota Virgilii*, which became a commonplace in medieval rhetoric, 'distinguishes three styles, to which certain occupations, trees, and animals correspond, and which were based upon Virgil's *Bucolics*, georgics, and the *Aeneid* respectively' (1953, 201–35). Using what were considered to be the first four lines of the *Aeneid*, the three styles also became the three stages that the poet must master in his literary career, thus establishing the 'myth' of the poet, one that entailed a specific career pattern. The poet must begin with pastoral, move to the farming fields of georgics, and end in the martial field of epic. His final epic triumph is also the triumph of empire, for Virgil traces in his origins the origins of the Roman Empire, beginning with Aeneas's flight from Troy and ending with the predicted Golden Age of Augustan rule. Cervantes, I believe, consciously follows this career pattern in his prose fiction. He begins with pastoral (*La Galatea*), continues with an apprenticeship in epic (*Don Quixote*), and culminates his career with an epic in imitation of Heliodorus (*Persiles y Segismunda*). This is not the place to discuss this project, but simply to summarize how the pastoral interpolation in his *Don Quixote* serves to emphasize that he is still embarked on this Virgilian career pattern.[7]

A clear indication of the link between Cervantes and Virgil in this interpolation occurs towards the end of the tale. Learning that Grisóstomo had ordered that his poetry be destroyed at his death, Vivaldo argues that it ought to be preserved, giving as an example Augustus Caesar's decree disallowing the clause in Virgil's will where he ordered that his *Aeneid* be burned: 'Y no le tuviera bueno Augusto

César si consintiera que se pusiera en ejecución lo que el divino Manguano dejó en su testamento' (Augustus Caesar would have been out of his mind if he'd agreed to what the divine Mantuan poet ordered in his will) (1978, 1.13.171; 102). This anecdote was so important to the Renaissance that Raphael executed a grisaille painting of it, placing it under the *Parnassus* in the Vatican Stanze. Such was the textual and pictoric authority of this passage that, unable to counter it, Grisóstomo's friend, Ambrosio, allows some of the poems to be rescued from the blaze. Cut down in the prime of his life, Grisóstomo's poetic works consist of some sacred poems and plays written earlier in life and his amorous poems to Marcela composed while disguised as a shepherd. His disguise would link these poems with the first and lowest Virgilian career move, the eclogue.

These two Virgilian gestures, the writing of amorous poetry by a youthful 'shepherd' and the order that his poetry be destroyed, alert us to the presence of a Virgilian *cursus* in Part 2 of Cervantes' 1605 novel. It may be argued that, since Grisóstomo's life is cut short, the text may be challenging the notion of an ideal career. After all, how can a poet plan to fulfil a *cursus* when the length of life is uncertain? But I would claim that such a challenge is countered in the works written by and about Grisóstomo, texts that evince his ability to follow the ancient *cursus* in spite of his short life. Grisóstomo's first significant career move is the composition of pastoral amatory works. He does this as he disguises himself as shepherd. As part of his new identity, Grisóstomo uses the appropriate Virgilian locale, the pasture, the corresponding animal, the sheep, as well as the appropriate tree, the beech: 'No está muy lejos de aquí un sitio donde hay casi dos docenas de altas hayas, y no hay ninguna que en su lisa corteza no tenga grabado y escrito el nombre de Marcela' (Not far from here is a place where there are almost two dozen lofty beeches, and there is not one on whose smooth bark is not engraved the name of Marcela') (1978, 1.12.166; 93). Furthermore, the notion of writing on the beech tree is clearly Virgilian. In Eclogue V, Mopsus states: 'Nay I will try these verses, which the other day I carved on the green beech-bark, and set to music, marking words and tune in turn' (1978, 5.13–14; 1.35). Thus we have writing within writing, carved trees within Virgilian and Cervantine pastorals.

More important, in asking that his poetry be burned at his death, Grisóstomo is also, as noted, following the lead of Virgil – specifically of the poet who had already written his epic. And, when Grisóstomo's last poem is saved from the fire, as Virgil's *Aeneid* was saved by Varius and

Augustus, the work turns out to be contaminated by epic, evincing Grisóstomo's move from low to high style.[8] Grisóstomo's 'Canción desesperada' (Song of Despair), which is read aloud by Vivaldo, focuses on the lament for a lost love. But the amatory poem is replete with epic images. The vision of the underworld in these verses is intended to rival Aeneas's catabasis in the sixth book of the *Aeneid*, from where Cervantes had borrowed the funeral rites for Grisóstomo. Virgilian epic images of the three-headed Cerberus, of Tityus tormented by a vulture who gnaws at his liver, of Egion stretched on a wheel, and of Sisyphus rolling a huge stone, become in Grisóstomo's poem dreaded visions and torments that the dying lover expects to encounter. And indeed, as in the *Aeneid*, Grisóstomo could well find himself in the Mourning Fields where 'those whom stern Love has consumed with cruel wasting are hidden in walks withdrawn, embowered in a myrtle grove' (1978, 1.537; 6.441–4). It is here that he may expect to find his Marcela as Aeneas discovered Dido in a less than happy reunion. Thus, Grisóstomo is not only a new Virgil, but also a new Aeneas, one who, like his epic predecessor, abandons the feminine.[9]

By utilizing the sixth book of the *Aeneid*, Grisóstomo elicits an expectation of prophecy. After all, it is in the underworld that Aeneas found out about his future. There are no prophetic remarks in Grisóstomo's poem, except the expectation of his own death. This mournful prophecy contrasts with Don Quixote's triumphant vision of the return of a Golden Age and serves as foreshadowing for the knight's failures. In an ironic twist typical of Cervantes' style, the epic images of Grisóstomo's last poem do not always derive from Virgil. There are some that imitate Lucan's *Pharsalia*, a work that 'counters' many of Virgil's ideals, structure, and style. As with the *Aeneid*, it is the sixth book of the epic poem that becomes the model for Grisóstomo. In the *Pharsalia*, the witch Erichto, in order to perform a necromantic resurrection, screams at a dead body with sound 'untunable and far different from human speech. The dog's bark and the wolf's howl were in that voice; it resembled the complaint of the restless owl and the night-flying screech owl, the shrieking and roaring of wild beasts, the serpent's hiss ...' (1988, 355; 6.687–90).

In Grisóstomo's 'Canción desesperada' it is the poet-lover himself who uses these witching sounds in order to express the disharmony created in his heart by Marcela's alleged cruelty. Grisóstomo makes use of Lucan's necromancy in a metaphoric sense. First of all, Grisóstomo's poem contains a voice that will be heard after death. It represents his lament emerging from the grave. Not only is he revivifying his own voice, but also that of the ancient epic poets. He not only wishes to bring back to life Virgil's epic body, but he seeks to combine it with that of Lucan, Virgil's rival. Claiming that in order to express his inordinate grief he needs 'nuevos modos' (novel tones) (1978, 1.14.181; 104), the poet shocks his audience (and his beloved) with witching sounds, necromantic resurrections, and the 'unnatural' blending of two opposing epic voices in one work or body. The result is a carefully 'untunable' poem which not only dares to rival the greatest of all epic poets, but also his opponent. This disinterment of two great ancients shows that in death, Grisóstomo has more than fulfilled the Virgilian *cursus*. His new song combines eclogue and epic, Virgilian and counter-Virgilian voices, in a tour de force that seeks to show how even in a short work and in a brief life a poet can emulate the career of the most canonical of ancient poets.

But what Grisóstomo had not counted on in his tour de force imitation of the Virgilian career in life, death, and verse, was that the object of his (poetic) desire would become a subject that would rival his own artistic creations. As the group gets ready to read more of Grisóstomo's poetry at his funeral, Marcela appears to them upon a mound or rock above the grave. What the shepherds and friends witness is a 'maravillosa visión' (miraculous vision) of inimitable beauty (1978, 1.14.185; 108). Ambrosio immediately accuses her of cruelty and disdain, comparing her appearance upon the heights to Nero's happy contemplation of the burning of Rome. But Marcela answers his accusation with a speech of great force and impact, a harangue that certainly rivals Grisóstomo's imitation of the ancients. If readers and critics often judge Marcela along gender lines, as both Ruth El Saffar (1993, 158) and Anne J. Cruz (1999, 145) have argued, it is also true that the text places Marcela within a patriarchal story that is 'told and retold by men' (Gabriele 2003, 516), one that makes Marcela's struggles 'to achieve textual and contextual authority' much more poignant, as John P. Gabriele has shown (2003, 522).

More important for the purposes of this chapter is how Ambrosio's interpretation of Marcela as Nero has been countered by a host of other classical and Christian analogies. Pierre Ullman (1971), for example, has analysed the plot as a secularized version of a Christian miracle tale. Others have shown how the character and actions of Marcela recall a pagan goddess. She has been described as a new Diana, the chaste deity of the hunt who shuns the company of men; as the nymph Daphne who runs away from Apollo's attentions; and as a new Astraea, the goddess who lived on earth the longest after the end of the first or mythical Golden Age.[10] Some feminist studies, however, have turned away from the mythological since they claim that this aspect dehumanizes Marcela (Jehenson 1990).

Although it has been claimed that we are faced once again with woman as either angel or demon, goddess or destructive force, I believe that we cannot discard the associations between Marcela and the goddess on the grounds of dehumanization. I will give four reasons for this: (1) Marcela carefully chooses where she will speak to the assembled men, thus countering Grisóstomo's epic move with her own epic-theatrical move which places her in the realms above, in the realms of positive authority; in this manner Marcela wants to be perceived as goddess. (2) The goddesses of the Greeks and Romans were much more like human beings. They took sides in wars and disputes and acted much like courtiers in an ancient or Renaissance palace, and thus their link to Marcela does not dehumanize her. (3) Her placement above recalls two epic devices, theophany and (to a lesser degree) *teichoskopia*, used both in the Homeric epics and in Virgil, thus rendering her an epic figure. And, (4) by deliberately fusing a number of perspectives, those of different goddesses, Marcela exhibits a multifaceted self, a humanity that has been denied to her by her male suitors. Cervantes' perspectivism is thus related to the artistic technique of anamorphosis, prevalent in Renaissance art.

Theophany is a device of epic, although it is not restricted to this genre. Here the invisible becomes visible, as a human being comes face to face with a deity. In most cases, this god or goddess assumes a disguise. We need only recall the many metamorphoses of Zeus in order to deceive mortal women. Perhaps the most famous theophany of a goddess takes place in the *Aeneid*. Here Venus, Aeneas's mother, decides she must give him counsel and advice. Among other things, she will help him to discover Dido's kingdom. But as she appears to her own son, she takes on a disguise. She is a huntress with bow and arrow, and wearing appropriate attire for this pursuit. Although Venus cannot fully disguise her divinity, she can appear as her rival, the goddess Diana. When she prophesies to Aeneas, pointing to the twelve swans in the heavens, he is certain she is a goddess. As she departs, 'her ambrosial tresses breathed celestial fragrance' (1978, 1.269; 1.403). Only then does Aeneas realize that he has spoken to his own mother Venus.[11] This double vision of his mother as both huntress/Diana, goddess of chastity, and Venus, goddess of love, creates a kind of anamorphosis in the text, adding texture to the apparition. The same can be said of Marcela. Like Venus, she appears disguised – we must remember that she has taken on the dress of a shepherdess. Furthermore she, on the one hand, is the object of love, her beauty linking her to Venus, while on the other, she is the shepherdess and huntress who wishes to live away from men, associating her with Diana. This type of anamorphosis, as Michel Jeanneret explains, stems from the fact that artists were aware that 'to escape from oblivion, the work had to keep on developing. They deliberately made room in their texts and paintings for the reader or spectator and left him the task of completing, arranging, elucidating' (2001, 257). It is precisely this collaboration between reader and text that is being elicited in the pastoral digression by Cervantes. The reader can fill in her image of Marcela and thus keep imparting new meaning to the episode.

Cervantes imitates the Virgilian theophany when depicting Marcela, not only because it is anamorphic, or because it derives from the very epic with which Marcela is competing, but also because the way Venus is disguised in the *Aeneid* caused much critical debate during the Renaissance. Pedro M. Cátedra has shown that Donatus's notion of Venus as the ideal both of beauty and virtue changed in a number of cases.[12] He explains how Santillana moves away from the portrayal in Virgil, since his description of Venus casts doubt on this deity's virtue (Cátedra 1996, 157). When she meets Aeneas, Virgil has her appear with her hair flowing in the wind and 'her knee bare, her flowing robes gathered in a knot' (1978, 1.263; 1.320). Enrique de Villena explains that Venus's indecorous attire shows that Aeneas is an illegitimate child from an immoral woman. He adds that the hunt represents a lustful goddess chasing after men (Cátedra 1996, 157–8). Given the arguments concerning Venus dressed as an unchaste Diana, it is very telling that Cervantes' text does not describe Marcela's attire. She only appears as a 'maravillosa visión.' It is up to the reader (and the spectators) to decide who she may be, thus confirming the collaborative aim of anamorphosis.

Another curious aspect of the text is that in her speech from up high, Marcela/Venus/Diana is not talking to either her son (Aeneas) or her would-be lover. Grisóstomo is dead. She is speaking to his friends, desiring to justify her actions. Indeed, as Roberto González Echevarría has explained, this scene as well as the whole episode, resembles a trial: 'The conflict, involving injury, restitution, possible revenge, accusations, defense, judgment, and release from culpability, unfolds and is resolved in a decidedly judicial manner' (2005, 79). And there is a body of evidence – the corpse of Grisóstomo – for all to view.

Perhaps it is time to ask if there is another aspect to Grisóstomo other than his embodiment of the Virgilian epic. Often in Cervantes, Christian and classical elements coalesce in a type of syncretism that was prevalent in the Renaissance.[13] As Américo Castro has shown, Cervantes was well aware of, and often pointed to the pagan substratum of Christianity: 'Cervantes sabe, y lo dice claramente, que hay aspectos fundamentales de la religión cristiana que son mero trasunto de la pagana ... El culto a la Virgen, ¿guarda, pues, relación con el de Venus, como el de los santos con los dioses? Así lo creía el humanismo, en su afán de buscar un común denominador que uniese el mundo pre- y poscristiano' (Cervantes knows, and states clearly, that there are fundamental aspects of the Christian religion that are mere copies of paganism ... The cult of the Virgin – does it, then, preserve a connection with the cult of Venus, like the one of the saints with the gods? Humanism believed it so, in its desire to find a common denominator that would unite the pre- and post-Christian world) (1972, 271). The 'maravillosa visión' can thus refer both to the ancient Venus/Diana and to the Christian Virgin Mary. This move from classical antiquity to Christianity leads us to wonder who, then, is Grisóstomo? He is more than just an emblem for the Virgilian career. A number of critics have mentioned in passing that his name ties him to St John Chrysostom.[14] Carroll Johnson had emphasized the irony in Cervantes' naming of Grisóstomo: 'To say the least, Chrysostom goes well beyond Saint Paul in recommending celibacy over marriage. His work enjoyed great influence, and *On Virginity* is one of the standard sources of support for the dogma of the virginity of Mary. The name of Marcela's ill-fated lover, in other words, leads the reader, through an ironical Cervantine about-face to an unimpeachable source of justification for the life-style that Marcela herself has adopted' (1983, 97). Thus, we come to the vision of Marcela as a Christianized Venus/Diana and as a figure akin to the Virgin Mary to whom this saint was devoted. And the very name Chrysostom recalls the Christ. Like Christ, Grisóstomo suffered a passion, and this brought about his death. Again, we have an anamorphic scene, which, when viewed from different perspectives, yields different results. In a Christian context, Marcela can be the Virgin looking down on the death of the crucified Christ – no matter that Grisóstomo's burial rites 'parecen de gentiles' (they're more like what pagans get up to) (1978, 1.12.162; 89–90).

This added element, the notion of the Virgin looking down at the dead Christ, serves to nullify the image of Marcela as a Nero who looks down at burning Rome. It also takes us from Virgil's epic to mannerist painting in the Italian Renaissance. Although this term has been strenuously debated throughout the twentieth-century, and although it is a misnomer,[15] Frederick Hartt believes that it is useful in considering 'the tensions and distortions, the visual and emotional surprises of the years around 1520' (1994, 535), years subsequent to the apogee of High Renaissance art.[16] In this chapter we will consider two of the main artists associated with mannerism: Jacopo Carucci da Pontormo (1494–1557) and Francesco Mazzola, called Parmigianino (1503–40). The first, as Frederick Hartt, explains, 'opens for us a world of fantasy, poetry and torment that is unprecedented in the history of Italian Renaissance art' (1994, 550); the second is filled with spatial anomalies, hermetic and alchemical images, and oneiric spaces. It is not my argument that any one painting or fresco by these artists served as a model for Cervantes. In that sense, there is no specific ekphrasis here. Instead, it is a combination of motifs, manners, visions, and images that suggest a mannerist perspective in Cervantes' pastoral scene.

Before turning to their representations of the Virgin Mary, it should be noted that both Pontormo and Parmigianino were keenly interested in the portrayal of Diana, one of the faces of Marcela. While Parmigianino was chiefly concerned with the representation of Diana and Acteon, showing his metamorphosis in a mannerist and almost grotesque mode,[17] Pontormo shows the clothed and chaste Diana in a fresco for the Villa Medici at Poggio entitled *Vertumnus and Pomona* (fig. 9.1). This lunette is the only fresco he was able to execute at the Villa Medici, since Pope Leo X was overtaken by death and the project was abandoned (Vasari 1996, 2.353). While the goddess of fruits in the right foreground is linked to the god of the harvest in the left foreground through garlands under the window, in the upper spaces two other deities seem also to be linked – this time by the laurel. On the right side of the fresco, Diana seems to hover above Pomona and a maiden. She holds on to laurel branches, symbol of both the Medici and the epic – let us recall that the *Rota Virgilii* assigned a plant to each of the three main genres. Since the laurel connects her to Apollo, this also recalls that he is the god of poetry of which epic is the highest form. The second genre, georgics, is here represented by the god of harvest, the goddess of fruits, and the vegetation that connects them.[18] Perhaps the golden air surrounding the scene with the light from the oculus window recalls the golden moment of a golden age, the age of eclogue and pastoral, the age that Cervantes linked so clearly to the Marcela and Grisóstomo episode through Don Quixote's discourse on 'la edad de oro' (the age of gold). Thus, Pontormo summarizes in his fresco many of the Cervantine concerns in Part 1 of the 1605 novel: the importance of a Virgilian *cursus*; the representation of Diana who stands above, presiding over a pastoral and epic mode; and the strong features of mannerism, including the use of space: 'the ground is nonexistent, space is nowhere defined, the figures are poised on the horizontals as if balanced on wires ...' (Hartt 1994, 553).[19] Space is indeed very fluid in Cervantes' pastoral episode, as Marcela/Diana seems to almost float upon a rock or hill as a miraculous vision.

Marcela's spatial positioning, in many ways, reflects what Don Quixote attempts to do throughout the novel, that is, the superimposition of planes – the imaginative or dreamlike level that the knight seeks to impose upon the quotidian real or even grotesque landscape. Discussing a painting by El Greco, Américo Castro explains: 'Cervantes llevó a cabo la máxima proeza de reducir a uno los dos planos del *Entierro del conde de Orgaz*; los armonizó secularmente de tal forma que la ensoñación ilusoria pareciera incluida en la realidad de este mundo' (Cervantes accomplished the great feat of reducing to one the two planes of the *Burial of the Count of Orgaz*; he created a secular harmony such that the dreamlike illusion would appear as being a part of the reality of the world) (1966, 107). In spite of the fact that Marcela's speech utilizes strong arguments grounded on vivid images and facts, it is as if she has not been heard, what David Castillo calls the 'collective deaf ear to Marcela's voice' (81). While they do not listen to her, they seem almost mesmerized by the use of space, by her poignant presence in the realms above thus adding the emotional surprise typical of mannerism.

Marcela may well be seen as a Madonna, sometimes depicted in the Renaissance in imitation of Venus and Cupid as in Parmigianino's *Madonna of the Rose* or even in Raphael's *Madonna della Sedia*. Indeed, Raphael's Madonna seems to be akin to his *Donna Velata*, which depicts his mistress as a new Venus (Jones and Penny 1883, 167, 170). But Cervantes is presenting us with a dead lover.

Turning to what is considered to be Pontormo's masterpiece, *The Entombment* (fig. 2), we witness, as in Cervantes' funereal scene, a female presence that looks down from on high.[20] The *teichoskopia* is both affirmed and distorted by the use of space. The wall becomes a wall of women who prevent us from seeing the landscape. We do not know where she stands or if she is suspended above the ground. In the foreground below is the body of Christ being carried by two youths. One could view the Madonna above as Marcela, looking down upon the dead body of Christ/Grisóstomo after the 'passion.' The two youths carrying the body of Christ can recall the two main speakers in Cervantes' scene, Ambrosio, Grisóstomo's friend, and Vivaldo, the guest who does not wish his papers to be burned. The handsome figure of the dead Christ, with wounds almost healed, recalls the deceased Grisóstomo, who, 'aunque muerto, mostraba que vivo había sido de rostro hermoso y de disposición gallarda' (even though he was dead, it was plain to see that in life he'd had handsome features and a gallant disposition) (1978, 1.13.178; 101). Their age is also similar. In the middle and falling away from her son, with legs in an almost impossible position, is the image of Mary, further destabilizing time and space, as the earthly mixes with the heavenly, reality with dreams. We come to realize that, if the figure above is also the Madonna, she is a much younger one, envisioning her future and the future of her son.

What this painting is not is a theophany for the people below facing each other, Christ, or the spectator. They are unaware of the young Madonna who looks down upon them – if anything it is a *teichoskopia*, where the ascended Mary looks back upon a scene where she herself is in mourning for her son. But there is also a second figure which looks on in contemplation. The bearded young man, a small and almost floating head and torso on the upper right, is none other than a portrait of Pontormo himself. This portrait of the artist within his work leads us to consider that Grisóstomo's life, his career, may well represent the ambitions of Cervantes. Grisóstomo's death can well represent a wish-fulfilment dream of a writer who has not yet succeeded in becoming a figure akin to Virgil.

The notion of dreams and the relation between above and below, between a beatific vision and a seemingly dead human being, is more clearly viewed in Parmigianino's *The Madonna and Child with Saints John the Baptist and Jerome* (fig. 9.3).[21] Here, the foreshortened body of an older Jerome on the right seems to be a corpse. But death and sleep imitate each other, and Jerome, who is asleep, is having a dream vision. The inclusion of oneiric phenomena within a painting is a characteristic of mannerism much like the young Madonna in Pontormo. It can also be observed in Pontormo's *Joseph in Egypt*, which includes in the upper right, the dream of Pharaoh.[22] In Parmigianino, we have St John, with his index finger pointing to a rock above, as mediator between spectator and painting, between Jerome and the Virgin. Here, the dead Grisóstomo is replaced by a sleeping Jerome, and the mourners at Grisóstomo's funeral are metamorphosed into the spectators of the painting. From the rock above, the Virgin looks down with an incomprehensible gaze, but showing herself truly as a miraculous and sublime apparition.

But this painting, famous for its elongated figures and for the ambiguity of space, also contains another break with the High Renaissance, one that turns the sublimity of a celestial dream into what Frederick Hartt calls a 'lascivious and perverse' depiction (1994, 518). Parmigianino 'has emphasized the Child's genitals and with unprecedented daring has shown the Virgin's nipples erect against the tight, sheer fabric of her tunic' (Hartt 1994, 564). That Jerome would be having both a sublime and sexual dream should come as no surprise. As Patricia Cox Miller has noted, he was a prolific dreamer, often poised between asceticism and sexual desire. She stresses that 'his visions – of dancing girls and other urban delights – were not prophetic but rather reflective of the struggle of the ascetic with persistent sexual desire' (1994, 205). This painting, then, is akin to an ancient theophany, for here the Virgin is disguised as a lustful Venus and vice versa.

There are some very suggestive parallels between Jerome's dreams and those of Don Quixote. The knight is as tormented as the dreaming Jerome, imagining many a night with the chaste Dulcinea, but knowing her to be Aldonza. In the 1615 *Quixote*, the episode of the Cave of Montesinos seems also to be a dream, one with sexual implications. Although Don Quixote seeks to Platonize his desire for the ever-elusive Dulcinea, he is constantly tempted, be it by the allure of false princesses at the inn or by the disguised Dorotea. In many ways, Marcela corresponds to Don Quixote's dreams. She is the most beautiful and chaste Diana and, through the male gaze, she becomes an alluring Venus. Parmigianino's sexualized Virgin with child is a clear echo of this plight. Thus, at the end of the episode Don Quixote prevents other shepherds from following Marcela, but he himself wishes to follow, albeit for supposed altruistic motives of protecting a damsel in distress (who does not want protection). Miller concludes her study of Jerome by showing how he attempted to cure his body through language, how his library of classical works was both a boon and a torment. This is not very different from Don Quixote, whose desires also become textualized, and whose library, even when destroyed, keeps producing images through the art of memory – images that are superimposed upon reality.

But in all of these texts and paintings the reader and the spectators within have been looking to the 'maravillosa visión.' Cervantes also shows the view from above, as Marcela speaks to the crowd. Her own lookout and perception of the men below as potential enemies whom she must persuade recalls another famous epic device. The *teichoskopia*, or view from the wall, will serve as an ending to this chapter. Two such views are imitated in the Cervantine episode, merging in *contaminatio*. The most famous *teichoskopia* in literature is that of Helen in book 3 of the *Iliad*. Here she rushes to the ramparts by the Scaean gates as she is informed by Iris that Paris and Menelaus are about to engage in single combat. Priam and the elders of Troy, on seeing her arrival, remark on how 'wondrously like is she to the immortal goddesses' (1988, 1.129; 3.158). And Priam leads her to speak of the men below – Agamemnon, Odysseus, and Aias. This *teichoskopia* of Helen looking down (as the elders gaze upon her), has much in common with Marcela. Marcela, like Helen, appears to be a goddess of beauty and splendour, and she also gazes down on a man who loves her. While Marcela gazes upon a corpse, Helen believes that either her husband Menelaus or her abductor, Paris, is bound to die in single combat that very day (although Paris will be saved by Aphrodite). While Marcela views the men below so as to defend her self and her self-sufficiency, Helen is racked with guilt and self-recrimination and calls herself a loose woman or dog-faced woman. At the same time, such suffering imparts on Helen a kind of heroic quality. And although Helen does not defend herself as Marcela does, others do it for her. Priam, for example, blames the gods for the conflict. Matthew Gumpert wonders: 'The text of the *teichoskopia* is haunted by the specter of competing and contradictory Helens. Which Helen is the right one?' (2001, 9). The reader of Cervantes' pastoral interlude might also ask herself the same question. Who is the 'real' Marcela? Through competing myths and paintings, through artistic anamorphoses, the many aspects of Marcela are revealed to the careful reader. The theophany reveals both Venus and Diana; the chaste Christian Virgin, and the sexualized sacred vision of St Jerome. Marcela looks down towards men who would battle with her image, and they look up at a miracle and at a monstrous and desirable being.

The second *teichoskopia* is found, predictably, in Virgil's *Aeneid*, thus reminding us of Grisóstomo as follower of the Virgilian *cursus*. While Aeneas's arrival in Carthage is auspiciously presaged by the appearance of Venus in a theophany, his departure is viewed by love-sick Dido from above a tower, in the form of a *teichoskopia*. This departure of Aeneas will lead her to curse the hero who is abandoning her before she commits suicide. Arturo Marasso is one of the few critics who have noted the imitation of the Dido episode in Virgil in Cervantes' pastoral digression: 'Dido murió por Eneas; Grisóstomo por Marcela. Una misma crueldad y una idéntica desventura arrastran al suicidio a los dos enamorados' (Dido died for Aeneas; Grisóstomo for Marcela. A same cruelty and an identical fate move the two lovers to suicide) (1954, 85). Thus, Cervantes' scene reverses the gender roles. While Aeneas was the cruel one, here Marcela is said to share this fault; and while Aeneas departs to become an epic hero, Marcela turns away to become a goddess of the forests, both embodying their own genre (epic and pastoral). The death of Grisóstomo, although freeing Marcela, paradoxically makes Grisóstomo into a new Virgil, whose works are rescued from the fire. Marcela's supposed cruelty is part of Grisóstomo's plan to gain fame. He defames her in order to fulfil his poetic career. But his poetry does not sing of a new empire, unless it is the territory of Marcela's body, which is denied to him. His, then, is an epic of the defeated, which evokes Virgilian triumph in a Pharsalian lament.

Although pastoral suggests the harmony of the primordial Golden Age, or even the return of an imperial Golden Age through Augustus's *Pax Romana*, such an event is denied in Grisóstomo's prophetic poem. The ending of the Cervantine digression is thus very different from its beginning, where Don Quixote had spoken of a coming Age of Gold. The pastoral episode may serve to prove him wrong. For, the future is in the past. It is the past not only of Augustus Caesar, but of Charles V, who is accompanied by Astraea in Ariosto. It is the past of a would-be world emperor. As Marcela moves away from humanity and enters deep into the forest, she follows Astraea, goddess of the Golden Age, who abandons earth during the worst of ages. Don Quixote is too late. The world is not moving towards an age of perfection, but away from it. All that is left is separation, suspicion and thwarted sexuality. Marcela, as a marvellous vision, as theophany, reminds her viewers and listeners of immense potential, of wondrous complexities. She is Diana, Venus, and the Virgin Mary. Anamorphosis makes her into a complex figure that strides across pagan fields and Christian paintings. But as she looks down in a manner akin to a *teichoskopia*, she becomes the unknowable Helen, emblem of war and the Iron Age. In a gender reversal, she is also the departing Aeneas going to claim new lands. And Aeneas as Grisóstomo points to the fulfilment of a strange new *cursus* which combines defeat and triumph. Finally, Marcela is the Virgilian Astraea, who was conflated in Christian times with the Virgin Mary.[23] But, looking down at mankind, this miraculous vision decides that she does not belong upon this earth. Don Quixote's last move, to follow Marcela/ Astraea, shows that he is not the predestined hero to bring back the Age of Gold, for he cannot find her. Furthermore, he has rejected her desire not to be followed. Thus, the knight is a figure akin to Grisóstomo, forever bound to seek a woman's body, an imperial land, a quest that his conflicted dreams will not allow him to fulfil. The triumph of the written word is built upon a mock-epic of the defeated, which lauds the anamorphic visions of woman's complex domain.

10 Dulcinea and the Five Maidens: Zeuxis

When he [Zeuxis] was going to produce a picture for the city of Girgenti to dedicate at the public cost in the temple of Lacinian Hera he held an inspection of maidens of the place paraded naked and chose five, for the purpose of reproducing the most admirable points in the form of each.

Pliny, *Natural History*

While Part 2 of the 1605 *Quixote* is dedicated to digression, Part 3 returns to the adventures of the deranged knight of La Mancha. Chapter 15 forms a kind of buffer between the amorous (albeit epic) interpolation of Part 2 and the return to 'epic' or chivalric exploits. Here, the reader is treated to the passions of Rocinante. Don Quixote's horse, freed to graze in some meadows, would rather enjoy the pleasures of mating with some Galician mares guarded by carriers from Yanguas. Very much like the reaction Marcela had to Grisóstomo, the mares ignore and reject Rocinante, who becomes more and more of a nuisance to them. It is at this point that the carriers start to intervene while Don Quixote decides to stand up for Rocinante and battle the Yanguensans. Nothing good, of course, comes of this adventure. But it is important because it both looks back in parody at the Grisóstomo and Marcela episode and looks forward to the continuing adventures of the knight. Part 3 of the 1605 novel includes an example of what may be called epic *teichoskopia*, as Don Quixote beckons Sancho to climb upon a hillock (albeit not a wall) in order to witness a major battle between two great foes – the Christian prince Pentapolín and the Moslem emperor Alifanfarón, whom Don Quixote refers to as a 'foribundo pagano' (wild pagan) (1978, 1.18.219; 139). Of course, what they are witnessing is in reality two clouds of dust generated by two flocks of sheep. This once again takes us to the epic, since in Ajax, when he went mad at not being given Achilles' shield, battled with a flock of sheep thinking them to be an enemy army.[1] There is a proliferation of epic devices following the *teichoskopia* of chapter 18, including a catalogue of principal warriors and armies and the enumeration of them according to the river that runs through their land (1978, 1.18.221).[2] Just as *teichoskopia* is a marker for epic, so is theophany. In the following chapter, Don Quixote witnesses some strange lights coming towards him in the middle of the night. This frightful vision ('temerosa visión' [fearful vision] [1.19.230; 148]) certainly contrasts with the 'maravillosa visión' (miraculous vision) of Marcela, and turns theophany into a demonic apparition. Of course, Don Quixote is once again wrong and is excommunicated for having attacked a holy man.

The epic thrust of Don Quixote's adventures in Part 3 is attenuated in chapter 20. Here, dreaded sounds in the night bespeak of another adventure. But in this case, Don Quixote is not able to paint over reality. The dreaded noise is viewed simply as six fulling-hammers from a watermill. The question arises as to why the knight is unable to make this into one of his epic adventures. The answer might be found in the water that surrounds the landscape. From the start of the chapter, Sancho points to its proximity: 'Alguna fuente o arroyo que estas yerbas humedece' (All this grass ... must be a sign that there's a spring or a stream near here watering it) (1.20.237; 153). By eventually viewing a river with its mill, the dryness of the knight's constitution, which is the cause of his imaginings, dissipates. Thus, he is not able to recreate the landscape. This episode also serves to point out the importance of digressions in the novel. The lengthy interpolation of Part 2, in spite of epic reminiscences, had helped to humidify the novel through the passions of the heart. In the prologue to the novel, the fictive author had proclaimed his work to be too dry and in need of adornment. Dryness is a masculine quality that, in excess, can lead to both choler and melancholy, and to imagined visions. In order to attenuate the dryness caused by male adventures, the novel introduces 'adornments' or feminine digressions. Thus, there is a gendering of material in the novel. On the one hand, we have the epic and dry adventures of the knight, and on the other, the amorous digressions or interpolations that add 'adornment' and feminine humidity. This gendering of fiction recalls the gendering of art already discussed. While some artists were thought to be masculine, emphasizing design (Michelangelo, Raphael), others used the feminine technique of colour (Titian). In this novel, both sets of artists are used to adorn the text, their work thus becoming feminine even if they are masculine in technique. Cervantes replicates the gendered opposition of art in his novel, alternating dry and humid parts. While Parts 1 and 3 are dry and dedicated to knightly adventures, Parts 2 and 4 are more humid and turn with greater frequency to digressions and matters of the heart.

We have stated that Part 2 begins with a buffer between feminine digression and masculine adventure. The same can be said for its ending. Don Quixote turns away from the path to adventure to go deep into the mountains, the Sierra Morena, where he will perform penitence for his lady-love, Dulcinea del Toboso. In so doing, he points to the proliferation of amorous digressions that will be at the heart of the last section of the novel. It should come as no surprise that this moment of introspection and passion in Don Quixote's journey should be adorned by paintings from the Italian Renaissance.

Among the many pictures we can discover amidst the narrative of Cervantes' *Don Quixote,* there is a particular group that relates to Dulcinea. In answer to the question posed by Javier Herrero: 'Who was Dulcinea?' this chapter will examine how Don Quixote painted in his mind an image of his lady.[3] While disagreement on who Dulcinea was abounds, many critics do agree that in chapter 25 of Part 1 Don Quixote gives us the first major indication as to her identity. Before that moment in the novel, as Ruth El Saffar asserts: 'Dulcinea serves only as a point of reference' (1984, 58). In the twenty-fifth chapter, as Herrero explains: 'Don Quixote gives us a surprising insight into the workings of his mind, we hear him assert that he is aware that Dulcinea is in a certain way a creation of his will in order to make possible the world of adventure' (1985, 7). In order to understand Don Quixote's composition in this chapter, I will turn to an anecdote from art history, Giambattista Della Porta's treatise on the art of memory, a Spanish and an Italian text with woodcuts and, of course, paintings from the Italian Renaissance.

In chapter 25, Don Quixote explains to Sancho how he has created Dulcinea: 'Píntola en mi imaginación como la deseo, así en la belleza como en la principalidad, y ni la llega Elena, ni la alcanza Lucrecia, ni otra alguna de las famosas mujeres de las edades pretéritas, griega, bárbara o latina' (I depict her in my imagination as I wish her to be, both in beauty and in rank, and Helen cannot rival her, nor can Lucrecia or any other of the famous women of past ages, whether Greek, Barbarian or Roman, equal her) (1978, 1.25.314; 216). The reference to Helen, the use of five examples (Helen, Lucretia, a Greek, a Barbarian, and a Roman), and the notion that no one woman can embody the perfection of beauty found in Dulcinea, brings to mind a classical anecdote. In his attempt to paint the perfect woman, Don Quixote follows the example of the Greek painter Zeuxis. The attentive reader would have been alerted to this painter's importance in the work since he is one of the many authorities listed by the friend in the prologue (1978, 1.53). His manner of painting perfection is found in Pliny's *Natural History* (1952, 309; xxxv.64). This story was often quoted in the early modern period, both in Italy and Spain. It is included in influential treatises such as Alberti's *On Painting* (Book ii, ch. 56; Rubin 1995, 240), Castiglione's *The Book of the Courtier*,[4] and Francisco Pacheco's *Arte de la pintura*.[5] It is also found in a work much utilized by Cervantes, Pedro Mexía's *Silva de varia lección* (1989, 1.643). It even became the subject of two paintings by Giorgio Vasari. In Pliny's anecdote, the Greek painter Zeuxis chose five women as models when asked to paint a beautiful image of woman for the temple of Juno in the city of Girgenti. While Pliny does not specify who the woman may be, and seems to confuse the city, Cicero in *De Inventione* asserts that Zeuxis was given his commission by the citizens from Croton. The Greek artist decides 'to paint a picture of Helen so that the portrait though silent and lifeless might embody the surpassing beauty of womanhood' (Cicero 1960, 167; 2.1). In order to accomplish this task he chose five women from that city 'because he did not think that all the qualities he sought to combine in a portrayal of beauty could be found in one person, because in no single case has Nature made anything perfect and finished in every part' (Cicero 1960, 169 2.1–2).[6]

In a similar fashion, Don Quixote creates Dulcinea in his imagination from a series of models. Like Zeuxis, he will point to five key models, all of which appear in chapter 25. But unlike the Greek painter, he does not choose all his models from nature. Instead, he attempts to surpass Zeuxis by using texts and paintings – and only one example from nature. Cervantes' text, with all its mixtures of text, art, and nature, seems to flaunt imitation, thus challenging Pliny, who criticized Zeuxis because he 'produces unaesthetic works precisely because he places himself within the limits of the real' (Barkan 1999, 85). Don Quixote follows the sense of Cicero's *De Inventione*, for the Roman writer uses the anecdote to show the importance of imitating several textual models when composing his treatise on rhetoric: 'I did not set before myself some one model which I thought necessary to reproduce in all details ... but ... culled the flower of many minds (1960, 169; 2.2).[7] Chapter 25 of

Cervantes' work also focuses on imitation and also asserts that one should imitate the best models. Indeed, the knight expressly mentions painting in his discussion of imitation: 'Cuando algún pintor quiere salir famoso en su arte, procura imitar los originales de los mas únicos pintores que sabe; y esta mesma regla corre por todos los oficios o ejercicios de cuenta que sirven para adorno de las repúblicas' (When a painter wants to become famous for his art, he tries to copy originals by the finest artists he knows. And this same rule holds good for nearly all the trades and professions of importance that serve to adorn a society) (1978, 1.25.303; 207).

By intimating that Don Quixote is following Zeuxis, the Cervantine text also exhibits its knowledge of Renaissance artistic and literary theory. In a letter to Castiglione, Raphael explains how his *Galatea* was created and how other beautiful women may be drawn: 'To paint a beauty, I must see more beautiful women, with this condition, that your Grace assists in selecting the best' (Hulse 1990, 86). As Clark Hulse asserts: 'The method espoused by Raphael is instantly recognizable as that of the ancient painter Zeuxis' (1990, 87). Indeed, Francisco Pacheco cites Raphael's letter in his *Arte de la pintura* immediately before discussing the five maidens from Croton (1982, 43). By turning to a classical anecdote, Raphael shows himself 'dependent on the simultaneous imitation of the classical past and of present nature' (Hulse 1990, 87). By alluding to painting and by having Don Quixote draw Dulcinea in the manner of Zeuxis, Cervantes exhibits his imitation not only of the classics, but also of Renaissance artists such as Raphael. Indeed, Cervantes' text acknowledges that the tale of the maidens of Croton is also about invention and composition, which are key to both painting and literature. Francisco Pacheco uses the story as an example of *inventio*. But Hulse argues that Zeuxis's tale was also 'a *locus classicus* in humanist discussions of decorum. As Zeuxis could spot the best anatomical feature of each maiden, and arrange these disparate parts into a single harmonious body, so the able poet could arrange or dispose perfectly the elements of his composition' (Hulse 1990, 88). Don Quixote is certainly capable of *inventio* as described by Pacheco, but his choice of subjects may be conflictive and thus inappropriate in creating a harmonious whole. The knight is also unable to follow the concept of compositional decorum. His imitation of chivalry would, if we follow the canon of Toledo's logic as developed in chapter 47 of the 1605 novel, impede him from understanding that the 'parts of the body must work together' (Hulse 1990, 195).[8] After all, his bookish models are monstrous:

'No he visto ningún libro de caballerías que haga un cuerpo de fábula entero con todos sus miembros ... sino que los componen con tantos miembros, que mas parece que llevan intención a formar una quimera o un monstruo que a hacer una figura proporcionada' (I've never seen a book of chivalry that could be regarded as a whole body complete with all its members ... on the contrary, their authors give them so many members that their intention seems more to produce a chimera or a monster than a well-proportioned figure) (1978, 1.47.565; 440).[9]

In contradistinction to the Greek painter, Don Quixote will draw Dulcinea in his mind, and thus create one more ur-ekphrasis, one that will be based on allusion. For this, he will follow the dictates of the art of memory. As noted in chapter 2, the Renaissance was intent on rediscovering and developing what it considered an important contribution of the ancients, as found in Quintilian's *Institutio Oratoria*, Cicero's *De Oratore*, and the *Ad Herennium* – the art of recalling through artificial memory 'discovered' by Simonides of Ceos (Yates 1966, 1–2; Carruthers 1990, 71–9). As noted before, Giambattista Della Porta was one of its Renaissance practitioners. *L'Arte del ricordare* was published only four years before Cervantes' arrival in Naples, a city that viewed Della Porta as one of its greatest writers. Many authors of mnemonic treatises (including the Spaniard Juan Velázquez de Azevedo) argue that five is the ideal number of images to place together.[10] Following this trend, Della Porta gives an example of five figures that form one mnemonic image (1996, 8.72–3) and claims that there are only five ways of altering a word for mnemonic purposes (1996, 13.82). The consistent use of the number five in memory treatises is particularly fortuitous since it coincides with the number of women that Zeuxis utilizes in his painting. Furthermore, Della Porta asserts that artificial mnemonics should rely on painting, and particularly the best of Italian art: 'It is useful to take pictures by good artists as memory images for these are more striking and move more than pictures by ordinary painters. For example, pictures by Michelangelo, Raphael, Titian, stay in the memory' (Yates 1966, 206).[11] This concern with painting may derive from the ancient relation between this art and memory. For example, Aristotle in his *Memory and Reminiscence*, a treatise that Thomas Aquinas thought was sufficiently significant to write a commentary on (Flor 1996, 30), calls memory 'something like an impression or picture' (1941, 609). Memory, then, is not an actual event or object, but a picture or representation of it. Don Quixote is so concerned with painting, constantly painting over reality with images from his memory, that these images may indicate his conscious ability to pick specific topics from his artificial memory. Although he would generally create images from the texts he was reading and place them in his memory,[12] it is very likely, given his continued reference to painting, that he also utilized paintings, including Italian art. And it is precisely works by Titian, Raphael, and one of his disciples that help to create Dulcinea. But would this *hidalgo* from La Mancha have any interest in Italy and its art? In chapter 8 of the 1615 novel, Don Quixote evinces a rather detailed knowledge of Roman architecture, providing us with the possibility that he may have visited the city and enjoyed its art. Such a pre-history for Don Quixote would certainly be in keeping with Cervantes' fictional creations. After all, his famous man of glass travelled extensively through Italy before going mad. Given the constant textualizing of Cervantes' own biography in *Don Quixote*, it would be more than plausible to assume that the knight, like Cervantes, had spent time in Italy and had become interested in its art and architecture.

Since Don Quixote is engaged in 'painting' Dulcinea in his mind, he will choose many of his models from painting although he will also turn to its sister art, poetry. There is no conflict here for, as Frances Yates reminds us, the relationship between poetry and painting is a very ancient one. Simonedes of Ceos, she tells us, believed that 'the poet and the painter both think in visual images which the one expresses in poetry and the other in pictures' (1966, 28).[13] The transposition of the visual and the verbal, then, was based on the supremacy of sight. And in a number of places in the novel, both the narrator and Don Quixote use the term 'to paint' instead of 'to narrate.'[14] The first two portraits utilized by the knight appear to be textual. But they could very well derive from woodcuts or paintings based on these texts. After all, the manuscript in which the story of Don Quixote appears includes at least one illustration, that of the knight fighting his Basque adversary.[15]

Don Quixote wishes to convert his visit to Sierra Morena into a prolonged meditation on Dulcinea. But he does not know which model to follow: should he do penance like Amadís for the jealous Oriana, or should he imitate the madness that seized Orlando when he discovered Angelica's love for Medoro? (1978, 1.25.304–5). Thus, as several critics have pointed out, Don Quixote uses the notion of imitation to become the artist or writer of his own life. Sancho, however, finds fault with the knight's thinking: both Orlando and Amadís had reason for their 'necedades y penitencias' (antics and ... penances) (1978, 1.25.305; 208), but Don Quixote does not. The knight replies: 'Ahí esta el punto ... y esta es la fineza de mi negocio ... dar a entender a mi dama que, si en seco hago esto, ¿qué hiciera en mojado?' (That is the whole point ... and therein lies the beauty of my enterprise ... have my lady think: if I do all this when dry, what would I not do when wet?) (1978, 1.25.305; 208). Although Don Quixote agrees with Sancho that he has no cause for his penance or madness, this is not entirely true. The two knights and the two ladies he has chosen have a deep connection to Don Quixote's fears and desires. His painting of Dulcinea will thus partake of both Oriana and Angelica.

Don Quixote tells Sancho that there are two things that arouse love in man, 'la mucha hermosura y la buena fama' (great beauty and good repute) (1978, 1.25.314; 216). The loyal and beautiful is often portrayed in the woodcuts of editions of the *Amadís de Gaula* that Don Quixote would have read, and he may have placed her in his memory as such (fig. 10.1). In a woodcut accompanying chapter 125, Oriana is seen in front of an arch. This is the 'arco encantado de los leales amadores' (enchanted arch of faithful lovers) (Rodríguez de Montalvo 1987, 1619), standing next to a magical chamber where only the most beautiful of women may enter. Oriana triumphs in both of these trials – of fidelity and beauty. As she approaches the arch, the image above it, 'comenzó el dulce son. Y como llegó so el arco, lançó por la boca de la trompa tantas flores y rosas' (commenced the sweet sound. And as she arrived under the arch, many flowers and roses were flung through the mouth of the trumpet) (Rodríguez de Montalvo 1987, 1622), confirming her loyalty to Amadís. Immediately following this magical test, a disembodied arm and hand seizes her and leads her into the 'Cámara Defendida' (Defended Chamber), thus confirming that she is the most beautiful of all women, 'en quien toda la fermosura del mundo ayuntada era' (in whom all the beauty of the world was gathered) (Rodríguez de Montalvo 1987, 1625). Don Quixote, then, may wish to place her in his memory in the moment of triumph. And indeed, the architecture surrounding Oriana in the woodcut and in the text actually recalls the placement of images in architectural loci. Della Porta recommends that they be placed in sites such as 'camere' and 'portichi' – chambers and porticos (1996, 4.63). But this is not the only way to recall Oriana. Amadís, as Don Quixote reminds Sancho, did penance in Peña Pobre when his lady, Oriana, thought he was unfaithful with Briolanja.[16] Like Amadís, Don Quixote is not totally without blame. Acting like Beltenebros, like a melancholy knight, Don Quixote is acknowledging his culpability.

He balances this, however, with the story of Orlando's love for

Angelica. Here the woman turns away from the valiant knight in order to love another. And in both Orlando's and Don Quixote's eyes, this Other is unworthy. But, in the pictoric tradition, from woodcuts of early editions to Renaissance paintings, these two figures are often idealized as in the works of Benedetto Lutti and Pellegrini.[17] Don Quixote does see himself as Orlando becoming crazed with jealousy over Angelica's love for Medoro. Although he acknowledges her beauty and thus places her in his memory, she stands in contrast to Oriana since she is far from loyal or faithful. Furthermore, Don Quixote refuses to visualize Medoro as either the perfect lover or an ideal knight. His image of the Moor breaks with idealized paintings and borrows from burlesque ballads on the subject: 'Angelica había dormido más de dos siestas con Medoro, un morillo de cabellos enrizados' (Angelica had enjoyed more than a couple of siestas with Medoro, a young Moor with curly hair) (1978, 1.26.319; 220).[18] For the Christian knight, the lover is an unworthy Moor. By turning from Oriana to Angelica, Don Quixote is transferring his guilt to the woman. The knight concludes that he will not imitate Orlando's madness since 'mi Dulcinea del Toboso pasaré yo a jurar que no ha visto en todos los días de su vida moro alguno' (I would venture to swear that my Dulcinea del Toboso has never seen a real Moor ... in all her life) (1978, 1.26.319; 221). Once again, Don Quixote is lying to himself and to Sancho; he is dissembling. The town of El Toboso, where Aldonza/Dulcinea resides, at least doubled in population after many moriscos settled there 'obligados a salir del reino de Granada de resultas de su levantamiento en el año de 1569' (obligated to depart from the kingdom of Granada as a result of its uprising in the year 1569) (Clemencín 1833, 1.332–3).[19] Américo Castro claims that Cervantes thus makes Dulcinea into a 'morisca.'[20] Whatever our view on this subject may be, the inclusion of El Toboso in the narrative raises the morisco question only four years before their final and tragic expulsion and shows Don Quixote's conscious denial of the problem at a crucial time in history. As Carroll Johnson asserts: 'The story that has emerged of the hundred years from the conversions of 1501 through the revolt in the Alpujarra and consequent expulsion of moriscos from Granada in 1570, to the final expulsion of all moriscos from Spain in 1609–1614, is the story of a struggle between oppression and resistance. The expulsion may be read as a confession of defeat on the part of the authorities' (2000, 53).

These two texts, Rodríguez de Montalvo's *Amadís* and Ariosto's *Orlando furioso*, and their pictoric representations, then, have provided the knight with traits with which to paint his picture of Dulcinea. This is a complex and conflictive drawing, one that points to both his and her guilt; one that delights in the noble provenance of the lady and casts doubts as to her and her lover's religion. It arouses in Don Quixote the two humours that have made him lose his mind: with Amadís he becomes melancholic, and with Orlando he is prone to a choleric temperament.[21] But Zeuxis tells us that five models are needed. Don Quixote, as we have noted, mentions two others: Helen and Lucretia (1978, 1.25.314). Since the knight alludes to these women of antiquity while explaining that he is painting Dulcinea in his imagination, we are certainly tempted to assume that his image of these classical figures may derive from famous paintings. And we have also noted that Cicero asserts that it was Helen whom Zeuxis was painting.

Don Quixote may wish to place Helen in his memory as she was drawn by Zeuxis. But the knight has neither the painting nor a description of it available to him. In spite of Zeuxis's depiction of Helen, she did not become one of the more popular subjects in Renaissance art, perhaps because, as Lessing argues, Homer conveys 'an idea of her beauty which far surpasses anything [visual] art is able to accomplish toward that end' (1984, 111; Heffernan 1993, 126).[22] Most Renaissance paintings dealing with the abduction of Helen show her transported by force. Indeed, the Spanish painter Juan de la Corte portrays her thus (fig. 10.2). Helen is held by a soldier and is guarded by Hercules, wearing lion skins, as she is transported by boat to a galleon at sea.[23] Don Quixote thus sees Helen as a lady in distress and even transgenders Sancho at one point, comparing him to the most beautiful of women and assuring him that he will save him: 'Y hubiera hecho en tu venganza más daño que el que hicieron los griegos por la robada Elena' (I should have returned there and avenged you by wreaking more havoc than the Greeks did for the rape of Helen) (1978, 1.21.256; 169). Thus, the knight establishes a link between the inn and Troy and between Sancho and Helen. But just as soon as he paints this picture of Sancho as his Helen, he sets out to erase the humorous overstatement and the homoerotics of friendship. Don Quixote turns to his imagined Dulcinea and argues that if she had been of Helen's time, she would be reputed as the most beautiful.

In the 1615 novel, we find a very different portrait of Helen, as Don Quixote views a tapestry at an inn: 'En una dellas estaba pintada de malísima mano el robo de Elena, cuando el atrevido huésped se la llevó a Menelao ... Elena no iba de muy mala gana, porque se reía a socapa y a lo socarrón' (On one of them some clumsy hand painted the rape of Helen, at the moment when the audacious guest carried her off from Menelaus ... Helen wasn't too sorry to be stolen away, because she was laughing to herself on the sly) (1978, 2.71.574; 965). A tapestry from a famous series on the Trojan War now hanging at the church of Zamora shows Helen being joyfully taken (López Torrijos 1985, 193).[24] But it is Paris, not Helen, who seems joyful, and the tapestry's model is a medieval text that talks of Sibyls and seeks to exonerate Paris.[25]

The tone of the quixotic image comes much closer to that of a Renaissance fresco. Giorgio Vasari in his *Lives of the Artists* speaks admiringly of Raphael's disciple, Giulio Romano, and of his work at the Ducal Palace in Mantùa. This artist 'in one hall caused the whole of the story of Troy and the Trojan War to be painted' (1996, 2.132). One of Giulio's frescoes in the Sala di Troia is *The Rape of Helen*. In order to mirror the 'hedonistic and sometimes irreligious temperament' of the court of Federigo Gonzaga (Saslow 1986, 65), Giulio's fresco shows how Helen enters her captor's boat willingly,[26] beckoning her servants, so as to hurry them along. There is no rape of Helen, but a joyous departure to be with Paris. There is a kinship, then, between the badly painted cloth seen by Don Quixote and Giulio's famous fresco. In the Italian painting, her lips are parted in what could be taken as the beginnings of a smile. Her exposed breast confirms an erotic intent which is allegorized by a winged cupid above. But why is Giulio called a wretched dauber in Cervantes' text? Perhaps it is because he draws female joyous eroticism and pagan or hedonistic abandon. The painted Helen, like the textual Angelica, is thus interpreted by the knight as sites of culpability.

If this was Don Quixote's third model for Dulcinea, the fourth could not be more opposite. Lucretia was often conceived as the epitome of the chaste woman, who chose suicide over dishonor after being raped. It is most fitting that Don Quixote choose her for the palace of his mind since Della Porta gives a lengthy description of how to place this story in the memory (1996, 8. 72–3).[27] Della Porta's idealized depiction contrasts with the mocking view of Lucretia in Aretino and Machiavelli.[28] Some Spanish Golden Age playwrights even revel in the rhyme Lucrecia/ necia. But this perspective was more the exception than the rule.[29] It did not enter into the pictorial tradition. Perhaps the most famous Renaissance representation of the rape is a painting by Titian (fig. 10.3) which shows Sextus's 'violent and erotically charged attack' (Spear 1997, 88).[30] This painting came into the possession of Phillip II in 1571.[31] Could Don Quixote be picturing the ideal and chaste Lucretia at the moment of rape? There are elements in the painting that recall Don Quixote's encounter with Maritornes in chapter 16, an episode that has been mainly studied for its ludic and carnivalesque features or as a bedroom farce. In the painting, Sextus holds on to Lucretia's arm while she reclines on the bed. On seeing the Asturian maid, Maritornes, the knight 'la asió fuertemente de una muñeca, y tirándola hacia sí, sin que ella osase decir palabra, la hizo sentar sobre la cama' (seized her by her wrist and pulled her towards him and made her sit on his bed, and she did not dare utter a word) (1978, 1.16.203; 126). The similarities are thus striking. Furthermore, the knight decides to paint over[32] this rather grotesque looking servant into a princess from the romances. Again, her description fits Titian's Lucretia. Maritornes's hair becomes as golden as that pictured by Titian. Lucretia's arms in the Italian canvas are adorned with bracelets that could fit the double description by Don Quixote: they are encrusted with glass beads (jewels) and with fine pearls from the Orient. In Titian's painting, Lucretia attempts to disengage herself from the threatening Sextus. With one arm she pushes him away, while he holds on to her other arm. Maritornes also battles the knight while he perseveres in his attempts to hold her down, 'la moza forcejeaba por desasirse y don Quixote trabajaba por tenerla' (the girl struggling to break free and Don Quixote doing what he could to cling on her) (1978, 1.16.204; 127). And finally, the painting shows a figure at the foot of the bed, a slave watching the scene.[33] This voyeur also appears in the novel. The muleteer, who was awaiting Maritornes's visit, on seeing her with Don Quixote, 'se fue llegando más al lecho de don Quixote' (had crept up close to Don Quixote's bed) (1978, 1.16.204; 127).

Thus, Dulcinea partakes of the image Don Quixote had formed of Maritornes, and of his own struggle with his sexual impulses. Memory images, according to Della Porta, are strongly retained if they are either idealized or move to laughter (1996, 9.78). The classical *Ad Herennium* also points to this opposition,[34] adding that both 'exceptional beauty' and 'singular ugliness' are useful for recollection. All these elements (beauty versus ugliness; idealized and comic images) coalesce in the composition created by Don Quixote from the conflation of Titian's painting with the farce at the inn. Della Porta also claims that lewd images are easily remembered (1996, 9.78). The painting has as theme Lucretia's chastity but it also displays Lucretia's body. Comparing Titian's work to Artemisia Gentileschi's *Tarquin and Lucretia*, Donaldson concludes that Artemisia did not move away from the male point of view represented by Titian.[35] Like Titian's painting, there is in Artemisia 'the suggestion of display in the disposition of Lucretia's body' (1982, 20); and there is also the presence of a slave who observes the scene. His presence and her pose are an 'invitation to male voyeurism,' which 'hint at a central conflict in purpose' (1982, 20). Although Cervantes would not have known Artemisia's painting, he would be familiar with Titian's. Don Quixote reflects the conflict in the painting. He both idealizes the chaste Dulcinea and is tempted to hold on to the female body against her will (as in the case of Maritornes).

Even if Don Quixote placed this painting in his memory, he would never acknowledge that he could be threatening to women or that he cared to view them in revealing postures. After all, he considers himself a Platonic lover and a defender of ladies in distress. In addition, he would have Sancho imagine that he is viewing Dulcinea/Lucretia as a protosaint, as the embodiment of chastity. Other Renaissance paintings show Lucretia alone after the rape. A knife like the one Tarquin holds in Titian's painting is now in her hand. This is the moment when she wills her own death. Marcantonio Raimondi's engraving of Raphael's drawing *The Death of Lucretia* (1510?) (fig. 10.4) is perhaps the most famous. Giorgio Vasari, in his *Lives of the Painters*, relates that Marcantonio 'having arrived in Rome ... engraved on copper a most lovely drawing by Raffaello da Urbino, wherein was the Roman Lucretia killing herself, which he executed with such diligence and in so beautiful a manner that Raffaello, to whom it was straightway carried by some friends, began to think of publishing in engravings some designs of works by his hand' (1996, 2.82). As Arthur M. Hind reminds us, this *Death of Lucretia* induced Raphael 'to acquire the co-operation of Marcantonio, which lasted till the death of the former in 1520' (1963, 94).

And yet, many of the martyred descendants of Raphael's and Marcantonio's work have been viewed in a different light. While Marcantonio drew her clothed, Lucas Cranach removes the clothing from his Lucretias so as to pander 'to male voyeurism with their teasingly transparent garments' (Spear 1997, 89). But to better understand this version of the pictorial Lucretia, it is best to look at one of Guido Reni's depictions, although his works were painted more than twenty years after the publication of the first part of *Don Quixote*.[36] As Richard E. Spear explains, Reni 'designed at least ten different representations of Lucretia and Cleopatra committing suicide' (1997, 84), all of which were 'phenomenally popular' (83). This popularity may have had to do with the bringing together of opposing elements: 'the mood of a quasi-

Christian martyrdom' (Spear 1997, 89) with an expression 'of detachment from reality and an inward bliss that can suggest sexual gratification' – as she holds the phallic knife (Spear 1997, 98). Don Quixote's Dulcinea can thus exude the perfection of approaching martyrdom. Just as Reni's woman has her eyes averted, entranced in a beatific vision, so Don Quixote can imitate her rapture and look upwards to the heavens, in search of celestial beauty and perfection.[37] In this he would be a typical lover since, as James F. Burke states: 'Late medieval and Renaissance writers often portrayed their male lovers as experiencing mystical rapture when beholding the beloved' (2000, 35–6). This intimation of perfection can sanction a different type of male pleasure, which Spear describes as 'the iniquitous excitement derived from watching women suffer *in extremis*' (Spear 1997, 86).

Even though nowhere in the text do we find Don Quixote acknowledging this type of hidden pleasure, a crucial moment in the interpolated story of the *Curioso impertinente* (*Tale of Foolish Curiosity*), which is narrated while the knight is asleep, may be a manifestation of the knight's unconscious desire. Camila, in order to show her husband her alleged faithfulness, plunges a knife into her own body as Anselmo watches 'cubierto detrás de unos tapices donde se había escondido' (hiding behind the tapestries) (1978, 1.34.432; 325). Spear discusses Reni's paintings of Lucretia in terms of staging, calling them 'emblematic soliloquies' with Reni as producer-director (1997, 83). Cervantes' novel is replete with theatrical techniques as Jill Syverson-Stork and Jay Farness have pointed out.[38] In the tale of the *Curioso impertinente*, we also have a theatrical act, one produced and directed by Camila so that the spectator (or voyeur), Anselmo, would be convinced of her faithfulness. Indeed, she models her most dramatic moment after Lucretia, and even refers to her before her fake attempted suicide (1978, 1.34.430). Of course, Camila's distress is a faked one, a parody of Lucretia's plight. But this is not the only woman with knife in hand in Cervantes' novel who threatens suicide before an audience.[39] Thus, the reader, like Don Quixote, is offered several pictorial embodiments of beauty at the moment of greatest distress.

Indeed, Lucretia's 'female distress' (Spear 1997, 86) is central to Don Quixote's view of the world. Ruth El Saffar has explained that Don Quixote, while fearing the body, emphasizes 'to an extraordinary degree man's uncontrollable lust, and the dangers to which young women are subject in the present age ... Don Quixote finds menaced women everywhere ... Ironically the only real virgin in need of protection in

Don Quixote's life is the unmarried niece he has left at home under the care of his housekeeper' (1984, 55). Don Quixote creates an image of Dulcinea that has many facets for contemplation: Lucretia the martyr, the woman in distress, and the woman *in extremis*; and Lucretia the Maritornes whom he held against her will in his own bed. They are accompanied by Helen, the most beautiful, seeker of erotic pleasures; the sinned against Oriana, and the sinful Angelica, attracted by Moorish pleasures. But there is one element missing, the fifth element, the fifth woman, who must complete the image of Dulcinea that Don Quixote will place in the memory palace of his mind.

Don Quixote tells Sancho that Dulcinea is the daughter of Lorenzo Corchuelo and Aldonza Nogales. From this information, Sancho concludes that Don Quixote's Dulcinea is none other than Aldonza Lorenzo. We are now moving from pictoric and literary models to one from 'nature.' Don Quixote gives us even more information. He states that he has seen his beloved only four times, because her parents have kept her in seclusion. The number four, as we have seen, is key to the Pythagorean conception of the universe. It represents the number of elements, humours, directions, winds, etc. In seeing her four times, Don Quixote admits that he has been engaged in a Pythagorean creation. Pythagorean numerology was used by Plato, and it is the knight's 'Platonic' love that is also foregrounded here. It may well be that she has never noticed his loving glances (1978, 1.25.311).

On hearing this, Sancho asserts that he knows her well and gives his own version of Aldonza/Dulcinea, one that contrasts with Don Quixote's idealized vision. For him, she is a rustic, strong woman with a manly voice who is not at all shy or modest and was never kept at home. Indeed, Sancho calls her a courtesan (1978, 1.25.312). But, scrutinizing this description,[40] Mary Gossy concludes that she is 'not a heterosexual female, that is, not an object or participant in male desire' (1995, 21).[41] Gossy thus argues that Aldonza 'does not participate in the objectifying structures of traditional narrative ... her body is represented but not transgressed. She is not coupled with Don Quixote, but rather with Dulcinea' (1995, 24). If Gossy is correct, then this fifth element is important because it guarantees that the knight will never be able to possess her. This possibility both soothes Don Quixote, who fears the female body, and forever defers his desire for her. In addition, Aldonza as a fifth element stands as something beyond that which can be grasped, as something unearthly, as something beyond the Pythagorean tetrad. And yet, she is useful to the knight's composition because a strong emotion is key to memory and recollection, according to Della Porta and Quintillian (Carruthers 1990, 148–9). Even San Juan de la Cruz argues that for devotion, one should 'escoger [la imágen] que mas mueve' (choose [the image] that most moves them) (Flor 1996, 36 note 30). The image must be accompanied by a feeling. Thus, the knight's fear/desire for that which he cannot have forms the last element in the construction of Dulcinea. Her image is now painted forever in his memory.

But why construct and forever recollect this complex and unattainable figure? In answer to Sancho's description of Aldonza/Dulcinea, Don Quixote tells a story whose message is that many of the women sung by poets are constructions which serve the poet's purposes (1978, 1.25.313–14). What is Don Quixote's purpose? True, his books of chivalry reveal that Don Quixote must have a lady if he is to be an exemplary knight. But in choosing five women with which to paint an ideal picture, the knight has actually drawn an image of multiple desires, one that allows him to see a beautiful and chaste princess as well as an alluring and erotic figure. While Don Quixote can feel the pains of guilt when he turns away from the princess, he can also portray her as the guilty one, the courtesan, the woman who can be enjoyed and shunned. Even his most chaste depictions contain elements of display and voyeurism. His contemplation then leads him to places of pain and desire, of lewdness and sublimity. In fashioning his woman, he has become subject to the treacherous and unstable erotic landscape of his mind. Furthermore, while attempting to paint the perfect beauty according to the notions of Zeuxis, following his *inventio*, he has actually succeeded in drawing a monstrous body. This image reflects the compositional problems of the romances of chivalry as defined by the canon of Toledo. Thus, the knight's monstrous readings have led him to create a monstrous woman. But there are, perhaps, less problematic purposes in this creation. Don Quixote does not want to be an ordinary knight; he wants to reestablish the Golden Age, to become emperor (of the world). Henry Higuera finds the purpose of Dulcinea to be rather straightforward: 'Don Quixote wants to conquer the world out of love for Dulcinea del Toboso, his ladylove. His love for her, he thinks, inspires his whole imperial project' (1995, 185). Lisa Rabin also sees Dulcinea as a companion of empire: 'In these texts, the Petrarchan desire to possess the woman translates into a desire to possess new territory' (1994, 84).

Indeed, the complex portrait of Dulcinea can be turned into a map of empire. Don Quixote's allusion to 'las edades pretéritas, griega, bárbara o latina' (past ages, whether Greek, Barbarian or Roman) (1978, 1.25.314; 216) speak of *translatio imperii*. Inhabitants of the Greek and Roman Empires, as Sebastián de Covarrubias notes, always spoke of those who were not members as barbarians (1987, 194). Antonio de Nebrija, whose grammar contains the famous phrase 'Siempre la lengua fue compañera del imperio' (Language always was companion of empire) (Navarrete 1994, 19), surveys the power of language, of the poets, and relates them to the strength of a kingdom, thus linking political, military, and linguistic accomplishments. He lists in succession the empires of the Chaldeans, the Hebrews, the Greeks, and the Romans, hoping that Spain will be the next heir. In Don Quixote's feminine map of empire, only the two more recent great empires of the past are listed – both are European. Helen represents the Greeks and Lucretia the Romans. Both women are in a rather unstable position in regards to the land they embody, mirroring the ancient view of the feminine as trigger for violence. In the locus classicus of historical causality, Herodotus's *History*, we are told that wars, and in particular, wars between Greeks and barbarians, have as their cause the ravishing of women. His *History* begins with a series of abductions: the Phoenicians abducted Io; then the Greeks carried off Europa. It was the Greeks again who indulged in another wrong, stealing Medea. This 'double wrong' led Paris to steal a Greek woman, Helen. This is but the beginning of Herodotus's tale, which goes on to recount how Gyges stole Candaules's kingdom of Sardis as well as his wife. In Rome, Livy follows closely Herodotus's links between abduction of women and epic conquest. The most salient example is, of course, the rape of the Sabine women. At a second key moment in the history of Rome, Livy resorts to the tale of Lucretia.[42] Thus, Don Quixote's imperial expansionism is based on two of the women that are central to historical accounts of martial conquest and empire building.

Don Quixote's five women, then, take on in this episode the role of the women in Raphael's *stanze* at the Vatican. They are allegorical figures. The men, on the other hand, represent through action the appropriation of the qualities or places these women symbolize. Indeed woman as place was a common icon. Cesare Ripa, whose illustrated version of his *Iconologia* was published in Rome in 1603, could have served as model for Don Quixote's allegorizations. Ripa personifies as women all four known continents of the time, Europe, Asia, Africa, and America. He links Europe with Rome: 'The richly dressed woman who here represents Europe is modeled chiefly on the personification of

Rome or on Minerva, goddess of wisdom' (1971, 102). Numerous instruments at her feet serve to map the globe, as she is seen as leader, discoverer, and conqueror of the world. But the male-dominated message of this illustration is clear. It is not this allegorical woman who accomplishes the deeds propounded by Ripa, but the men of the continent. In Don Quixote's mind, then, both Helen and Lucretia are allegorizations of Europe and part of the *translatio imperii*, of the move of empire from Greece to Rome.

The other three women represent a map of the present. The first and the last can also be included within the allegorization of Europe. Oriana, as daughter of the king of Great Britain, symbolizes Spain's rival at sea, England. Her place in Don Quixote's mnemonic gallery may be due, in part, to the fact that Philip II had indeed married an English queen, and that on the death of Mary Tudor in 1558, he proposed marriage to Elizabeth (Kamen 1997, 72). If Don Quixote was to be like Amadís and the Spanish Habsburgs,[43] he could indeed consider an English wedding. But this English Dulcinea would ignore the knight. Elizabeth would not marry Philip, and even though he tried to remain at peace with England, this turned out to be impossible. Oriana as England would also bring to mind not only the defeat of the Armada, but also the English sack of Cadiz.[44] Angelica represents the non-European Other. She is daughter of the ruler of Cathay (Asia) and loves an African Moor, Medoro. In Ripa, she can be seen as both the 'bejeweled woman' of Asia who stands for the 'fierce and barbarous peoples adhering to the religion which Mohammed taught' (1971, 103) and the dark-skinned native of Africa who portrays a region 'filled with superstition' and that also honor Mohammed 'above all' (1971, 104). Angelica thus stands for Cervantes' continuing concern with Algerian corsairs and Islamic control of the Mediterranean.

The fourth continent, America, is not represented in Cervantes imaginative image of Dulcinea, something that should not come as a surprise given the conflictive view of the newly encountered continent during the Spanish Golden Age. To conquer America may have meant for Don Quixote to take her gold and riches. And this is certainly not commensurate with the knight's vision of himself. The last woman represents the European present, much like Oriana. Aldonza must represent the Spanish empire, thus completing the *translatio imperii* started with Greece and Rome. Not surprisingly, she is the most conflictive figure in the map, and not at all the proud woman of Titian's allegory *Spain Coming to the Aid of Religion*. She is both an exalted princess and a manly peasant who evinces Moorish ancestry. She even espouses a sexuality that rejects the hierarchical power structure of male-female. Rather than representing the univocal empire suggested by the prophecy of the River Duero in *La Numancia*, she is the stuff of diversity; she is that which the Spanish rulers sought to squelch.

From the start, then, Don Quixote's imperial project, his desire to 'conquer' Dulcinea, is doomed. The knight is as conflicted about women's bodies as he is about his own home and his imperial project. His portrayal of Dulcinea draws on a classical anecdote and on Renaissance art and literature in order to create a perfect beauty, a goddess. But the result of his *inventio* seems to be a monstrous and conflictive body, which he constantly denies. Even though Don Quixote fails to create his perfect Dulcinea, he succeeds in making her unforgettable. She is housed in the palace of his memory in such a way that she becomes impossible to dislodge. Her image carries with it all the attributes necessary for artificial mnemonics to create indelible images: chaste perfection and lewd depictions, the brutish[45] and the beautiful (Della Porta 1996, 9.79), the emotional and the imaginative. Dulcinea's image must be captured,[46] must be enchanted, must be restrained, for, in her memory palace, she holds sway over the violent, exotic, and erotic demons of the knight's mind.

11 Love's Architecture: Giulio Romano

'Should you like to go to the Farnesina, Dorothea? It contains celebrated frescoes designed or painted by Raphael, which most persons think it worth while to visit.'

'But do you care about them?' was always Dorothea's question.

'They are, I believe, highly esteemed. Some of them represent the fable of Cupid and Psyche, which is probably the romantic invention of a literary period, and cannot, I think, be reckoned as a genuine mythical product ...'

George Eliot, *Middlemarch*

With Part 4 of *Don Quixote* we not only have a proliferation of chapters, but also of adventures. While Part 3 consisted of thirteen chapters, Part 4, the longest, includes twenty-five. Most of these are once again dedicated to digression, as with Part 2. But while the second part featured one pastoral interpolation, Part 4 has six distinct digressions, which are not in the main told as a whole but are narrated in segments, weaving into other interpolations and even quixtoic adventures in order to produce a texture akin to the romances, which relish in the device of interlacing. This manner of telling a story, which begins a digression, brings it to a halt to pass to either the main action or another digression, and then picks up yet another thread is certainly key to works from the medieval romances to Renaissance epics such as Ariosto's *Orlando furioso*. David Quint refers to these texts as 'baggy monsters' (2003 ix), and explains that this first impression gives way to connections and correspondences. These links, he argues, become more pronounced in *Don Quijote*. Indeed, as prelude to these digressions, Don Quixote, in the Sierra Morena episodes, makes numerous references to Ariosto, also pointing to the difficulty in following the 'thread' of adventures. These threads will serve to weave a most complex tapestry of interpolations, one that is replete with analogies and correspondences. One of the digressions is very different from the rest, since it has nothing to do whatsoever with the events being narrated or with the characters in Cervantes' novel. This tale is one found in a trunk at the inn and is simply read to those who are present.

Although found towards the beginning of Part 4, *El curioso impertinente*'s placement is almost at the centre of the 1605 novel. Thus, it seems as if the whole novel is an elaborate frame that contains this curious tale. Pointing to the shield of Achilles in Homer, on which the circling ocean serves as border or frame to the figures within the shield, Françoise Meltzer argues: 'The ocean stream frames the scene depicted on the shield, and it also "frames off," delimits, the story of the shield from the larger story of the *Iliad*. In this sense, ecphrasis may be seen as an early version of the intercalated story' (1987, 22–3). Like Homer's shield and like the figures depicted in the manuscript from Toledo in chapter 9, the *Curioso* is framed by an ekphrasis, the description of a trunk filled with manuscripts and three large tomes (1978, 1.32.394). While the large books elicit a discussion of the difference between history and fiction, the manuscripts excite the curiosity of both Cardenio and the priest. Among them is one consisting of eight folios and written in excellent handwriting. The title in large lettering, *Novela del curioso impertinente* (*Tale of Foolish Curiosity*) and the attention it receives by Cardenio and others leads the priest to read it aloud to the others 'por curiosidad siquiera' (if only out of curiosity) (1978, 1.32.399; 295). Thus, curiosity exists both within the frame and within the tale. Later we will see that it extends to the novel as a whole. The description of the trunk and of the manuscript serves as an initial ekphrasis, much as the one of the manuscript from Toledo that contained the adventures of Don Quixote. This first ekphrasis can be seen as frame for the second or metaekphrasis, the stop in the narrative to read the *novela*. It is like the ocean that frames the figures in Achilles' shield. And yet, the situation is even more complex, for this tale is also framed by two interlaced episodes, those of Fernando and Lucinda and of Cardenio and Dorotea, which are in turn interwoven around Don Quixote's adventures. The frame is thus much larger, consisting of two other amorous tales. And they lie within the story of the adventures of Don Quixote. These frames within frames as well as the double ekphrasis serve to demarcate the *novela* as something of great importance, something as important as the very novel itself, whose manuscript had been discovered in chapter 9. The artfulness of the interpolation serves to exhibit not only its complex intertextuality but also its ekphrastic qualities.

The *Curioso* is, at its core, a work that tests its protagonists through curiosity. Anselmo wants to test the faithfulness of his wife, Camila. In order to do this, he asks his best friend to serve as bait. Just as we have a double ekphrasis, we have a double test, one of the faithfulness of the wife and the second of the bonds of friendship. In order to emphasize the literariness of the test, Lotario reminds his friend Anselmo how Rinaldo, in the *Orlando furioso*, rejected such a test. Lotario, thus admonishes his friend to be prudent since nothing would be gained by such an 'impertinent' endeavour (1978, 1.33.407). This explicit reference to Ariosto highlights once more the importance of interlacing in the fourth part of Cervantes' novel, since the Italian author was a master at this technique. However, there are at least two other textual models for the *Curioso*. The main one is the myth of Cupid and Psyche, an interpolated story in the ancient romance by Apuleius, *The Golden Ass*, which, like Cervantes' tale, is ekphrastic in the sense that it stops the narrative to tell a tale that seems totally unrelated to the action of the novel.[1] Cervantes was well aware of this ancient tale, as he refashioned it into the story of Ruperta and Croriano in the *Persiles y Sigismunda*.[2] In Apuleius's story, Venus wishes to bring down Psyche for her amazing beauty. It is demanded that Psyche be given to a monster to marry. Carried by the wind, Psyche dreads her death at the hands of such a creature, but awakens to find herself in an amazingly beautiful meadow at the centre of which stands a magnificent palace, her home and that of her husband. Surrounded by incredible luxury and pleasures, she has but to follow one command. Psyche is ordered never 'to try to discover what her husband looked like or to allow impious curiosity to hurl her down to destruction from the heights on which Fortune had placed her and so forever deprive her of his embraces' (1990, 57). Curiosity to see what must remain invisible brings about Psyche's downfall, much in the same manner as Anselmo's desire to render visible his wife's invisible qualities (her fidelity) brings about his destruction. A key difference between the tales is found in the reversal of roles. While in the Cupid and Psyche story it is the woman who in biblical fashion indulges her curiosity, in Cervantes' interpolation it is the male who succumbs to this desire.[3]

Most critics accept the fact that the theme of *improspera curiositas* (Apuleius 1990, 15) is central not only to the Cupid and Psyche tale but also to the *Golden Ass* as a whole. Lucius, the protagonist of the work, suffers a fate very much like that of Psyche as E.J. Kenney explains: 'His downfall and his many ordeals are the result ... of his debased curiosity which led him to pry into magic instead of devoting himself to the liberal studies and beneficent mysteries' (Apuleius 1990, 11). A similar link can be discovered between the *Curioso* and *Don Quixote.* This link is consciously fashioned after Apuleius's work. Don Quixote, like Lucius, eagerly pursues a type of learning that is not suited to his station in life. His assiduous reading of chivalric romances leads him to believe in the power of enchanters, much in the same way as Lucius seeks out the knowledge possessed by witches. Both Lucius and Don Quixote must eventually renounce these pursuits and devote themselves to the deity, the Christian God in the case of Don Quixote in the 1615 novel, and the mysteries of Isis in the case of Lucius.

The tale of the *Curioso* is interrupted by an episode in which Don Quixote slashes at some wineskins thinking they are a giant. For Juergen Hahn (1972), this serves to point to a relationship between Anselmo in the tale and Don Quixote in the novel. While the first is ruled by his curiosity and must test his wife's faithfulness, the knight seems to be totally faithful to a lady he has never seen. And yet, when he slashes at the giants/wineskins in order to help Princess Micomicona regain her kingdom, he is also being tempted by her offer of marriage. While for Hahn, the *Curioso* becomes a countertale to Don Quixote's actions, it is only so if we accept that Don Quixote is indeed forever faithful to Dulcinea. Another important point to be added is that the wineskins episode is modelled after Apuleius's *Golden Ass,* in which Lucius, like Don Quixote, battles three wineskins which he describes as giants (Scobie 1976, 75). Diana de Armas Wilson asserts that the link between Apuleius and Cervantes is thus reinforced by what she calls 'the rhetoric of double interpolation' (1994, 89), where both the *Curioso* and the wineskins interruption derive from *The Golden Ass*. This leads the reader to further contemplate the links not only between the tales but between ancient and modern novels. In the wineskins episode, both Don Quixote and Lucius are blinded to the reality of the situation and wield their swords valiantly against mock-enemies, the first against the giant that took Micomicona's kingdom, and the second against thieves that threatened the home of his friend Milo. In Cervantes' text, laughter is the response elicited by Don Quixote's deeds: 'Quién no iba a reir con los disparates de los dos, amo y mozo? Todos reían sino el ventero' (Who could have failed to laugh at the nonsense of these two, master and servant? And laugh they did, all except the innkeeper) (1978, 1.35.440; 332). In Apuleius's work, Lucius comes to discover (after being tried for murder) that it was all a hoax created expressly 'for the public holiday which we regularly celebrate after the passage of a year in honour of Laughter, the most pleasing of gods' (Apuleius 1989, 1.147; 3.11). The novelistic episodes then stimulate laughter when men think of themselves as heroes by mistaking what they see, and by fighting that which does not threaten them or their society. While in the novelistic episodes in *The Golden Ass* and *Don Quixote*, not seeing correctly leads to laughter, the interpolated stories provide the opposite response. In *Cupid and Psyche* and the *Curioso*, seeing what should remain invisible (a god or an intangible virtue) brings about great suffering. Thus, the tales serve to highlight the character of the protagonist in the frame.

But the situation is much more complex, since the remnants of the tale of 'Cupid and Psyche' in the Cervantine text also contain pictoric allusions to this myth as it was depicted during the Italian Renaissance, particularly by Raphael and his disciple Giulio Romano. Indeed, the first instance of 'Cupid and Psyche' paintings to decorate a villa or palace can be found at the very inception of Cervantes' trip to Italy, since Luca Cambiaso, together with Giovanni Battista Castello, executed frescoes on the subject at the Palazzo Imperiale in Genoa (Suida Manning and Suida 1958, 88). The pleasurable and hedonistic ambience of the 'Cupid and Psyche' paintings contrasts with the more moralistic tone of Apuleius's interpolation, and the claustrophobic and tragic mood of Cervantes' tale. In order to fully view the images within the *Curioso*, it is necessary to consider the hedonistic impetus of ekphrasis within the ekphrasitic interpolation. To these paintings should be added the very architecture of love, of the pleasure villa. It should be recalled that one of the models for Cervantes' *La Galatea*, as Edward Dudley has shown, was the painting by Raphael, *The Triumph of Galatea*, located at the Galatea Loggia of the Villa Farnesina in the outskirts of Rome. There is a second important loggia at this Villa, the Psyche Loggia. Dudley explains: 'In fact until the twentieth century the two famous loggias were open to public perusal, just as the Loggia della Signoria in Florence still is. In this sense the Farnesina loggias serve a type of proto-museum for ambitious artists to display their wares' (1995, 33).

Cervantes seems to have used loggias as places to meditate on artistic images. Not only did he use the Galatea Loggia but also the Loggia della Signoria in Florence, which he reconceived in the six women of the prologue to the 1605 *Don Quixote*. Other public places were also sites of imitation, like the Piazza della Signoria. Cervantes inscribed its artistic and political battles also in the prologue to the novel. Thus, *Don Quixote* replicates the notion of a museum, rapidly passing in review images and forms from Italian works he had witnessed. This hidden artistic museum, revealed through flickers of pictorialism, rivals the libraries which are also a key to the novel. Indeed, the private museum rivalled during the sixteenth-century the private library. As Anthony Grafton has noted: 'The rooms they devoted to their acquisitions often followed the existing pattern of the scholar's study as given ideal form in Dürer's engraving of Saint Jerome: a harmonious realm, with beamed ceiling and leaded windows, where the owner of the house and his guest could withdraw for quiet work or intimate conversation. But their contents could not have been in sharper contrast with the neat book stand and shelves under which Jerome's lion sleepily crouched' (1998, 14). The startling art objects in Cervantes' museum of the mind would certainly have created a greater sense of wonderment than a glimpse at Don Quixote's library. Indeed, Dürer's picture of Jerome recalls how Don Quixote placed, in the museum of his mind, Parmigianino's *The Madonna and Child with Saints John the Baptist and Jerome*, which allowed him to represent Marcela – and even Dulcinea – as both sublime and sexualized Virgins. The knight's room of books was an ancient concept. It coalesces in the novel with a new type of site, the museum. Even if Don Quixote's library is burnt, its dying embers serve as a basis for the knight's imagination. And, even though the pictorial and architectonic museum is concealed and often subverted through distortion, inversion, and fragmentation, it serves to enrich the texture of the verbal tapestries in the novel – let us recall that in the *Curioso impertinente* Anselmo hides behind some tapestries in his home to view that which he should not see.[4] What is also concealed in this and other episodes are, as we have seen, the many pictorial images gathered by Cervantes in Italy. While the pictorial museum of the *Galatea* borrows from the garden loggia at the Farnesina, the central interpolated tale of the fourth part of *Don Quixote* makes use of the entrance loggia.

The Farnesina was built between 1509 and 1511 by Baldassare Peruzzi and surrounded by gardens that stretched all the way to the Tiber. Here were placed ancient statues, while a banqueting loggia faced the river. As for the house, its square plan, following ancient models, was set off by two loggias. Indeed, Peruzzi had been sent to Naples to study famous houses there which followed classical form and, in particular, the Villa de Poggio Reale, the most famous, built between 1487 and

1489.[5] For the loggia facing the river, Peruzzi had painted mythological scenes dealing with the horoscope of the owner, Agostino Chigi. It is for this loggia that Raphael had painted his *Galatea* (circa 1512). Chigi was a famous merchant and banker, his power unequalled among his peers. The activities of his trading and banking house extended to the whole of Europe and beyond – Italy was known for its commerce with the East. Indeed, as D'Ancona records: 'His business turnover was huge and continually increased by loans to eminent people of the time, such as Charles VIII of France, Caesare Borgia, Julius II, Leo X, and others ... The kings of Spain, France, England and Germany sent him letters and presents, and the Sultan wrote to him addressing himself to 'The Great Merchant of Christendom' (1955, 22). Once again the merchant and the visionary are set face to face. But in this case, it is not a Don Quixote battling mercantilism. Instead, we have a Raphael who paints in praise of this most prominent of merchants.

It was not until 1518 that Raphael returned to the Chigi villa, this time to decorate the second, or entrance loggia. The selection of the myth of Cupid and Psyche links art, architecture, biography, and literature. This tale of love, secrecy, and suffering may have been selected, first of all, to comment on Agostini Chigi's personal life. His relationship with Francesca Ordeasca gave him a number of children, but their union was not legitimized until 1519, eight years after its inception. As Roger Jones and Nicholas Penny state: 'It is tempting to connect the fable of Cupid and Psyche in which a clandestine relationship comes to a respectable conclusion with Chigi's personal life' (1983, 184). The Farnesina, then, became an abode of love and as such recalls Eros's palace in the interpolated tale of *The Golden Ass*. The description given by Apuleius must have been truly tantalizing to those in the Renaissance who wanted to imitate classical architecture. As Psyche awakens from her aerial voyage, she finds herself in 'a park planted with great tall trees and a spring of crystal-clear water. In the very centre of the garden ... a palace had been built, not by human hands but by arts divine. You could be sure at your first entry that you were looking at the splendid and delightful country-house of some god' (1990, 51). It is this type of divine and pleasurable country villa that the Renaissance wished to duplicate. In fact, Nicolo de Correggio had adapted the tale of Cupid and Psyche in his poem *Fabla Psiches et Cupidinis* (1491), which was in its fifth edition in 1518 when Raphael started his decorations of the loggia. In Correggio, the Apuleian description of the palace of love becomes a visionary example of the ideal villa in the Renaissance. Michael P. Fritz has shown that Correggio's architectural narrative bears a striking resemblance to the descriptions of the Villa de Poggio Reale in Naples (1997, 38). Thus, Chigi's life, Neapolitan architecture, ancient descriptions of a myth and of a palace of love in Apuleius, and a modern poem by Correggio intersect in the construction and decoration of the Farnesina. It is out of this intersection of love's architectures and arts that Cervantes begins to fashion his *Curioso*.

Even Raphael's own life seems to have a bearing on this new palace of love. As Giorgio Vasari describes it, both artist and merchant had a commonality of vision here, since both were enmeshed in amorous and sensual delights. Since Raphael would not abandon his mistress long enough to make progress on the loggia decorations, Agostini Chigi 'worked things out in such a way that he finally managed to bring this woman of Raphael's to come and stay with him on a constant basis in the section of the house where Raphael was working, and that was the reason why the work came to be finished' (1991, 328). Amorous passion unites artist and patron so that the resulting work is as much in praise of Chigi's union with Francesca as of Raphael's desire for his mistress, the difference being that the artist would not marry any of his mistresses, while Chigi acquiesced to the legitimization of his union with Francesca after a passionate affair with the beautiful and cultured courtesan Imperia (D'Anconna 1955, 22). The tale of Cupid and Psyche, then, extols the power of love, which is central to both Chigi and Raphael. But it also shows the legitimization of passion, something that pointed to Chigi and not to Raphael. Cervantes, who must have read Vasari's *Lives* and Apuleius's *Golden Ass* and viewed both the loggia at the Farnesina and the Villa de Poggio Reale in Naples, would have noted the many erotic, architectural and artistic permutations of the villa as palace of love. Cervantes' own tale will deal with a sanctioned love – that between Anselmo and Camila. It also includes the secret affair between Lotario and Camila, and between the maid Leonela and her lover, and the conflicted relationship between the two best friends, Anselmo and Lotario. Thus, his 'palace' of love was as filled with amorous permutations as the one constructed and decorated by Peruzzi, Raphael, and other artists for Chigi.

But there are two more elements needed in the construction of Cervantes' palace of love in the *Curioso*, a palace by Giulio Romano and a poem by Ludovico Ariosto. The second great rendering of the myth of Cupid and Psyche as associated with the architecture of love, was performed by one of Raphael's former assistants. While helping to decorate the Psyche loggia in 1518, Raphael's foremost disciple, Giulio Romano, aged only nineteen at the time, was called to Naples. On his return to Rome he may have added his impressions of the Villa de Poggio Reale, together with descriptions from Correggio's poem and even figures from the Farnesina loggia as part of the decorated loggia behind the portrait of Isabel de Requesens of Naples (Fritz 1997, 41ff). Giulio Romano, who participated in the decoration of the Chigi palace of love and evoked it in the Isabel portrait, would later have to decorate a palace of love. In 1524, four years after the death of his teacher, Giulio, shortly before departing Rome for Mantua, composed his *I Modi* (*The Positions*), 'sixteen drawings of similar format and composition, each of which displayed a heterosexual couple engaged in the sexual act' (Talvacchia 1999, 4). When Marcantonio Raimondi made engravings of these works in Rome, he was sent to jail and the prints destroyed (Talvacchia 1999, 4). But this scandal was followed by a second. For Pietro Aretino, who like Giulio had left papal Rome for Mantua, would eventually publish his *Sonetti lussuriosi*. These sonnets comment upon the forbidden engravings, which are reproduced above the poems. In Mantua, Giulio went to work for Federigo Gonzaga, who asked him to erect the famous Palazzo del Té (1526–35). The Roman artist combined architecture and painting, breaking with the majestic art of the Renaissance in order to exhibit the exuberance of mannerism. During the sixteenth century there was 'an island paradise' (Hartt 1958, 1.92), just outside of Mantua. Here many came to enjoy nature's beauty. It was on the island of Té that Giulio built the pleasurable and divine palazzo which was reached by a bridge from Mantua. It was a country palace that could well be compared to the divine home of Eros in Apuleius's myth, where both nature and art combined to bring about all possible joy.

Cervantes, who borrows from the Room of the Giants for the windmill episode, turns once again to Giulio Romano, this time to his Sala di Psique for a model (fig. 1). Indeed, Hartt shows that both the Room of the Giants and the Psyche rooms form a whole: 'What in the form of love is rewarded in the Sala di Psiche is punished when it assumes the shape of rebellion in the Sala dei Giganti. In each case the theme is the same: the ascent of the individual to Olympus' (1958, 1.157). The program is even more ambitious than the one at the Farnesina, consisting of twenty-three scenes divided into octagons, lunettes, wall frescoes, and a central scene of the marriage. There are even other paintings, some unrelated to the tale (Hartt 1958, 1.130). But once again, the paintings can be linked to amorous passion, to Federigo's passion for Isabella Boschetta. The vengeful image of Venus in the frescoes represents Isabella d'Este, Federigo's mother, who tried to block any legal union since she had a different political agenda. In the end, as Frederick Hartt explains, the legitimization of the relation between Isabella and Federigo took place only in art: 'For Federigo was never able to marry Isabella Borschetta, and when Maria Palologa died he married her sister Margherita with indecent rapidity, after some dispute inheriting the Monferrato' (Hartt 1958, 1.140).

In all these tales, love and politics, desire and wealth, art and patronage come together in a delicate weave of hues and forms in order to inform the art of the Renaissance. From these delicate yet powerful weaves Cervantes derived elements of plot and imagery for his tale of the *Curioso.* What is curious, however, is that Cervantes sets his tale in Florence rather than in Rome, Naples, or Mantua, thus seemingly invalidating connections with these earlier versions of the Apuleian palace of love. Not that Naples is silenced. Luigi Tansillo, some of whose verses are translated in the *novela,* was from Venosa in southern Italy, and spent much of his life at the service of the Spanish viceroys of Naples. Indeed, his *Clorida* contains a 'vivacious description of villa life on the Bay of Naples' (Wilkins 1966, 246). The Neopolitan villas of love, then, do have a textual entrance in Cervantes' tale. More important, the evocation of Florence serves to point to the locus of artistic endeavours in Renaissance Italy. Although there was no such prominent villa of (illicit) love where Cupid and Psyche reigned supreme in Florence, there could well have been. Florence and its surroundings were, after all, replete with villas constructed by its great financiers and leaders, such as the Medici. And Florence owes its name to the goddess Flora, who was not only the deity of flowers but also of prostitution. It is no wonder that Florence was known for its permissiveness. It was also considered the city of sodomitic passions.[6] Thus, Cervantes chooses a city where the fulfilment of desires is even in its very name. It is a city that subsumes the hedonistic desire of all others. By negating previous models, Cervantes encompasses all of them in the careful depiction of love's architectures.

In fact, there is one Italian site in Cervantes' tale that is particularly significant for the pictorial elements. As noted above, one of the models for the *Curioso* is actually alluded to in the *novela.* When Anselmo asks Lotario to test his wife, the latter reminds him of the tale of Rinaldo as related in Ariosto's *Orlando furioso.* In cantos 42 and 43, he is invited to spend time at an opulent palace where he is shown a goblet with remarkable properties: 'The man whose wife is chaste may drink from it, but not the man whose wife is adulterous: then the wine he expects to drink spills out to splash his chest' (1983, canto 43, 512). Rinaldo refuses to drink and then is told of the woeful tale of the knight who had confronted his wife's infidelity only when he had tested her to the extreme. This knight with his fabled pleasure palace, a structure now turned an instrument of torture for him, was from Mantua and the palace he inherited was not far from that city.[7] Ariosto's tale and beautiful palace with its many sculpted marbles and paintings (1983, canto 42, 505) may have led Cervantes to imagine yet another such palace in Mantua – the Palazzo del Té, where Giulio Romano painted his Sala di Psique. But in contradistinction to the owner of the Palazzo del Té, Ariosto's knight was abiding in a palace of pleasure without the pleasure of his beloved. The knight has lost his love by testing his wife, much in the same way that Anselmo would lose Camila. The amorous emptiness of this palace would be echoed in the halls of Cervantes' Florentine abode, where, after the marriage celebrations, the newly wed are left to their private spaces. A contrastive situation would take place in the Palazzo del Té, where Federigo would hold a feast for his mistress, inviting many friends and powerful political figures, who entered into the hedonistic pleasures of the villa.

Cervantes transforms the amorous emptiness of the pleasure palace into loneliness within marriage. The first few days after the wedding, the house still resembles the pleasure palace, for there is happiness in the company of friends, and in particular, the company of Lotario: 'Los primeros días, como todos los de boda suelen ser alegres, continuó Lotario como solía la casa de su amigo Anselmo, procurando honralle, festejalle y regocijalle con todo aquello que a él le fue posible (A wedding celebration is a time of happiness, so for the first few days Lotario continued to frequent his friend Anselmo's house, doing all he could to honour, regale and delight him) (1978, 1.33.400; 296). *The Banquet of the Gods* (fig. 2), one of two ceiling paintings at the Psyche Loggia of the Farnesina, or the wall fresco of *The Wedding Banquet of Amor and Psyche* (fig. 3) at the Sala di Psiche at the Palazzo del Té, depicts how the gods rejoice at a wedding feast. Anselmo's feast would have been far more modest – for it required modesty (thus transposing the Spanish manner into an Italian tale) and was held with modest means. It is true that these paintings are reflections of Renaissance conspicuous consumption, and that they celebrate, in Lisa Jardine's words, 'the culture's new access to a superfluity of material possessions' (1996, 15) but the Renaissance vision of pagan pleasure, which was fully realized only sporadically, had passed with the arrival of the Counter-Reformation. None of the guests at Anselmo's wedding feast could be equated with the nudes and seminude figures of Raphael and Giulio Romano, whose amorous glances and gestures of desire filled the walls and ceilings in these pleasure palaces. Indeed, the sexual pleasures of these pagan gods were even represented in Giovanni da Udine's festoons of fruits and flowers. As Jones and Penny have noted, the ceiling of the Farnesina exhibits, among these gifts of nature, a 'parody of sexual intercourse painted directly above the raised hand of the figure of Mercury' (1983, 185).

The fruits of marriage do not bring contentment to Anselmo. He cannot abide the new solitude of marriage, wishing instead to spend time with his best friend, Lotario. The latter no longer visits him regularly: 'Pero acabadas las bodas y sosegada ya la recuencia de las visitas y parabienes, comenzó Lotario a descuidarse con cuidado de las idas en casa de Anselmo' (But once the celebrations were over and the congratulatory visits had abated, Lotario began to be careful to neglect to go to see Anselmo) (1978, 1.33.400; 296). This curious loneliness comes as a faint echo from the Cupid and Psyche tale. There, Psyche is indeed alone since she cannot see her husband, and all the servants at the palace are invisible. She thus requests and is granted a visit from her sisters. Their envy of Psyche's fortune is the beginning of her downfall. In the *Curioso impertinente,* the fault lies not with Lotario, the visitor, but with Anselmo himself, who is not content with a life of amorous passion in his secluded abode of love. This heterosexual union deprives him of his most cherished homosocial bond, that of his best friend Lotario. Anselmo's test of his wife's faithfulness through Lotario becomes a way of having, in Diana de Armas Wilson's words 'two men sharing a woman who somehow intrudes on their original bond' (1987, 12). This type of 'trafficking in the body of a woman without her leave' (De Armas Wilson 1987, 15) is a motif encountered from biblical times when David, lamenting for Jonathan, states: 'very pleasant have you been to me / your love to me was wonderful / passing the love of women' to Borges' *La intrusa,* which uses this quote as an epigraph (De Armas Wilson, 1987, 11).

Some critics of *El curioso impertinente,* such as Francisco Ayala and Louis Combet, have delved deeper into the relationship between the two friends. They argue that the homosocial bond conceals a homosexual desire at a time in history when such unions were forbidden and at times even punished by death.[8] It may be, then, that Cervantes takes the notion of the Renaissance villa of love, which imitated its classical counterpart, one step further. He recalls the love between men that was so prevalent in ancient times – a bond forbidden by early modern Christian society. In both the Farnesina and in the Palazzo del Té, the artists inscribe this ancient love in their decorations. At the Farnesina, the main image of *The Banquet of the Gods* celebrates not only heterosexual pleasures by having the Graces pour perfumes on Cupid and Psyche's hair while Bacchus pours wine; it also shows Ganymede kneeling by Jupiter and handing him his cup. In itself, these images may appear as simply a part of the festivities. But it should be recalled that Jupiter's bisexuality was often represented in his rape of the youthful Ganymede, a handsome Trojan boy whom Jupiter in the form of an eagle abducted and took to the heavens to become his cupbearer. As James M. Saslow has shown, 'a persistent substratum of erotic associations adhered to the myth from classical times; the very word *ganymede* was used from medieval times well into the seventeenth century to mean an object of homosexual desire' (1986, 2). The figure at the Farnesina is surrounded by a feast of desire. Thus, it is nearly impossible to escape its sexual implications. Equally important is the fact that one of the lesser pictures in the loggia is a spandrel depicting *Jupiter Kissing Cupid*. Saslow explains: 'The gesture of Jupiter's left hand, which caresses the youth's chin with one finger extended, was a conventional indicator of tenderness and sexual love. Although it seems unlikely that Raphael meant Jupiter's gesture here to imply actual physical attraction – the god is, after all, blessing Cupid's impending marriage – the scene is so similar to the god's parallel action towards his beloved cupbearer that it was in the past mistakenly identified as *The Kiss of Ganymede* (1986, 132).

But one may go further than Saslow in this assessment. After all, Jupiter never respected his own marriage to Juno, often visiting earth to enrapture beautiful maidens – or youths. Indeed, his cupbearer was with him together with his wife Juno. Jupiter, in Raphael's interpretation of these scenes of pagan passion, may not have seen it as imperative to restrain his feelings towards the very god of love, in whom he may have seen a more perfect image of his beloved Ganymede. In Cervantes' *Curioso impertinente* it is shortly after the wedding feast that a new desire is revealed. Anselmo tries to explain this to Lotario, 'porque no sé qué días a esta parte me fatiga y aprieta un deseo tan estraño y tan fuera del uso común de otros, que yo me maravillo de mí mismo, y me culpo y me riño a solas, y procuro callarlo y encubrirlo de mis propios pensamientos' (because for I don't know how long now I've been assailed and tormented by a desire that's so peculiar and so unusual that I'm astonished at myself, and accuse and scold myself when alone, and try to stifle it and hide it from myself) (1978, 1.33.402; 297). The wording could well be that of a man tormented by the desire for a forbidden love. Anselmo may be unconsciously expressing the desire of a Jupiter, no longer abiding in ancient times, but in the constrictive ambience of the Counter-Reformation, for his beloved Lotario/Ganymede. As it turns out, the desire is deflected. Anselmo wants Lotario to test his wife, and probably, make love to his wife. The totally forbidden passion is channelled into a strange sharing of a woman's body.

The Farnesina was not the only palace of pleasure where the myth of Cupid and Psyche coexisted with that of Ganymede. While in Mantua, Giulio Romano became almost obsessed with the portrayal of Ganymede. Saslow records that 'besides the lost *Neptune,* during his years in Mantua Giulio designed six other compositions that include Ganymede' (1986, 137). Curiously, Ganymede's presence and sexuality are as bold in the ducal palace of Federigo Gonzaga as in his pleasure villa. At the Sala di Troia in the ducal palace, the ceiling painting is dedicated to *Venus Swoons in the Arms of Jupiter*. But here, Ganymede as a 'sensual nude male ... occupies the center of the composition despite his irrelevance to the immediate narrative' (Saslow 1986, 139).[9] The cupbearer is also the central ceiling figure in the Camerino dei Falconi, where he 'is manifestly an object of erotic desire' (Saslow 1986, 138).[10] Ganymede appears at least four times at the Palazzo del Té. He is shown in *Neptune Taking Possession of the Sea,* which is preserved only as a print. Here Jupiter's hands are on the cheeks of both Ganymede and Cupid, recalling the Farnesina's *Jupiter Kissing Cupid* (Saslow 1986, 137). The figure of Ganymede can also be glimpsed in the ceilings of the Sala dei Venti[11] and the Room of the Giants.[12] In the Sala de Psiche, he is shown in a lunette where Venus pleads with Jupiter to grant her the aid of Mercury. Here Jupiter, regally dressed, has his arm on a nude Ganymede, who in turn fondles an eagle (Jupiter's bird). Even more curious is the fact that underneath this lunette we read 'Federicus.' It is as if Giulio is forcing the viewer to link the duke of Ferrara with forbidden sexualities. Furthermore, the notion of male love appears again as part of the bacchanal feast depicted in the *Wedding Banquet of Amor and Psyche* (fig. 11.3). Giulio's marriage feast departs from Apuleius and from the banquet depicted at the Farnesina in that it takes place on earth rather than in heaven. Exotic animals reveal the lower plain and the lower passions, for here we have in addition to elephants and camels the goats of Silenus and the tigers of Bacchus. The painting revels in excess and exhibits 'husky nymphs and incontinent satyrs' (Hartt 1958, 1.135) seeking sexual satisfaction, and even 'attempting the chastity of divinities' (Hartt, 1958, 1.136). An old man – perhaps a god – embraces a satyr, exhibiting his sodomitic desire.

But, behind them, an ass brays. Hartt asks a most pertinent question: 'Why can he not be the Golden Ass, Apuleius himself, who in this unfortunate shape was forced to listen to the fable of Cupid and Psyche as narrated by the old woman who cooked in the cave for the band of thieves that had stolen him?' (1958, 1.136). Indeed, if on the one hand both the villas of passion and Cervantes' tale exhibit the permutations of desire, they also contain an opposite movement of which the transformation of Lucius into an ass is emblematic. Studying the Loggia of Psyche at the Farnesina, Jones and Penny warn that the fable was 'commonly regarded as an allegory of the immortality of the soul' (1993, 184). Psyche, after all, can be translated as soul. Indeed, there are several religious renditions of the myth in the Spanish theatre of the Golden Age. José de Valdivielso wrote an *auto sacramental* entitled *Psiquis y Cupido*, while Calderón de la Barca was the author of two *autos* based in the myth. These works often show Cupid as Christ and Psyche as the soul.

Although Cervantes' tale is not a part of this allegorical tradition,[13] the tale does include an opposition between amorous pursuits and retribution, together with the notion of punishment for excessive curiosity, be it for reading books, practising witchcraft, or engaging in amorous pleasures. The opposition between licence and exemplarity is inscribed in Cervantes' tale in many guises. Included in the Spanish *novela* are some verses from Tansillo's *Lagrime di San Pietro* (1978, 1.33.407), a work written as a palinode to this poet's youthful 'bachanalian' work *Il vendemmiatore* (Wilkins 1966, 246). The villas of love and the tale of Cupid and Psyche bring with them their own warnings. Surrounding the hedonistic pleasures, in the Palazzo del Té, Giulio Romano includes numerous tales of amorous infidelities by gods and men. Present is Venus 'who having betrayed her husband with the god of war, then betrays her lover with the beautiful huntsman Adonis; Ariadne, half-sister to the Minotaur, who is betrayed by her lover and finds comfort in the god of wine' (Hartt 1958, 1.136). Giulio thus warns of the innumerable betrayals and tragedies brought about by excess. It is, then, Anselmo's excess that brings him down. He will perish together with Lotario and Camila. The braying ass in both Apuleius and Giulo Romano warns against the excess of passion, but the beast is not heeded since Lucius becomes such an animal in the novel, while the frescoes show the old man and the satyr as they are filled with drink and desire.

Cervantes' *Curioso impertinente,* then, is a tale that both sings of excess and denies desire. Although the ending warns of the consequences of pagan excesses, the architecture of love found in the villas and paintings of the Renaissance shine through a textualized oppressive environment and a tormented psyche which are signs of the Counter-Reformation. The reader is left to confront oppositions and to discern the boundaries between eros and excess. But the brilliant renderings of Raphael and Giulio Romano serve as reminders of Psyche's final triumph and of the presence of Ganymede at the feast of the gods.

12 The Last Enchantment: Epilogue

Among the many images from the frescoes and canvases from Italian Renaissance art that are exhibited in the 1605 *Don Quixote*, a vast majority are anthropomorphic. The text renders depth and perspective to its portrait of character through the many figures found in Italian painting. The prologue begins by depicting the fictive author in a specific pose and mood. He is the melancholy writer whose demeanour parallels that of Michelangelo's as found in Raphael's *School of Athens*. In praising Michelangelo, Raphael is also showing his own anxiety and rivalry. The harmonious works of the latter contrast with Michelangelo's *terribilitá*, his rebelliousness at church dictates and classical strictures, leading him to become a model for later mannerist art. By portraying himself as a new Michelangelo, Cervantes signals that *Don Quixote* will differ significantly from his early works such as *La Numancia* and *La Galatea*, in which the art of Raphael was a key to his themes and structures. He is also signalling his awareness that Michelangelo's works, particularly *The Last Judgment*, were censored by Counter-Reformation dictates. Thus, Cervantes' *Quixote* will feature a form of self-censorship, contrasting the figure of the fictive author (a new Michelangelo) with the constant preoccupations of his characters – the priest and the barber – to censor libraries and books of entertainment.

While the fictive author's self-portrayal inscribes the rivalry between two great Renaissance artists, the portrayal of the crazed knight derives from a canvas by Titian, a painter known for his colourist style. Accused by many of being inferior to the greatest artists because colour was feminine as opposed to the great designs of artists like Michelangelo, Titian not only drew sensual mythological scenes, but was also the portrait artist of Charles V. His *Charles V at Mühlberg* is an epic and bellicose painting that draws upon the determination of the emperor and transforms his deformed jaw through a careful attention to decorum. The image of Don Quixote as a new Charles V will repeatedly appear throughout Cervantes' novel in a way that defies Titian's decorum and seems to point to the physical and political inadequacies of the emperor and his Habsburg successors. The repeated perspectivism and the problematic nature of the link between knight and emperor trigger an active reader to attempt to decipher who is being parodied. Is it the Golden Age that Charles sought to bring through wars with the Protestants, the French, and the Islamic foes? Or does the novel parody, instead, the decline after Charles, due to the ineptness of his successors, Philip II and Philip III? The impotence of the knight calls upon the failings of Spain, while the Habsburg jaw of determination cuts both ways: it can indicate the greatness of an imperial vision or the folly of indiscriminate territorial wars.

Since Don Quixote sallies forth to defeat foes, a number of them are also portrayed through images from Italian art. The merchants from Toledo may well recall the merchants of Trebizond, and the famous fresco by Luca Cambiaso in Genoa, which glorifies the mercantile city's successes over the ancient empire. Don Quixote battles the merchants because he envisions empire as a universal and univocal land ruled by a Catholic leader. Genoa and Venice, on the other hand, are mercantile empires that prefer accommodation with supposed enemies of Christianity, particularly the Ottoman Empire and the corsair havens of the North African coast. A second essential foe for a Christian knight is the giant, often seen as a demonic and pagan force. It is no wonder, then, that the knight sees the windmills as hundred-armed giants such as Briareus. His battles with this mythical foe recall both Dante's *Divine Comedy* and Botticelli's illustrations of this Italian epic. They also recall Giulio Romano's famous Sala dei Giganti at the Palazzo del Té in Mantua, where Jupiter's thunderbolts are destroying the rebellious creatures. This room, built to honour Charles V (a new Jupiter), who was conquering Italian rebelliousness, is another example of the link between Charles V and Don Quixote. While the emperor is able to spread his influence throughout Italy, the knight is impotent to defeat just one giant or windmill. This battle with the windmills also suggests the difficult relationship between chivalry and technical advancement. Through the use of artistic and scientific *techné*, Cervantes problematizes the link, pointing on the one hand, to the wonders of a pastoral Golden Age exalted by Don Quixote (which may only exist in books and myths), and on the other, to Charles V's ability to utilize chivalry, art, and technical advancement for the benefit of an imperial quest. Other foes easily materialize: sheep become armies in an epic pseudo-teichoskopia, while dead bodies assume the role of a demonic theophany.

While battling foes, Don Quixote as would-be knight must also assist the needy. The image of the half-nude Andrés being flogged by Juan Haldudo and complaining that he was being flayed alive elicits images from Michelangelo, where, in *The Last Judgment*, St Bartholomew displays his flayed skin. And yet, Don Quixote is far from being a new Christ/Apollo, dispenser of justice. In the same manner, it is difficult to ascertain the innocence of Andrés. The problematics of justice is one more element that must be inscribed in the discourse of Spanish rule, as Don Quixote consistently betrays the ideals of justice, although he himself is the subject of the harsh justice of the priest and the barber, who, in an inquisitional scene, burn most of his books. Both the problem of justice and the question of censorship are presented in such a way that the reader is unable to see directly what is meant. In this manner, the text wards off Counter-Reformation controls such as were shown in Michelangelo's work, where the forbidden nudes are covered by veils. In Cervantes, what Andrés fails to say is up to the reader to discover. Finally, the impulse for portraiture is once again felt, since the woeful figure depicted in St Bartholomew's skin from Michelangelo's fresco can be related to Don Quixote himself, who becomes the 'Caballero de la Triste Figura' (Knight of the Sorry Face). It is as if both the fictive Cervantes and his protagonist share in some way the melancholy and tortured vision of the Renaissance's most powerful artist.

All knights, according to Don Quixote, must have a lady. But once again, the desire for a lady is as conflicted in Don Quixote as is the acquiring of new territories and gaining fame. Although his Platonic musings over Dulcinea arise from the beginnings of the novel, other women seem to evince both Don Quixote's fear and desire for a woman's body. His vision of Marcela, the lovely shepherdess who appears on high as in a theophany, is filled with both sublimity and desire, thus recalling the mannerist art of Parmigianino in which the Virgin Mary is both an oneiric apparition that calls forth the celestial dream to a human body, and a sexualized woman who imparts fear in ascetic renunciates. As the text advances, it becomes clear that Dulcinea is even more difficult to portray in the knight's mind than Marcela. Chapter 25 clearly shows that she is made from remnants of famous women: Oriana and Angelica, from textual models; Helen of Troy and Lucretia, from

Renaissance art works. A fifth model, Aldonza, completes the picture, recalling Zeuxis's portrait of Helen, which was composed from the five most beautiful maidens from Croton. Although Zeuxis's portrait produced one of the most beautiful figures in ancient art, Don Quixote was only able to place in the palaces of his mind a most conflictive Dulcinea, one that was both loyal and traitorous; alluring and chaste; Christian and Moorish. As if this were not enough, the readers, as well as the guests at the inn, are treated to an interpolated story, *El curioso impertinente*, that seeks to foreground the nature of desire through the myth of Cupid and Psyche and the Renaissance artistic depictions of this tale. Both Raphael and Giulio Romano included depictions of them in palaces where desire and illicit passions were to be given free reign. While the Italian artists delved into passion in expansive palaces, Cervantes focuses on an almost claustrophobic abode in the midst of Florence, a city named after the goddess Flora, who ruled over prostitutes. It is also a city famed for its sodomitic practices during the Renaissance. Thus, Cervantes, while pointing to the openness of Florence, shows the closed nature of sexuality in Spain, where suspicion prevails. In the architecture of love constructed by Italian artists and imitated through both parallel and contrast in Cervantes' interpolated tale, desire moves from heterosexual abandon to the possibility of sexual dalliance among males. Since Don Quixote, in a comical, poignant, and revealing moment, once associated saving his squire to rescuing Helen of Troy, the incertitude of desire foregrounded in Cervantes' *novela* has echoes in the main action of Cervantes' text.

Interpolation is one more form of ekphrasis, a stop in the narrative to describe an image. The many Renaissance frescoes included in the tale further complicate this device, creating a metaekphrasis which is also surrounded by numerous digressions. These digressions, along with the ekphrastic description of the trunk in which the manuscript of *El curioso impertinente* is found, serve as frame. And it is this frame that will lead us to the conclusion of the novel. Among the six interpolated tales that are interwoven in Part 4 of *Don Quixote*, the one of Fernando and Dorotea is particularly interesting, since it contains a story within a story. Having been deceived and abandoned by Fernando, Dorotea leaves her home dressed as a man. When the priest and the barber discover her in Sierra Morena, they will again use her abilities at disguise to deceive Don Quixote. She will become Princess Micomicona, who was driven from her kingdom by the giant Pandafilando. Although her story seems derived from the romances of chivalry, numerous elements in her tale point to the evil magician Armida in Tasso's *Jerusalem Delivered* (Ruiz Pérez 1995). Needless to say the crazed knight is determined to help this lady in distress. The plan is to have her lead him past his village, where he will be forced to stay by the priest and the barber. In many ways, Dorotea/Micomicona/Armida captivates the knight much as the Italian enchantress captivates Godfrey's knights in the poem. Dorotea is as much a 'mistress of deception' as her pagan counterpart (Tasso 2000, 104; 5.61).

However, when it turns out that Fernando reappears and is willing to marry her, the priest and the barber seek another method to bring Don Quixote home (1978, 1.46.574). At any rate, it would have been difficult to continue the deception, since Don Quixote believes he has killed Pandafilando, slashing the wineskins at the inn in his sleep. Since the knight has followed Apuleius's footsteps in his madness, a new method to take him home has to be formulated. Don Quixote is placed in a cage upon a cart drawn by oxen, where he is told he is being held captive by enchanters. What Ruiz Pérez fails to note in his important essay on Tasso and Cervantes is that, in many ways, the Micomicona adventure ends as it had with Armida, since she had led her love-captives to a real fortress where she would keep them in chains.[1] In addition, it should come as no surprise that one of the more famous Italian illustrators of Tasso's poem, who draws Armida ensnaring the Christian troops, is none other than Giovanni Battista Castello (Bernini 1985, 59–60, figs 51d and 51e; Suida Manning and Suida 1958, 88), who had worked with Luca Cambiaso on frescoes dealing with Cupid and Psyche at the Palazzo Imperiale in Genoa and other projects. Once again textual interpolations are infused with ekphrastic materials.

But perhaps the most telling ekphrasis is the final one – Don Quixote enchanted in the cart led by the slothful and slow oxen ('perezosos y tardios animals' [heavy, slothful beasts] [1978, 1.47.557; 433]). This means of transport recalls an image from the heavens. Ever since antiquity, planetary gods were depicted as riding in chariots, led by the animals assigned to them. Venus, for example, is often seen in a chariot drawn by either doves or swans, while Saturn, the furthest and slowest of planets according to Ptolemaic astrology, is portrayed in a cart drawn by slow and slothful oxen.[2] The ox-drawn Saturn can be found in works as different as Boccaccio's *Genealogia deorum* (*Genealogy of the Gods*) and Baccio Baldini's account of a Medici wedding in Florence in 1565 (Fajardo 1986, 249). When depicted as a malefic or world-changing planet, Saturn is conducted by terrifying dragons, creatures that would certainly impress Don Quixote more than the oxen.[3] And yet, the knight is quite aware that his enchantment has to do with a malefic planet. When he is unable to free yet another captive (a statue of the Virgin in procession), he accepts his place in the heavenly cart stating: 'Será gran prudencia dejar pasar el mal influjo de las estrellas que agora corre' (It will be wise indeed to wait for the presently prevailing malign influence of the stars to dissipate) (1978, 1.52.601; 472). Saturn is also the planet of melancholy. Thus, Don Quixote is 'enchanted' by his own melancholy temperament, one that is prone to create alluring visions and terrifying apparitions. As the incarcerated knight arrives in his village he is described as 'flaco y Amarillo' (thin and pale) (1978, 1.52.602; 472), conditions typical of the melancholic.

To the iconography of Saturn, planet of melancholy in *Don Quixote*, must be added the fact that astrologers considered Saturn as a marker of great changes in empires and religions. This belief goes back to Abu Ma'shar, a ninth-century astrologer who studied in Baghdad. His theories were well known in medieval and Renaissance Europe, where he was often referred to as Albumasar, provoking furious debates in scholarly settings such as the University of Paris. In the Spanish Golden Age, this Arabic astrologer was at times used against himself by sermon writers who prophesied the end of Islam.[4] Indeed, in 1603, two years before the publication of *Don Quixote*, a major conjunction of Saturn and Jupiter could be seen in the skies. Coupled with the appearance of a *nova* or new star the following year, this created a furore of astrological predictions, culminating in the notion of 'nova stella, novus rex' (new star, new king).[5]

But in Cervantes' text, Don Quixote is trapped by Saturn, by his melancholy temperament, and is unable to fight the demonic Armida, the magician Micomicona, and the evil enchanters who hold him fast to the cart. Instead of prophesying great political or religious changes, Don Quixote's saturnine cart shows his impotence as a marker of earthly transformations (except in his own imagination). He is no Charles V, nor will he bring about a new Golden Age, leading the reader to wonder if he represents one of the emperor's less successful successors.[6] Trapped in his own imaginings Don Quixote is an icon of Saturn, a pagan deity of incarceration and suffering. While this final ekphrasis debilitates the knight, it paradoxically renders the author of his tale much more powerful, for he is showing us the influence of the fabric of the heavens. The notion of *Deus pictor*, of god as painter of the universe and of the heavens, was widely disseminated and was used to make painting a worthy liberal art rather than a mere mechanical craft.[7] To further emphasize this connection, painters of the Italian Renaissance and Spanish Golden Age covered ceilings with pictures of the heavens. They could simply represent the twelve signs of the zodiac and the twelve months of the year, or the artist could choose a specific moment in time, pointing to a patron's horoscope or a key moment in history. Finally, some portrayed a particular way to divide the heavens, be it Manilius's divergent configurations or the division of months into three parts or Decans.[8] In the novel, the last ekphrasis belongs to the heavens. It is as if the author, after painting emperors, pagan deities, Christian saints, sublime and seductive Virgins, abducted beauties, Roman maidens, sodomitic friends, and melancholy authors is finally ready to compete not only with his main character, who is constantly painting over reality, but also with the deity. As a melancholy visionary, he will depict that which God alone can envision, the planetary chariot and the baneful influence of the highest of planets, a planet that also brings about visions as unique as those of *Don Quixote*.

Notes

1 The Exhilaration of Italy

1 'Embarca en Sevilla y visita Italia. Los otros viajes hacia el Oriente no me parecen verosímiles, y participan más bien de un tema literario. Sin embargo, no es razón suficiente para no admitir el viaje a Italia, que por entonces era corriente entre los españoles' (He embarks in Seville and visits Italy. The other voyages towards the East do not seem to me verisimilar, and they are better seen as part of a literary theme. However, it is not a sufficient reason to not admit the voyage to Italy that at that time was common among the Spaniards) (Rojas 1977, 1.xv).

2 *Desiring Italy* is the title of a recent anthology edited by Susan Cahill of women writers who celebrated their Italian sojourn.

3 The Conde de Lemos, Cervantes' patron, was named Viceroy of Naples in 1610. Avalle-Arce explains: 'Cuando Lemos fue nombrado virrey de Nápoles, Cervantes soñó con una vuelta a Nápoles en la comitiva virreinal, que no se cumplió para bien de la posteridad' (When Lemos was named Viceroy of Naples, Cervantes dreamt of a return to Naples in the viceroyal retinue, which was not fulfilled for the good of posterity) (*Novelas ejemplares* 1982, 1.65).

4 'Cervantes durante su paso por Florencia tuvo que haber visto las esculturas y pinturas de Miguel Angel, que también repiten el mismo movimiento indicado por Lisandro y Carino' (Cervantes during his visit to Florence had to have seen Michelangelo's sculptures and paintings which also repeat the same movement pointed out by Lisandro and Carino) (Issacharoff 1981, 331).

5 Ludovico tells this tale in the fourth act of Lope de Vega's *La Dorotea* (1968, 343). It is probably based on a similar account of a sleeping Cupid found in Vasari (1991, 423).

6 According to Thomas M. Greene, the concept of imitation can be related to necromancy. The student of *imitatio* must ask of a text that imitates a classical model 'whether the necromantic disinterment is brought off, whether the Latin text emerges mummified from the tomb, or shrunken and thin, or merely ornamented, or whether rather an authentic resurrection has occurred (1982, 37–8). On *La Numancia*'s necromantic imitation of Lucan, see De Armas 1996.

7 Citing the reference to Raphael and Michelangelo, Canavaggio wonders if Cervantes 'limited himself to accumulating the readings, the images, the memories in this fashion, or whether he took advantage of his free time to start writing again' (1990, 73).

8 Karl-Ludwig Selig argues that this passage is not an example of Cervantes' interest in antiquarianism: 'Contextually one is on much more solid ground when one realizes that the passage employs the topos of a catalogue and reflects a literary tradition and convention; its source is in Ariosto' (1973, 309). However, this is not the only example of Cervantes' interest in antiquarianism. For example, Ortel Baledre's tale in the *Persiles* is recounted near the town of Talavera, which was then preparing to celebrate the feast of Monda. The story connects this Christian feast with a pagan festival for Venus: 'La gran fiesta de la Monda, que trae su origen de muchos años antes que Cristo naciese, reducida por los cristianos a tan buen punto y término, que si entonces se celebraba en honra de la diosa Venus por la gentilidad, ahora se celebra en alabanza de la Vírgen de las vírgenes' (The great festival of Monda, which traces its origin many years before Christ was born, reduced by the Christians to such a good point and end, that if then one celebrated in honour of the goddess Venus by the pagans, now one celebrates in praise of the Virgin of the virgins) (1969, 312). See de Armas 1993, 407.

9 As Alfonso E. Pérez Sánchez has noted, in most sixteenth- and seventeenth-century Spanish references to Raphael he is paired with Michelangelo: 'Se le halla siempre – al menos en el siglo XVI y hasta mediados del XVII – estrechamente asociado a Miguel Ángel, pero ocupando el segundo lugar ...' (One finds him always – at least in the sixteenth century and until the middle of the seventeenth – strictly associated with Michelangelo, but occupying a second place ...) (1985, 34). He cites, among others, Francisco de Quevedo's *Silva al pincel,* Fray Hortensio Félix Pallavicino's *Oraciones evangélicas,* and Vicente Carducho's *Diálogos de la pintura.* Francisco Pacheco's *Arte de la pintura* and Jusepe Martínez's *Discursos practicables del nobilísimo arte de la pintura,* on the other hand, praise Raphael's art above Michelangelo's (1985, 37).

10 I am borrowing this term from Thomas Greene, who utilizes it to describe notions of imitation.

11 Tamar Yacobi asserts: 'Over the last decades, ekphrasis has become an exciting topic.' But this critic also speaks of a 'healthy unrest' that has arisen: 'But one can also read the signs of a deeper thrust in the question marks that have lately begun to surround the field's very premises and inherited practices' (1998, 21).

12 Steven Wagschal is the first to coin the term 'veiled ekphrasis' in his essay.

13 This termed was coined by John Hollander (1988, 209) and is further described by James Heffernan (1993, 7).

14 'But the availability of the painting allows us to see how the poem reconstructs it, how the poet's word seeks to gain its mastery over the painter's image' (Heffernan 1993, 17).

15 Murray Krieger has explained: 'The early meaning given "ekphrasis" in Hellenistic rhetoric ... was totally unrestricted: it referred most broadly to a verbal description of something, almost anything, in life or art' (1992, 7). Philostratus was the first to apply it exclusively to a work of art.

16 This episode is carefully described by both Michael Gerli and William Worden.

17 Citing Auden's 'Letter to Byron': 'All Cézanne's apples I would give away / for one small Goya or a Daumier,' Tamar Yacobi asserts: 'The poet thus bundles into one synecdochic and familiar detail 'apples', his rejection of Cézanne's entire thematic material ...' (1998, 24). Yacobi labels this 'the ekphrastic model,' a subdivision of ekphrasis which 're-presents in language some visual common denominator (topos, theme, style, traditional figure) as distinct from a unique work of art' (1998, 23). But his category also fits within my 'umbrella' term of allusive ekphrasis.

18 Thus, any object – or even a person, an animal, a plant, or a landscape can be described (object ekphrasis).

19 Francoise Meltzer has argued that 'ecphrasis may be seen as an earlier version of the intercalated story' (1987, 22).

20 Jonathan Brown has documented how 'the voracious demand of seventeenth-century collectors turned the art of painting into a mercantile commodity' (1995, 247).

21 María Asunción Gómez has adapted Zatlin's definition to a study of theatrical works of the Golden Age. She argues that allusions to art in Lope and Calderón 'van mucho mas allá de lo puramente ornamental. Constituyen reflexiones intertextuales, mediante las que se subraya la función mimética del arte pictórico, e implícitamente, del dramático' (go much further than the purely ornamental. They constitute intertextual

reflections that serve to underline the mimetic function of the pictorial art, and implicitly of the dramatic) (1997, 289).

22 It may seem as if Don Quixote wants to return to the Middle Ages through his use of the chivalric romances. In reality, it is a return to the age of Charles V, an emperor who wished to revive the practice of chivalry as well as renew the world through the knowledge of reformers such as Erasmus. Charles was also keenly interested in the art of the Italian Renaissance: Titian was his portrait artist and he marvelled at the inventions of Giulio Romano.

2 A Museum of Memories: From *Numancia* to *La Galatea*

1 It is said that Simonides 'called painting mute poetry and poetry painting that speaks.' Yates cites from Plutarch's *Glory of Athens* (1966, 28).

2 Treating 'magical' images and perfumes associated with them, Ficino asserts: 'Accordingly, it is my opinion that the intention of the imagination does not have its power so much in fashioning images or medicines as it does in applying and swallowing them' (1989, ch. 20, 353). On the subject, see also Scaramuzza Vidoni 1998, 29.

3 For Huarte, 'human mental ability or *ingenio* excelled in three categories: imagination, judgment, and memory. A superabundance of heat (choler) would create a strong imagination capable of producing poets, artists, inventors, and such, depending on the degree of excess' (Heiple 1991, 124).

4 Pedro Mexía states: 'Plinio y Quintiliano dizen que fue inventor deste arte memorativa Simonides' (Pliny and Quintillian say that Simonides was the inventor of this memorative art) (1990, 2.59).

5 'para que las musas más estériles se muestren fecundas ...' (so that the most sterile muses show themselves fertile) (1978, 1.50)

6 There have been critical attempts to explain this problem. For Chester Halka, Don Quixote suffers from adust melancholy, which can change from cold to hot. This 'dual humoral complexion' (1981, 11), can explain his lucidness and madness. For Robert Folger, Don Quixote 'possesses not only a precise memory of his pre-psychotic life and the reading that caused his mental derangement, but perfectly remembers everything he perceives during his *vueltas* as a knight errant' (2002, 237).

7 'La memoria andante de don Quijote es tan poderosa que las imágenes que percibe y los lugares por los que transita pasan a identificarse inmediatamente en ella con los lugares e imágenes que guardaba en su mente' (Don Quixote's errant memory is so powerful that the imagines he

perceives and the places through which he travels become immediately identified in his memory with the places and images that he kept in his mind) (1994, 101–2).

8 On textual pictures see Carruthers (1990, 230).

9 The *Ad Herennium* addresses these points. For example, the treatise points to theatre when asking how to remember certain verses. The image chosen is that of 'Aesopus and Cimber being dressed as for the roles of Agamemnon and Menelaus in *Iphigenia*' (1954, 3.21; 217). The text also explains that images should be 'strong and sharp and suitable for awakening recollection' (3.21; 129). They can be of opposing qualities: 'base, dishonourable, extraordinary, great, unbelievable or laughable' (3.21; 129).

10 The *Ad Herennium* also discusses light: 'Then the backgrounds ought to be neither too bright nor too dim, so that the shadows may not obscure the images nor the luster make them glitter' (1954, 2.19.32; 213).

11 Pedro Mexía also refers to 'lugares señalados y muy conoscidos' (marked and well known places) (1990, 2.58).

12 It is curious to note that Raphael is omitted from the Italian translation of Della Porta's *Art of Memory*. He does appear with Michelangelo and Titian in the Latin original which was not published until 1602. Lodovico Dolce also recommends the use of images from Italian art, giving as an example Titian's painting on the rape of Europa (Yates 1966, 164).

13 In the *Ad Herennium*, attributed to Cicero, Publius Cornelius Scipio (Africanus) is listed among the great orators, together with Cato and others (1954, 4.5.7; 245).

14 Pedro Mexía relates an anecdote in which Scipio and Apius Claudius were competing for a post in Rome. While Apius knew everyone by name Scipio could hardly remember anyone. He thus stated: 'La verdad es, Apio Claudio, que yo nunca he procurado conoscer a muchos, sino que ninguno aya que no me conozca a mí' (The truth is, Apius Claudius, that I have never attempted to know many people, but that there would be no one who would not know me) (1990, 2.54). According to Mexía's editor, Antonio Castro, this anecdote appears in Plutarch and in Erasmus.

15 Vasari dscribes the painting as 'Galatea in a cart on the sea drawn by two dolphins and surrounded by Tritons and many sea-gods' (1996, 1.723). Cervantes' knowledge of the painting is much more detailed. Lodovico Dolce also speaks of Raphael's *Galatea* (Roskill, 1968, 169).

16 Pilar Berrio asserts: 'La zampoña, instrumento rústico perteneciente al tipo óboe, es decir, de boquilla provista con dos cañas, aparece con frecuencia en libros de género bucólico ... Escritores del XVI, como Montemayor y Gil Polo, identificaban flauta y zampoña ...' (The *zampoña*, rustic instrument

belonging to the oboe family, which means, with a mouthpiece equipped with two reeds, appears frequently in books of the bucolic genre ... Writers of the sixteenth century, like Montemayor and Gil Polo, identified flute and *zampoña* ...) (1995, 239 note 21).

17 Goffen also argues that 'Galatea's triumph is ephemeral, and the Cyclops will avenge himself, crushing his rival, Galatea's beloved Acis. The shadow foreshadows this tragedy' (2002, 324). There is also a somewhat ominous ending to the first part of Cervantes' *Galatea*, as her father seeks to marry her to a foreign shepherd against her will.

18 For a detailed analysis of the relationship between Galatea and Florisa, see De Armas 2000. The blush is also taken from Raphel's *Galatea*.

19 The ball game is a sport that was related to friendship as an art of giving and receiving as symbolized in catching and throwing the ball. As Van Lohuizen-Mulder has noted, there are images of the Graces playing ball (1977, 92–3).

20 It is curious to note that in spite of his reluctant praise of Botticelli's whimsical art, Vasari does admit that *The Birth of Venus* and the *Primavera* are 'expressed very gracefully' (1996, 1.537).

3 At School with the Ancients: Raphael

1 On the Lucretian concept of *clinamen* as a form of anxiety of influence, see Bloom 1973, 44–5.

2 Whenever I refer to the character in the prologue, the terms 'Cervantes' and 'author' should not be confused with the writer of *Don Quixote*. Rather, it refers to the fictionalized representation of the author.

3 Christiane L. Joost-Gaugier uses the inventory of Julius's library as a way to identify figures in Raphael's *School of Athens* (1998, 764, 776).

4 Marasso (1954, 83), Murillo (Cervantes 1978, 179), and many others have speculated as to Cervantes' source for this story. It may well derive from his having viewed Raphael's painting.

5 Hersey may have derived this comment from Vasari who describes him as having 'a youthful head and a very modest appearance' (1991, 313).

6 Hersey asserts that they are from Greece 'and one or two other countries; but note that Rome doesn't rate' (1993, 135).

7 Diana de Armas Wilson shows how 'other, more philosophic authorities are being interrogated throughout Cervantes' writings ... What about those avowed "Platonic loves" that motivate Don Quixote's pure but rigid holding actions? What about the "written word" of Aristotle himself, the two-term system for organizing discourse available to Cervantes? ...

Cervantes is hostile to overly schematic oppositions, to Janus-faced dualisms ...' (1992, 49–50).

8 Vasari mentions St Thomas's presence in the fresco (1991, 316).

9 The altarpiece of Santa Caterina in Pisa shows Plato and Aristotle on a lower level while the evangelists are above. Christ is at the top. St Thomas sits at the centre of this pyramidal composition. In Filippino Lippi's fresco, Averroes sees a reflection of a theological controversy at the University of Paris in 1270. At this time, St Thomas refuted Averroes's interpretation of Aristotle's *On the Soul* in his treatise on the *Unity of the Intellect* (Geiger 1982, 226).

10 Later in the novel he will create Cide Hamete Benengeli, the Arabic historian who writes of the adventures of Don Quixote. Although he is described as a liar, his text becomes authoritative, since it is the one that preserves the Christian knight's adventures.

11 Although the text ascribes 'Non bene pro toto libertas venditur auro' (Freedom should not be sold for all the gold in the world) to Horace (1978, 1.55; 983 note 4), it actually derives from an Aesopian fable (1978, 1.55). No author is given for the second maxim, 'Pallida mors aequo pulsat pede pauperum tabernas, Regumque turres' (Pale Death with impartial foot knocks at the doors of poor men's hovels and of kings' palaces) (1978, 1.55; 983, note 5), but it derives from Horace's *Odes* 1.4 (1978, 1.55).

12 This figure has also been identified as Aeschylus (Jones and Penny 1983, 72).

13 The Pythagorean and numerological elements of Raphael's *stanza* will be discussed in the next chapter.

14 This figure has also been identified as St James Major and as St James the Less. If the figure is indeed St Matthew, it is no coincidence that he sits next to Abraham. Matthew begins his gospel by calling Christ the son of David and the son of Abraham.

15 The friend had actually begun his advice by telling the fictional Cervantes how to add preliminary sonnets. The elements needed by Cervantes and provided by the friend are four in number, thus foregrounding once again the importance of quaternity: (1) preliminary verses, (2) annotated maxims (*acotaciones*), (3) footnotes (*anotaciones*), and (4) bibliography (*citación de los autores*). Only the middle two contain material relevant to the Stanza della Segnatura.

16 The river Tagus also appears. In the *Canción de Grisóstomo* (*Song of Grisóstomo*), the lover claims that his laments will not be heard in the usual places (on the shores of the Tagus and the Betis), but instead his wild torments will be heard through dark valleys, the plains of Libya, etc. (1978, 1.14.180–2).

17 Cacus appears twice in the 1605 *Don Quixote*, the first comparing the innkeeper to a thief (no menos ladrón que Caco' (no less a thief than Cacus) [1978, 1.2.84; 33]) and the second labelling Reinaldos de Montalban's friends as 'más ladrones que Caco' (worse thieves than Cacus) (1978, 1.6.113; 54).

18 'Pero la Santa Escritura, que no puede faltar un átomo en la verdad, nos muestra que los hubo, contándonos la historia de aquel filisteazo de Golías, que tenía siete codos y medio de altura, que es una desmesurada grandeza' (Yet the scriptures, which cannot be anything less than the absolute truth, show us that they did exist, by recounting the history of that immense Philistine, Goliath, who was seven and a half cubits tall, a vast height) (1978, 2.1.50; 495).

19 In Lope's *El peregrino en su patria* (1604), a work that may have been directly satirized in Cervantes' prologue, the defeat of Goliath is mentioned (Vosters 1977, 1.234). Vosters comments: 'En la tipología cristiana de Lope y de Euchario existe una trinidad de héroes bíblicos interrelacionados y hasta intercambiables: David degollador de Goliat, Cristo, matador del diablo, y María, pisadora de serpientes' (In Lope's and Eucharius's Christian typology there exists a trinity of biblical heroes interrelated and even interchangeable: David the beheader of Goliath, Christ, killer of the devil, and Mary, who steps on snakes) (Vosters 1977, 1.234). It may be that one of Dulcinea's images is that of Mary.

20 It could also be argued that the Castalian spring under Apollo and his muses in the *Parnassus* is metamorphosed into the river Tagus in Cervantes' prologue.

21 As Joost-Gaugier has explained, the attribution to Zoroaster goes back to Vasari. Joost-Gaugier identified the figure with its crown and its back to the viewer as Zoroaster. However, this figure has consistently been regarded as Ptolemy. Zoroaster's identity was then transferred in the late nineteenth-century to the figure with a globe facing the viewer (1998, 763).

22 See, for example, the Basle 1540 and the Venice 1511 editions.

23 The Tagus features prominently in other classical works. In Pliny's *Natural History*, for example, one reads that 'the Tagus is famous for its auriferous sands' (1942, 2.209; 4.22.115). Pliny also mentions that Lisbon lies at the point where the Tagus meets the sea (1945, 2.209; 4.22.116). Both of these points are mentioned by the friend in Cervantes' prologue. Thus, although the pictorial allusion is to the Ptolemy of *The School of Athens*, the actual locus classicus of Cervantes' description may well be Pliny's *Natural History*.

24 The three prostitutes are taken from Antonio de Guevara's *Epistolas familiares*. Their names are derived from classical prostitutes and goddesses. See Nadeau 1995 and 1997.

25 The presence of Sappho in the *Parnassus* also serves to evince the belief that beauty is never allied to wisdom. Her poetic ability contrasted with her lack of physical beauty.

26 According to Yvonne Jehenson, Marcela's 'knowledge of the best Western tradition of oratory, her impeccable presentation, her courageous stance within the text itself, her refusal to play the role of *mujer esquiva* within her cultural context are in danger of being lost or suppressed from the collective memory ... She can either be 'immortalized' as the men have *wanted* her to be or she is to be suppressed and even maligned in subsequent publications for exhibiting "inappropriate" behavior' (1990, 30).

27 But even here, some connections remain. The friend conjures up two great warriors from antiquity. Alexander appears in a grisaille painting, while Pope Julius II, who commissioned the stanze, was praised by Raphael as a new Julius Caesar. The reader will note that these figures must have been particularly pleasing to the fictional Cervantes since he chooses to include them along with the giants (Cacus and Goliath) in his novel.

28 As Hersey states: 'There is less agreement about the characters' identities' (1993, 136) who stand on the lower level of the *Disputa*. He may be one of the bishops portrayed there.

29 During the Middle Ages, there was prolonged debate as to which was the most important virtue of the epic hero, *sapientia* embodied in Ulysses or *fortitudo* personified in Achilles. Cervantes is well aware of this debate and refers to Ulysses's 'predencia' (prudence) (1978, 1.25.303; 207) while Aquiles is singled out for his 'valentía' (courage) (1978, 1.47.566; 441). Thus, the 'valorous' Don Quixote is humorously portrayed as a figure akin to Achilles.

4 The Fourfold Way: Raphael

1 Pope-Hennessy follows H.B. Gutmann when he asserts that the program of the wall frescoes is based on St Bonaventure. The *School of Athens* as well as the *Disputa* reflect 'Bonaventure's distinction between the natural and rational sciences' (1970, 139). However, Pope-Hennessy also points to failures in this theory and emphasizes Raphael's archeological impulses (1970, 139–41).

2 Redig de Campos understands Plato's gesture as pointing to the realm of

Ideas: 'Platone ... indica con la diestra l'empireo delle Idee, ultima realtà' (Plato ... indicates with his right hand the realm of the Idea, the ultimate reality) (1965, 15).

3 The Stanza della Segnatura and the Hall of Heliodorus were originally painted by Piero della Francesca with later decorations by Lucas Signorelli and Giovanni Antonio Bazzi (Sodoma). But Pope Julius II interrupted the work of Signorelli and Sodoma and had the earlier work of Piero della Francesca destroyed so as to redo these stanze (Nesselrath 1992, 36). He agreed, on Donato Bramante's counsel, to give a young artist a chance: 'So pleased was the pope with Raphael's work that he was put in charge' (Hersey 1993, 129). Raphael is said to have saved the framework: 'Vasari's report that Raphael saved ... Sodoma's framework in the Stanza della Segnatura invites the speculation that Raphael was trying to avoid making himself totally unpopular with his colleagues' (Nesselrath 1992, 37).

4 James Beck claims that the number eight is the key structuring principle: 'The central octagon seems to have given rise to the scheme of the entire ceiling. The eight main scenes are each related to one of the sides ... Furthermore, there are tiny depictions, four in imitation of Antique marble reliefs (perhaps executed by Sodoma) and four related to mosaic, again reinforcing the number eight' (1993, 19). Considering the importance of the tetractys in *The School of Athens* and following Wind's interpretation of the eight scenes as representing the four elements, I would argue for the four elementals as key. The ceiling has four sets of pictures with four paintings each. We thus have a quaternity of a quaternity, further emphasizing the elemental four.

5 This was the Camera di Torre Borgia, which Vasari calls 'camera del fuoco' (the hall of fire) (Rubin 1995, 368).

6 The middle halls are the more difficult to discern in terms of elements. The Stanza della Segnatura also contains numerous references to air. The ceiling in this hall, as well as the vault in the Hall of Heliodorus depict all of the four elements.

7 In *A Treatise on Angel Magic* from the seventeenth century we read under the number four: 'Pythagoras preferred this Number as the root and foundation of all Numbers, from whence all foundations in artificial as well as divine things are quadrate, and signify solidity' (McLean 1990, 92).

8 Using the Pythagorean harmonies, Mario Praz has attempted to trace 'parallels between the structure of a poem and that of a painting or a building' during the Renaissance (1970, 89).

9 Indeed, the idea of cosmos in the Renaissance was best expounded in the *quatrivium*, that is, through the disciplines of arithmetic, music, geometry,

and astronomy. Since all four are 'mathematical disciplines' (Heninger 1974, 149), the importance of number and numerology is foregrounded.

10 As Curtius explains, '"God as painter" is an old topos, which first appears in Empedocles and Pindar' (1953, 562). It is no coincidence, then, that Empledocles appears in *The School of Athens*. He leads us both to the theory of the four elements and to the question of authority in painting.

11 'Esto podría constituir o al menos sugerir e indicar posiblemente un aspecto sintomático y revelador de la técnica de la parte primera ... y ofrecer tal vez una de varias llaves para distinguir por medios técnicos del arte de la narrativa las dos partes de la obra' (This perhaps would constitute or at least suggest and possibly indicate a symptomatic aspect and revealer of the technique of the first part ... and to offer perhaps one of the various keys to distinguish the narrative art of the two parts of the work through technical means) (Selig 1989, 629).

12 Of course, several other names for the *hidalgo* will appear later in the novel, concluding with his final Alonso Quijano 'el bueno' (the Good) (1978, 2.74.588; 977). On critical approaches to these names see chapter 7.

13 In staying up late, Don Quixote stirs up the imagination to excess according to Marsilio Ficino: 'Phantasy or imagination ... is distracted and upset by many long and contrary imaginations, cogitations, and cares while it is awake. This distraction and confusion are too contrary to someone pursuing contemplation and requiring a completely tranquil and serene mind. Only during the quiet of night is that agitation finally calmed and put to rest' (1989, 129).

14 Soufas (1990), García Gibert (1997), and Folger (2002) echo Heiple (1979) in showing that Don Quixote suffers from an excess of melancholy. All three critics differ from Otis H. Green's assessment that 'Alonso Quijano is described as a man in whom *choler* (yellow bile) prevails over blood, melancholy (black vile) and phlegm. He is thus a person more akin to the element *fire* (1970, 172).

15 'La razón de la sinrazón que a mi razón se hace, de tal manera mi razón enflaquece, que con razón me quejo de la vuestra fermosura' (The reason for the unreason to which my reason is subjected so weakens my reason that I have reason to complain of your beauty) (1978, 1.1.72; 26). Don Quixote's reason becomes debilitated very much like this passage suggests.

16 For Iventosch, the fact that he names his horse before naming himself or his lady is not pure parody: 'Sabida es la importancia del caballo en el mundo medieval y caballeresco' (The importance of the horse in the medieval and chivalric world is well known) (1963–4, 60).

17 'Our imagination is able to be so disposed, composed, and conformed, especially to Mars or to the Sun ... that it might instantly be a proper receptacle for Martial or Phoeban influence' (Ficino 1989, ch. 21, 365).

18 There is a debate as to whether Don Quixote's madness stems from his faulty imagination or from the dryness of his memory. For Avalle-Arce, 'la venta es recibida por el alma de don Quijote por un castillo por el desajuste de su imaginativa, y una vez que se imprime en su alma la imagen de un castillo acude su lesionada fantasía a perfeccionarla "con todos aquellos adherentes que semejantes castillos se pintan"' (the inn is received by Don Quixote's soul as a castle due to the maladjustment of his imaginative faculty, and once the image of a castle is imprinted on his soul, his lesioned fantasy responds by perfecting it 'with all those accessories with which such castles are painted') (Avalle-Arce 1976, 100). Teresa Soufas, on the other hand, stresses that Avalle-Arce and others are using 'a more modern concept of the imagination. In Cervantes's portrayal, the interpretation that don Quijote's intellect makes of the images his imagination receives and his memory retrieves leads to his folly, but only because his memory is damaged by the dryness of his system' (1990, 25). More recently, Aurora Egido has stressed the importance of memory in Cervantes: 'La de los molinos es una clara confirmación de cómo las imágenes de la memoria se superponen de tal modo a la realidad que ciegan la percepción en la imaginativa de los sentidos de don Quijote' (The adventure of the windmills is a clear confirmation of how the images of memory are superimposed in such a way on reality that they blind the perception of the senses in the imaginative faculty of Don Quixote) (1994, 104). But she clarifies that memory alone does not characterize the text (135). Mariarosa Scaramuzza Vidoni defends the role of imagination in *Don Quixote* by quoting Pero Mexía, who argues that the imagination 'es capaz de mover pasiones, de hacer enfermar o curar, de provocar cambios y monstruosidades en el cuerpo propio o ajeno' (is capable of moving the passions, of making one sick or being cured, of provoking changes and monstrosities in one's own body or another's) (Scaramuzza Vidoni 1998, 34). She also cites López Pinciano who claims that imagination is 'un sentido muy conveniente para la poética' (a sense greatly convenient for poetics) (Scaramuzzi Vidoni 1998, 37).

19 The text actually says that his kind is famous for lying: 'Siendo muy propio de los de aquella nación ser mentirosos' (It's a well-known feature of Arabs that they're all liars) (1978, 1.9.144; 76).

20 There is a famous portrait of Elizabeth with an ermine at her side. The animal wears a collar in the form of a crown which is 'expressive of both

the triumph of her reformed imperial rule and of her personal triumph as a chaste Petrarchan heroine' (Yates 1975, 114).

21 My translation.

22 Cornelius Agrippa asserts: 'The *Pythagoreans* call eight the number of justice and fullness ... Hence the custome of *Orpheus*, swearing by eight deities, if at any time he would beseech divine justice' (1986, 206).

23 The whole question of *Don Quixote* as carnival has been studied from Bakhtin (1984, 22–3) to Redondo. The latter sees the knight's initiation as a parody, since Don Quixote becomes a son of the innkeeper and a son of the prostitutes: 'De esta manera la degradación burlesca llega al punto cumbre, pero al mismo tiempo se va delineando la trayectoria vital del personaje principal ... Don Quijote supera esa degradación por el poder de la imaginación, que transforma la realidad más trivial ...' (In this manner the burlesque degradation arrives at its high point, but at the same time the text continues delineating the vital trajectory of the main character ... Don Quixote overcomes that degradation by the power of his imagination, which transforms the most trivial reality) (1998, 304).

24 Morgante is one of the few 'good' giants in Cervantes. In Pulci's *Morgante maggiore* we learn that he was once an enemy of Roland who killed his two companions but led Morgante to be converted to Christianity. Don Quixote clearly shows that this giant is meant to be an exception to the rule, 'porque, con ser de aquella generación gigantea, que todos son soberbios y descomedidos, él sólo era afable y bien criado' (because, despite belonging to a proud and insolent breed, he alone was affable and well-mannered) (1978, 1.1.74; 27).

5 Textual Terribilitá: Michelangelo

1 'Nell'afresco della *Scuola d'Atene* é la figura di un uomo pensieroso ...' (In the fresco of the *School of Athens* there is a figure of a melancholy man) (Redig de Campos, 1946, 83).

2 My translation.

3 For a study of the romantic approach to *Don Quixote*, see Anthony Close 1978.

4 Giorgio Vasari writes that Michelangelo's character 'took pleasure in solitude, as a man deeply enamoured of his art, which wants a man to be alone and pensive for its own purposes' (1991, 472).

5 In the 1615 *Don Quixote* the knight has an encounter with a lion, which recalls Hercules' defeat of the Nemean lion and his wearing its skin in triumph. In addition, Maese Pedro refers to Don Quixote as a Hercules

(1978, 2.25.235), while Don Quixote suggests to the duchess that he may be a new Hercules who can kill a new Acteon (1978, 2.32.292).

6 On the *Apollo Belvedere* as model for Raphael, see chapter 1. Let us recall that, according to Loren Partridge, Michelangelo also utilized this statue for the Christ of his *Last Judgment* (1996, 136).

7 Let us recall that when Don Quixote first sallies forth, he immediately evokes and invokes Apollo: 'Apenas había el rubicundo Apolo ...' (Scarce had ruddy Apollo ...) (1978, 1.2.80; 30). Linking his adventures to the course of Apollo/Sol, Don Quixote begins his quest at dawn 'una mañana, antes del día' (one morning, before dawn) (1978, 1.2.79; 30). He also goes forth at dawn after being knighted by the innkeeper: 'La del alba sería ...' (It must have been about daybreak) (1978, 1.4.94; 41).

8 As I was finishing this book manuscript, I was fortunate to review for publication Roberto González Echevarría's astounding new book, *Love and the Law in Cervantes*. The initial chapter on the galley slaves is unsurpassed in its insights on Cervantes. This critic gleans a number of important interpretations from the veiled and legalistic answers of these convicts. In a brilliant and subtle reading of the discourse of one of the galley slaves, González Echevarría discovers the narcissistic and perverse impulses hidden within the slave's rhetoric.

9 *The Golden Legned* already tells of the similarity between these two saints. After narrating a miracle performed by St Bartholomew, the text adds: 'A very similar story is told about Saint Andrew' (Voragine 1993, 2.114).

10 According to Vecchio, these critics included 'the most finicky Messer Biagio da Cesena, the writer Pietro Aretino, the theologian Ambrogio Catarino and the ecclesiastic Giovanni Andrea Gilio' (1996, 216).

11 On the interaction between Don Quixote and the galley slaves, see the excellent studies of Redondo (1998, 347–62) and González Echevarría (in press).

12 Edgar Wind states: 'While Michelangelo professed to have turned away from the pagans, and to have become as *chietino* as Vittoria Colonna herself, his work was still of pagan inspiration, and his imagery pagan in disguise' (1968, 188–9).

13 Michael Hasbrouck has noted the numerous links between Don Quixote and the devil. He claims: 'El protagonista, después de haber sido un don Quijote poseído por el demonio, ha vuelto a ser Alonso Quijano tras someterse a un lento proceso de exorcismo' (The protagonist, after having been a Don Quixote possessed by the devil, has returned to being Alonso Quijano after submitting himself to a slow process of exorcisim) (1992, 126). Following Hasbrouck's argument it is possible to conceive of the

cleric's excommunication of Don Quixote in chapter 19 as a signpost of the knight's demonic possession. Hilaire Kallendorf also points to 'a connection between Don Quixote and the devil' (2003, 172). She also points to Don Quixote's self-exorcism as a sign of the rise of the autonomous novelistic character. Henry Sullivan rejects possession, claiming that 'Cervantes's protagonist is in need of spiritual cleaning or purgation, as shown throughout the process of his transformation. So, in my view, "possession" fails to describe the condition of Don Quixote's soul (psyche) in Part II of the novel' (1996, 104). Sullivan emphasizes instead the notion of purgatory 'enthusiastically promoted in the Counter Reformation by Catholic polemicists, particularly the Jesuits' (1996, 67). For this critic, Don Quixote undergoes purgation in a purgatory of this world. The cleric's excommunication, then, would signal only a temporary separation from the church.

14 There are, of course, other ways of looking at the 'triste figura' (sorry face). The term may be humorous, pointing to Don Quixote's disfigured countenance after so many misadventures; or it may point to the enchanters that bedevil the knight. Kallendorf affirms this: 'One explanation for this marginalization or even persecution of Don Quixote as a malevolent force might be his physical appearance, which contains indicatory signs of demonic possession' (2003, 172).

6 The Merchants of Trebizond: Luca Cambiaso

1 This artist has been called 'Liguria's greatest painter of the Renaissance and the central figure of the Genoese school of painting' (Suida Manning and Manning 1974, 9).

2 'cuanto más bien será bastante para defenderme de alguna pedrada' (since it will certainly be adequate to protect me against stonings) (1978, 1.21.255; 168).

3 David Quint has recently returned to this topic: 'For the realism of the world of the inn, or what we could call the novelistic world, encroaches upon and infects the other domains as well. The informing principle of this world is money ... Both hidalgo and squire, though to be sure in different ways, regard free hospitality as the recompense due to them for their knightly calling: it is the novel's principal emblem of how Don Quixote's re-creation of a chivalric past attempts to escape from a modern world of money' (2003, 65).

4 Studying the beginnings of the chivalric romances, particularly *Amadís de Gaula*, Juan Bautista Avalle-Arce contrasts it with that of *Lazarillo de Tormes* in *Nuevos deslindes cervantinos* (1975). Both works evince a genealogical

interest which displays the determinism of the main character – while Amadis's royal birth will lead him to heroism, Lázaro's picaresque parentage will propel him to delinquency. By eschewing any mention of Don Quixote's genealogy, Cervantes provides his protagonist with free will.

5 Clemencín asserts: 'En los libros de caballerías se habla frecuentemente de Emperadores de Trapisonda, como Amadís de Grecia, Esferamundi, Lindadelo, d. Renaldos, y Teodoro, padre de la princesa Claridiana señora del Caballero del Febo. Todavía se repite más en la biblioteca caballeresca la mención de Emperadores de Constantinopla ... Los autores de muchos libros caballerescos hablaron de ambos imperios como coexistentes, por lo cual aparece que quisieron referir sus historias al tiempo que medió entre la fundación de Trapisonda que fue por los años de 1220, hasta el de 1453, en que se perdió Constantinopla' (The emperors of Trebizond are frequently talked about in the books of chivalry, like Amadis of Greece, Esferamundi, Lindadelo, don Renaldos, and Teodoro, father of the princess of Claridiana, lady of the Knight of Phoebus. The mention of emperors of Constantinople is repeated even more in the chivalric library ... The authors of many chivalric books talked about both empires as coexistent, from which it appears that they wanted to refer their stories to the time between the foundation of Trebizond around the 1220s, until 1453, when Constantinople was lost) (Cervantes 1833, 2.429–30).

6 One of Cervantes' biographers, Navarro y Ledesma, minimizes Cervantes' interest in the art and architecture of Italy: 'Más que las catedrales y los monumentos le seducen de Italia ... la vida libre, la *libertad de Italia*' (More than the cathedrals and monuments what he finds seductive in Italy is ... the free life, the *liberty of Italy*) (1944, 52).

7 If *Thetis at Vulcan's Forge Receiving the Arms of Achilles* (Suida Manning and Suida 1958, 99–100, figs 14, 78) was known to Cervantes, it could have helped to shape certain episodes of the *Quixote*.

8 There is a drawing of *The Emperor of Trebisonda* in the Manning Collection and another one in the National Museum, Stockholm (Manning 1967, no. 45). On the popularity of Cambiaso's drawings Robert L. Manning states: 'Evidently, Cambiaso's drawings found widespread appreciation even during his own lifetime, and were frequently used by others to copy and study. Tintoretto at one instance ... warns, that only a master may study these drawings – a young man without knowledge could be ruined forever by copying them' (Manning 1967, n.p.).

9 'Luca Cambiaso's drawings reveal a flight or artistic genius to whose height Cambiaso the painter could rise but rarely, be it owing to the

limitation of medium or of artistic freedom in the execution of commissioned works' (Manning 1967, n.p.).

10 These dates provided by Miller are the most reliable (1969, 35). Manning and Suida give a date of 1300 (1958, 90). Others have given 1380 as the date.

11 The *fondaco* seems to be a development of the Byzantine Empire: 'The physical facilities given to merchants followed the example established by the Byzantines in the early Middle Ages in the *mitata* of Constantinople. The Byzantine government customarily grouped merchants for a particular region together so that their activities could more easily be monitored and controlled by imperial officials. From these merchant compounds developed the framework of the *fondaco*, or merchants' compound, found throughout Moslem lands' (Day 1988, 5–6).

12 Discussing the nine panels of Caro Crivelli's *Demidoff Altarpiece* painted in 1476, and particulary *The Annunciation with Saint Emidius*, Jardine states: 'This meticulous visual inventory of consumer goods is not merely a record of acquisitiveness limited to Italy ... They announce with pride Italian access to markets from northern France to the Ottoman Empire. Here is a world which assembles rugs from Istanbul, tapestry hangings from Arras, delicate glass from Venice, metalwork from Islamic Spain ... celebrating global mercantilism' (1996, 9–10).

13 As Miguel de Unamuno has stated, Don Quixote 'wanted to make those men, whose moneyed hearts could only see the material kingdom of riches, confess that there is a spiritual kingdom, and thus to redeem them in spite of themselves' (1976, 45).

14 In 1878 Nicolás Díaz de Benjumea stated: 'Cuando leemos el imperio con que manda Don Quixote a los mercaderes, creer sin ver ... sí viene a la memoria el procedimiento usado por los fanáticos para imponer la fe en dogmas religiosos, y no sólo en España sino en todo el orbe, aunque más en nuestra patria, notable por su mariolatría' (When we read the command with which Don Quixote orders the merchants, to believe without seeing ... what comes to mind is the procedure used by the fanatics to impose faith in religious dogmas, and not only in Spain but rather in all the world, although more in our country, notable by its worship of the Virgin Mary) (1878, 127).

15 This opposition is, of course, an oversimplification of the diverse nature of empires. Ferguson argues that there have been close to seventy empires, and, citing Dominic Lieven, he expresses some of the salient characteristics of empire: 'first and foremost, a very great power that has left its mark on the international relations of an era ... a polity that rules over wide

territories and many peoples since the management of space and multi-ethnicity is one of the great perennial dilemmas of empire' (2004, 10). The Habsburg Empire had to deal, at least with a multitude of languages: German, Dutch, Italian, Spanish, Catalan, the languages of the Americas, etc.

16 See, for example a pamphlet attributed to Quevedo which opposed the 'international capitalism fostered by the Genoese' (Cruz 1999, 103).

17 For example, he painted for the Church of San Lorenzo del Escorial *The Annunciation*, *The Coronation of the Virgin*, and the four Evangelists (and puttis) in different corners. And, for the lower cloister at the Escorial he painted *Peter and John at the Sepulchre* and the *Appearance to the Apostles in the Cenacle* (von Barghahn 1985, 1.83). Lauro Magnani discusses a number of paintings by Cambiaso at the Escorial, such as *The Martyrdom of St Ursula*, *St Lawrence*, *St Jerome*, etc. (2002, 109–25).

18 Although the king was satisfied by *The Holy Trinity*'s 'utter clarity and legibility,' many others (including Cambiaso) blamed it for its 'remarkable rigidity and lifelessness' (Brown 1991, 62).

19 R. Soprani published *Le vite de' pittori escoltori, et architetti genovesi* in 1674.

7 Drawing Decorum: Titian

1 As David Quint rightly points out, Don Quixote renounces marriage to Micomicona (which would provide him with wealth and social status). He chooses Dulcinea instead. For Quint, this means that 'the mad hidalgo ultimately renounces the modern desire for wealth and status barely disguised in his dreams of the princess. His choice is emblematic of his refusal of the modern world itself, however he may secretly be tempted by it' (2003, 90).

2 My translation.

3 Antonio Sánchez Jiménez studies Canto 27, a parenthesis in a more comprehensive poem that deals with García de Paredes: 'Zapata inicia aquí una pequeña digresión sobre la ingratitud de los gobernantes – concretamente de Carlos V, que no recompensó adecuadamente los servicios del marqués de Pescara – que quizá pudo ser la causa de la enemistad de Felipe II' (Zapata initiates here a small digression about the ingratitude of the rulers – concretely of Charles V, who did not adequately compensate the Marquis of Pescara's services – which perhaps could be the cause of the enmity of Philip II). I would like to thank Antonio Sánchez Jiménez for allowing me to see the manuscript of his text.

4 John Weiger contrasts the feminine ending of all the names of Don

Quixote in the first part with the masculine ending (Quijano) at the end of part 2 and concludes that 'there is good reason to be consistent and consider this final masculine version as evidence of an ability and a confidence to call himself at last a man' (1979, 44).

5 See, for example, Lascaris Commeno (1952) who discusses *quixote* as thighplate, a term often symbolic of erotic desire; Dámaso Alonso (1933) who relates Quixote to Camilote from the *Primaleón;* and Alfredo Baras Escolá (1992) who insists on an erotic reading of the name and many other elements in the novel: 'Se ha aludido siempre en el muslo del varón, por metonimia, a la potencia reproductora, cuando no al mismo sexo' (It has been always alluded to the thigh of the male, by metonymy, to the reproductive potency, when not to sex itself) (1992, 81).

6 For a different assessment of the carnivalesque elements, where Don Quixote is related to Pantalone (Pasquati) and Sancho Panza to Panzannini, see Vélez-Sainz 2000 (39ff).

7 'Ya no le llaman Don Quijote, sino el señor Martín Quijada, que era su propio nombre' (Already they don't call him Don Quijote, but rather Lord Martín Quijada, which was his own name) (1987, 59).

8 'Este personaje, célebre por su carácter, era soldado de Carlos V y tan querido del emperador, que fue a él a quien confió la crianza secreta de su hijo natural, Don Juan de Austria' (This personage, celebrated by his character, was a soldier of Charles V and so liked by the emperor, that it was to him Charles V confided the secret upbringing of his natural child, Don Juan de Austria) (Fernández-Cañadas 1985, 18). The physician Daza Chacón, praised by Cervantes in his 'Canto de Calíope' (Song of Calliope) tells of Quijada's heroic deeds of his near-death experience in Naples and his death by an *arcabuz* in Granada. We should recall that firearms are rejected by Don Quixote as antiheroic.

9 'Titian's work pleased the invincible emperor so much that once he had met him he never wanted to be painted by other painters' (Vasari 1991, 502).

10 In his poem 'Al Quadro y retrato de su Majestad que hizo Pedro Pablo de Rubens, Pintor excelentíssimo' (To the Painting of the Portrait of His Majesty that Peter Paul Rubens Made), Lope calls Rubens 'el nuevo Ticiano' (the new Titian) and compares his portrait of Philip IV with Titian's painting of Charles V. On Lope's praise of Titian's portrait, see De Armas 1978.

11 Elizabeth Gilmore Holt explains how Carducci rejects the new dramatic realism of Caravaggio and how he also disliked his contemporary, Velázquez (1947, 437).

12 Brown and Elliott claim that the portrait formed part of the decoration of the Pardo's antechamber by the year 1590 (1980, 151), but Wethey shows that it is listed as being in the Casa del Tesoro of the Alcázar in 1600 (1971, 89).

13 According to Brown and Elliott, the program of the room was based on three themes: battle pieces, family portraits, and four allegorical subjects (Faith, Hope, Charity, and Fame) (1980, 152).

14 The painting remained at the Hall of Mirrors until the Alcázar was destroyed by fire in 1734.

15 It may be that Avellaneda, in his 1614 continuation, chose this one name for his own knight, being aware of its ironic implications. As Rey Hazas notes: 'Martín Quijada, el contrahéroe avellanesco, no registra oscilación alguna en el nombre ni en los apellidos' (Martín Quijada, the antihero of Avellaneda, does not register any oscillation in the name nor in the last names) (1996, 151).

16 'First we are shown a character living a drably conventional existence; then, the transformation of his life by an external catalyst (*incitación*), which releases his individuality and volition' (Close 1978, 238).

17 In chapter 16 Benengeli is said to recount actions that are 'tan mínimas, tan rateras' (so petty and trivial) (1.16.201; 125).

18 As he sallies forth for the first time, Don Quixote, like the emperor, rides his horse ('sobre Rocinante' [mounted Rocinante] [1978, 1.2.79; 30] and brandishes a weapon, his lance or spear ('tomó su lanza' ['seized his lance'] [1978, 1.2.79; 30]).

19 In chapter 5 Don Quixote claims to have battled 'diez jayanes, de los más desaforados y atrevidos' (ten giants, the most lawless and reckless giants) (1978, 1.5.108; 51). There are many others, such as Brocabruno de la Gran Fuerza (1978, 1.21.258) and Pandafilando de la Fosca Vista (1978, 1.29.362). The famous Malambruno of Part 2 is a descendant of Pandafilando (1978, 2.39.335). On these and many other giants, see Urbina 1987, 329–31.

20 'El que guiaba las mulas y servía de carretero era un demonio feo' (Driving the mules and acting as carter was a hideous demon) (1978, 2.11.115; 553).

21 'Entre todos los que allí están, aunque parecen reyes, príncipes y emperadores, no hay ningún caballero andante' (Even though there might be kings, princes and emperors among them, there isn't a single knight errant there) (1978, 2.11.119; 556).

22 Ironically, in many cases, Don Quixote's violent madness is associated with demonic possession. See Hasbrouck (1992).

23 Panofsky casts doubt on this parallel, claiming that the Holy Lance 'looks altogether different' from Charles V's spear (1969, 85).

24 The citation is from the prologue of the *Tercera y cuarta parte del invencible píncipe Don Belianís de Grecia* (*The Third and Fourth Parts of the Invincilbe Prince Don Belianís of Greece*) (1579). This prologue was written by the author's brother, Andrés Fernández.

25 'y muchas veces le vino deseo de tomar la pluma y dalle fin al pie de la letra como allí se promete; y sin duda alguna lo hiciera, y aun saliera con ello, si otros mayores y continuos pensamientos no se lo estorbaran' (and often felt the urge to take up his quill and bring the story to a proper conclusion, as is promised there; and no doubt he'd have done so, and with success too, if other more important and insistent preoccupations hadn't prevented him) (1978, 1.1.73; 26).

26 In Cervantes' *El licenciado Vidriera* (*The Licentiate of Glass*), Venice is seen as Calypso, an alluring enchantress (1982, 2.114).

27 'sin el ornato de prólogo, ni de la innumerabilidad y catálogo de los acostumbrados sonetos, epigramas y elogios que al principio de los libros suelen ponerse' (undecorated by any prologue or the endless succession of sonnets, epigrams and eulogies that are usually put at the beginnings of books) (1978, 1.51; 12). On ornaments as related to the feminine, see Sohm 1995, 781.

28 This is typical of his middle period according to Panofsky (1969, 16).

29 For this reason, the 'inside scenes' of Part 1 take on such a striking ambience: the Maritornes episode and the tale of Impertinent Curiosity.

30 By choosing the ermine, Don Quixote may be foregrounding the symbol of his own defeat in battle.

31 The quote is from Wolfgang Lazius, *Fragmentum ... Methodi*. See Tanner 1993, 128.

32 Not all would see Charles V in this manner. For a fuller discussion of the emperor's imperial vision and symbols, see De Armas 1986, 24–7; Yates 1975, 20–8; Kleinschmidt 2004, 68–74.

33 Ávila y Zúñiga describes the colour red of the mounted emperor, 'llevaba un caparazón de terciopelo carmesí' (wearing a caparison of crimson velvet) and also 'la banda muy ancha de tafetán carmesí' (the widest sash of crimson taffeta) (1876, 441).

34 For a defence of Johnson's psychoanalytical approach as well as an opening of the question of desire in the novel, see Anne J. Cruz (2002, 191).

35 The humid and feminine is further enhanced by a number of interpolations dealing with amorous desire.

36 Charles V wrote his own *Commentaries* in imitation of those by Julius Caesar. According to Kleinschmidt, Charles attempts to present himself as superior to Caesar: 'Whereas Julius Caesar had gone on a single expedi-

tion to Gaul, Charles accomplished five journeys to France. Whereas Caesar had conquered nearby Gaul, Charles sacked distant Tunis. In other words, Charles credited his dynastic empire with more power than the Roman imperial institutions' (2004, 225).

37 Ávila y Zúñiga shows that Charles V was consciously imitating Julius Caesar since the emperor makes a statement that deliberately transforms the words and the context one of Caesar's most famous sayings: 'Y así, dijo aquellas tres palabras de César, trocando la tercera como un príncipe cristiano debe hacer, reconociendo el bien que Dios le hace: "Vine y ví, y Dios venció"' (And so, he said those three words of Caesar, truncating the third as a Christian prince should do, recognizing the good that God is doing for him: 'I came and I saw, and God conquered') (1876, 444).

38 When Sancho informs Don Quixote that many take him to be a 'grandísimo loco' (raging lunatic) (1978, 2.2.56; 500), the knight answers that many great heroes have been the object of similar calumnies, including Julius Caesar: 'Julio César, prudentísimo y valentísimo capitán, fue notado de ambicioso y algún tanto no limpio, ni en sus vestidos ni en sus costumbres' (Julius Caesar, a most spirited, wise and courageous leader, was criticized for being overambitious and not as clean as he might have been, either in his dress or in his personal habits) (1978, 2.2.57; 500).

39 Ávila y Zúñiga uses the term *determinación* not only in his comparison between Charles V and Julius Caesar, but repeatedly in his portrayal of the emperor: 'Era bien menester acompañar la determinación del Emperador con arte y fuerza' (1876, 440); 'Y cuando ha sido conveniente la fuerza y la determinación, se ha ejecutado con aquel ánimo y esfuerzo que es menester' (it was highly necessary to accompany the determination of the emperor with art and force; and when it has been convenient, force and determination were executed with that spirit and effort that is necessary) (1876, 449).

40 Although I am using the English version of Fernández Alvarez work, his more recent book in Spanish (1999) provides additional material for those interested in Charles V's biography.

41 Covarrubias connects *amarillo* with the latin *pallidus* (1987, 110).

42 Louis C. Pérez has commented on a text by Rey de Artieda where he describes colour symbolism as 'leonado escuro congoxa' (dark tawny anguish) (1967, 28).

43 For Kleinschmidt, the defeat of Charles's dream of empire comes when Philip waved 'his candidacy for succeeding Ferdinand as king of the Romans and heir to Ferdinand as future emperor. Philip did so, thereby annihilating the essence of the 1550 arrangements between Charles and Ferdinand' (2004, 217)

8 Dancing with Giants: Philostratus

1 Watt argues: 'The jousting with the windmills is unique in one respect, because it involves inanimate objects which are so huge and unmistakable that the encounter provides a starkly representative pictorial image for the myth' (1996, 65). And yet, the transformation of an inn into a castle also provides a huge and unmistakable object.

2 Augustin Redondo asks: 'Y ¿qué son los *molinos de viento* que se ven por el campo de Montiel sino *torres*, aunque destinadas no a la defensa sino a la molienda? Además, el movimiento giratorio de las aspas del molino, ¿no hace pensar en el voltear de la maza del gigante?' (And what are the *windmills* that are seen in the Plain of Montiel but *towers*, although destined not for defense but for milling? Also, the gyratory movement of the sails of the mill, doesn't it make one think about the swinging of the giant's mace?) (1998, 329). Redondo points to the *Amadís de Gaula* where Galaor, shortly after being armed a knight, goes on to defeat the giant of Peña de Galtares. This critic concludes: 'La visión que se le impone al narrador es la de una *torre*. Esta semejanza entre *gigante* y *torre* viene a ser un verdadero tópico de la literatura caballeresca, asimilado como tal por Cervantes y por don Quijote' (The vision that is imposed on the narrator is that of a tower. This similarity between *giant* and *tower* becomes a true *topos* of chivalric literature, assimilated as such by Cervantes and by Don Quixote) (193).

3 For a discussion of the link between Cervantes' perspectivism and anamorphosis, see Castillo (2001, 7–8; 73ff.).

4 According to F.E. Peters 'Plato has no theory of *techne* ... The contemporary usage of *techne* was to describe any skill in doing and, more specifically, a kind of professional competence as opposed to instinctive ability (*physis*) or mere change (*tyche*). And it is precisely in these senses that Plato uses the term (*Rep*. 381c; *Prot*, 312b, 317c)' (1967, 190). However, Peters does add that in the *Sophist* and the *Politicus*, the term enters 'technical philosophical discourse' (ibid.).

5 Aristotle speaks of *techné* in the sixth book of the *Nichomachean Ethics*. All human activity is either theoretical or practical. The latter can be divided into practically practical (doing) and practically productive (making). The first leads to ethics and politics, while the second leads to *techné*. The *techné* of art is its ability to imitate. This is what Cervantes does so well in this brief but highly allusive episode.

6 Martin Heidegger explains: 'One is that *techne* is the name not only for the activities and skills of the craftsman, but also for the arts of the mind and the fine arts' (1977, 13).

7 The setting for Philostratus's *Imagines* (*Eikones*) is a luxurious house in Naples. This villa was particularly splendid 'by reason of the panel paintings set in the walls' (1931, 7; 1.1). These, we are told, had been 'collected with real judgment. For they exhibited the skill of very many painters' (ibid.). Philostratus decides to use them to instruct the youth. His purpose is 'to describe examples of paintings in the form of an address which we have composed for the young, that by this means they may learn to interpret paintings and to appreciate what is esteemed in them' (1931, 5; 1).

8 These two paintings are based on Philostratus's *Imagines* 1.6 and 1.25 (Wilson 1992, 185–6 note 32). Carlo Ridolfi, in his seventeenth-century biography of Titian, already points to this connection (1996, 67–9). Other works that may have utilized notions and images from Philostratus are *Martyrdom of St Lawrence* in its use of torchlight, and *Adlocution of Alfonso d'Avalos* in its use of perspective (Kennedy 1964, 165).

9 In France, Blaise de Vigenére, secretary to the Duc de Nevers, translated Philostratus (1614) (Hulse 1990, 119); in England his *ekphrases* were related by Franciscus Junius the Younger in *The Painting of the Ancients* (1638) (Hulse 1990, 162) and may have even led Shakespeare in his *Rape of Lucrece* to tell how a painting of war deceives the viewer (Heffernan 1993, 82).

10 In the Spanish Golden Age, Pedro Mexía makes a number of references to this more famous Philostratus in his *Silva de varia lección* (*Silva of Varied Topics*). Cervantes' allusion to the gymnosophists in *Don Quixote* (1978, 1.47; 561) could possibly be a nod to the elder Philostratus.

11 He is mentioned in the Latin version of the text, not in the Italian. In chapter 19 of the *Ars Reminiscendi* Della Porta explains how to remember images of vices and virtues and, after giving a number of examples from Ovid, Virgil, and other classical writers, he sends the reader to Philostratus (1996, 43).

12 In his description of 'quickness' as a key narrative technique, Italo Calvino points to the importance of objects in narrative, even alluding to Mambrino's helmet in *Don Quixote* (1988, 33).

13 Frederick Hartt calls the *David* 'Michelangelo's first adventure in gigantism' (1984, 20).

14 My translation.

15 As Avalle-Arce has repeatedly asserted, 'Don Quixote sale al mundo para vivir la vida como una obra de arte' (Don Quixote sallies forth into the world to live life as a work of art) (Avalle-Arce and Riley, 1973, 51), but he also creates living works of art utilizing media such as theatre and the visual arts.

16 Euripides refers to this story in his *Hecuba* (v. 838), and Callistratus dis-

cusses the matter in depth when describing a statue of Memnon seen in Ethiopia. He claims that it surpasses those of Daedalus in that it can speak and show emotion: 'Daedalus did indeed boldly advance as far as motion, and the materials of which they were made and to move in the dance; but it was impossible and absolutely out of the question for him to make statues that could speak' (Philostratus et al. 1931, 9; 409).

17 Coomonte's picture appears in John J. Allen's Cátedra edition of *Don Quixote* (1985, 1.8. 147).

18 The Sierra Morena is conceived by Don Quixote as the labyrinth designed by Daedalus. He thus tells Sancho that he must devise a mnemonic device to find his way back. He suggests using 'retamas' (broom-branches) instead of the mythical thread (1978, 1.25.317; 219).

19 The Andalucian inkeeper in chapter 2, as well as Reinaldo de Montalbán and his companions in chapter 6, are tied to the thieving qualities of Cacus (1978, 1.2.84, 1.6.113). The innkeeper is called a new Cacus due to his 'picaresque' past and many thieving adventures which succeeded because of 'la ligereza de sus pies, sutilezas de sus manos' (the dexterity of his hands and the nimbleness of his heels) (1978, 1.3.89; 37). But he proves to be benevolent to Don Quixote, and allows him to undergo a chivalric initiation.

20 'The notion of a great heretic, like Luther, appearing under the mantle of a huge giant was a prevalent one that harks back to the story of David and Goliath. Since the Philistine was a giant who lived outside the law of Israel ... all important foes of the pope were likened to Goliath appearing on the plain to do battle with David' (Camamis 1991, 240).

21 Titian again uses the gesture of the praying David in a St George. Rubens, however, will have a David with arms raised 'not in order to pray but, significantly, in order to behead Goliath' (Panofsky 1969, 35).

22 Although the knight does not attack them in chapter 20 of Part 1, he does battle with them in chapter 29 of Part 2, picturing them as 'la ciudad, castillo o fortaleza donde debe estar algún caballero oprimido, o alguna reina, infanta o princesa malparada' (the city, castle or fortress that must hold some knight under duress or some distressed queen, infanta or princess) (1978, 2.29.265; 685).

23 Cervantes was certainly acquainted with Archimedes since he read Pedro Mexía's *Silva de varia lección*, where the life and accomplishments of this inventor are discussed at length (1989, 1.826–33).

24 'La idea de progreso, en suma, tuvo uno de sus puntos de partida en la exaltación de lo moderno frente a lo antiguo en el terreno de la técnica. Los españoles del siglo XVI, como hombres de su tiempo, se sentían a ese

respecto superiores a los clásicos' (The idea of progress, in sum, had one of its points of departure the exaltation of the modern in contrast with the ancient in the realm of technology. Spaniards of the sixteenth century, like men of their time, felt in that respect superior to the classics) (López Piñero 1979, 159–60). Another important work, focusing on technology in Philip II's Spain, is that of David C. Goodman. See, in particular, chapter 3 where he discusses the technology for war (1988, 88–150).

25 In his *Cartas* (*Letters*), Lope de Vega compares a woman's subtlety to Juanelo's artifice (February/March 1616). In 1622, Andrés de Ocaña speaks of a curious astrological instrument designed by Turriano where one could see the movements of all ten spheres of the heavens. He also praises a miniature clock made by Turriano which would fit in the space of a stone within a ring worn on the finger (1622, 164). Seven years later, Calderón de la Barca alludes to Juanelo in *La dama duende* (*The Phantom Lady*).

26 Although in the past most have agreed that Juanelo is the author of this manuscript, more recently José A. García-Diego (1983), the editor of Turriano's work, rejects this authorship. He argues that the language of the manuscript suggests that it was written by an Aragonese. It has very few Italianisms and we know that Juanelo spoke Spanish with a strong dose of Italian. Furthermore, there is little said of Toledo where Juanelo presumably wrote the text. However, it is possible to counter these assertions by arguing that Juanelo had a Spaniard write down his ideas. However, García-Diego suggests that the work was written by another Italian engineer, Giovanni Francesco Sitoni, born in Milan in 1532. He worked for Philip II in irrigation canals for the Tagus and for the plains of Lérida.

27 Among other elements discussed are boats for crossing rivers (Libro de las barcas que sirven en lugar de puente para passar los rios y de otras puentes' [Book of barges that serve in place of a bridge to cross rivers and of other bridges], wooden and stone bridges, maritime works (de hazer defensas a puertos para que armadas no puedan entrar' [for making defenses at ports so that armadas cannot enter]), fortifications, waterclocks, etc. (Turiano 1983).

28 Julio Caro Baroja seems to misquote Juanelo when he states: 'Afirma que ni en España ni en Italia hay molinos de viento y ello "a causa de la irregularidad y fuerza de los vientos (!!)." Por su época (1500 (?) – 1585) ya estaban en pie cantidad grande de molinos, no sólo en el S. de la Península, sino también en La Mancha, bien cerca de Toledo' (He affirms that there are neither in Spain nor in Italy windmills and that 'was due to the irregularity and force of the winds (!!).' During his time (1500 (?) – 1585) already there were standing a great quantity of mills, not only in

the south of the Peninsula, but also in La Mancha, very close to Toledo) (Caro Baroja 1983, 153). But Juanelo only criticizes such mills. He does not say that they do not exist in Spain.

29 Of course, the use of Renaissance mechanical contraptions did not cease with the reign of Philip II. They appear at the feast for the birth of the future Philip IV in 1605. As Ferrer Valls asserts: 'El creciente gusto por las invenciones mecánicas se manifiesta en la figura dorada de la Fama tocando su clarín. No voy a insistir sobre la utilización de carros y nubes ...' (The growing zeal for mechanical inventions manifests itself in the golden figure of Fame playing its trumpet. I am not going to insist on the utilization of carts and clouds ...) (1990, 130).

30 Dante's ekphrasis was noted by Botticelli, who chose it for one of his illustrations of the *Divine Comedy* entitled *Briareus and Giants*. Vasari mentions these drawings but complains that Botticelli 'wasted a great deal of time on this, neglecting his work and disrupting his life' (1991, 227). It is doubtful that Cervantes would have seen these drawings, scattered throughout Europe. But the knowledge of their existence may have impelled him to enter into this battle between the verbal and the visual, between Dante's ekphrasis and Botticelli's drawing.

31 Cervantes knew Dante well. Alban Forcione points to Cervantes' use of Dante in *Pedro de Urdemalas*: 'He uses his inventive powers to conjure forth a vision of the sister's suffering in Purgatory ... As if the reminiscences of Dante were not enough to suggest Pedro's affinities with the poet ... he begins his speech with an invocation of memory ... traditionally invoked by the epic poet' (1970, 330–1). Werner Friederich finds a reference to Dante in Cervantes' *Galatea* as well as a borrowing from the *Inferno* in Don Quixote 2.69 (1950, 49). Henry Sullivan points to the fact that there was only one translation of the *Commedia* into Spanish during the Golden Age, but thinks there may be an allusion to Dante in the Clavileño episode when this horse is described as *el Alígero*, which is how Lope refers to Dante in the *Arte nuevo de hacer comedias*: 'Dante Alígero' (Sullivan 1996, 75).

32 Arturo Marasso points to the *Aeneid* as model for the windmills episode citing the translation of Virgil by Hernández de Velasco. He believes that the windmills actually derive from the episode of the Cyclops in the *Aeneid* and thus fails to link the figure of Briareus with false dreams (1954, 56–7). Avery, however, connects Sancho's advice to Don Quixote with the Sybil's counsel to Aeneas upon entering the underworld (1961–2, 2). Briareus also appears in Homer's *Iliad* where he is much more heroic and less threatening (1988, 1.401–6). The giant also figures at the very begin-

ning of Apollodorus's *Library*, where his ancestry is described: 'Sky was the first who ruled over the whole world. And having wedded Earth, he begat first the Hundred-handed, so they were named: Briareus, Gyes, Cottus, who were unsurpassed in size and might, each of them having a hundred hands and fifty heads' (1976, 1.1).

33 Ruben's *The Fall of the Giants* in the Torre de la Parada, El Pardo (1636–8) is one of the few works that seeks to compete with Giulio Romano's fantasy.

34 Rubin believes that the use of the term 'ekphrasis' for Vasari is misleading. She states that although it was 'reintroduced to the west by Byzantine humanists in the first half of the fifteenth century ... Ekphrasis is not included in fifteenth- or sixteenth-century Latin or Italian rhetorical manuals or treatises, and ekphrastic compositions were not a standard part of the rhetorical curriculum as they were in the east' (1995, 275). This is not to say that the term was not used in the Spanish Golden Age, where it can be found even in the title of works on botany.

35 Next to Jupiter and Juno, on their right, stands Cybele with her lions, and almost behind her, Hercules (Hartt 1958, 1.155, 2.fig. 347). With his mace and a furious expression he merely watches the destruction. Although his expression is fierce, he has to step back and allow Jupiter to complete the destruction.

36 On *contaminatio*, see Greene 1982, 39; De Armas 1998, 14.

37 The poem states: 'a guisa di maciulla' (34.56), which is explained as: "an instrument that crushes hemp stalks and separates the fiber' (Dante 1972, 305). For an image of Lucifer that may have been the model for Dante, see the depiction in the Baptistry of Florence. I would like to thank Lloyd Howard and Janice Elliott for pointing this out to me.

38 On this subject, see Hartt 1950, 181, 186–7. Hartt also shows that this Sala was next to the handball court, at which Charles V played. Thus 'the act of throwing the ball becomes divinized in the figure of Jupiter hurling the thunderbolt' (186).

9 A Mannerist Theophany / A Cruel *Teichoskopia*

1 According to the 'Advertencias' from D. Juan Oldfield at the beginning of the 1738 English edition, the frontispiece depicts Cervantes disguised as Hercules: 'Hércules llamado Musagetes a quien atribuyó la Mitología la guía de las Musas' (Hercules called Musagetes to whom Mythology attributed the role of guide of the Muses). His lyre represents his knowledge of the art, while Spain is the theatre of his actions. He uses satire,

represented by a mask, as one of his weapons (Cervantes 1738, ii). Of course, this Hercules has many of the qualities of Apollo, protector of poets and a deity surrounded by bards and the muses in Parnassus, as we have seen in the fresco by Raphael on the subject. On Cervantes as both Hercules and Apollo in this frontispiece, see De Armas 2005a.

2 Agustín García Arrieta (1805), Francisco María Turbino (1862) and Ramón León Maínez (1876) are among those who questioned Vincente de los Ríos's conclusions. (For a summary of their views, see Drake 1974.)

3 Ríos had alluded to Virgil, but found Homer preferable. For example, he finds a stronger causality in the gift of weapons in the *Iliad* than in those prepared for the protagonist of Virgil's *Aeneid* (1819, 61). Perhaps Ríos's preference for Homer blinds him to the closer kinship between Cervantes and Virgil.

4 *The Theory of the Novel* was first published in 1916 and is one of Lukács's principal pre-Marxist works. It was translated into English by Anna Bostock in 1971. His theory that the novel resulted from the difficulty in reaching towards the Christian God in an age where religion was in decline finds some support here, since the religious images of Parmigianino and others exhibit a transcendent being tainted with human subjectivity. Anthony Cascardi expands upon the process of secularization in *Don Quixote* arguing that 'we must regard this process not just as the result of a change in the patterns of religious belief but as a master-trope for the problem of authority as it is figured within literary history' (1997, 211).

5 Susanne Lidgren Wofford (1992) discusses *Don Quixote* in terms of figuration, while Chester L. Wolford has shown that two qualities of the Homeric hero as typified by Achilles are also present in *Don Quixote*: *areté*, 'which demands that he strive ceaselessly for the first prize' (1986, 198), and *menos*, 'or the fierce battle-rage into which Homer's warriors whip themselves' (1986, 202).

6 On the archaeology of Numancia based on Troy and Rome, see Johnson (1981) and De Armas (1998).

7 For a full discussion of Cervantes' Virgilian project, see De Armas (2002) as well as other essays in the *Yearbook for Comparative and General Literature* 49 (2001) by Anne J. Cruz and Álvaro Molina.

8 There is, of course, the problem of the middle style. Where are the *Georgics*? Perhaps it is merely sufficient for Cervantes to point out that both Marcela and Grisóstomo are children of rich farmers. They do not write georgics since they are living embodiments of this style. It should also be noted that the three steps of the *Rota Virgilii* were not always

followed. Indeed, Traugott Lawler claims: 'Nor has any poet ever followed the pattern altogether strictly: neither Spenser nor Milton produced anything really comparable to the Georgics' (1977, 54).

9 For Marasso, there is a clear relationship between Dido and Grisóstomo (1954, 85).

10 Both Herman Iventosch (1974) and Ruth El Saffar (1984) underline the resemblances between Marcela and the goddess Diana. Using the Jungian theories, the latter argues: 'She belongs very much to the Diana archetype' (1984, 61). Thomas Austin O'Connor uses the myth of Diana/Artemis to discover instead the mythical move from maiden to wife (2005, 373). Michael McGaha stresses the parallels with the Apollo/Daphne episode (1977); and Erna Berndt-Kelley (1989) and Carolyn Nadeau (1995) have argued that she resembles the goddess Astraea.

11 There is also something in her demeanour and certainly in her words that tells Aeneas that he is speaking to a goddess, 'for thy face is not mortal nor has thy voice a human ring' (1978, 1.265; 1.327–8).

12 However, she remains admirable although unclothed in a number of Renaissance works. Studying Agostino Veneziano, Cartari, and others, Daniel L Heiple concludes: 'A common element in some of these representations is that Venus is not fully armed, or even fully dressed ... As stated by Ariosto and Hurtado de Mendoza, the real armor of Venus is her nudity' (1994, 375–7).

13 One of the most obvious examples is found in the *Persiles y Sigismunda*, in which Cervantes shows his archaeological interests. He tells the readers that the present feast of Monda at Talavera, which honours the Virgin of the Fields, used to be a pagan festival for the goddess Venus (1969, 312).

14 Anthony Cascardi, for example, states: 'Like his friend Ambrosio, Grisóstomo bears a saintly name; they recall Saint John Chrysostom and Saint Ambrose' (1997, 229).

15 It comes from the word *mano* or hand and was used disparagingly in the seventeenth and eighteenth centuries. Only in the twentieth century did it acquire a positive connotation, as some writers 'thought that in Mannerism they had found a new period to be set between the High Renaissance and the Baroque, forming a Hegelian succession of thesis, antithesis and synthesis' (Hartt 1994, 535).

16 Within the category of mannerism, Hartt places the later works of Michelangelo, as well as Giulio Romano's art, in spite of the fact that the latter was a disciple of Raphael. Those who view the term as negative see mannerism as taking Michelangelo's experiments to an extreme.

17 In 1523 Parmigianino undertook a fresco decoration at the Rocca di

Fontanellato near Parma, dealing with Diana and Acteon. For Freedberg, it is intended as an allegory of the high summer season, the dog days of August (1950, 51). The mannerism of the work is seen in the fact that 'the spectator's space and the space of the frescoes are intimately interpenetrated' (Freedberg 1950, 52).

18 To confirm the importance of Virgil's *Georgics*, there is an inscription from this text (1.21) above the oculus.

19 *Vertumnus and Pomona* evinces other eccentricities such as the representation of a naked Apollo 'with his legs spread wide, above a dog with its back arched, also stretching itself' (Hartt 1994, 553).

20 This panel was executed 1525–8 for the Capponi family chapel in Santa Felicita. It is praised by Vasari. Afterwards Pontormo 'seems to have become morose and warped, ingrown and strange' (Hartt 1994, 554).

21 It was painted for the Buffoni chapel in San Salvatore in Lauro in Rome. It was later transported to Citta di Castello and eventually ended up at the National Gallery in London.

22 Pontormo's painting includes a number of other mannerist features. Executed for a Florentine villa, *Joseph in Egypt* astounds with its 'crowds of nervous figures, statues pulsating ... uncertain and unprotected staircases spiraling into nowhere ...' (Hartt 1994, 552).

23 Constantine proclaimed that the Virgin who returns in Virgil's *Fourth Eclogue* is none other than Mary. The prophesied child is Jesus, the serpent that shall cease to be is the devil, and the balsam which will grow is the Christian race (Comparetti 1929, 100).

10 Dulcinea and the Five Maidens: Zeuxis

1 It has been suggested that the episode of the battle of the sheep may be derived from Sophocles' *Ajax*. However, if this were the case we have to contend with the fact that this tragedy 'was not translated into Spanish until long after Cervantes' time; the first translation into a modern language was the Italian one published in Venice in 1603' (McGaha 1991, 158). Consequently, a later model for the episode, Apuleius's *Golden Ass*, has seemed to be a more probable subject of imitation (Selig 1974/5 and 1983, 286).

2 On enumeration in *Don Quixote*, see Selig (1989).

3 This is, of course, a question that has puzzled readers of *Don Quixote* for centuries. In the nineteenth century, Díaz de Benjumea compared Don Quixote's love for her with devotion to the Virgin Mary, equating Dulcinea with 'luz, sabiduria, verdad, libertad' (light, wisdom, truth,

liberty) (1986, 137). This is the Dulcinea who became 'the cornerstone of his (Unamuno's) Quixotic Christianity' (Close 1978, 248). But for Anthony Close, she is a simulacrum of sublimity, an 'ironic facsimile' (1978, 248). And attempting to bring opposites together, Javier Herrero speaks of Dulcinea's split into 'a lady of light and a woman of darkness' (1985, 5).

4 In book 1, Cesare Gonzaga argues that physical gives more pleasure to he who understands it best, and thus gives the example of Zeuxis: 'Have you not read that those five girls of Crotone, whom the painter Zeuxis chose from among all the others of that city for the purpose of forming from all five a single figure of consummate beauty, were celebrated by many poets because their beauty had won the approbation of one who must have been the most perfect judge?' (Castiglione 1967, 102).

5 Although alluding to Pliny, Pacheco gives Cicero's version of the story: 'Con el ejemplo del antiguo Zeusis, que para la bellísima Helena que se le ofreció pintar al pueblo de Agrigento, eligió cinco hermosas doncellas, y de cada una de ellas fue escogiendo lo más perfecto' (With the example of the ancient Zeuxis, who offered to paint the most beautiful Helen for the town of Agrigento, he selected five beautiful maidens, and from each one of them was choosing the most perfect elements) (1982, 43). Pacheco also includes a poem by Melchor del Alcázar on this subject, although the painter is now called Protógenes.

6 For a discussion of Vasari's painting in relation to Cicero's account, see Patricia Lee Rubin 1995, 240.

7 Cicero imitates Aristotle and Isocrates in particular, combining the philosophical 'sect' or 'family' with the one 'devoted entirely to the study and teaching of oratory' (1960, 173; 2.3). In *De Oratore* Cicero will stress the importance of the ethical trustworthiness of the orator, the fact that he must know and practise moral philosophy.

8 As Charles M. Rosenberg has shown, the notion of proportion in the human body was derived from Alberti, who warns that 'care should be taken above all that all the members accord well with one another' (Rosenberg 1986, 182). Hulse relates this compositional decorum in painting to Horace's view of poetry (1990, 195).

9 Eduardo Urbina speaks of 'lo grotesco monstruoso' (the monstrous grotesque) as a way to satirize 'los defectos de estilo y forma que se encuentran en los libros de caballerías, es decir, su carácter disparatado y extravagante, su fealdad y deformidad grotescas' (the defects of style and form that are found in the books of chivalry, that is to say, their disparate and extravagant character, their grotesque ugliness and deformity) (1989, 674).

10 According to Fernando de la Flor 'el mejor modo de hacer la distribución del espacio conocido o inventado se basa en el número cinco' (the best method for making the distribution of the known or invented space is based in the number five) (1996, 63). Azevedo's *El Fénix de Minerva y arte de Memoria* was published in 1626. For an illustration of his five places in each 'trascendente' where images are to be placed see Flor 1996, 231.

11 It is curious to note that Raphael's name appears in the Latin version of the work published in 1602 but not in the Italian 'translation' of 1566.

12 Della Porta utilizes what has been called 'architectural mnemonics,' arguing that the practitioner must place the images to be remembered in appropriate loci, which in many cases means that they are to be set on walls in a room of a building. This should be a fairly large building with many halls in order to contain the variety of images necessary to remember a lengthy text.

13 It is said that Simonides 'called painting mute poetry and poetry painting that speaks.' Yates cites from Plutarch's *Glory of Athens* (Yates 1966, 28).

14 When describing Ulysses, for example, the knight states: 'Pinta Homero un retrato vivo de prudencia' (Homer painted for us a living portrait of these two qualities [prudence and long-suffering]) (1978, 1.25.303; 207).

15 For a fascinating discussion of the four retellings of the battle with the Basque (including an ekphrasis of the painting in the manuscript), see Michael Gerli 1995, 61–81.

16 Indeed, Amadís was even tempted by other women such as Madásima. It is thus no coincidence that Queen Madásima is the subject of a heated debate between Cardenio and Don Quixote in the previous chapter (1978, 1.24.298). Cardenio claims that Madásima was the mistress of Elisabat. This is not true, and it has been supposed that Cardenio confuses Madásima with Grasinda (who did favour Elisabat). What is important is that the name brings up in Don Quixote's mind the possible infidelity of Amadís. As Juan Manuel Cacho Blecua asserts in his edition of the *Amadís*: 'Por ello Amadís deberá resistir las tentaciones que se le ofrecen y que en algún caso pueden salvarle de una situación peligrosa para su vida, casos de Madasima, señora de Gantasi, o de Briolanja' (For that reason Amadis must resist the temptations that are offered to him and that in some cases can save him from a dangerous situation in his life, cases such as that of Madásima, lady of Gantasi, or of Briolanja) (1987, 1.125). Madásima appears in book 1, chapter 33.

17 Titian, however, presents a typically chivalric scene in which Angelica is saved from a dragon by Medoro. This seems to be a false identification since the saviour was Ruggero.

18 The term 'morillo' recalls the diminutive used for Medoro in a *romance*, 'Medorillo,' which seems to announce 'una obra de estilo satírico o burlesco' (a work of satirical or burlesque style) (Chevalier 1986, 255). Perhaps the most famous burlesque version of the story is told by Quevedo in *El Parnasso español* (*The Spanish Parnassus*): 'Quitándose está Medoro ...' (Medoro is taking off ...) (Chevalier 1986, 317–18).

19 Henry Kamen describes how the morisco rebellion began when Granada, with the support of the crown, decided 'to put into effect the existing laws (above all, those of 1526), prohibiting Moorish customs, language and dress' (1997, 129). Once the rebellion was put down in 1570, the king's council decided 'to expel a part of the Muslim population of Granada to other parts of Spain' (1997, 131).

20 Castro's statement in *Cervantes y los casticismos españoles* (1966, 93–4) is criticized by Avalle-Arce and Riley, claiming that this is guilt by association, 'porque en el Toboso había muchos moriscos, Dulcinea tenía que serlo también' (because in Toboso there were many Moors, Dulcinea had to be one also) (1973, 51 note 9).

21 'imitar a Roldán en las locuras desaforadas que hizo, o Amadís en las malencólicas' (imitating Orlando and his outrageous madness, or Amadis and his melancholy madness) (1978, 1.26.318; 220).

22 According to both Lessing and Heffernan, what is important is that the Homeric poem eschews her description. Instead, she has an old man upon the wall say: 'Small blame that Trojans and well-grieved Achaeans should for such a woman long time suffer woes; wondrously like is she to the immortal goddess to look upon' (Homer 1988, 129; 3.156–60).

23 Juan de la Corte painted several abductions of Helen. He always included the figure of Hercules, something that, according to Rosa López Torrijos, gives the canvas a medieval tone, although 'en ninguna de estas obras figura Hércules como parte de la expedición que raptó a Elena' (in none of these works is Hercules depicted as part of the expedition that abducted Helen) (1985, 208). She adds that Juan de la Corte, in general terms, follows 'un grabado italiano que inspiró también a los artistas de Fontainebleau y otros muchos flamencos, como Franken II, contemporáneo de Juan de la Corte, cuyo *Rapto de Helena*, del museo de Tours, fechado en 1629, está compuesto de la misma manera ...' (an Italian drawing that also inspired the artists of Fontainebleau and many other Flemish ones, like Franken II, contemporary of Juan de la Corte, whose *Rape of Helen*, of the museum of Tours, dated in 1629, is composed in a similar manner ...) (1985, 209).

24 The French text included in the tapestry states that Paris 'Ravit denuit

Helanie amoult grant joie.' However, this joy is not at all clear in the tapestry itself. Neither Helen nor Paris, who holds her by the arm, appears to be particularly happy. While the French text appears at the top of the tapestry, a Latin version is found at the bottom.

25 'Aparece el "Temple dy Chitarae" con su Sibila sentada que contempla cómo los troyanos se llevan las riquezas de la Isla y a Helena que monta en una embarcación' (The Temple of Cythera appears with its seated Sibyl who contemplates how the Trojans are carrying away the riches of the Island and Helen who is placed in a boat) (Ramos de Castro 1982, 483). Cythera was an island said to be the birth place of Aphrodite/Venus, the goddess who had promised Helen to Paris. It belonged to Sparta and thus can be seen as a place for Helen's abduction. In Leomarte's *Sumas de historia troyana* (*Compendia of Trojan History*), Paris goes to the island of Cythera where a festival for the goddess Diana is underway. Here, he abducts Helen and takes untold treasures. His action is in response to the Greeks' abduction of Usiona (1932, 159–68).

26 Discussing the Sala di Troia, Frederick Hartt asserts: 'No character is convincing, no situation human, no alarm real ... The wall paintings contain many salty and amusing elements ... the happy departure of Paris and Helen in an impossible boat adorned with grinning masks ...' (1958, 182).

27 Della Porta, like Don Quixote, views her first as naked, being raped by Tarquin; and later, with a knife in hand ready to commit suicide. He also has a third moment, absent from Cervantes, Tarquin wearing a crown.

28 For a lucid discussion of Machiavelli's *Mandragola*, see Donaldson 1982, 90–4.

29 For the comical view of Lucretia in Spain, see Joseph E. Gillet (1947) who traces this back to a question from Augustine: If she was adulterous, why praise her? If chaste, why did she slay herself? But the chaste Lucretia appears in a number of Golden Age plays and is the subject of a tragedy by Francisco de Rojas Zorrilla.

30 Another exception is Marcantonio Raimondi's engraving based on Raphael where 'the stoic potential of the story as an allegory of political liberty' emerges (Spear 1997, 89).

31 It is documented at the Alcázar in Madrid starting with 1626. Juan de Piña describes the painting in detail in *Caso prodigioso y cueva encantada* (*Prodigious Event and Enchanted Cave*) (1628); Pacheco mentions it in *Los diálogos de la pintura* (1633); and Vicencio Juan de Lastanosa has a copy of it in his museum (Vosters 1990, 154, 266, 309).

32 'La pintó en su imaginación' (He depicted her in his imagination) (1978, 1.16.203; 126).

33 In Ovid's *Fasti*, one of the key models for the painting, there is no slave-voyeur. But Tarquin threatens Lucretia: 'I, the adulterer, will bear false witness to thine adultery. I'll kill a slave, and rumour will have it that thou wert caught with him' (1989, 115; 2.808–9).
34 'or by assigning certain comic effects to our images ...' (Cicero 1954, 221; 3.22).
35 It is surprising that she would draw this rape shortly after her own attempted rape by her art teacher Agostino Tassi. Donaldson concludes: 'Artemisia was attempting to place at some distance a subject painfully close to her own experience' (1982, 20).
36 One of his Lucretias became the subject of a poem by Manuel Gallegos, published in Madrid in 1637. While Gallegos underscores the 'piedad' elicited by the suicide (MacCurdy 1974, 304), Reni foregounds the alluring sexuality of the suicide victim.
37 'alzó los ojos al cielo y, puesto el pensamiento ... en su señora Dulcinea ...' (he raised his eyes to heaven and, fixing his thoughts ... on his lady Dulcinea) (1978, 1.3.91; 38).
38 Commenting on the Cardenio/Dorotea episode, Syverson-Stork asserts that it 'is replete with dramatic technique. The author has blocked his characters' movements as if they were performing on stage' (1986, 124).
39 Lucinda faints while holding a knife. The hidden Cardenio, the voyeur, shuns her because she does not follow through with her intention to use the knife instead of marrying Fernando. In another episode, Marcela seems to confuse her Tarquins in her speech on liberty (1978, 1.14.185).
40 Gossy takes as a point of departure for her analysis an explanation by Augustín Redondo. He claims that 'tirar la barra' (pitches a bar) (1978, 1.25.312; 214) 'que puede tomar el significado de *futuere*, como lo demuestran otros textos del Siglo de Oro' (can mean *futuere*, as other Golden Age texts demonstrate) (Redondo 1998, 244–5). Gossy stresses that *futuere* is 'to have sexual intercourse (with a woman)' (1995, 20).
41 Since she is a butch, she is on the lookout for a femme, and, of course, this is the image of Dulcinea created by Don Quixote.
42 On this subject, see Patricia Joplin (1990).
43 Curiously, even though Amadís was from Brittany, he was often though to be from England since he did battle in Wales. When Philip II went to England to wed Mary Tudor, Henry Kamen relates: 'The Spanish nobles were excited by England. For them it was the legendary island of chivalry, the home of King Arthur and of Amadís' (1997, 58).
44 Cervantes describes the sack of Cádiz by the English in 1596 in one of the

Novelas ejemplares (*Exemplary Novels*), 'La española inglesa' (The English Spaniard).

45 In his description of an idealized romance of chivalry, Don Quixote uses the term 'brutesco' (grotesque) (1978, 1.50.584; 457). This term is a corruption of 'grutesco,' the origin of what today we call the grotesque. Don Quixote's Dulcinea will later be studied under this rubric since her image foregrounds the conflict between centre and margins; the disproportion of parts; the decorative and the ugly.

46 It is for this reason that Don Quixote sends Sancho to find Dulcinea. He can no longer deal with his mind's image and must find a counterpart.

11 Love's Architecture: Giulio Romano

1 For the interweaving of the tales of Giges in Herodotus and Cupid and Psyche in Apuleius in order to fashion *El curioso impertinente*, see De Armas (1992a). De Armas Wilson (1987) also foregrounds some of the key models of the *novela*: the *Orlando furioso*, the tale of Giges from Herodotus, and the tale of the two friends.

2 Forcione has shown that 'Cervantes turns to the realm of classical myth to enrich the texture of the scene' in the *Persiles* (1972, 134). For Diana de Armas Wilson, 'Cervantes deallegorizes the Cupid and Psyche story and, in the process, gives Psyche (Soul) back the body that over a millennium of allegorical readings ... had so relentlessly erased' (1994, 94).

3 The reversal of the Cupid and Psyche story led to the creation of what I have labelled as the plot of the 'Invisible Mistress.' The first instance of this reversal occurs in the twelfth-century French romance *Partonopeu de Blois*. The Spanish theatre of the Golden Age revelled in the presentation of this Invisible Mistress as in Calderón's *La dama duende* (*The Phantom Lady*) and Ana Caro's *El conde Partinuplés* (*The Count Partinuples*). See de Armas (1976).

4 'Todo lo miraba Anselmo, cubierto detrás de unos tapices donde se había escondido' (Anselmo, hiding behind the tapestries, was watching it all) (1978, 1.34.432; 325).

5 This villa was destroyed in the eighteenth century (Fritz 1997, 36–7).

6 According to Alain Saint-Saëns: 'Paradoxically, it was to struggle against the practice of sodomy among young men, common in Tuscany, that the city of Florence accepted to tolerate the existence of brothels' (2000, 11).

7 The knight states he was born 'a Mantuan of good family' (1983, canto 43, 510) and that his city is 'surrounded by a clear river, as by a lake, which

flows from Lake Garda and extends to run into our Po' (1983, canto 43, 510). This 'clear river' is the Mincio, which passes through Mantua on its way to merging with the Po.

8 Comparing this interpolated tale with the 'Isla Bárbara' (Barbaric Island) episode in the *Persiles*, Diana de Armas Wilson sees it as emblematic of Cervantes' 'homosocial landscape' in the sense ascribed to it by Eve Sedgewick: 'a far-ranging continuum which includes not only the elements of homosexuality in male-male relationships but also such other elements as male bonding which may be characterized by intense homophobia' (De Armas Wilson, 1987, 22). Thomas Pavel, on the other hand, prefers to avoid such interpretations in order to concentrate on character and verisimilitude (2005, 114–15).

9 For different interpretations of this painting, see Hartt (1958, 1.181) and Talvacchia (1989, 410).

10 For an illustration of this Ganymede, see Berzaghi (1989, 396). Giulio Romano's drawing, he states, is found at the Pierpont Morgan Library in New York.

11 Among the twelve signs of the zodiac, we discover Aquarius often depicted as Ganymede or cupbearer in the form of a water-bearer. This image contains only astrological significance (Hartt 1958, 1.115–18).

12 Jupiter's eagle, the transformation he used in the rape of Ganymede, is seen in his temple at the very top and centre of the composition.

13 There are some, however, who do read the *Curioso* as a tale of Christian exemplarity. For Kenneth Brown, for example: 'El *curioso* es un sermón ... Si quedamos conformes con que la falta de fe en el amor sirve de tema principal ... tal pudiendo equivaler al desagradecimiento del hombre mortal ante los sacrificios del Señor' (The *Tale of Foolish Curiosity* is a sermon ... If we agree that the lack of faith in love serves as the principal theme ... it can be the equivalent to the ingratitude of mortal man before the sacrifices of the Lord) (1981, 794–5).

12 The Last Enchantment: Epilogue

1 The captives are eventually saved by Rinaldo.

2 Juan Pérez de Moya asserts that the planet Saturn is always painted as slow and lazy: 'Píntanle pereçoso, en quanto planeta, porque es el que más tiempo gasta en cumplir su revolución,según su movimiento propio en que gasta treynta años' (They paint him lazy, as a planet, because it is the one that spends the most time in completing its revolution, according to its own movement which takes thirty years) (1996, 374).

3 Perugino, as explained below in note 8, painted Saturn's cart as drawn by two dragons. A rather terrifying dragon is seen in Noel Coypel's *The Triumph of Saturn* (1670–2) at Versailles.

4 For the sermon of Martín García, bishop of Barcelona, see Vernet 1974, 23. For a discussion of the impact of Albumasar in Spain up to the times of Lope de Vega, see De Armas 1992b.

5 The mock prophecy that leads Don Quixote to accept his enchantment is carefully described, along with its implications, by Fajardo (1986, 239ff). He contrasts the name given to the knight 'león manchado' (tainted lion or lion of La Mancha) (1978, 1.46.555; 432) to the epithet used to refer to the king of Spain in prophecies: 'león coronado' (crowned lion). It would be interesting to connect the prophecies of 1603–5 with the mock prophecy given to Don Quixote.

6 Saturn was not only considered the most malefic of planets, but also the planet of painters and philosophers; and as god, he was often seen presiding over the Golden Age. For Don Quixote, Saturn may be just a planet of frightful visions and melancholy. It also rules his temper as a temperamental artist who paints over worldly realities.

7 The notion of *Deus artifex* and *Deus pictor* passed through many permutations, starting with Plato, where God as demiurge is architect and maker of the cosmos, and continuing with Empedocles and Pindar, who envisioned God as painter (Curtius 1953, 544, 562). This image of *Deus pictor* became a prevalent motif in the Spanish Golden Age, and as such it appears in many of the writers of the time including Lope de Vega and Calderón de la Barca. For the latter, 'the divine Logos is not only a painter, but also architect, musician, poet' (Curtius 1953, 568).

8 At the Palazzo Schifanoia in Ferrara, a group of Ferrarese painters with 'expressive and bizarre style' (Roettgen 1996, 410), painted at the end of the fifteenth century the Hall of the Months. 'The gods are seated here on lavishly decorated triumphal cars ... Each of the enthroned deities is identified by his or her common attributes' (Roettgen 1996, 414). Here we see Venus, for example, in a cart drawn by swans. At the Sala di Udienza at the Collegio del Cambio in Perugia, Pietro Perugino adorned the vault with the seven planets: 'Each of the gods stands or sits enthroned on a car drawn by his or her attendant animals. The wheels of their car are ornamented with the appropriate constellations of the zodiac' (Roettgen 1997, 260). In this cycle, Saturn has two dragons as his attendant animals, while Venus is led by doves. At the Palazzo del Té, studied in this volume for its Sala dei Giganti and Sala de Psiche, there is also a Sala dei Venti with its sixteen medallions arranged under the twelve signs of the zodiac. Accord-

ing to E.H. Gombrich: 'They are based on a doctrine propounded in the fifth book of Manilius' famous Astronomica which ascribes an influence not only to the zodiacal signs themselves but also to the various constellations which rise together with these signs' (1972, 109). Finally, at the Villa Farnesina, home to Raphael's *Triumph of Galatea* and the loggia of Psyche, we also encounter Peruzzi's decoration of complex astrological subjects, which depicts the horoscope of Agostino Chigi.

Works Cited

Agrippa, Cornelius. 1986. *The Three Books of Occult Philosophy*. London: Chthonios Books.

Allen, John J. 1969. *Don Quixote: Hero or Fool?* Gainesville: University of Florida Press.

– 1976. 'Autobiografía y ficción: El relato del *Capitán cautivo*.' *Anales Cervantinos* 10:23–31.

Alonso, Dámaso. 1933. 'El hidalgo Camilote y el hidalgo Don Quijote.' *Revista de Filología Española* 20:391–7.

Alter, Robert B. 1975. *Partial Magic: The Novel as a Self-Conscious Genre*. Berkeley and Los Angeles: University of California Press.

– 1981. 'Mirror of Knighthood, World of Mirrors.' In Miguel de Cervantes, *Don Quixote, the Ormsby Translation*, ed. Joseph R. Jones and Kenneth Douglas. 955–74. New York: W.W. Norton.

Apa, Cristina, ed. 1998. *Rabisch. Il grotesco nell'arte del Cinquecento. L'accademia della Val di Blenio, Lomazzo e l'ambiente milanese*. Milan: Skira.

Apollodorus. 1976. *The Library*. Trans. James George Frazer. 2 vols. Cambridge, MA: Harvard University Press.

Apuleius. 1989. *Metamorphoses*. Ed. and trans. J. Arthur Hanson. Loeb Classical Library. 2 vols. Harvard: Harvard University Press.

– 1990. *Cupid and Psyche*. Ed. and trans. E.J. Kenney. Cambridge, MA: Harvard University Press.

Ariosto, Ludovico. 1983. *Orlando furioso*. Trans. Guido Waldman. Oxford: Oxford University Press.

Aristotle. 1941. *The Basic Works of Aristotle*. Ed. Richard McKeon. New York: Random House.

Avalle-Arce, Juan Bautista. 1974. *La novela pastoril española*. Madrid: Ediciones Istmo.

– 1975. *Nuevos deslindes cervantinos*. Barcelona: Ariel.
– 1976. *Don Quijote como forma de vida*. Valencia: Fundación Juan March y Editorial Castalia.
– 1979. 'Estudio Preliminar.' In Miguel de Cervantes, *Don Quijote de la Mancha*, 3–43. Madrid: Alhambra.
Avalle-Arce, J.B., and E.C. Riley. 1973. 'Don Quijote.' In *Suma Cervantina*, ed. J.B. Avalle-Arce and E.C. Riley. 147–79. London: Tamesis.
Avery, William T. 1961–2. 'Elementos dantescos del Quijote.' *Anales Cervantinos* 9:1–28.
Ávila y Zúñiga, don Luis de. 1876. *Comentario de la guerra de Alemania*. In *Historiadores de sucesos particulares*, ed. Cayetano Rosell. *Biblioteca de autores españoles*, vol. 21. Madrid: Rivadeneyra.
Ayala, Francisco. 1965. 'Los dos amigos.' *Revista de Occidente* 3:287–306.
Bailey, Martin. 1995. *Dürer*. London: Phaidon.
Bakhtin, Mikhail. 1984. *Rabelais and his World*. Trans. Helene Iswolsky. Bloomington: Indiana University Press.
Baras Escolá, Alfredo. 1992. 'Una lectura erótica del *Quijote*.' *Cervantes* 12:79–89.
Barkan, Leonard. 1999. *Unearthing the Past: Archeology and Aesthetics in the Making of Renaissance Culture*. New Haven, CT: Yale University Press.
Beck, James. 1993. *Raphael: The Stanza della Segnatura*. New York: George Braziller.
Bell, Shannon. 1994. *Reading, Writing, and Rewriting the Prostitute Body*. Bloomington: Indiana University Press.
Bergmann, Emilie. 1979. *Art Inscribed: Essays on Ekphrasis in Spanish Golden Age Poetry*. Cambridge, MA: Harvard University Press.
Berndt-Kelley, Erna. 1989. 'En torno a la maravillosa visión de la pastora Marcela y otra ficción poética.' In *Actas del IX Congreso de la Asociacion Internacional de Hispanistas*, ed. Sebastian Neumeister. 1:367–71. Frankfurt: Vervuert Verlag.
Bernini, Dante, ed. 1985. *Luca Cambiaso e la sua cerchia: Disegni inediti da un album palermitano del '700*. Genoa: Sagep.
Berrio, Pilar. 1995. 'Música en *La Galatea*: De nuevo sobre la presencia de Orfeo en la obra cervantina.' In *Actas del III Congreso Internacional de la Asociación de Cervantistas*, ed. Giuseppe Grilli. 231–42. Naples: Instituto Universitario Orientale.
Berzaghi, Renato. 1989. 'I camerini degli Uccelli e dei Falconi.' In *Giulio Romano*, ed. Ernst H. Gombrich et al. 396–7. Milan: Electa.
Bloom, Harold. 1973. *The Anxiety of Influence: A Theory of Poetry*. Oxford: Oxford University Press.

Brown, Jonathan. 1991. *The Golden Age of Painting in Spain*. New Haven, CT: Yale University Press.

– 1995. *Kings and Connoisseurs: Collecting Art in Seventeenth-Century Europe*. Princeton, NJ: Princeton University Press.

Brown, Jonathan, and J.H. Elliott. 1980. *A Palace for a King: The Buen Retiro and the Court of Philip IV*. New Haven: Yale University Press.

Brown, Kenneth. 1981. '*El curioso impertinente*: Una homilia novelesca.' In *Cervantes: Su obra y su mundo*, ed. Manuel Criado de Val. 783–6. Madrid: Edi-6.

Burke, James F. 2000. *Vision, the Gaze, and the Function of the Senses in* Celestina. University Park: Pennsylvania State University Press.

Burrow, J.A. 1986. *The Ages of Man: A Study in Medieval Writing and Thought*. Oxford: Clarendon Press.

Cahill, Susan, ed. 1997. *Desiring Italy*. New York: Fawcett Columbine.

Calvino, Italo. 1988. *Six Memos for the Next Millennium*. Cambridge, MA: Harvard University Press.

Camamis, George. 1988. 'The Concept of Venus-*Humanitas* in Cervantes and Botticelli.' *Cervantes* 8:183–223.

– 1991. *Beneath the Cloak of Cervantes: The Satanic Prose of 'Don Quijote de la Mancha.'* New York: Senda Nueva de Ediciones.

Canavaggio, Jean. 1990. *Cervantes*. Trans. J.R. Jones. New York: W.W. Norton.

– 2001. 'Cervantes y Roma.' *Cervantes en Italia: Actas del X Coloquio Internacional de la Asociación de Cervantistas*, ed. Alicia Villar Lecumberri. 53–63. Palma de Mallorca: Asociación de Cervantistas.

Caro Baroja, Julio. 1983. *Tecnología popular española*. Madrid: Editora Nacional.

Carruthers, Mary. 1990. *The Book of Memory: A Study of Memory in Medieval Culture*. Cambridge: Cambridge University Press.

Cascardi, Anthony J. 1997. *Ideologies of History in the Spanish Golden Age*. University Park: Pennsylvania State University Press.

Castiglione, Baldesar. 1967. *The Book of the Courtier*. London and New York: Penguin.

Castillo, David R. 2001. *(A)Wry Views: Anamorphosis, Cervantes and the Early Picaresque*. West Lafayette, IN: Purdue University Press.

Castro, Américo. 1961. *De la edad conflictiva*. Madrid: Taurus.

– 1966. *Cervantes y los casticismos españoles*. Madrid: Alfaguara.

– 1972. *El pensamiento de Cervantes*. Ed. Juan Rodriguez-Puertolas. Barcelona: Noguer.

Cátedra, Pedro M. 1996. 'El sentido involucrado y la poesía del siglo XV: Lecturas virgilianas de Santillana con Villena.' In *Nunca fue pena mayor: Estudios de literatura española en homenaje a Brian Dutton*, ed. Ana María

Colleras and Victoriano Romero López. 149–62. Cuenta: Universidad de Castilla-La Mancha.

Cervantes, Miguel de. 1738. *Vida y hechos del ingenioso caballero Don Quixote de la Mancha*. London: J. and R. Jonson.

– 1833. *El ingenioso hidalgo don Quijote de la Mancha*. Ed. Diego Clemencín. 3 vols. Madrid: Aguado.

– 1969. *Los trabajos de Persiles y Sigismunda*. Ed. Juan Bautista Avalle-Arce. Madrid: Castalia.

– 1978. *El ingenioso hidalgo don Quijote de la Mancha*. Ed. Luis Murillo. 2 vols. Madrid: Castalia.

– 1982. *Novelas ejemplares*. Ed. Juan Bautista Avalle-Arce. 3 vols. Madrid: Castalia.

– 1983. *Don Quijote de la Mancha*. Ed. John Jay Allen. 2 vols. Madrid: Cátedra.

– 1984a. *La Numancia*. Ed. Robert Marrast. 2nd ed. Madrid: Cátedra.

– 1984b. *Poesías completas, I: Viaje del Parnaso y Adjunta al Parnaso*. Ed. Vicente Gaos. Madrid: Castalia.

– 1995. *La Galatea*. Ed. Francisco López Estrada and María Teresa López García-Berdoy. Madrid: Cátedra.

– 2000. *The Ingenious Hidalgo Don Quixote de la Mancha*. Trans. John Rutherford. New York: Penguin.

Chastel, André. 1983. *The Sack of Rome, 1527*. Trans. Beth Archer. Princeton, NJ: Princeton University Press.

Checa, Fernando. 1994. *Tiziano y la monarquía hispánica*. Madrid: Nerea.

Checa Cremades, Fernando. 2002. 'Pittori genovesi al servizio del re di Spanga: dal Bergamasco a Luca Cambiaso.' In *Genova e la Spangna*, ed. Piero Boccardo, José Luis Colomer, and Clario Di Fabio. 89–107. Milan: Silvana Editoriale.

Cherry, Peter. 1999. *Arte y naturaleza: El bodegón español en el Siglo de Oro*. Madrid: Fundación de apoyo al arte hispánico.

Chevalier, Maxime. 1986. *Los temas ariostescos en el romancero y la poesía española del Siglo de Oro*. Madrid: Castalia.

Cicero. 1923. *De senectute. De amicitia. De divinatione*. Trans. W.A. Falconer. Loeb Classical Library. Cambridge, MA: Harvard University Press.

– 1954. *Ad Herennium*. Trans. H. Caplan. Loeb Classical Library. Cambridge, MA: Harvard University Press.

– 1960. *De Inventione. De optimo genere oratorum. Topica*. Trans. H.M. Hubbell. Cambridge, MA: Harvard University Press.

Cirillo, Teresa. 1995. 'Nápoles en el *Viaje del Parnaso* cervantino y en dos parnasos partenopeos.' In *Actas del II Congreso Internacional de la Asociación de Cervantistas*, ed. Giuseppe Grilli. 65–73. Naples: Instituto Universitario Orientale.

Clemencín, Diego, ed. 1833. *Miguel de Cervantes: El ingenioso hidalgo don Quijote de la Mancha*. 3 vols. Madrid: Aguado.

Clements, Robert J. 1966. *The Poetry of Michelangelo*. New York: New York University Press.

Close, Anthony. 1978. *The Romantic Approach to 'Don Quixote.'* Cambridge: Cambridge University Press.

Clubb, Louise George. 1965. *Giambattista Della Porta Dramatist*. Princeton, NJ: Princeton University Press.

Combet, L. 1980. *Cervantes: Les incertitudes du desir*. Lyons: Presses Universitaires de Lyons.

Commeno, Láscaris. 1952. 'El nombre de Don Quijote.' *Anales Cervantinos* 2:361–4.

Comparetti, Domenico. 1929. *Virgil in the Middle Ages*. Trans. E.F.M. Benecke. New York: G.E. Stechert.

Conte, Gian Biagio. 1994. *Latin Literature*. Trans. Joseph B. Solodow; revised by Don Fowler and Glenn W. Most. Baltimore: Johns Hopkins University Press.

Cornini, Guido, et al. 1993. *Raphael in the Apartments of Julius II and Leo X*. Milan: Electa.

Covarrubias, Sebastian de. 1987. *Tesoro de la lengua Castellana o Española*. Ed. Martín de Riquer. Barcelona: Alta Fulla.

Cozad, Mary. 1988. 'Cervantes and *Libros de entendimiento*.' *Cervantes* 8:159–82.

Crane, Susan A. 2000. 'Curious Cabinets and Imaginary Museums.' In *Museums and Memory*, ed. Susan A. Crane. 60–80. Stanford, CA: Stanford University Press.

Creuzer, Friedrich. 1835. *Religions del l'Antiquité, considérées principalement dans leurs formes symboliques et mythologiques*. Trans. J.D. Guigniaut. 2 vols. Paris: Treuttel et Wurtz.

Cruz, Anne J. 1999a. 'Cervantes and His Feminist Alliances.' In *Cervantes and His Postmodern Constituencies*, ed. Anne J. Cruz and Caroll B. Johnson. 134–50. New York: Garland.

– 1999b. *Discourses of Poverty: Social Reform and the Picaresque Novel in Early Modern Spain*. Toronto: Toronto University Press.

– 2002. 'Psyche and Gender in Cervantes.' In *Cervantes*, ed. Anthony J. Cascardi. 186–205. Cambridge: Cambridge University Press.

Cull, John T. 1990. 'The "Knight of the Broken Lance" and His "Trusty Steed": On Don Quixote and Rocinante.' *Cervantes* 10:37–54.

Curtius, Ernst. 1953. *European Literature and the Latin Middle Ages*. Trans. Willard R. Trask. New York: Harper and Row.

Dacos, Nicole. 1969. *La découverte de la Domus Aurea et la formation des grotesques a la Renaissance*. London: Warburg Institute.

Damiani, Bruno. 1983. *'La Diana' of Montemayor as Social and Religious Teaching*. Lexington: University Press of Kentucky.

Damonte, Mario. 1991. 'Cervantes y Génova.' In *Actas del II Congreso de la Asociación de Cervantistas (Alcala de Henares 6–9 de noviembre 1989)*. 301–6. Barcelona: Anthropos.

D'Ancona, Paolo. 1955. *The Farnesina Frescoes at Rome*. Milan: Edizioni del Milione.

Dante Alighieri, 1972. *La Divina Commedia*. Ed. C.H. Grandgent and Charles S. Singleton. Cambridge, MA: Harvard University Press.

– 1980. *Inferno*. Trans. Allen Mandelbaum. New York: Bantam.

– 1982. *Purgatorio*. Trans. Allen Mandelbaum. New York: Bantam.

Darst, David H. 1985. *Imitatio: Polémicas sobre la imitación en el Siglo de Oro*. Madrid: Orígenes.

Day, Gerald W. 1988. *Genoa's Response to Byzantium 1155–1204*. Urbana and Chicago: University of Illinois Press.

De Armas, Frederick A. 1976. *The Invisible Mistress: Aspects of Feminism and Fantasy in the Golden Age*. Charlottesville, VA: Biblioteca Siglo de Oro.

– 1978. 'Lope de Vega and Titian.' *Comparative Literature* 30:338–52.

– 1986. *The Return of Astraea: An Astral-Imperial Myth in Calderón*. Lexington: University Press of Kentucky.

– 1992a. 'Interpolation and Invisibility: From Herodotus to Cervantes's *Don Quixote*.' *Journal of the Fantastic in the Arts* 4:8–28.

– 1992b. 'Saturn in Conjunction: From Albumasar to Lope de Vega.' In *Saturn from Antiquity to the Renaissance*, ed. Massimo Ciavollela and Amilcare A. Iannucci. 151–72. University of Toronto Italian Studies 8. Ottawa: Dovehouse.

– 1993. 'A Banquet of the Senses: The Mythological Structure of *Persiles y sigismunda, III*.' *Bulletin of Hispanic Studies* 70:403–14.

– 1996. 'The Necromancy of Imitation: Lucan and Cervantes' *La Numancia*.' In *El arte nuevo de estudiar comedias: Literary Theory and Spanish Golden Age Drama*, ed. Barbara Simerka. 246–58. Lewisburg, PA: Bucknell University Press.

– 1998. *Cervantes, Raphael and the Classics*. Cambridge: Cambridge University Press.

– 2000. 'Ekphrasis and Eros in *La Galatea*: The Case of the Blushing Nymphs.' In *Cervantes for the Twenty-first Century: Studies in Honor of Edward Dudley*, ed. Francisco La Rubia Prado. 33–47. Newark, DE: Juan de la Cuesta.

– 2001a. 'The Eloquence of Mercury and the Enchantments of Venus: *Humanitas* in Botticelli and Cervantes's *Don Quixote*.' In *Humanism and the Humanities in the Twenty-first Century*, ed. William S. Haney and Peter Malekin. 118–36. Lewisburg, PA: Bucknell University Press.

– 2001b. 'Painting Dulcinea: Italian Art and the Art of Memory in Cervantes' *Don Quijote.' Yearbook for Comparative and General Literature* 49:3–19.

– 2002. 'Cervantes and the Virgilian Wheel: The Portrayal of a Literary Career.' In *European Literary Careers: The Author from Antiquity to the Renaissance*, ed. Patrick Cheney and Frederick A. de Armas. 268–85. Toronto: University of Toronto Press.

– 2005a. 'Cervantes ante el Parnaso: Auto-retratos textuales y pintura italiana.' *Ínsula* 697–8.

– 2005b. 'Cervantes and Della Porta: The Art of Memory in *La Numancia, El retablo de las maravillas, El Licenciado Vidriera,* and *Don Quijote.' Bulletin of Hispanic Studies* 82:83–97.

De Armas Wilson, Diana. 1987. '"Passing the Love of Women": The Intertextuality of *El curioso impertinente.' Cervantes* 7:9–28.

– 1992. '"Unreason's Reason": Cervantes and the Frontiers of Difference.' *Philosophy and Literature* 16:49–67.

– 1994. 'Homage to Apuleius: Cervantes' Avenging Psyche.' In *The Search for the Ancient Novel*, ed. James Tatum. 88–100. Baltimore: The Johns Hopkins University Press.

De la Flor, Fernando R. 1996. *Teatro de la memoria: Siete ensayos sobre mnemotecnia española de los siglos XVI y XVII*. Junta of Castille and León: Consejería de Educación y Cultura.

De los Ríos, Vicente. 1819. 'Juicio crítico o análisis del Quijote.' In *El ingenioso hidalgo don Quijote de la Mancha, de Miguel de Cervantes Saavedra*. 4th edition. 1:13–159. Madrid: Imprenta Real.

Della Porta, Giambattista. 1996. *Ars Reminiscendi: Agiunta L'Arte di ricordare tradotta da Dorandino Falcone da Gioia*. Ed. Raffaele Sirri. Naples: Editione Scientifiche Italiane.

Díaz de Benjumea, don Nicolás. 1878; rpt. 1986. *La verdad sobre el Quijote*. Madrid: Gaspar; Barcelona: Ediciones Rondas.

Donaldson, Ian. 1982. *The Rapes of Lucretia*. Oxford: Clarendon Press.

Doody, Margaret Anne. 1996. *The True Story of the Novel*. West Lafayette, IN: Purdue University Press.

Doré, Gustave. 1983. *Don Quichotte*. Paris: SACELP.

Drake, Dana B. 1974. *Don Quijote (1894–1970): A Selective Annotated Bibliography*. Vol. 1. Chapel Hill: North Carolina Studies in the Romance Languages and Literatures.

Dudley, Edward. 1995. 'Goddess on the Edge: The Galatea Agenda in Raphael, Garcilaso and Cervantes.' *Calíope* 1:27–46.

– 1997. *The Endless Text: Don Quixote and the Hermeneutics of Romance*. Albany: State University of New York Press.

Durán, Manuel. 1996. 'Picaresque Elements in Cervantes's Works.' In *The Picaresque Tradition and Displacement*, ed. Giancarlo Maiorino. 226–47. Minneapolis: University of Minnesota Press.

Egido, Aurora. 1994. *Cervantes y las puertas del sueño*. Barcelona: Promociones y Publicaciones Universitarias.

Eisenberg, Daniel. 1982. *Romances of Chivalry in the Spanish Golden Age*. Newark, DE: Juan de la Cuesta.

El Saffar, Ruth. 1984. *Beyond Fiction: The Recovery of the Feminine in the Novels of Cervantes*. Berkeley, Los Angeles, and London: University of California Press.

– 1993. 'In Marcela's Case.' In *Quixotic Desire: Psychoanalytic Perspectives on Cervantes*, ed. Ruth El Saffar and Diana de Armas Wilson. 157–78. Ithaca, NY: Cornell University Press.

Fajardo, Salvador J. 1986. 'The Enchanted Return: On the Conclusion of *Don Quijote*, I.' *Journal of Modern and Renaissance Studies* 16:233–51.

Fajardo-Acosta, Fidel. 1989. 'Don Quijote y las máquinas infernales: Vanidad del ejercicio de las armas.' *Hispanic Journal* 10.2:15–25.

Ferguson, Niall. 2004. *Colossus: The Rise and Fall of the American Empire*. New York: Penguin.

Fernández Alvarez, Manuel. 1975. *Charles V: Elected Emperor and Hereditary Ruler*. London: Thames and Hudson.

– 1999. *Carlos V; el César y el hombre*. Madrid: Espasa-Calpe.

Fernández-Cañadas de Greenwood, Pilar. 1985. 'Los médicos del "Canto de Calíope."' *Quaderni Ibero-Americani* 39:1–19.

Fernández de Avellaneda, Alonso. 1971. *El ingenioso hidalgo don Quijote de la Mancha, que tiene su tercera salida y es la quinta parte de sus aventuras*. Ed. F. García Salinero. Madrid: Castalia.

Ferrer Valls, Teresa. 1990. *La práctica escénica cortesana: De la época del Emperador a la de Felipe III*. London: Tamesis.

Fichter, William. 1927. 'Color Symbolism in Lope de Vega.' *Romantic Review* 18:220–31.

Ficino, Marsilio. 1989. *Three Books on Life*. Ed. Carol V Kaske and John R. Clark. Binghamton, NY: Medieval and Renaissance Texts and Studies.

Findlen, Paula. 2000. 'The Modern Muses: Renaissance Collecting and the Cult of Remembrance.' In *Museums and Memory*, ed. Susan A. Crane. 161–78. Stanford, CA: Stanford University Press.

Folger, Robert. 2002. *Images in Mind: Lovesickness, Spanish Sentimental Fiction and* Don Quijote. Chapel Hill: North Carolina Studies in the Romance Languages and Literatures.

Forcione, Alban. 1970. *Cervantes, Aristotle and the* Persiles. Princeton, NJ: Princeton University Press.

– 1972. *Cervantes' Christian Romance: A Study of* Persiles y Sigismunda. Princeton, NJ: Princeton University Press.

Foucault, Michel. 1970. *The Order of Things: An Archeology of the Human Sciences*. New York: Random House.

Freedberg, Sydney J. 1950. *Parmigianino: His Works in Painting*. Westport, CT: Greenwood Press.

Friederich, Werner P. 1950. *Dante's Fame Abroad, 1350–1850*. Rome: Edizione di Storia e Letteratura.

Fritz, Michael P. 1997. *Giulio Romano et Raphael: La vice-reine de Naples*. Paris: Service culturele du musée du Louvre.

Gabriele, John P. 2003. 'Competing Narrative Discourses: (Fe)male Fabulation in the Episode of Grisóstomo and Marcela.' *Hispanic Review* 71:507–24.

García Gibert, Javier. 1997. *Cervantes y la melancholia: Ensayos sobre el tono y actitud cervantinas*. Valencia: Alfons el Magnanim, Generalitat Valenciana.

García Simón, Agustín. 1995. *El ocaso del emperador: Carlos v en Yuste*. Madrid: Nerea.

Gaylord Randel, Mary. 1983. 'Cervantes' Portrait of the Artist.' *Cervantes* 3:83–102.

Geiger, Gail L. 1982. 'Filippino Lippi's *Triumph of Saint Thomas Aquinas*.' In *Rome in the Renaissance: The City and the Myth*, ed. P.A. Ramsey. 224–36. Binghamton, NY: Center for Medieval and Early Renaissance Studies.

Gerli, Michael. 1995. *Refiguring Authority: Reading, Writing and Rewriting in Cervantes*. Lexington: University Press of Kentucky.

Gillet, Joseph E. 1947. 'Lucrecia-*Necia*.' *Hispanic Review* 15:120–36.

Goffen, Laura. 2002. *Renaissance Rivals: Michelangelo, Leonardo, Raphael, Titian*. New Haven, CT: Yale University Press.

Gombrich, E.H. 1972. *Symbolic Images. Studies in the Art of the Renaissance II*. Chicago: University of Chicago Press.

Gómez, María Asunción. 1997. 'Mirando de cerca "mujer, comedia y pintura" en las obras dramáticas de Lope de Vega y Calderón.' *Bulletin of the Comediantes* 49:273–94.

Góngora, Luis de. 1990. *Fábula de Polifemo y Galatea*. Ed. Alexander A. Parker. Madrid: Cátedra.

González Echevarría, Roberto. 2005. *Love and the Law in Cervantes*. New Haven, CT: Yale University Press.

Goodman, David C. 1988. *Power and Penury: Government, Technology and Science in Philip II's Spain*. Cambridge: Cambridge University Press.

Gossy, Mary. 1995. 'Aldonza as Butch: Narrative and the Play of Gender in *Don Quixote*.' In *¿Entiendes? Queer Readings, Hispanic Writings*, ed. Emilie Bergmann and Paul Julian Smith. 17–28. Durham: Duke University Press.

Graf, Eric. 1999. 'When an Arab Laughs in Toledo: Cervantes's Interpellation of Early Modern Spanish Orientalism.' *Diacritics* 29:68–85.

Grafton, Anthony. 1997. 'The Rest vs. the West.' *The New York Review of Books* 44.6:57–64.

– 1998. 'Believe It or Not.' *The New York Review of Books* 45.17:14–18.

Green, Otis H. 1970. *The Literary Mind of Medieval and Renaissance Spain*. Lexington: University Press of Kentucky.

Greene, Thomas M. 1982. *The Light in Troy: Imitation and Discovery in Renaissance Poetry*. New Haven, CT: Yale University Press.

Gumpert, Matthew. 2001. *Grafting Helen: The Abduction of the Classical Past*. Madison: University of Wisconsin Press.

Hagstrum, Jean H. 1958. *The Sister Arts: The Tradition of Literary Pictorialism and English Poetry from Dryden to Gray*. Chicago: University of Chicago Press.

Hahn, Juergen. 1972. '*El curioso impertinente* and Don Quijote's Symbolic Struggle Against *Curiositas*.' *Bulletin of Hispanic Studies* 49:128–40.

– 1973. *The Origins of the Baroque Concept of Peregrinatio*. University of North Carolina Studies in the Romance Languages and Literatures 131. Chapel Hill: University of North Carolina Press.

Halka, Chester S. 1981. '*Don Quijote* in the Light of Huarte's *Examen de Ingenios*: A Reexamination.' *Anales Cervantinos* 19:1–13.

Hartt, Frederick. 1950. 'Gonzaga Symbols in the Palazzo del Té.' *Journal of the Warburg and Courtauld Institutes* 13:151–88.

– 1958. *Giulio Romano*. 2 vols. New Haven, CT: Yale University Press.

– 1984. *Michelangelo*. New York: Harry N. Abrams.

– 1994. *History of Italian Renaissance Art*. 4th ed. New York: Harry N. Abrams.

Hasbrouck, Michael D. 1992. 'Posesión demoníaca, locura y exorcismo en el *Quijote*.' *Cervantes* 12:117–26.

Haskell, Francis. 1993. *History and Its Images: Art and the Interpretation of the Past*. New Haven, CT: Yale University Press.

Heckscher, William S. 1987. 'The Anadyomene in the Medieval Tradition.' In *Art and Literature: Studies in Relationship*, ed. Egon Verheyen. 127–64. Durham: Duke University Press.

Heffernan, James A.W. 1993. *Museum of Words: The Poetics of Ekphrasis from Homer to Ashbery*. Chicago: University of Chicago Press.

Heidegger, Martin. 1977. *The Question Concerning Technology and Other Essays*. Trans. William Lovitt. New York: Harper & Row.

Heiple, Daniel L. 1979. 'Renaissance Medical Psychology in *Don Quijote.*' *Ideologies and Literature* 2:65–72.

– 1991. 'Profeminist Reactions to Huarte's Misogyny in Lope de Vega's *La prueba de los ingenios* and María de Zayas's *Novelas amorosas y ejemplares.*' In *The Perception of Women in Spanish Theater of the Golden Age*, ed. Anita K. Stoll and Dawn L. Smith. 121–34. Lewisburg: Bucknell University Press.

– 1994. *Garcilaso de la Vega and the Italian Renaissance*. University Park: Pennsylvania State University Press.

Heninger, S.K. 1974. *Touches of Sweet Harmony: Pythagorean Cosmology and Renaissance Poetics*. San Marino, CA: The Huntington Library.

Hermetica: The Greek Corpus Hermeticum *and the Latin* Asclepius *in a New Engligh translation, with notes and introduction*. 1992. Ed. Brian P. Copenhower. Cambridge: Cambridge University Press.

Herrera, Fernando de. 1985. *Poesía castellana original completa*. Ed. Cristóbal Cuevas. Madrid: Cátedra.

Herrero, Javier. 1985. *Who Was Dulcinea?* New Orleans: Graduate School of Tulane University.

Hersey, George L. 1993. *High Renaissance Art in St. Peter's Vatican*. Chicago: University of Chicago Press.

Hibbard, Howard. 1974. *Michelangelo*. 2nd ed. New York: Harper & Row.

Higuera, Henry. 1995. *Eros and Empire: Politics and Christianity in Don Quixote*. London: Rowman and Littlefield.

Hind, Arthur M. 1963; rpt. 1923. *A History of Engraving & Etching from the Fifteenth Century to the Year 1914*. New York: Dover.

Holt, Elizabeth Gilmore. 1947. *Literary Sources of Art History*. Princeton, NJ: Princeton University Press.

Hollander, John. 1988. 'The Poetics of Ekphrasis.' *Word and Image* 4:209–19.

Homer. 1988. *The Iliad*. Trans. A.T. Murray. 2 vols. Cambridge, MA: Harvard University Press.

Hulse, Clark. 1990. *The Rule of Art: Literature and Painting in the Renaissance*. Chicago: University of Chicago Press.

Iamblichus. 1986. *Life of Pythagoras*. Trans. Thomas Taylor. Rochester, VT: Inner Traditions International.

Imperiale, Louis. 1997. *La Roma clandestina de Francisco Delicado y Pietro Aretino*. New York: Peter Lang.

Issacharoff, Dora. 1981. 'Imágenes manieristas en *La Galatea* de Cervantes.' In *Cervantes: Su obra y su mundo*, ed. Manuel Criado de Val. 327–36. Madrid: Edi-6.

Iventosch, Hermann. 1963–4. 'Dulcinea, nombre pastoril.' *Nueva Revista de Filología Hispánica* 17:60–81.

– 1974. 'Cervantes and Courtly Love: The Grisóstomo-Marcela Episode of *Don Quixote*.' *PMLA* 89:64–76.

Jaksic, Iván. 1994. 'Don Quijote's Encounter with Technology.' *Cervantes* 14:75–96.

Jardine, Lisa. 1996. *Worldly Goods: A New History of the Renaissance*. New York: Macmillan.

Jeanneret, Michel. 2001. *Perpetual Motion: Transforming Shapes in the Renaissance from da Vinci to Montaigne*. Trans. Nidra Poller. Baltimore and London: Johns Hopkins University Press.

Jehenson, Yvonne. 1990. 'The Pastoral Episode in Cervantes' *Don Quijote*: Marcela Once Again.' *Cervantes* 10:15–35.

Jiménez Patón, Bartolomé. 1993. *Elocuencia española en arte*. Ed. Francisco J. Martín. Barcelona: Puvill.

Johnson, Carroll B. 1981. '*La Numancia* y la estructura de la ambigüedad cervantina.' In *Cervantes: Su obra y su mundo. Actas del I Congreso Internacaional sobre Cervantes*, ed. Manuel Criado de Val. 309–16. Madrid: EDI-6.

– 1983. *Madness and Lust: A Psychoanalytical Approach to Don Quijote*. Berkeley and Los Angeles: University of California Press.

– 2000. *Cervantes and the Material World*. Urbana: University of Illinois Press.

Johnson, Leslie Deutsch. 1976. 'Three Who Made a Revolution: Cervantes, Galatea and Calíope.' *Hispanófila* 57:23–34.

Johnson, W.R. 1984. 'Virgil's Bees: The Ancient Romans' View of Rome.' In *Roman Images*, ed., Annabel Patterson. 1–22. Baltimore: Johns Hopkins University Press.

Jones, Roger, and Nicholas Penny. 1983. *Raphael*. New Haven, CT: Yale University Press.

Joost-Gaugier, Christiane L. 1993. 'Sappho, Apollo and Neopythagorean Theory, and *Numine Afflatur* in Raphael's Fresco of the *Parnassus*.' *Gazette des Beaux Arts* 122:123–34.

– 1996. 'Pindar on Parnassus: A Neopythagorean Impulse in Raphael's Stanza della Segnatura.' *Gazette des Beaux Arts* 127:63–80.

– 1998. 'Ptolemy and Strabo and Their Conversation with Apelles and Protogenes: Cosmography and Painting in Raphael's *School of Athens*.' *Renaissance Quarterly* 51:761–87.

Joplin, Patricia. 1990. 'Ritual Work on Human Flesh: Livy's Lucretia and the Body Politic.' *Helios* 17:51–70.

Kallendorf, Hilaire. 2003. *Exorcism and Its Texts: Subjectivity in Early Modern Literature of England and Spain*. Toronto: University of Toronto Press.

Kamen, Henry. 1997. *Philip of Spain*. New Haven, CT: Yale University Press.

Kennedy, Ruth Wedgwood. 1964 'Apelles Redivivus.' In *Essays in Memory of*

Karl Lehmann, ed. Lucy Freeman Sandler. 160–71. New York: Institute of Fine Arts, New York University.

Kermode, Frank. 1987. 'Introduction to the New Testament.' In *The Literary Guide to the Bible*, ed. Robert Alter and Frank Kermode. 375–86. Cambridge, MA: Harvard University Press.

Kleinschmidt, Harald. 2004. *Charles V: The World Emperor*. Phoenix Mill, UK: Sutton.

Krieger, Murray. 1992. *Ekphrasis: The Illusion of the Natural Sign*. Baltimore, MD: Johns Hopkins University Press.

Lambert, Royston. 1988. *Beloved and God: The Story of Hadrian & Antinous*. New York: Carol.

Láscaris Commeno, Constantino. 1952. 'El nombre de Don Quijote.' *Anales Cervantinos* 2:361–4.

Lawler, Traugott. 1977. 'The *Aeneid*.' In *Homer to Brecht: The European Epic and Dramatic Traditions*, ed. Michael Seidel and Edward Mendelson. New Haven, CT: Yale University Press.

Leomarte. 1932. *Sumas de historia troyana*. Ed. Agapito Rey. Madrid: S. Aguirre.

Leonardo da Vinci. 1989. *Leonardo on Painting*. Ed. Martin Kemp. New Haven, CT: Yale University Press.

Lessing, G.E. 1984. *Laocöon: An Essay on the Limits of Painting and Poetry*. Trans. and ed. Edward Allen McCormick. Baltimore, MD: Johns Hopkins University Press.

Lexicon Iconographicum Mythologiae Classicae. 1990. Vol. 6. Zurich and Munich: Artemis Verlag.

Lida de Malkiel, María Rosa. 1974. *Dido en la literatura española: Su retrato y defensa*. London: Tamesis.

Livy. 1971. *The Early History of Rome*. Trans. Aubrey de Sélincourt; intro. R.M. Ogilvie. New York: Penguin.

Lope de Vega, Félix. 1968. *La Dorotea*. Ed. Edwin S. Morby. 2nd ed. Madrid: Castalia.

– 1971. *El arte nuevo de hacer comedias en este tiempo*. Ed. Juana de José Prades. Madrid: Consejo Superior de Investigaciones Científicas.

– 1975. *La Arcadia*. Ed. Edwin S. Morby. Madrid: Castalia.

– 1985. *Cartas*. Ed. Nicolás Marín. Madrid: Castalia.

López, Ignacio. 2002. *Práctica escénica cortesana del siglo XVI: El Palacio de los duques de Calabria*. PhD. Dissertation. Universidad Complutense de Madrid.

López Estrada, Francisco. 1948. *La 'Galatea' de Cervantes: Estudio crítico*. Tenerife: Universidad de La Laguna.

López Piñero, José María. 1979. *Ciencia y técnica en la sociedad española de los siglos XVI y XVII*. Barcelona: Editorial Labor.

López Torrijos, Rosa. 1985. *La mitología en la pintura española del Siglo de Oro*. Madrid: Cátedra.

Lucan. 1988. *Pharsalia. The Civil War*. Trans. J.D. Duff. Cambridge, MA: Harvard University Press.

Lukács, George. 1971. *The Theory of the Novel*. Trans. Anna Bostock. Cambridge, MA: Massachusetts Institute of Technology Press.

MacCurdy, Raymond. 1974. 'On the Uses of the Rape of Lucretia.' In *Estudios literarios de hispanistas Norteamericanos dedicados a Helmut Hatzfeld con motivo de su 80 aniversario*. 297–308. Barcelona: Hispam.

MacCurdy, Raymond R., and Alfred Rodríguez. 1978. 'Algo más sobre los apellidos "verdaderos" de D. Quijote.' *Romansiche Forschungen* 90:448–57.

Madrigal, José Antonio. 1981. 'El símbolo y su función temática en los primeros capítulos de *Don Quijote*.' In *Cervantes: Su obra y su mundo*, ed. Manuel Criado de Val. 569–74. Madrid: Edi-6.

Magnani, Lauro. 2002. 'Luca Cambiaso "pintor famoso," "facilísimo en el arte."' In *Genova e la Spangna*, ed. Piero Boccardo, José Luis Colomer, and Clario Di Fabio. 109–25. Milan: Silvana Editoriale.

Maiorino, Giancarlo. 1992. *Leonardo da Vinci: The Daedalian Mythmaker*. University Park: Pennsylvania State University Press.

– 2003. *At the Margins of the Renaissance: The Picaresque Art of Survival and the Practice of Everyday Life in* Lazarillo de Tormes. University Park: Pennsylvania State University Press.

Manning, Robert L. 1967. *Drawings of Luca Cambiaso*. New York: Finch College Museum of Art.

Marasso, Arturo. 1954. *Cervantes: La invención del* Quijote. Buenos Aires: Hachette.

Maravall, José Antonio. 1948. *El humanismo de las armas en* Don Quijote. Madrid: Instituto de Estudios Políticos.

– 1991. *Utopia and Counterutopia in the* Quixote. Trans. Robert W. Felkel. Detroit, MI: Wayne State University Press.

McGaha, Michael. 1977. 'The Sources and Meaning of the Grisóstomo-Marcela Episode in the 1605 *Quijote*.' *Anales Cervantinos* 16:1–37.

– 1980. 'Cervantes and Virgil.' In *Cervantes and the Renaissance*, ed. Michael McGaha. 34–50. Newark, DE: Juan de la Cuesta.

– 1991. 'Intertextuality as a Guide to the Interpretation of the Battle of the Sheep (*Don Quixote* I, 18).' In *On Cervantes: Essays for L.A. Murillo*, ed. James A. Parr. 149–62. Newark, DE: Juan de la Cuesta.

McKendrick, Melveena. 1974. *Women and Society in the Spanish Drama of the Golden Age*. Cambridge: Cambridge University Press.

McLean, Adam, ed. 1990. *A Treatise on Angel Magic*. Grand Rapids, MI: Phanes Press.

Meltzer, Françoise. 1987. *Salome and the Dance of Writing*. Chicago: University of Chicago Press.

Mexía, Pedro. 1989 and 1990. *Silva de varia lección*. Ed. Antonio Castro. 2 vols. Madrid: Cátedra.

Miller, Patricia Cox. 1994. *Dreams in Late Antiquity: Studies in the Imagination of a Culture*. Princeton, NJ: Princeton University Press.

Miller, William. 1926; rpt. 1969. *Trebizond: The Last Greek Empire of the Byzantine Era 1204–1461*. Chicago: Argonaut.

Mitchell, W.J.T. 1994. *Picture Theory*. Chicago: University of Chicago Press.

Montero Reguera, José. 1996. 'Humanismo, erudición y parodia en Cervantes: Del *Quijote* al *Persiles*.' *Edad de Oro* 15:87–109.

Morales, Ambrosio de. 1791. *Crónica general de España*. Madrid: Benito Cano.

Muccini, Ugo. 1997. *Painting, Sculpture and Architecture in the Palazzo Vecchio of Florence*. Florence: Le Lettere.

Murillo, L.A. 1975. *The Golden Dial: Temporal Configuration in Don Quijote*. London: Dolphin.

Nadeau, Carolyn Amy. 1995. 'Evoking Astraea: The Speeches of Marcela and Dorotea in *Don Quijote I*.' *Neophilologus* 79:53–61.

– 1997. 'Recovering the Hetairae: Prostitution in *Don Quijote I*.' *Cervantes* 17:4–24.

– 2002. *Women of the Prologue: Imitation, Myth and Magic in Don Quixote, I*. Lewisburg: Bucknell University Press.

Nájera, Antonio de. 1632. *Suma astrológica y arte para enseñar prognósticos de los tiempos, y por ellos conocer la fertilidad o esterilidad del año*. Lisbon: A. Alvarez.

Navarrete, Ignacio. 1994. *Orphans of Petrach: Poetry and Theory in the Spanish Renaissance*. Berkeley, Los Angeles, and London: University of California Press.

Navarro y Ledesma, Francisco. 1944. *El ingenioso hidalgo Miguel de Cervantes Saavedra*. Madrid: Espasa-Calpe.

Nesselrath, Arnold. 1992. 'Art-historical Findings during the Restoration of the *Stanza dell'Incendio*.' *Master Drawings* 30:31–60.

Neuerburg, Norman. 1964. 'Raphael at Tivoli and the Villa Madama.' In *Essays in Memory of Karl Lehmann*, ed. Lucy Freeman Sandler. New York: J.J. Augustin.

Ocaña, Andrés de. 1622. *Primera parte de los discursos eucharísticos compuestos por el Padre fr. Andrés de Occaña [sic] Predicador y Padre de la Provincia de S. Ioseph de los descalços de nuestro Padre S. Francisco*. Vol. 1. Madrid: En la Imprenta Real, a costa de su Majestad.

O'Connor, Thomas Austin. 2005. 'Marcela, seguidora de Ártemis: El fundamento social, cultural y mítico del episodio de Marcela y Grisóstomo.' In *Cervantes y su mundo*, ed. Kurt Reichenberger and Darío Fernández-Morera. 2:369–390. Kassel: Edition Reichenberger.

Orso, Steven N. 1986. *Philip IV and the Decoration of the Alcázar of Madrid*. Princeton, NJ: Princeton University Press.

Ovid. 1971. *Metamorphoses*. Trans. Frank Justus Miller. 2 vols. Cambridge, MA: Harvard University Press.

– 1989. *Fasti*. Trans. James George Frazer; rev. G.P. Goold. Cambridge, MA: Harvard University Press.

Pacheco, Francisco. 1982. *Arte de la pintura*. 2nd ed. Barcelona: Las ediciones de arte.

Panofsky, Erwin. 1969. *Problems in Titian: Mostly Iconographic*. New York: New York University Press.

Pardo Tomás, José. 1991. *Ciencia y censura: La Inquisición Española y los libros científicos en los siglos XVI y XVII*. Madrid: Consejo Superior de Investigaciones Científicas.

Parr, James. 1984. 'Extrafictional Point of View in *Don Quijote*.' In *Studies in* Don Quijote *and other Cervantine Works*, ed. Donald W. Bleznick. 20–30. York, SC: Spanish Literature Publications.

– 1988. *Don Quixote: An Anatomy of Subversive Discourse*. Newark, DE: Juan de la Cuesta.

– 1991. 'Plato, Cervantes, Derrida: Framing Speaking and Writing in *Don Quixote*.' In *On Cervantes: Essays for L. A. Murillo*, ed. James A. Parr. Newark, Delaware: Juan de la Cuesta, pp. 163–88.

Partridge, Loren. 1996. *The Art of Renaissance Rome 1400–1600*. New York: Harry M. Abrams.

Pavel, Thomas. 2005. *Representar la existencia: El pensamiento de la novela*. Trans. David Roas Deus. Barcelona: Crítica.

Pedrocco, Filippo. 2001. *Titian*. New York: Rizzol: International Publications.

Percas de Ponseti, Helena. 1975. *Cervantes y su concepto del arte: Estudio crítico de algunos aspectos y episodios del* Quijote. 2 vols. Madrid: Gredos.

– 1988. *Cervantes the Writer and the Painter of* Don Quijote. Columbia: University of Missouri Press.

Pérez, Louis C. 1967. 'Color en la Comedia.' *Bulletin of the Comediantes* 19:28–9.

Pérez Botero, Luis. 1981. 'La concepción del mundo en las tres salidas de don Quijote.' In *Cervantes: Su obra y su mundo*, ed. Manuel Criado de Val. 515–19. Madrid: Edi-6.

Pérez de Moya, Juan. 1996. *Comparaciones o símiles para los vicios y virtudes:*

Philosophia secreta. Ed. Consolación Baranda. Madrid: Fundación José Antonio de Castro.

Pérez Sánchez, Alfonso E. 1985. 'Rafael en los tratadistas españoles.' In *Rafael en España: Museo del Prado, Mayo-Agosto 1985*. 29–42. Madrid: Ministerio de Cultura.

Peters, F.E. 1967. *Greek Philosophical Terms: A Historical Lexicon*. New York: New York University Press.

Philostratus the Elder, Younger Philostratus, and Callistratus. 1931. *Imagines, Imagines*, and *Descriptions*. Trans. Arthur Fairbanks. Cambridge, MA: Harvard University Press.

Pietrangeli, Carlo. 1996. *Paintings in the Vatican*. Boston: Little, Brown and Company.

Pliny. 1942–52. *Natural History*. Trans. H. Rackham. Loeb Classical Library. 10 vols. Cambridge, MA: Harvard University Press.

Plutarch. 1966. *The Lives of the Noble Grecians and Romans*. Trans. John Dryden; rev. Arthur Hugh Clough. New York: The Modern Library.

Pope-Hennessy, John. 1970. *Raphael*. New York: New York University Press.

Portús Pérez, Javier. 1999. *Pintura y pensamiento en la España de Lope de Vega*. Guipúzcoa: Nerea.

Praz, Mario. 1970. *Mnemosyne: The Parallel between Literature and the Visual Arts*. Princeton, NJ: Princeton University Press.

Predmore, Richard L. 1973. *Cervantes*. New York: Dodd, Mead and Co.

Ptolemy. 1966. *Geographia*. Ed. Sebastian Munster; intro. R.A. Skelton. Basle, 1540; rpt. Amsterdam: Theatrum Orbis Terrarum.

– 1969. *Geographia*. Venice, 1511; rpt. Amsterdam: Theatrum Orbis Terrarum.

Putnam, Michael C.J. 1998. *Virgil's Epic Designs: Ekphrasis in the* Aeneid. New Haven, CT: Yale University Press.

Quint, David. 1983. *Origin and Originality in Renaissance Literature: Visions of the Source*. New Haven, CT: Yale University Press.

– 2003. *Cervantes's Novel of Modern Times: A New Reading of* Don Quijote. Princeton, NJ: Princeton University Press.

Rabin, Lisa. 1994 'The Reluctant Companion of Empire: Petrarch and Dulcinea in *Don Quixote de la Mancha*.' *Cervantes* 14:81–92.

Ramos de Castro, Guadalupe. 1982. *La catedral de Zamora*. Zamora: Fundación Ramos de Castro.

Redig de Campos, D. 1946. *Raffaello e Michelangelo: Studi di sotria e d'arte*. Rome: G. Bardi.

– 1965. *Raffaello nelle stanze*. Milan: Aldo Martello.

Redondo, Augustín. 1998. *Otra manera de leer el Quijote: Historia, tradiciones culturales y literatura*. Madrid: Castalia.

Rey Hazas, Antonio. 1996. 'El *Quijote* y la picaresca: La figura del hidalgo.' *Edad de Oro* 15:141–60.
Rhodes, Elizabeth. 1988. '*La Galatea* and Cervantes' "Tercia Realidad."' *Cervantes*. Special Issue: 17–28.
Ridolfi, Carlo. 1996. *The Life of Titian*. Ed. Julia Conaway et al. University Park: Pennsylvania State University Press.
Riley, E.C. 1962. *Teoría de la novela en Cervantes*. Madrid: Taurus.
– 1986. *Don Quixote*. London: Allen and Unwin.
Ripa, Cesare. 1971. *Baroque and Rococo Pictorial Imagery*. Ed. Edward A. Maser. New York: Dover.
Riquer, Martín de. 1969. 'El 'Quijote' y los libros.' *Papeles de Son Armadans* 160:5–24.
Rivers, Elias L. 1981. 'Cervantes y Garcilaso.' In *Cervantes: Su obra y su mundo*, ed. Manuel Criado de Val. 963–8. Madrid: Edi-6.
Rodríguez de Montalvo, Garci. 1987. *Amadís de Gaula*. Ed. Juan Manuel Cacho Blecua. 2 vols. Madrid: Cátedra.
Rodríguez Marín, Francisco. 1947. *Estudios cervantinos*. Madrid: Ediciones Atlas.
Roettgen, Steffi. 1996. *Italian Frescoes: The Early Renaissance*. New York: Abbeville Press.
– 1997. *Italian Frescoes: The Flowering of the Renaissance*. New York: Abbeville Press.
Rojas, Fernando de. 1974. *La Celestina*. Ed. Bruno Mario Damiani. Madrid: Cátedra.
Rojas Villandrado, Agustín de. 1977. *El viaje entretenido*. Ed. Jacques Josset. Madrid: Espasa-Calpe.
Rosenberg, Charles M. 1986. 'Raphael and the Florentine *Istoria*.' In *Raphael Before Rome*, ed. James Beck. 175–87. Washington: National Gallery of Art.
Roskill, Mark W. 1968. *Dolce's 'Aretino' and Venetian Art Theory of the Cinquecento*. New York: New York University Press.
Rowland, Beryl. 1973. *Animals with Human Faces: A Guide to Animal Symbolism*. Knoxville: University of Tennessee Press.
Rowland, Ingrid D. 1998. *The Culture of the High Renaissance: Ancients and Moderns in Sixteenth-Century Rome*. Cambridge: Cambridge University Press.
Rubin, Patricia Lee. 1995. *Giorgio Vasari: Art and History*. New Haven, CT: Yale University Press.
Ruiz Pérez, Pedro. 1995. 'La hipóstasis de Armida: Dorotea y Micomicona.' *Cervantes* 15:147–63.
Saint-Saëns, Alain. 2000. 'Homoerotic Suffering, Pleasure, and Desire in Early

Modern Europe (1450–1750).' In *Lesbianism and Homosexuality in Early Modern Spain*, ed. María José Delgado and Alain Saint-Saens. 3–86. New Orleans, LA: University Press of the South.

Sánchez, Jiménez, Antonio. (unpublished manuscript) *El Sansón de Extremadura: Diego García de Paredeas en la literatura española del siglo XVI.*

Saslow, James M. 1986. *Ganymede in the Renaissance: Homosexuality in Art and Society*. New Haven, CT: Yale University Press.

Scaramuzza Vidoni, Mariarosa. 1998. *Deseo, imaginación, utopía en Cervantes.* Roma: Bulzoni.

Schmidt, Rachel. 1999. *The Canonization of Don Quixote through Illustrated Editions of the Eighteenth Century*. Montreal and Kingston: McGill-Queen's University Press.

Scobie, A. 1976. '*El curioso impertinente* and Apuleius.' *Romanische Forschungen* 88:75–6.

Segal, Charles. 1989. *Orpheus: The Myth of the Poet*. Baltimore: Johns Hopkins University Press.

Selig, Karl-Ludwig. 1973. '*Persiles y Segismunda*: Notes on Pictures, Portraits and Portraiture.' *Hispanic Review* 41:305–12.

– 1974/5. 'The Battle of the Sheep (*Don Quijote*, I, xviii).' *Revista Hispánica Moderna* 38:64–71.

– 1983. 'Apuleius and Cervantes: *Don Quixote* (I, XVIII).' In *Aereum Saeculum Hispanum*, ed. Kart-Hermann Corner and Dietrich Brisenmeister. 285–7. Wiesbaden: Franz Steiner Verlag.

– 1989. '*Enumeratio*/enumeración en *Don Quijote*.' In *Actas del IX Congreso de la Asociación Internacional de Hispanistas*, ed. Sebastian Neumeister. 629–34. Frankfurt: Vervuert Verlag.

Shepherd, J.C., and G.A. Jellicoe. 1993. *Italian Gardens of the Renaissance*. New York: Princeton Architectural Press.

Shoemaker, Innis H., and Elizabeth Brown. 1981. *The Engravings of Marcantonio Raimondi*. Lawrence, KS: The Spencer Museum.

Sohm, Philip. 1995. 'Gendered Style in Italian Art Criticism from Michelangelo to Malvasia.' *Renaissance Quarterly* 48:759–808.

Sola-Solé, Josep M. 1981. 'Sobre el *Quejana* de *Don Quijote*.' In *Cervantes. Su obra y su mundo*, ed. Manuel Criado de Val. 717–22. Madrid: Edi-6.

Soufas, Teresa Scott. 1990. *Melancholy and the Secular Mind in Spanish Golden Age Literature*. Columbia: University of Missouri Press.

Spear, Richard E. 1997. *The 'Divine' Guido. Religion, Sex, Money and Art in the World of Guido Reni*. New Haven and London: Yale University Press.

Spence, Jonathan D. 1985. *The Memory Palace of Matteo Ricci*. New York: Penguin Books.

Spike, John T. 1996. *Fra Angelico*. New York: Abbeville Press.

Spitzer, Leo. 1955. 'The 'Ode on a Grecian Urn,' or Content vs. Metagrammar,' *Comparative Literature* 7.3: 203–25.

Stagg, Geoffrey. 1972. 'A Matter of Masks: *La Galatea*,' *Hispanic Essays in Honour of Joseph Manson*, ed. Dorothy M. Atkinson and Anthon H. Clarke. Oxford: Dolphin, pp. 255–267.

Stamm, James R. 1981. '*La Galatea* y el concepto de género: un acercamiento,' *Cervantes. Su obra y su mundo*, ed. Criado de Val. Madrid: Edi-6, pp. 337–43.

Suetonius. 1989. *The Twelve Caesars*. New York: Penguin.

Suida Manning, Bertina, and Robert L. Manning. 1974. *The Genoese Renaissance, Grace and Geometry: Paintings and Drawings by Luca Cambiaso from the Suida-Manning Collection*. Houston: The Museum of Fine Arts.

Suida Manning, Bertina, and William Suida. 1958. *Luca Cambiaso: La vita e le opere*. Milan: Casa Editrice Ceschina.

Sullivan, Henry W. 1996. *Grotesque Purgatory: A Study of Cervantes's* Don Quixote, *Part II*. University Park: Pennsylvania State University Press.

Syverson-Stork, Jill. 1986. *Theatrical Aspects of the Novel: A Study of Don Quixote*. Valencia: Albatross.

Talvacchia, Bette. 1989. 'La sala di Troia.' In *Giulio Romano*, ed. Ernst H. Gombrich. 406–11. Milano: Electa.

– 1999. *Taking Positions: On the Erotic in Renaissance Culture*. Princeton, NJ: Princeton University Press.

Tanner, Marie. 1993. *The Last Descendant of Aeneas: The Hapsburgs and the Mythic Image of the Emperor*. New Haven, CT: Yale University Press.

Tasso, Torquato. 2000. *Jerusalem Delivered*. Trans. Anthony M. Esolen. Baltimore, MD: Johns Hopkins University Press.

Taylor, René. 1976. 'Arquitectura y magia: Consideraciones sobre la 'idea' de El Escorial.' *Traza y Baza* 6:5–62.

Taylor, Valerie. 1999. 'Giulio Romano as Court Artist to Federico Gonzaga in the Early 1530s: Studies for Decorations in the *Camera di Attilio Regolo* and the *Camera dei Giganti*, Palazzo Té.' In *Giulio Romano: Master Designer*, ed. Janet Cox-Rearick. 74–97. Seattle: University of Washington Press.

Thoenes, Christof. 1986. 'Galatea: Tentativi di Avvicinamento.' *Raffaello a Roma*. 59–72. Rome: Elefante.

Thomas, Henry. 1952. *Las novelas de caballerías españolas y portuguesas*. Trans. Esteban Pujals. Madrid: Consejo Superior de Investigaciones Científicas.

Turriano, Juanelo. 1983. *The Twenty-One Books of Devices and of Machines*. Ed. José A. García Diego. Madrid: Colegio de Ingenieros de Caminos, Canales y Puertos.

Ullman, Pierre. 1971. 'The Surrogates of Baroque Marcela and Mannerist Leandra,' *Revista de Estudios Hispánicos* 5:307–19.

Unamuno, Miguel de. 1976. *Our Lord Don Quixote: The Life of Don Quixote and Sancho with Related Essays*. Princeton, NJ: Princeton University Press.

Urbina, Eduardo. 1987. 'Gigantes y enanos: De lo maravilloso a lo grotesco en *Don Quijote*.' *Romanistisches Jahrbuch* 38:323–38.

– 1989. 'Tres aspectos de lo grotesco en el "Quijote."' In *Actas del IX congreso de la Asociación de Internacional de Hispanistas*, ed. Sebastian Neumeister. 1:673–79. Frankfurt: Vervuert Verlag.

Valdivielso, José de. 1616. *Sagrario de Toledo. Poema heroico. Por el Maestro Joseph de Valdivielso, Capellán del Ilustrissimo de Toledo*. Madrid: Por Luis Sanchez, Impressor del Rey.

Van Lohuizen-Mulder, Mab. 1977. *Raphael's Images: Justice – Humanity – Friendship*. Wassenaar: Mirananda.

Vasari, Giorgio. 1991. *The Lives of the Artists*. Trans. Julia Conaway Bondanella and Peter Bondanella. Oxford: Oxford University Press.

– 1996. *The Lives of the Painters, Sculptors and Architects*. Trans. Gaston du C. de Vere, intro. David Ekserdijan. 2 vols. New York: Alfred A. Knopf.

The Vatican Collections: The Papacy and Art. 1982. New York: Metropolitan Museum of Art.

Vecchi, Pierluigi de, with Gianluigi Colalucci. 1996. *Michelangelo: The Vatican Frescoes*. New York: Abbeville Press.

Vélez-Sainz, Julio. 2000. 'El *Recueil de Fossard*, la compañía de los Gelosa y la génesis de *Don Quijote*.' *Cervantes* 20:31–52.

Vercelloni, Virgilio. 1990. *European Gardens: An Historical Atlas*. New York: Rizzoli.

Verheyen, Egon. 1977. *The Palazzo del Té in Mantua: Images of Love and Politics*. Baltimore, MD: Johns Hopkins University Press.

Vernet, J. 1974. *Astrología y astronomía en el Renacimiento*. Barcelona: Ariel.

Villamediana, Conde de. 1992. *Poesía*. Ed. Maria Teresa Ruestes. Barcelona: Planeta.

Virgil. 1978. *Eclogues. Georgics. Aeneid*. Trans. H.R. Fairclough. 2 vols. Cambridge, MA: Harvard University Press.

Von Barghahn, Barbara. 1985. *Age of Gold, Age of Iron: Renaissance Spain and Symbols of the Monarchy*. 2 vols. Lanham, MD: University Press of America.

Voragine, Jacobus de. 1993. *The Golden Legend: Readings on the Saints*, trans. William Granger Ryan. 2 vols. Princeton, NJ: Princeton University Press.

Vosters, Simon A. 1977. *Lope de Vega y la tradición occidental*. 2 vols. Madrid: Castalia.

– 1990. *Rubens y España: Estudio artístico-literario sobre la estética del Barroco*. Madrid: Cátedra.

Wagschal, Steven. 2004. 'Writing on the Fractured 'I': Góngora's Iconographic Evocations of Vulcan, Venus, and Mars.' In *Writing for the Eyes in the Spanish Golden Age*, ed. Frederick A. de Armas. 130–50. Lewisburg: Bucknell University Press.

Watson, Paul F. 1988. 'To Paint Poetry: Raphael on Parnassus.' In *Renaissance Rereadings: Intertext and Context*, ed. Maryanne Cline Horowitz, Anne J. Cruz, and Wendy Furman. 113–41. Urbana: University of Illinois Press.

Watt, Ian. 1996. *Myths of Modern Individualism: Faust, Don Quixote, Don Juan, Robinson Crusoe*. Cambridge: Cambridge University Press.

Weiger, John C. 1979. *The Individuated Self: Cervantes and the Emergence of the Individual*. Athens: Ohio University Press.

Weimer, Christopher B. 2004. 'The Quixotic Art: Cervantes, Vasari, and Michelangelo.' In *Writing for the Eyes in the Spanish Golden Age*, ed. Frederick A. de Armas. 63–84. Lewisburg: Bucknell University Press.

Wethey, Harold. 1971. *The Paintings of Titian*. Vol. 2, *The Portraits*. London: Phaidon.

Wilkins, Ernest Hatch. 1966. *A History of Italian Literature*. Cambridge, MA: Harvard University Press.

Wilson, N.G. 1992. *From Byzantium to Italy: Greek Studies in the Italian Renaissance*. Baltimore, MD: Johns Hopkins University Press.

Wind, Edgar. 1938. 'The Four Elements in Raphael's Stanza della Segnatura.' *Journal of the Warburg Institute* 2:75–9.

– 1968. *Pagan Mysteries in the Renaissance*. 2nd ed. New York: Norton.

Winner, Matthias. 1993. 'Projects and Execution in the Stanza della Segnatura.' In *Raphael in the Apartments of Julius II and Leo X*, ed. Roberto Caravaggi. 247–91. Milan: Electa.

Wittkower, Rudolf. 1952. *Architectural Principles in the Age of Humanism*. London: Alec Tiranti.

Wofford, Susanne Lidgren. 1992. *The Choice of Achilles: The Ideology of Figure in the Epic*. Stanford, CA: Stanford University Press.

Wolford, Chester L. 1986. 'Don Quixote and the Epic of Subversion.' In *Cervantes and the Pastoral*, ed. José J. Labrador Herraiz and Juan Fernández Jiménez. 197–212. Cleveland, OH: Cleveland State University Press.

Woodbridge, Linda. 1994. *The Scythe of Saturn: Shakespeare and Magical Thinking*. Urbana and Chicago: University of Illinois Press.

Worden, William. 2005. 'The First Illustrator of *Don Quixite*: Miguel de Cervantes.' In *Ekphrasis in the Age of Cervantes*, ed. Frederick A. de Armas. 144–55. Lewisburg: Bucknell University Press.

Yacobi, Tamar. 1998. 'The Ekphrastic Models: Forms and Functions.' In *Pictures into Words: Theoretical and Descriptive Approaches to Ekphrasis*, ed. Valerie Robillard and Els Jongeneel. 21–34. Amsterdam: VU University Press.

Yates, Frances A. 1964. *Giordano Bruno and the Hermetic Tradition*. Chicago: University of Chicago Press.

– 1966. *The Art of Memory*. Chicago: University of Chicago Press.

– 1975. *Astraea: The Imperial Theme in the Sixteenth Century*. London: Routledge and Keagan Paul.

Zatlin, Phyllis. 1990. 'Ekphrastic Theatre and the Contemporary Spanish Stage.' *Journal of Interdisciplinary Literary Studies* 2:201–13.

Index

Abraham, 41, 43
Acquaviva, Giulio (Cardinal), 5, 22
Acteon, 163
Acuña, 3
Agrippa, Cornelius, 65
Alberti, Leon Battista, 173; *De Pictura* (*On Painting*), 27, 173
Albumasar (Abu Ma'shar), 210
Aldana, Francisco de, 3
Alemán, Mateo, 109–10; *Guzmán de Alfarache*, 109–10
Alexander the Great, 118
Alexios (Emperor), 105
Alfonso V (Aragon), 4
Allen, John J., 120
Alter, Robert B., 38
Amadís de Gaula. *See* Rodríguez de Montalvo, Garci
Ammannati, Bartolommeo, 78; *Biancone*, 78
Andronicus, 105
Angelico, Fra, 98; *Expulsion and Stoning of St Stephen*, 98–9
Anteus, 147
Apelles, 118
Apollo, 37, 47, 56, 63, 64, 69, 82–3, 127, 128, 160, 163, 207
Apollo Belvedere, 6, 7, 8, 82
Apuleius, 30, 33, 191–3, 195, 196, 197, 198, 202–3, 204, 209; *The Golden Ass*, 33, 191–3, 195–6, 203, 204
Archimedes, xii, 144–7, 150, 151, 152
Arcimboldo, xvi, 33
Aretino, Pietro, 90, 180, 197; *Sonetti lussuriosi*, 197
Argensola (brothers), 3
Ariosto, Ludovico, 126, 138, 139, 168, 189, 196, 198–9; *Orlando furioso*, 11, 33, 113, 139, 176, 177–9, 184, 187, 189, 191, 198–9, 207
Aristotle, 14–15, 21, 27, 38, 39, 49, 67, 125, 137, 175; *Ethics*, 39; *Memory and Reminiscence* (*De memoria et reminiscentia*), 14, 21, 175
Artemis. *See* Diana
Astraea, 127, 160, 169
Avalle-Arce, Juan Bautista, 57
Avellaneda, Alonso Fernández de, 117
Averroes, 35, 39
Ávila y Zúñiga, Luis de, 115–16, 125–6, 128, 129–31; *Comentario de la guerra de Alemania hecha por Carlos V … en el año 1556*, 125–6, 129–30

Ayala, Francisco, 200

Bacchus, 201, 203
Baldini, Baccio, 209
Bandinelli, Baccio, 76–80; *Hercules and Cacus*, 76–80
Bartholomew, St, 85–7, 89–91, 95, 207
Basil, St, 49
Bernini, Dante, 111
Boccaccio, Giovanni: *Genealogia deorum* (*Genealogy of the Gods*), 27, 209
Bosch, *Temptation of St Anthony*, 135
Boschetta, Isabella, 198
Bottarga, 116, 119
Botticelli, xvi, 23, 26, 27, 150, 206; *Primavera*, 27, 28, 48–9
Briareus, 144–51, 206
Brown, Jonathan, 5, 110
Burke, James F., 183
Byzantium, 105–6

Caballero del Febo, 58
Cacus, 43, 44, 45, 68–9, 70, 75, 76–80, 89, 142, 143–4
Caesar, Augustus, 127, 156–7, 168; *Pax Romana*, 127, 168
Caesar, Julius, 64, 129–31, 156, *Commentaries*, 131
Calderón de la Barca, Pedro, 203
Callistratus, 137; *Descriptions*, 137
Calypso, 47, 48
Camamis, George, 26, 143
Cambiaso, Luca (Luchetto), xv, 93–112, 116, 193, 206, 209; *Combat between Aeneas and Turnus*, 104; *The Departure of the Armada from the Port of Messina*, 110; *The Emperor of Trebisonda Constructing a Fondaco for Megollo Lercari*, 105–6, 109, 110, 112, 116; *Episode of Ulysses and Poliphemus*, 104; *Galatea*, 103; *La Gloria*, 110, 111; *Guidizio finale*, 94–5, 111; *Marco Curzio*, 104; *Martyrdom of St Bartholomew*, 96, 111; *Rape of the Sabines*, 104; *The Return of the Armada*, 110; *Return of Ulysses*, 104; *The Stoning of St Stephen*, 96; *terribilitá*, 94–5, 111; *The Withdrawal of the Turks*, 110
Camillo, Giulio, 22
Carducci, 118
Carpio, Bernardo del, 68
Carruthers, Mary, 15
Casena, Biagio da, 88
Castello, Giovanni Battista (Bergamasco), 95, 193, 209
Castiglione, Baldassare, 173, 174; *The Book of the Courtier*, 173
Castillo, David, 164
Castro, Américo, xi, 119, 136, 162, 164, 178
Cátedra, Pedro M., 161
Cato, 42
Cellini, Benvenuto, 78, 80
Cervantes Saavedra, Miguel de: *Adjunta al Parnaso*, 44; *Canción de Calíope*, 4; *La Galatea*, xii, xv, 4, 5, 8, 9, 12, 13, 14–28, 29, 30–1, 33, 34, 36, 75, 96, 156, 193–4, 205; *El licenciado vidriera*, 93, 96, 176; *Novelas ejemplares*, 5, 12; *La Numancia*, xi–xii, xv, 3, 8, 11, 12, 14–28, 29, 30–1, 33, 34, 38, 52, 55, 75, 104, 156, 188, 205; *Ocho comedias y ocho entremeses*, 5; *Los trabajos de Persiles y Sigismunda*, xii, 5, 8, 9, 12, 15, 156, 191; *El trato de Argel*, 20; *Viaje del Parnaso*, 104
Cetina, Gutierre de, 3

Charlemagne, 122
Charles V (Spain), xii, xiv, 47, 107, 110, 111, 113–33, 145, 146–7, 151, 168, 205–6, 210
Checa, Fernando, 125, 128, 131
Chigi, Agostino, 195–7
Chrysostom, St John, 162
Cicero, xiii, 16, 17, 19, 49, 173, 175, 179; *Ad Herennium*, xii, 16, 17, 20, 175, 181; *De Inventione*, 173; *De Oratore*, xii, 16, 175
Cid, El, 68
Circe, 47, 48
Clemencín, Diego, 103
Clement VII (Pope), 77, 79
Close, Anthony, 155
Clubb, Louise George, 17
Colonna, Ascanio, 4, 22
Columbus, Christopher, 97
Combet, Louis, 200
Condivi, Ascanio, 85
Constantine, 7
Coomonte, Pilar, 142
Correggio, Nicolo de, 195, 196; *Fabla Psiches et Cupidinis*, 195
Cosimo, Duke (Medici), 78, 79
Council of Trent, 8, 88, 91
Counter-Reformation, xiv, 6, 7, 26, 28, 36, 45, 87, 88, 89, 90, 91, 101, 111, 133, 200, 202, 204, 207
Covarrubias, Sebastián de, 45, 107, 131–2, 140, 186; *Tesoro de la lengua*, 45
Cozad, Mary, 36
Cranach, Lucas, 118, 182
Crane, Susan A., 32
Cruz, Anne J., 106, 109–10, 159
Cull, John, 120
Cupid, 191–204, 208, 209
Curtius, Ernst, 156
Curtius, Mettius, 104

Daedalus, xii, 140, 147, 151–2
Damonte, Mario, 96
D'Ancona, Paolo, 195
Dante Alighieri, xv, 37, 147, 150, 152; *Divine Comedy*, 206; *Inferno*, 147, 150; *Purgatorio*, 147
Daphne, 159–60
Darst, David, 5–6
David, 43, 45, 76–9, 143, 200
Da Vinci, Leonardo, xiv, 29, 34, 151
Day, Gerald W., 105
De Armas Wilson, Diana, 192, 200
De la Corte, Juan, 179
De la Cruz, San Juan, 185
De la Flor, Fernando R., 16
Delicado, Francisco, 3
Della Porta, Giambattista (Giovanni Battista), 17, 18, 19, 20, 21, 63, 172, 175, 177, 180, 181, 185; *L'Arte del ricordare*, xii, xiii, 17, 20, 21, 138, 172, 175; *De furtivus literarum*, 17; *Magiae*, 17; *La Turca*, 17, 20
Della Rovere, Francesco Maria, 35
De los Ríos, Vicente, 154–5
Democritus, 74
d'Este, Alfonso, 138
d'Este, Isabella, 198
Diana, 73, 159, 160–1, 162, 163–4, 166, 167, 168
Díaz de Benjumea, N., 114
Dolce, Ludovico, 20, 22, 24, 71; *The Dialogue on Painting*, 71
Donaldson, Ian, 181
Donatello, 77; *David*, 78
Donatus, 161
Doody, Margaret Anne, 32
Doré, Gustave, 135–6, 142
Dudley, Edward, xii, 23, 193

Dürer, Albrecht, 121–2, 133, 194; *The Knight, Death, and the Devil*, 121–2

Egido, Aurora, 18
Elizabeth I (England), 66, 126, 187
Elliot, George, 189
El Saffar, Ruth, 55, 128, 159, 172, 183–4
Empedocles, 35, 53, 54, 59–60, 61
Euclid, 45

Faenza, Marco de, 79; *Hercules and Cacus*, 79
Farness, Jay, 183
Ferdinand (Charles V's brother), 114, 132, 133
Ferdinand I (Naples), 66
Ferdinand and Isabella, 107
Fernández, Jerónimo de, 61; *Don Belianís de Grecia*, 59, 104, 122–3
Fernández Alvarez, Manuel, 132
Ficino, Marsilio, 15, 24, 33, 53, 63
Fichter, W.L., 132
Figueroa, Francisco de, 3
Flora, 198, 208
Forcione, Alban, xi
Foucault, Michel, xi, 29–30
Francis I (France), 114, 133
Fritz, Michael P., 195–6

Gabriele, John P., 159
Galaor, 58
Gálvez de Montalvo, Luis, 4, 22; *El pastor de Fílida*, 4, 22
Ganassa, 116, 119
Ganymede, 201–2, 204
Garcilaso de la Vega, xiii, xv, 3; *Third Eclogue*, 23
Gattinara, Mercurino, 120
Gaylord, Mary, 34
Gentileschi, Artemisia: *Tarquin and Lucretia*, 181–2
George, St, 120–1
Giulio Romano, xv, 28, 33, 96–103, 112, 148–52, 180, 189–204, 206, 208; *architettura rustica*, 99; *The Banquet of the Gods*, 199–201; Camerino dei Falconi, 202; *The Cross Appearing to Constantine the Great, flanked by portraits of two popes*, 21; *Jupiter Kissing Cupid*, 201–2; *I Modi (The Positions)*, 197; *Neptune Taking Possession of the Sea*, 202; Palazzo del Té, 197, 199, 201, 202, 203, 206; *The Rape of Helen*, 180; Sala dei Giganti, 149–51, 197, 202, 206; Sala di Constantino, 148; Sala di Psiche, 197, 199–200, 202–3; Sala di Troia, 148, 180, 202; Sala dei Venti, 202; *Stoning of St Stephen*, 96–103; *Thetis Buckling on Achilles' Shield*, 148; *Venus Swoons in the Arms of Jupiter*, 202; *The Wedding Banquet of Amor and Psyche*, 199–200, 202–3
Goffen, Rona, 25
Goliath, 42–3, 75, 76–9, 142–3
Gonzaga, Federigo, 148, 151, 180, 197–9, 202
González Echevarría, Roberto, 161–2
Gossy, Mary, 184
Grafton, Anthony, 13, 22, 29, 194
Greco, El, 164
Green, Otis, 62
Guevara, Antonio de, 47, 115
Guiccardini, Francesco, 120
Gumpert, Matthew, 167

Habsburg (Empire), 79, 106, 118, 127, 206

Hagstrum, Jean, 135
Hahn, Juergen, 192
Hakewill, James, 96
Hartt, Frederick, 87, 89, 90, 94, 97, 100, 101, 148, 149, 150, 163, 166, 197, 198, 203
Hasbrouck, Michael, 121–2
Hebreus, Leo, 36; *Diálogos de amor*, 36
Heffernan, James, 141
Heiple, Daniel L., 60
Heliodorus: *Aethiopica*, 33
Heninger, S.K., 52, 55, 59, 60
Hephaestus, 141
Heraclitus, 72–4, 77
Hercules, 44, 68–9, 76–9, 89, 90, 154, 179
Hermes Trismegistus, 53–4; *Ascelpius*, 53; *Corpus Hermeticum*, 53
Herodotus, *History*, 186
Herrero, Javier, 172
Hersey, George L., 35, 38, 39, 74, 88
Hibbard, Howard, 78
Higuera, Henry, 185
Hind, Arthur M., 182
Hollanda, Francesco da: *Tractado de Pintura Antigua*, 128
Homer, xiii, 37, 45, 66, 104, 148, 154–5, 160, 179, 190; *Illiad*, 11, 141, 153, 167, 179–80, 184, 186, 187, 190, 207–8
Horace, 24, 30, 31, 40, 42; *Ars Poetica*, 24
Huarte de San Juan, Juan, 15, 63
Hulse, Clark, 174

Iamblicus, 52
Icarus, 142, 147
Isis, 192
Iventosch, Hermann, 57

Jaksic, Iván, 144
Jardine, Lisa, 93, 106, 108, 199–200
Jeanneret, Michel, 161
Jerome, St, 165–6, 167
Jews, 107
John, St, 81
Johnson, Carroll, 102, 108, 128, 162, 178
Jonathan, 200
Jones, Roger, 72, 74, 195, 200, 203
Joost-Gautier, Christiane L., 46
Julius II (Pope), xv, 7, 35, 36, 37, 81
Juno, 201
Jupiter, 149–51, 201–2, 206, 210

Kallendorf, Hilaire, 122
Kenney, E.J., 192
Kepler, Johannes, 53
Krieger, Murray, 3, 12

Laertius, Diogenes, 65, 75
Laocöon, 81
Lawrence, St, 90, 98
Lazarillo de Tormes, 57, 108
Lemos, count of, 5
Leo X (Pope), 76, 163
Lepanto, battle of, 4, 110
Lercari, Megollo, 105
Lessing, G.E., 179
Lippi, Filipino: *St Thomas in Triumph over the Heretics*, 39
Livy, 104
Lope de Vega Carpio, Félix, 37, 38, 40, 42, 43, 44, 80, 94, 118; *Arte nuevo de hacer comedias* (*New Art of Writing Comedias*), 38; *Égloga a Claudio*, 94
López de Hoyos, Juan, 104
López Piñero, José María 145
Lucan, xiii, 158–9; *Pharsalia*, 158, 168

Lucretia, 179–83, 186, 187, 207
Luis Vives, Juan, 145
Lukács, Georg, 155
Lutti, Benedetto, 178

MacCurdy, Raymond R., 117
Machiavelli, Niccolo, 180
Madrigal, José Antonio, 57
Maffei, Raffaello, 47
Maiorino, Giancarlo, 108, 145
Manilius, 211
Manutius, Aldus, 137–8
Marasso, Arturo, 155, 168
Maravall, José Antonio, 47, 114–15
Marcellus, 144, 152
María de Portugal, 147
Marín, Rodríguez, 117
Mars, 62–3, 65, 128
Marsyas, 90
Matthew, St, 41, 42, 43, 76, 80–1
Mayans y Sicar, Gregorio, 154
Mazzola, Francesco. *See* Parmigianino
McGaha, Michael, 155
Medea, 47, 48
Medici, 76, 78, 79
Medina, Luis de: *Flores del Parnaso: Octava Parte*, 107
Medrano, Francisco de, 3
Meltzer, Françoise, 190
Mendoza, Hurtado de, 3
Menéndez Pidal, Ramón,114
Mercury, 202
Metrodorus of Scepsis, 19
Mexía, Pedro, 16–17, 145, 173; *Silva de varía lección*, 16, 173
Michelangelo, xii, xiv, xv, 7, 8, 25, 71–92, 93, 94–6, 98, 104, 111, 124, 128, 133, 139–40, 171, 205, 207; *David*, 76–80, 90, 92; *The Last Judgment*, 7, 8, 81–2, 84–92, 94–5, 101, 111, 205, 207; *Saint Matthew*, 81; *terribilitá*, 25, 33, 71–92, 94–5, 205
Miciano, Theodoro, 136–7
Miller, Patricia Cox, 166
Mitchell, W.J.T., 11
Montalbán, Reinaldos de, 68
Montemayor, Jorge de: *La Diana*, 36
Morales, Ambrosio de, 3, 146
Moriscos, 178
Moses, 41
Murillo, Luis Andrés, 107, 115–16
Muslims, 107

Nadeau, Carolyn, 49
Nebrija, Antonio de, 186
Neptune, 78
Nero, 159, 163

Ordeasca, Francesca, 195–6
Ortega y Gasset, José, 119
Ottoman (Empire), 106, 206
Ovid, 42; *Tristia*, 42

Pacheco, Francisco, 20, 22, 173, 174; *Arte de la pintura*, 20, 173, 174
Palmerín de Inglaterra, 37, 58
Panofsky, Edwin, 113, 117–18, 120, 123
Parmigianino (Francesco Mazzola), xv, 153–69, 194, 207; *Madonna and Child with Saints John the Baptist and Jerome*, 165–6, 194; *Madonna of the Rose*, 164
Parr, James, 65, 117
Pasiphae, 147
Patridge, Loren, 7
Paul III (Pope), 133
Pellegrini, 178

Penny, Nicholas, 72, 74, 195, 200, 203
Percas de Ponseti, Helena, 31, 122
Pérez Botero, Luis, 119
Pérez de Oliva, Fernán, 145
Peruzzi, Baldassare, 25, 194–6
Peter, St, 81, 98
Philip II (Spain), xv, 17, 109–12, 114, 118, 132, 180, 187, 206; Escorial, 109, 110, 111
Philip III (Spain), 206
Philistines, 143
Philostratus, Flavius, 138; *Life of Apollonius of Tyana*, 138
Philostratus, Lemnius (the Elder), xiii, xv, 134–52; *Imagines*, 137
Philostratus (the Younger), 137, 140–2; *Imagines*, 9
Pico della Mirandolla, Giovanni, 53
Pindar, 40, 56
Pinturicchio, xvi
Piombo, Sebastiano del, 23, 25, 27; *Polyphemus*, 25
Plato, 36, 38, 39, 51, 52, 54, 55, 57, 64, 137, 166, 184, 207; *Timeus*, 39, 52, 57, 60
Pliny, 21, 170, 173; *Natural History*, 173
Plutarch, 30, 144–5; *Life of Marcellus*, 144
Pluto, 148
Poliziano, Angelo: *Orpheus*, 26
Pomona, 163
Pontormo, Jacopo Carucci da, xv, 153–69; *The Entombment*, 164; *Joseph in Egypt*, 165; *Vertumnus and Pomona*, 163
Portús Pérez, Javier, 9
Predmore, Richard L., 114
Protestant League, 122
Psyche, 191–204, 208, 209
Ptolemy, 45, 62–3, 69, 128, 209; *Geography*, 45–6
Pythagoras, 30, 33, 35, 41, 42, 51, 52–3, 54, 55, 64–5, 68, 71, 83, 125, 184

Quevedo, Francisco de, 3
Quijada, don Luis, 117, 118
Quint, David, 31, 102, 107, 189
Quintilian, 16, 175, 185; *Institutio Oratoria*, 16, 175

Rabin, Lisa, 185
Raimondi, Marcantonio, 37, 182, 197; *The Death of Lucretia*, 182
Raphael, xii, xiv, xv, 8, 13, 22, 25, 27, 29–51, 52–70, 71, 72, 74, 75, 76, 77, 80, 82, 83, 91, 93, 94, 96, 98, 104, 120–1, 148, 156, 157, 171, 174, 175, 176, 180, 182, 193, 195–7, 200, 201, 204, 205, 208; *Alexander the Great Places Homer's 'Iliad' in Safe Keeping*, 37; *Apollo and Marsyas*, 7; *Augustus Prevents the Burning of Virgil's 'Aeneid,'* 37; *The Cross Appearing to Constantine the Great, flanked by portraits of two popes*, 21; *Disputa*, 36, 39, 41, 45, 46, 49, 76, 80–1, 98; *Madonna della Sedia*, 164; *Parnassus*, 7, 34–5, 36–7, 39–40, 41, 45, 46, 49, 54, 56, 64, 69, 76, 157; *Poetry*, 35; *St George*, 120–1; *The School of Athens*, 7, 35, 36, 37–8, 39, 41, 42, 46, 47, 49, 52, 53, 55, 59–60, 61, 72, 75, 85, 90, 205; Stanza d'Eliodoro, 54; Stanza della Segnatura, 6, 8, 22, 33–4, 35, 36, 37, 39, 40, 41, 42, 45, 46, 48, 49, 50, 52, 54, 62, 64, 71, 72, 75, 76, 98, 101, 148, 157, 186; Stanza dell'Incendio,

54; Stanza di Constantino, 54; *The Three Graces*, 27, 28; *The Triumph of Galatea*, xii, 23, 25, 28, 96, 174, 193, 195; *The (Cardinal) Virtues*, 46, 47, 50, 51, 69
Redig de Campos, D., 74
Redondo, Augustin, 43, 116, 119, 134–5, 142
Remigio Noydens, Benito, 108
Reni, Guido, 182–3
Requesens, Isabel de, 197
Ripa, Cesare, 186–7; *Castitas*, 66; *Iconologia*, 186–7
Rodríguez de Montalvo, Garci: *Amadís de Gaula*, 36, 57, 58, 62, 113, 176–9, 184, 187, 207
Roettgen, Steffi, 39
Rojas, Fernando de, 72–4; *La Celestina*, 72–4
Rojas Villandrado, Agustín de, 3
Roland, 68
Romancero general, 107
Romberch, Johannes, 19; *Congestorium artificiose memorie*, 19
Rossellius, Cosmas, 19; *Thesaurus artificiosae memoriae*, 19, 20
Rossi, Vincenzo de', 79; *Hercules and Cacus*, 79
Rotterdam, Erasmus of, 121
Rubin, Patricia Lee, 9, 10–11, 41, 149
Ruiz Pérez, Pedro, 209

Santillana, Marqués de, 3, 161
Sappho, 46, 47, 56
Saslow, James M., 201–2
Saturn, 65, 73–4, 209–10
Schiaminossi, Raffaele, 96
Schmidt, Rachel, 154
Schön, Erhard, 133
Scipio, 21, 28
Selig, Kart-Ludwig, 56–7
Seneca: *De Beneficiis*, 27
Shakespeare, William, 138
Silva, Feliciano de, 59, 61, 104
Simonedes of Ceos, 14, 16, 17, 175, 176
Sistine Chapel, 6, 8, 133
Sixtus (Pope), 98
Sola-Solé, Josep M., 116–17
Soufas, Teresa, 61, 132
Spear, Richard E., 182–3
Spike, John T., 98
Spitzer, Leo, 136
Stephen, St, 97–102, 121
Strabo, 45
Syverson-Stork, Jill, 183

Tagus, 43, 44, 45
Tansillo, Luigi, 198; *Clorida*, 198; *Lagrime di San Pietro*, 203; *Il vendemmiatore*, 203
Tasso, Torquato, 209; *Jerusalem Delivered*, 209
Thomas Aquinas, St, 39, 175; *Summa contra gentiles*, 40
Titian, xv, 33, 48, 111, 113–33, 138, 143, 172, 176, 180–2, 205–6; *Bacchanal of the Andrians*, 138; *Charles V at Mühlberg*, 116, 118–31, 205–6; *David and Goliath*, 143; *Portrait of Charles V*, 125, 131; *Spain Coming to the Aid of Religion*, 187; *Tarquin and Lucrecia*, 180–2; *The Worship of Venus*, 138
Trebizond (Trapisonda), 93–112, 113, 117, 123, 206
Tudor, Mary, 187
Turner, Joseph, 96
Turriano, Juanelo, xii, 145–6, 150, 151, 152; *Veintiún libros de los*

ingenios y máquinas de Juanelo Turriano, 146

Udine, Giovanni da, 200
Ullman, Pierre, 159
Urbina, Eduardo, 43, 121

Valdés, Juan de, 3
Valdivielso, José de, 146, 203; *Psiquis y Cupido*, 203
Vanderbank, John, 154
Vasari, Giorgio, 7–8, 9, 10–11, 15, 22, 25, 27, 41, 76–9, 88, 117, 149, 173, 180, 182, 196; *The Infant Hercules Strangles the Snakes*, 79; *Lives of the Artists*, xiv, 7–8, 9, 10, 17, 41, 76, 93, 180, 182, 196
Vecchi, Pierluigi de, 7, 82, 90
Velázquez de Azevedo, Juan, 175
Veneziano, Agostino, 41
Venus, 160–1, 162, 164, 166, 167, 168, 191, 198, 202, 203, 209
Vidal, Pedro de, 103
Villacastín, Fray Antonio de, 111
Villamediana, Conde de, 3
Villena, Enrique de, 161
Virgil, xiii, xv, 30, 37, 45, 69, 71–2, 76, 88, 104, 127, 147–8, 150, 154, 155, 156–9, 160, 163, 167–9; *Aeneid*, 44, 147–8, 156–8, 160–3, 167–8; *Second Eclogue*, 26; *Fifth Eclogue*, 157; *Fourth Eclogue*, 127; *Rota Virgilii*, 156, 163
Volterra, Daniele da, 88

Watt, Ian, 134
Wethey, Harold, 118
Wind, Edgar, 48, 54
Winner, Matthias, 40
Wittkower, Rudolf, 55
Wofford, Susanne, 155

Yates, Frances, 14, 53, 176

Zapata, Luis, 116; *Carlo famoso*, 116
Zatlin, Phyllis, 11
Zeuxis, xv, 170–88, 208
Zoroaster, 45

www.ingramcontent.com/pod-product-compliance
Lightning Source LLC
LaVergne TN
LVHW090804070826
844660LV00022B/1073

* 9 7 8 1 4 4 2 6 1 0 3 1 6 *